TAM BLAKE & CO.

# TAM BLAKE & CO.
## The Story of the Scots in America

# JIM HEWITSON

CANONGATE

To Morag, Lindsey, David and Katy—for time and space.

First published in Great Britain in 1993
This edition first published in 1995
by Canongate Books Ltd, 14 High Street
Edinburgh EH1 1TE

*British Library Cataloguing-in-Publication Data*
A catalogue record for this book is available on request
from the British Library.

ISBN 0 86241 559 4

Photoset by The Electronic Book Factory Ltd, Fife.
Printed by
Cromwell Press Ltd, Broughton Gifford,
Melksham, Wiltshire, SN12 8PH.

# CONTENTS

Map of the United States of America      vi

Acknowledgments      vii

A Brief Chronology      viii

Chapter 1: The Way West      1

Chapter 2: Christopher Who?      11

Chapter 3: Cuddies, Coos and Coyotes      33

Chapter 4: Blazing A Quiet Trail      57

Chapter 5: Camped Beside A Good Thing      74

Chapter 6: Good Guys, Mad Guys and Bad Guys      96

Chapter 7: Clannish—Whit Us?      124

Chapter 8: Musket, Mainsail and Magic Bunnet      144

Chapter 9: The Chieftain's Eagle Feathers      164

Chapter 10: Slumberers—One Pace Forward!      186

Chapter 11: Ringing the Changes      205

Chapter 12: Log Cabins and Medicine Men      225

Chapter 13: Rifles By the Pulpit      243

Chapter 14: From City Hall to White House      259

Chapter 15: The Star-Spangled Saltire      274

Sources      284

Index      287

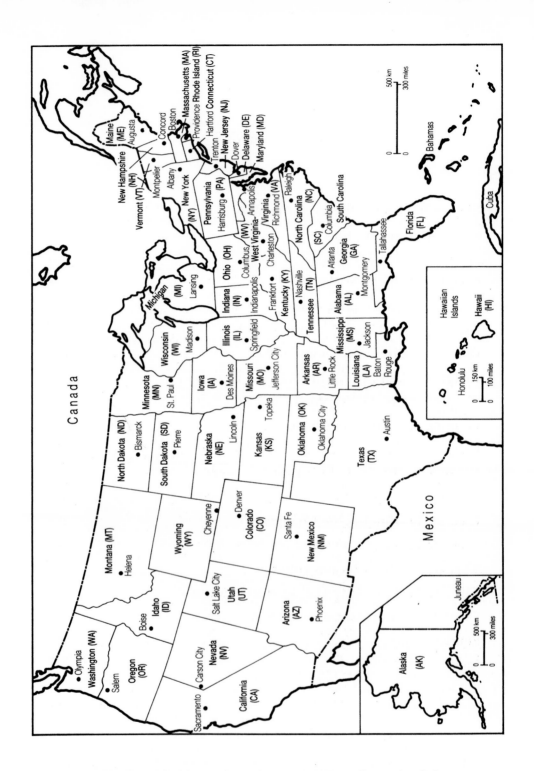

Map of the United States of America, showing all state lines and capitals.

# ACKNOWLEDGMENTS

Thanks are due to hundreds of kind individuals who responded to my research enquiries, as well as numerous historical societies, libraries, museums, newspapers and television stations, city halls, churches, Scots clan and family societies and other Scots interest-groups. Particular gratitude is expressed to:

Lori Davisson, Tucson (AZ); Bobby Leslie and his staff at the Orkney Library, especially Karen Miller and Maureen Drever; Harry Reid, Deputy Editor of *The Herald*; Jim Connor, *Herald* Picture Editor and the Photographic Library; Bob Barr, Orlando (FL); Wayne Rethford and Daniel Brown, Illinois Saint Andrew Society; Art Fischbeck, Mason City (IA); Paul Paulsen, Scotch Grove (IA); Mrs Bobette Orr, United States Consul-General for Scotland, Edinburgh; Betty Braddock, Kansas Heritage Centre, Dodge City (KS); Douglass Wallace, Topeka (KS); Carrie Autry, Fayetteville (NC); Jeannette Ackel, Monroe (LA); Nan Small, Lynn (MA); Flathead County Library, Kalispell (MT); History and Topography Department, Mitchell Library, Glasgow; The Library of Congress, Washington DC; Renetta Friesen, High Rolls-Mountain Park (NM); Todd Strand, State Historical Society of North Dakota; Fred Buchanan, University of Utah, Salt Lake City (UT); Corcoran Art Gallery, Washington DC; Ann Siebers, Tooele, (UT); Jack Scott and Betty Johnson, Princeton (WV); Paul Camp, University of South Florida Library; John Nolan, Farmington (NH); John Kerr Dean, Dearborn (MI); Alex Beaton, Woodland Hills (CA); Boston Museum of Fine Arts; the People of Lander (WY), especially Bill Duncan and Gladys and Pee Wee McDougall; Stephen Hague, Director of the Abraham Lincoln Museum, Harrogate (TN); The British Museum; The British Library; Gary E. Strong, California State Librarian; The New York State Historical Association; The New York Historical Society; Patricia Harpole, Minnesota Historical Society; Oregon Historical Society; United States Postal Service; National Park Service; University of Washington Libraries, Seattle (WA); American Heritage Center, University of Wyoming, Laramie (WY); Anaheim Public Library (CA); San Francisco Public Library; Eleanor Gehres, Western History Department, Denver Public Library (CO); Barbara Wolfe and the Logansport-Cass County Public Library, Logansport (IN); Pat McConnaughay Gregory, Indianapolis (IN); John Hallwas, Western Illinois University; Vivien Grant, Dunedin Historical Society (FL); Northern Indiana Historical Society, South Bend (IN); Lela J. Tindle, Fredonia (KS); Barbara Jobes, Pittsbburg (KS); The McDowell House, Danville, Kentucky; The US Embassy, London; Mowat Family International, Jackson (MS); Blaine Mills, St Andrews Society of Maine; John Grant, Oakland (MD); Commissioners of Aberdeen (MD); Neoma Laken, Breckenridge (MN); David L. Payne, Columbus (MS); John Thorburn, Tioga (ND); Presbyterian Church USA; Diane Bruce, Institute of Texan Cultures, San Antonio (TX) Ray McDonald of Arlington (TX) Diana and Joe Stein, Las Vegas (NM); John Driver, South Holland (IL); Floridel Bristow, Clinton (NC); Edwin C. Rangé, Merced (CA).

# A BRIEF CHRONOLOGY

501    Irish 'Scots' begin to arrive on the west coast of what is now Scotland.

843    Union of Picts and Scots in the Kingdom of Alba.

1314    Against the odds, Scots army under Robert the Bruce defeats vast English force at Bannockburn.

1320    Declaration of Arbroath, an assertion of Scottish freedom, also contained many elements later found in the American Declaration of Independence.

1398    Earl Henry Sinclair's expedition, which may have taken him as far as Massachusetts, begins.

1468    Orkney and Shetland islands acquired from Norway by Scotland.

1492    Columbus, looking for India, bumps into the West Indies.

1513    Battle of Flodden; death of James IV and most of the Scots nobility.

1540    Scotsman Thomas Blake joins Spanish expedition into present-day Arizona and New Mexico, in search of the fabled Seven Cities of Gold.

1541    Hernando do Soto reaches the Mississippi River.

1557    The First Bond or Covenant signed by Scots lords who declared their determination to overturn the Roman church.

1560    Latin mass and papal supremacy abolished and Reformed Confession of Faith authorised.

1579    Bible printed in Scotland for the first time.

1592    Presbyterian government first organised.

1598    Colonisation of Western Isles, in an attempt to subdue rebellious Highland landowners, is given the go-ahead by James VI.

1603    Union of the Crowns: Elizabeth of England dies and James VI goes to London to become also James I of England.

1607    English parliament rejects a union with Scotland, and flight of Catholic earls, signals start of Scots Protestant settlement of Ulster.

1608    French explorer, Samuel de Champlain, founds settlement at Quebec.

1609    James VI decides 'out of tindir affection' to let his Protestant subjects in Scotland in on the 'plantation' of Ulster.

1611    Large numbers of Scots begin to arrive in Ulster.

1619    First American parliament meets at Jamestown (VA) and the first shiploads of African slaves arrive in Virginia, which became a Crown Colony in 1624.

1626    Dutch found New Amsterdam, which was to become the city of New York.

1630    About 16,000 colonists from Britain begin to settle Massachusetts in a migration which lasted until 1642.

1638    Scots Presbyterians sign the Solemn League and Covenant.

1650    Scots defeated at the Battle of Dunbar; Covenanter prisoners begin to arrive in New England.

1651    Battle of Worcester, and another Scots defeat sees more Covenanters transported to the colonies.

1657    First Scots Association in America—The Charitable Society of Boston—founded specifically to ease the plight of Cromwellian prisoners.

1663    With the exception of indentured servants, all Scottish exports to the English colonies in America are barred.

1665    Scots parliament was shipping beggars, gypsies and thieves to the colonies.

1670    Hudson's Bay Company, which was to play an important role with the assistance of many Scots in the opening up of North America, founded.

1675    King Philip's War: Indians launch a major offensive against New England settlers.

1682    Scots colony in South Carolina for refugee Covenanters up and running.

1683    Colonists in their hundreds arrive at the Scots Quaker and Episcopalian outpost of East New Jersey.

1690    Decisive victory for King William of Orange at the Battle of the Boyne signals exodus of some 50,000 Scots to Ulster in a period of seven years.

1698    Five large vessels leave Leith with 1,200 immigrants bound for the ill-fated Scots colony of Darien, on the Isthmus of Panama.

1704    America's first newspaper—*The Boston News-letter*—published by John Campbell.

1707    Union of the Scottish and English parliaments; in what was seen by many as an omen, the bells of St Giles played: 'Why should I be sad on my wedding day.'

1716    Edinburgh-educated Ulster-Scots preacher, William Tennent begins his log college at Neshaminy (PA), an educational role model for the nation.

1717    Inventor Hugh Orr, a staunch patriot and gunsmith, born at Lochwinnoch, Renfrewshire.

1718    For the first time, Glasgow sent a vessel of its own to the American colonies; tobacco from Maryland and Virginia brought great prosperity to the city.

1718    Ulster-Scots immigration to America begins in earnest, with five shiploads of settler families arriving at Boston (MA).

1720    Poor French and Germans flood into Paris-based John Law of Lauriston's ill-starred Mississippi Valley colony in French Louisiana.

1729    Cape Fear River (NC) sees its Scots population boosted by the arrival of Jacobite refugees.

1736    Huge numbers of Ulster Scots said to be leaving Belfast for America, as earlier arrivals push westwards and southwards into the interior.

1740    Drift away from the land, first to Scottish towns then to America, had begun, prefacing the clearances which were well under way by the 1770s.

1744    Four-year 'King George's War' between Britain and the French colonies in America.

1746    Jacobite defeat at Culloden Moor signals end of the old clan system and brings thousands of Highland prisoners and refugees to the colonies.

1746    College of New Jersey (later Princeton University) is founded, with many Scottish connections.

1755    Ulster-Scots angered by the 'softly-softly' approach of the Quakers to the Indian problem at the commencement of the seven-year French and Indian War.

1758    Disastrous attack by the Black Watch on Fort Ticonderoga during French and Indian conflict.

1759    British forces capture Quebec; generals Montcalm and Wolfe killed.

1763    War ends with Britain gaining Canada and virtually all the land east of the Mississippi.

1763    Scots among a mob who hang six Indians at Harrisburg (PA), bringing 'lynch law', named after a Virginian farmer, into the English language.

1765    Stamp Act imposed by British parliament on all legal documents angers American colonists and is repealed the following year.

1768    Abortive attempt by Scots doctor, Andrew Turnbull, to establish a settlement at Mosquito Inlet, Florida, with hundreds of Mediterranean immigrants.

1770    Highland immigration to America at its height—during this year, fifty-four vessels sail across the Atlantic loaded with settlers.

1772    Great MacDonald exodus to America begins, lasting several years; Johnson and Boswell, visiting the Hebrides, witness 'the epidemick of wandering' in 1773.

1773    Boston Tea Party: citizens, including several Scots, disguised as Indians dump tons of tea into the harbour in a protest against British taxation.

1774    First Continental Congress meets at Philadelphia (PA) to protest a series of repressive acts against the American colonies.

1775    Patrick Henry, son of Aberdonian parents, makes famous 'Give me Liberty' speech; outbreak of Revolutionary War; divided loyalties among Scots and Ulster Scots.

1776    Leaders of American freedom movement—including nine Scots—sign Declaration of Independence.

1781    Dalkeith-born printer, Robert Aitken, publishes the first bible printed in America—war had halted the import of bibles from Britain.

1783    Treaty of Paris finally confirms American independence.

1787    New Constitution of the United States, with strong Scottish influences from the Presbyterian form of government, drawn up and signed in Philadelphia (PA).

1790    Scottish radicals begin to swell the tide of post-war immigrants to America, as unrest increases in the old country in the wake of the French Revolution.

1794    'Whisky war' provoked by US government's attempts to tax Ulster-Scots moonshiners in western Pennsylvania; whisky rebels retreat to Kentucky.

1800    New York presbytery orders that no slave-holder should be retained in their communion.

1803    Government-sponsored Lewis Clark expedition sets out to find a land route to the Pacific—Clark came from family of Virginia Scots; Louisiana 'purchase'.

1812    War between the United States and Britain over shipping and territorial disputes.

1814    Settlers from Sutherland, some of whom were to disperse to American Midwest and west coast, reach Lord Selkirk's Red River Colony, site of Winnipeg.

1824    Robert Owen acquires his pioneering settlement of New Harmony in Indiana.

1825    First Scots communities begin to spring up in the Midwest, as the great Western expansion gains momentum.

1836    American Scots fight and die at the Alamo as Texas struggles for independence from Mexico; Highland Society of New York holds first 'sportive' meeting.

1840    Scots immigrants celebrate Queen Victoria's marriage with forty-eight hour street party in New York.

1846    Potato famine in Ireland brings vast numbers of Catholic Irish to America, greatly outnumbering the Ulster Scots; all were simply known as 'the Irish'.

1847    America's first Burns Club founded in New York; former Ayrshire school-teacher, John Regan, publishes *Emigrant's Guide*—part survival guide, part travel book.

1848    Discovery of gold in California brings Scots fortune-hunters to the Far West.

1853    Scots mill girls imported in their hundreds to Holyoke (MA) to train as weavers; Boston the location for founding of first US Caledonian Club.

1861    American Civil War began, heralding an American industrial revolution which was to attract many thousands of Scots.

1862    Homestead Act, allowing any twenty-one year-old family head to claim 160 acres providing American citizenship could be proved, came into force.

1863    President Abraham Lincoln declares abolition of slavery in the United States.

1866    Ku-Klux Klan founded in Pulaski (TN) by a group of Confederate army veterans of Scottish origin.

1869    Wyoming becomes first US state to enact women's suffrage under its American-Scots governor, John A. Campbell.

1871    Infamous Camp Grant Massacre in Arizona in which American Scot, Will Oury, led settlers in slaughter of over a hundred men, women and children.

1871    Great Fire of Chicago sees ruination of businesses owned by Scots; two members of the Scots community died in the inferno.

1873    Large numbers of Scots corporations entered the investment field, as the railroad opened up the American West.

1875    Golf, thanks to the Scots pioneers in Yonkers (NY), was beginning to grasp the American imagination.

1886    Crofters Act, following work of Napier Commission, gives crofters in Scotland security of tenure and various other basic rights.

1888    Ship *Roger Stewart* sails from Greenock to New York with one hundred well-off immigrants who plan to become 'Lords of the Soil' in America's Far West.

1890    All across the United States, from New York to Oregon, Scots industrial immigrants are organising football teams and leagues.

1905    Tide of industrial immigrants from Scotland means that in many factories and workshops a case of 'Scots only spoken'.

1919    Airship R54 makes the first crossing of the Atlantic, a 108-hour flight from East Lothian to New York.

1923    Last great immigration of Scots to America, with depression in the old country.

1929    Wall Street stock market collapse leads to worldwide economic depression.

1934    Scottish National Party formed by the amalgamation of the National Party of Scotland and the Scottish Party.

1939    St Andrew's House, London government's headquarters in Edinburgh, opens.

1941    Japanese air attack on Pearl Harbor brings United States into WWII; in Glasgow, President Roosevelt's representative pledges US support against Nazi Germany.

1942    *Queen Mary* arrives at Gourock with nearly 10,000 US troops on board.

1945    Hundreds of Scots women wait for ships to take them to the US to marry servicemen who had proposed during war service—the famous GI brides.

1951    Stone of Destiny retrieved from Westminster Abbey by a group of young Scots patriots and left in Arbroath Abbey; some say the stone handed back on demand from England is a fake.

1955    Matador Cattle Company in Texas, one of America's most famous ranches with its headquarters in Dundee, finally passes out of Scottish control.

1969    American astronauts Armstong and Aldrin land on the moon, and the following year moon rock on display at the Royal Scottish Museum in Edinburgh.

~ *Chapter 1* ~

# THE WAY WEST

ISN'T IT STRANGE HOW EVENTS—insignificant in themselves—can combine to spark an idea? The morning mail brought a letter from a lady in Palm City, Florida. Having read one of my occasional despatches from Papa Westray to *The Washington Post*, she wanted to tell me that some 20,000,000 North Americans could, she thought, claim Scottish ancestry. Alas, so few knew or cared about their roots, she lamented. I filed the letter for unspecified future reference.

That same evening, however, staring at me from the TV screen at the height of the Gulf War, a senior US military man, a twentieth-century Scots émigré, was talking us through the latest phase in the campaign. Something was stirring in my subconscious, a notion was taking shape. Suddenly I wanted to learn more about those millions who had made the Atlantic crossing. Did they really forget their homeland, lose sight of their heritage? Not all, surely. Crockett and Carnegie, I knew a little about—but what of the rest?

Since migration from Scotland to the United States began to slow to a trickle after World War II, we have increasingly consigned great legions of immigrant men and women to the footnotes of history. Yet many of these people, I was to discover, still considered themselves as much Scots as American, even after decades in the New World, and while saluting the American flag their Caledonian roots held fast. Nowadays, family links between Scots and their American 'cousins' are generally very far removed. But however much the blood may have thinned, ties still exist. From almost every grimy city street or farming district , for over 250 years Scots chose America as their new home. It was in every sense the land of promise. From the sheep farms of the Borders, from the industrial heartland and the Highlands and Islands they left, and over the centuries their reasons for leaving have been consistent—economic, political or religious pressures forced them to seek land, opportunity, freedom of worship . . . and adventure.

Every journey of exploration must start somewhere, and what better place to begin my search than on my far-flung island home of Papa Westray. Even here, right on my own doorstep, I found that islanders were drawn, by the grind of life, to shake the glaur from their boots and exchange it, full of hope, for the more fertile soil of the New World. I've often walked of a summer's evening among the ocean-tumbled flagstones along the west shore, and as the sun lingers on the horizon west over the Atlantic, I've tried to recapture the parting emotions of folk like the Drever men from the farms of Ness and Bewing. John Drever, at the age of sixteen, set off in 1871 making landfall, the family believe, in New York, having crossed the ocean in a 'sidewheel steamship with sails'.

The teenager from Papay (the local name for the island) reached Chicago (IL) by train six weeks before the Great Fire then moved on to California to visit his brothers Andrew and David who had already settled on the West Coast. Eventually John Driver (the boys had mysteriously changed their name after arriving in the States) and four other brothers, Peter, William, Thomas and George, made their homes in the Windy City. John ran his own joinery business making wooden doors and window frames in what was then the peaceful suburban village of Englewood and is now a not-so-sought-after neighbourhood on the south side of Chicago.

Two of his brothers helped bring timber to Chicago for the business, one working in the logging camps and the other as skipper of a schooner-rigged sailing vessel which brought the timber across Lake Michigan. Their cousins, the Drevers o' Ness, William and Thomas, also chose America, Willie working as a 'pan and sluice box' prospector in the goldfields of California, near cousin Davie from Bewing, while Thomas settled in Chicago and (like his cousin of the same name, Thomas Drever) was a sailor on the Great Lakes.

The Drevers' unspectacular but intriguing story is typical in many respects of the experience of the Scots immigrants of the 1700s and 1800s. They got the head down and got on with the job. But since my researches began, I have been increasingly impressed by the quiet bravery, spirit and gritty determination of these pioneers, for that is what they were, whether in the industrial age or in the very earliest days of settlement.

From Thomas Blake (the first Scot we know to have ventured into what is now the southern United States, less than fifty years after Columbus made his historic 'discovery' in 1492) to the fortieth president of the United States, Ronald Reagan, the Scots and Ulster Scots (of whom much more later) have, for such a small nation, contributed dramatically to the development of what is now, indisputably, the most powerful nation on earth. Their story is a unique one and, I believe, forms an important yet sometimes underplayed chapter in the shaping of the USA we know today, with all its strengths and weaknesses.

Having established the fact that a large-scale exodus of Highland, Lowland and Ulster Scots took place over a period of more than two and a half centuries, how can it be that general histories often skip over this topic in a few sentences? Perhaps to examine in detail the role of various ethnic groups over-complicates the teaching of American history, or perhaps it's just out of fashion. Even the likes of Hugh Brogan (whose splendid history of the United States is the best general work on the subject

Paisley Place, a row of Renfrewshire weavers' cottages in the heart of what is now New York, occupied first in the 1830s. This lithograph dates from 1863. (New York Historical Society) *bottom* Abandoned nineteenth-century farm on the author's home isle of Papa Westray, Orkney. Even from this remote location young men, notably from the Drever family, immigrated to America. (Morag Hewitson)

I've read) seems content to lump the Scots, Irish and Welsh in with the English.

The Scottish influence has been undeniably impressive, even if it is occasionally understated. The skills and talents of the Scots were offered to literally thousands of small communities and growing cities. The bulk of stories contained here concern native-born Scots or first and second generation American Scots, still under the influence of parents and grand-parents, still considering what they called the 'land of the hills and heather' their spiritual home. When there were no longer native-born Scots in the family, my impression is that a subtle change overtook these people—no longer were they Scottish Americans but American Scots.

Few corners of this vast land were too remote for them, from the leafy glades of New England to the searing stone deserts of the south-west. There was no walk of life at which they failed to make their mark. And contrary to the music-hall stereotype of the canny, tight-fisted Scot, time and again we come across stories of how these immigrants were generous to their adopted homeland, giving their time and resources unstintingly to civic, religious and social projects.

Also, in a world daily more conscious of the fragility of our environment, it's inspiring to count through the many Scots who made early contributions to the conservation movement in America. Best known, unquestionably, is John Muir (1838–1914) of Dunbar, East Lothian, who liked to think of himself as a hobo but was one of history's most committed naturalists and an American hero. He was responsible for the concept of national parks and has a string of geographical features (glaciers, parks, lakes and peaks) named after him, from Alaska to California. In a land where the 'gobble, gobble' school of economics—the greedy scramble in mining, logging, ranching and trapping—had applied since the earliest days of settlement, he persuaded many Americans of the need to protect their priceless heritage. Muir's vision of nature, which he shared with the sorely pressed Indian tribes, was that the land was 'instinct with deity', a view at least a century ahead of its time.

Many of the earliest natural historians in America were Scots doctors, such as Alexander Garden, son of the parish minister at Birse in Aberdeenshire in the 1700s. After immigrating, Garden made regular trips into the interior of the Carolinas at a time when the frontier was almost within sight of the Atlantic. Botany and zoology were his specialities. Alexander Wilson, perhaps America's greatest ornithologist, was a Paisley weaver and political radical, and botanist, David Douglas, from Scone in Perthshire found a profusion of plants in the Pacific Northwest and some, notably the Douglas fir, carry his name.

However, just in case there's a hint of tartan jingoism creeping in at this point we should remember that many middle-class Scots made their fortune, or at least a comfortable living, off the backs of slaves who worked the farms and plantations. And our track record in dealing with the Red Indian, more

John Muir, America's pioneering environmentalist who introduced the concept of national parks and was born in Dunbar, East Lothian. (United States Postal Service)

commonly called the Native American today, is not unblemished. Among Scotland's 'ambassadors' were rough-and-ready characters not averse, it would appear, to lifting a scalp or two themselves. There were villains in our ranks.

A quick glance through the federal census papers for any US state reveals the pattern of this steady inflow of Scots to America. Tantalisingly, the stories of the overwhelming majority of these folk will never be told. They will remain as statistics.

What happened, for instance, to John Burmiss, a thirty-year-old Scots miner listed as resident in Arizona Territory in 1860? His property, according to the census, was 'nil'. Or later on that same list, Nathan Stevenson, a single man, a Scots-born mechanic who had been in the West for only two weeks? How did these adventurers fare? Perhaps the names will strike a chord in some family: someone might remember how great-uncle Nathan left to seek his fortune in America. We'll probably never know. But this book is dedicated as much to those anonymous millions as to the splendid characters who populate the following pages.

Some who travelled from within the geographical boundaries of Scotland may already have been indifferent to their nationality, ready for the melting pot. However, much of the material I have sifted suggests that while most folk were preoccupied with creating a new life for themselves and their families in the United States, they cherished their Scots background and tried to instil that same pride in subsequent generations. This is certainly the case with immigrants from Ulster, who can justifiably be described as Scotland's fourth immigrant tribe, as distinctively Scots as the Highlanders, Lowlanders and Borderers.

Transplanted to Northern Ireland from the early 1600s as part of a scheme of the English government to squeeze the Catholic Irish out of the north, these Protestant settlers, mainly from west-central Scotland, were still 'more Scottish than the Scots' when they began to drift to America a century later, forced to move on by political and religious, as well as economic pressures.

The vast exodus to America began in 1718 when five ships carrying 700 Ulster Scots arrived in Boston. During the entire colonial period it is thought that 250,000 Ulster Scots settled in America joined through the 1800s by perhaps another 500,000, although figures are clouded by the term 'Irish' often being applied to arrivals from the Emerald Isle, whether north or south. However, their 'Scottishness' was never in question. Soon after his arrival in America, the Rev. James MacGregor, minister to one of their first communities at Londonderry (NH), complained to the legislature: 'We are surprised to hear ourselves described as Irish'. As one old immigrant Ulster Scot, stressing his Scots origins, so neatly put it: 'If a man is born in a stable does that make him a horse?' Alternatively, it was suggested that Ulster Scots had been 'brewed in Scotland, bottled in Ireland and uncorked in America'.

There is no disputing the dynamic effect they had on the political and economic development of America. Always in the pioneering frontline defending the pacifist Quakers against what was seen as the Indian menace, they were among the first to declare for independence from Britain, providing the backbone of George Washington's fighting forces. Distinguished by their love of learning, religion, home and family, they have been described as the cheery people, but it should be noted that their critics found them contentious, hard to get along with, carrying the Scottish traits of stubbornness, clannishness and the liking for a good scrap. It seems an even more self-reliant, independent Scot had been created in the turmoil of the north of Ireland.

While many native Scots—surprisingly, even staunch Jacobites—were reluctant to join the Patriots in the Revolutionary War, the Ulster Scots, still carrying a bitter resentment over their treatment by the British establishment, happily threw in their lot with the freedom-fighters. Into the 1800s they were found throughout the developing nation. G.F. Black identified one large group of Ulster-Scots descendants in the mountain folk of Tennessee and Kentucky. Their Presbyterian background is conclusively shown in the warning used by mothers to bring unruly children into line: 'Behave, or Clavers will get you!' (referring, of course, to John Graham of Claverhouse, 'Bluidy Clavers', Scourge of the Covenanters.)

So the transatlantic traffic down the centuries can be seen to have ranged quite beyond what we are addressing here as a mainly Scottish-American connection. Indeed, it could be argued that any sectioning-off of the interchange of peoples across the Atlantic must entail some arbitrary element. This study does not touch on the history of the Scots in Canada—why not? After all, some will say the American-Canadian border, the 49th parallel, is perhaps the world's most artificial boundary. The answer is simple: the volume of material from colonial America and the United States alone is enormous. To have included the very special story of Canada would have meant that less than justice was done to either of the Scots communities.

One survey suggested that about half European Americans, including the Scots, have no consciousness of being connected with the Old World. In the race-memories of the American Scots must lie many thousands of stories which, as the blood thins and the memory fades will, sadly, be lost forever. Perhaps we can rescue a few here. As the family tree spread its branches through space and time, most of the Great Clan did indeed finally cut the umbilical cord linking them spiritually and intellectually to the old country. Yet the enthusiasm today of these Scots interest-groups keeps the connection alive, and more than makes up for the forgetful millions.

It should also be remembered that available biographical material is perhaps not representative of the great wedge of working-class immigrants, a largely anonymous people, who wrote little, if at all, and worked away quietly and largely unnoticed. This group form the bulk of American Scots and I hope that in our travels we will sense a little of their spirit and purpose.

Quotas were introduced in the 1920s by the US government anxious that the nation might be flooded with the poor and hungry of the world, but it was subsequent events—the Depression of the 1930s, with 9,000,000 unemployed in the US, World War II and the growing attraction of Commonwealth settlement—which finally slowed Scots immigration to the United States. By the mid 1960s, over ninety-five percent of the population of the United States was American-born.

Yet during the last decades of this century, Scots businesspeople, doctors, scientists, ministers, engineers, academics, sportsmen and women have been crossing the pond again, often for only a two or three-year secondment, occasionally for good. However, life for the non-professional techno-settler can still be very hard. The words of an elderly nineteenth-century native-born Scots settler on the plains of Iowa are, from time to time, echoed by Scots in the bars of New Jersey: 'I wish I'd never left home.'

For each story I have brought to the surface there must be a hundred waiting to be told. Inevitably there will be tales that should have been told and have not been. I can only apologise for this. This is neither an academic nor a genealogical work, although it does contain elements of both. Generally, books written about the Scots contribution in America fall into distinct categories—long lists of names with only the briefest of biographical detail, complex studies of development in tightly defined areas and important works of social anthropology or business enterprise. Working on a broad canvas is a style with which I am most comfortable. The search was for good stories and relevant background. Major topics, such as slavery and the Mormon Church regrettably are touched upon only lightly, simply providing a framework on which the Scottish anecdotes can be displayed. I hope the bibliography will enable anyone who wishes to pursue particular aspects of this remarkable and inspiring story to do so with relative ease.

For months I had scoured my notes for a story which summarised the Scots pioneering story in America, then the following tale ended up on my desk.

The McKenzie family were crossing the Rocky Mountains to begin a new life in Colorado. The year was 1884 and the col between Leadville and Aspen was still filled with snowdrifts, three or four feet deep in places. Spring sunshine, however, was slowly thawing the snow on the rough tracks—and the wagons were moving.

Little Jim McKenzie, aged eleven, trudged beside his father to lighten the load for the horses as they dragged the family's possessions on the way west. At one point, Jim fell headfirst into an icy pool of melt-water. As he was set up on the wagon, dripping wet, shivering and miserable, to dry off, the wee lad was introduced to the seldom-spoken motto of these sturdy Scots—a philosophy which saw many through the most trying of circumstances. His father told him: 'Laugh, son . . . and keep going.'

State of Indiana, _Cass_ County, ss:

To the Judge of the _Cass_ Circuit Court, in the State of Indiana:

_Walter Thompson_ Being an Alien, and free white person, makes the following report of himself; Upon his solemn oath declares that he is aged _28_ years, that he was born in the _County_ of _Dumfries Scotland_ that he emigrated from _Glasgow_ in the year one thousand eight hundred and _fifty four_ that he arrived in the United States at the _City_ of _New York_ in the State of _New York_ on the _18th_ day of _January_ eighteen hundred and _fifty four_ that he owes allegiance to _Victoria Queen of the United Kingdom of Great Britain and Ireland_ and that it is bona fide his intention to become a citizen of the United States of America, and to renounce forever all allegiance and fidelity to any foreign prince, potentate, state or sovereignty whatever; and particularly to _Victoria Queen aforsaid_ of whom he is a subject.

_Walter Thompson_

**Sworn to and Subscribed,** Before me, on the _9th_ day of _October_ A. D. 1860

_Noah S La Rose_ Clerk C. C.

A Declaration by Walter Thompson from Dumfriesshire seeking American citizenship in 1860. The document required Scots to renounce their allegiance to Queen Victoria and the UK and caused great anguish to many immigrants. (Indiana State Archives) *bottom* Aberdeen masons at the site of the Capitol building, Austin c.1887. Scores of Scotsmen immigrated in answer to newspaper adverts when a strike halted work on this impressive building. (Austin, Texas History Centre)

Time for a haircut. The gentleman receiving a trim outside his home at the Victoria colony in Kansas in the 1870s has been identified as T.F. Miller. (The Kansas State Historical Society, Topeka)

~ *Chapter 2* ~

# CHRISTOPHER WHO?

D URING 1992'S CELEBRATIONS of 500 years since America's discovery, the very reasonable claims—some twenty in total—made on behalf of alternative 'discoverers' of America were quietly put to one side while we hailed Christopher Columbus, the man who stumbled into the West Indies while looking for Cathay. Assuming there is some merit in examining the various claims, and that must be highly doubtful since it is widely accepted now that the first colonisers of America were a tribe of nomadic hunters who crossed the now-flooded land bridge between Siberia and Alaska, we can find at least three possible candidates who may, however speculatively, help tie northern Britain to the New World at a very early date.

St Brendan (484–577) has long been considered one of the earliest European travellers, setting out from his monastic outpost in the west of Ireland with a crew of monks in search of an 'earthly paradise' under the rim of the western horizon. He is likely to have used all available stepping-stones along the route, and that must surely include the Western Isles, Orkney and Shetland. George Mackay Brown, the Orcadian poet, has made reference to possible Brendan-linked place names in Shetland.

Next comes Leif Erikson, kinsmen of the Norse folk of Orkney. It is now generally accepted that some 500 years before Columbus, the swashbuckling Viking made a landfall in America, some say (from archaeological evidence) that it was in Labrador, others who cite the Saga stories of an abundance of grapes look further south. Could there have been Orkney men at his oars?

Most interesting of all—and taking us into medieval Scotland—is Earl Henry Sinclair. His epic voyage is said to have started from Orkney in 1398, and the only narrative of the voyage (by Haklyut) indicates the presence of Earl Henry and two Italian explorers in Greenland. Beyond that, guesswork comes into play. One theory has them landing at Guysborough in Nova Scotia and moving as far south as Massachusetts. This proposition is based on the discovery of a carved stone, originally thought to be an Indian relic, which experts at Cambridge University decided might depict a knight in armour. Research continues but this story seems set to run and run, and who knows, by 2092 Earl Henry may have moved up the league table to challenge that man Columbus.

Zuni Indian pueblos in New Mexico, the discovery of which almost certainly gave rise to rumours of the Seven Cities of Gold and prompted the Coronado Expedition. (Arizona Pioneers Historical Society)

SEVEN CITIES OF GOLD

After the North Atlantic explorations comes the first Scot to earn the title of a true American pioneer, the mercenary adventurer Tamas Blaque (Tam Blake), who was part of the famous Coronado Expedition which penetrated deep into what is now Arizona and New Mexico in 1540. As Spain's rich colonial empire flourished, the northern frontier of their Mexican lands lay a few hundred miles north of Mexico City—beyond was an unknown continent.

When three shipwrecked sailors arrived back after wandering for eight years, they brought with them stories of a fabulous land to the north where the streets of the large cities were

> lined with goldsmith's shops, houses of many storeys and doorways studded with emeralds and turquoises.

Reconnaissance parties returned with tales of the Seven Cities of Cibola. Presumably what they saw from a distance were the rock masonry Indian pueblos near what is now Gallup, New Mexico. Francisco Vasquez de Coronado, the thirty-year-old son of a Spanish aristocrat, was commissioned commander of the expedition and he set off with 300 soldiers, 800 Mexican Indian allies and four priests. With them was Tam Blake, who had married Franscisca de Rivera, widow of one of the first settlers in New Spain. Blake later identified himself as a citizen of the Kingdom of Scotland, son of William Blake and Agnes Mowat. In the statement made to the Spanish Viceroy in 1550, he explained that he had arrived in Mexico in 1534–35 after having taken part in the conquest of New Granada in 1532 with Alonso de Heredia, brother of the conquistador, Pedro de Heradia.

Unfortunately, Coronado's search for the seven cities of gold was in vain. He encountered, fought and conquered the Indians in their rock fortress towns—but there was no gold. One important outcome of the expedition, however, was the discovery of The Grand Canyon by his scouting parties. There seems a possibility that Tam Blake was among the group, the first Europeans to set eyes on the yawning mile-deep chasm.

Another Scot associated with the early exploration of the Grand Canyon—but more than 300 years later—was Andy Hall, born in Liddesdale in the

The 1540 Coronado Expedition into Arizona and New Mexico was joined by Scotsman Thomas Blake. (Arizona Historical Society Library)

13

Borders in 1848, who emigrated to Illinois with his family. While he was still a boy, Andy moved to the western frontier and joined a wagon train. He became an Indian-fighter of repute, known to his friends as 'Dare-Devil Dick' and once boasted in a letter:

> Many an Indian would be glad to get my scalp as my hair is about 14″ long.

He had told his family of his determination to explore the Colorado River and when John Wesley Powell, a Civil War veteran and geologist, decided to organise an expedition, Andy found himself recruited. All during that epic journey Andy remained cheerful and optimistic, although many of his companions—cold, wet and hungry—grew increasingly discouraged. It was Andy who named one of the Green River's most wild reaches as the Canyon of Lodore, after Southey's poem. His letters home were brief but gave some insight into the hardships and excitement of the expedition. In May 1869, he wrote to his mother announcing that he had joined Major Powell. He explains he had no time to write down any news at present and apologises:

> It is a long time since I wrote you but I am still alive and well and hope you are the same. You need not expect to hear from me for some time, 10 or 12 months at least.

The rigours and thrills of negotiating the Colorado are graphically outlined in a note to his brother in July of the same year:

> We had the greatest ride we ever got . . . the walls of the canone where the river runs through was 15 hundred feet in some places. I think we are through the worst of the water now.

By September he was able to write to his brother and explain that he had 'turned up all rite at last'. The expedition had lasted 111 days, and of the ten men who started only six made it through. Three men 'deserted' because of their dread of running the last of the rapids, but Andy reported 'We ran the rapid all rite and gave a loud cheer.'

COLONIAL ADVENTURES

Scotland's colonial exploits form only a minor part of our history, yet they show the first real efforts of a small nation to assert itself on the world stage. Certainly the best-known enterprise was the Darien Expedition, an attempt in the last years of the seventeenth century to establish a settlement in Panama, which failed due to the reluctance of the English government to lend assistance (a familiar story), the harsh jungle climate and the hostility of the Spanish in the region.

A century earlier, James VI tried to colonise the Western Isles of Scotland in a device to bring rebellious landowners to heel. To encourage interest, stories were put about of gold discoveries in Harris and North Uist and although a group of Fife adventurers took up the challenge and plans were laid for towns in Lochaber, Kintyre and at Stornoway, the scheme failed due to persistent and violent local opposition.

Another project, this time for the plantation of Ulster was to have far-reaching consequences for America and Scotland, as we'll see. After the Earls of Tyrone and Tyrconnel fled to the Continent in 1607, the English government decided to encourage non-Catholic settlement in Northern Ireland; but as it transpired, most of those who chose to cross the Irish Sea were from the central Lowlands of Scotland.

By the 1600s, however, Scotland, still with its own parliament although James was now in London, was desperate to make its presence felt on the international commercial scene and was looking west across the Atlantic. Almost every nation in Western Europe at that time was financing and organising settlements in the New World, and it was natural that Scotland should want to do likewise.

In the early 1600s the first Scots settlement, directed by Sir William Alexander, Earl of Stirling, a close friend of the king, was on the eastern seaboard of what is now Canada. Nova Scotia came into being only to fall relatively quickly under French sovereignty. Further attempts at establishing colonies were considered in Maine and New York but neither of these efforts met with success. It was difficult to persuade large numbers of Scots to abandon the homeland at this stage for the uncertainties of the New World.

Not until the 1680s—with the beginnings of 'improvement' which was to trim drastically the number of people on the land, a growing economy, the expansion of trade and a period of religious conflict in Scotland—were conditions right for large-scale investment of manpower and resources towards colonial enterprises, this time putting down markers more cautiously on already-established areas of English settlement. This decade saw the launch of two competing Scottish colonial ventures in America—a Covenanters outpost in Carolina and a Quaker-sponsored colony in East New Jersey. Again they were relatively short-lived but were by far the most significant of the early projects; planned at about the same time, the ventures could hardly have been more different in character.

The Carolina enterprise, which we first hear of when 12,000 acres were sold by the English proprietors to Sir John Cochran of Ochiltree and Sir George Campbell of Cessnock, was dominated by gentlemen and merchants from the south-west of Scotland, among whom religious motives were paramount. Persecution of the Covenanters had peaked in the previous decade and a number of the Carolina promoters were victims of this oppression. Their haven straggled along the River Royal, in what is now South Carolina, but numbers were never sufficient to sustain a permanent colonial presence.

A group of Presbyterian prisoners, banished for offences such as refusing to renounce the Covenant, was established in the colony by 1682. Among this group, whose descendants can still be found in the Carolinas, were names such as Buchanan, Inglis, Galt, Marshall, Machen, Paton, Gibson, Young, Cunningham, Smith and Dowart. In 1683, the colony was augmented by a group of Ulster Scots under a leader called Ferguson.

After long and complex negotiations with the proprietors the following year, Lord Cardross and William Dunlop, later Principal of Glasgow University, set off from Gourock to found their Covenanter outpost at Stuartstown 'in a very convenient place twenty miles from the mouth of the River Port Royall', south of the later town of Beaufort. Plans were ambitious but ill-fated. Six hundred acres of land was to be divided into 220 lots, each with an adjoining garden.

Nominally, Spain and Britain were at peace around this time but Port Royal lay on the Carolina-Florida frontier where warfare flickered intermittently. Strangely, this frontier post of Scots immigrants did not receive support from the largely English colony up the coast at Charleston, who might conceivably have seen the Scots as a useful buffer against the Spanish. Relations between the two communities were strained even before the Scots wives and families started to arrive at Stuartstown. At one point a warrant was issued for the arrest of Lord Cardross by the Grand Council at Charleston, simply over his failure to attend a meeting. But even this failed to dampen enthusiasm, and the Scots were joined by families from Antigua who believed the district would produce not only indigo but good sugar.

Crucial to the future of the settlement, with the ever-present threat of Spanish invasion, were good relations with the local Yamasee Indians. A deal was struck, and the Scots were even said to have equipped the tribe for a raid on the nearby Spanish colony of Santa Catalina. Some say the final destruction of Stuartstown in 1686 was precipitated by this raid.

Early in 1685, the uncertainties of frontier life were indicated by a plea from the Scots along the Port Royal River for six guns from the fort at Charleston to help in their defence. Whether they ever arrived, we do not know. But when the destruction of Stuartstown came, it came swiftly with a raiding party made up of Spanish, Indians and mulattos numbering about 150, moving north from the Spanish port of St Augustine in three galleys and overrunning the community which had only twenty-five fit men because of an outbreak of fever.

Before the descent of the Spanish on Cardross's 'very convenient place', the noble lord, disgusted by his treatment at the hands of the authorities in Charleston, had left to join the growing colony of Scots exiles in Holland. No attempt was made to revitalise the Covenanter haven.

One family closely connected with Port Royal were the Gibsons of Glasgow. James Gibson transported the Covenanter prisoners to the Carolinas while his brother Walter, Lord Provost of the city 1688–89 and perhaps the city's most successful merchant in the late 1600s, offered cheap passages to America and seventy acres at a penny an acre yearly rental.

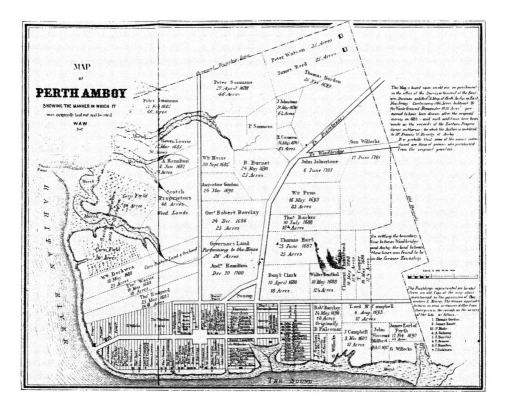

Town map of Perth Amboy, heart of the Scots colony of East New Jersey founded in the early 1680s. (New Jersey Historical Society)

ABERDEENSHIRE TRANSPLANTED

Generally speaking, the north-east of Scotland was the home ground of the families who picked the more convivial surroundings of East New Jersey as their target in America. Less of a frontier outpost, it soon overshadowed its counterpart in the south.

While it was the staunch Presbyterians from the south-west who had been the movers and shakers in the Carolina colonisation, most of the East New Jersey proprietors were either Quakers or members of the Episcopal Church. According to Landsman, in *Scotland and its First American Colony*:

> . . . the society they modelled their colony on was the northeast, where sons could acquire lairdships, a degree of religious diversity was tolerated and where economic expansion was the order of the day.

It was the Quaker William Penn who persuaded the leader of the East New Jersey Scots, Robert Barclay, laird of Urie near Stonehaven, to become involved in American colonisation. On condition that he could recruit four other Scots proprietors, Barclay was appointed nominal Governor of East New Jersey for life. The first task of the Scots team was to create their own enclave within the existing colony of New Jersey, giving them a foothold in the mid-Atlantic trading area. They successfully argued to be allowed to maintain trading links with Scotland using Scottish ships, and the decision to recruit Quakers and non-Quakers gave the new colony vitality and better social balance.

In the space of two years, from 1683, four major voyages were made to the colony with as many as 700 people leaving Leith, Montrose and Aberdeen in that first spurt, probably half of them as indentured servants.

At the mouth of the Raritan River the town of Perth Amboy, an early if dislocated example of a planned Scots village with its distinctive parallel street plan, sprang up. It was to this town that John Johnstone, an apothecary in Edinburgh but originally from the Borders, came to make his home. After marrying the daughter of another shareholder, he fell heir to his 'fraction' and was soon one of the colony's principal landowners with a seat on the Resident Board. He went on to found an important Perth Amboy dynasty. More typical, perhaps, of East New Jersey's residents would be John Hebron, who was on board the first Scots vessel to arrive in 1683. He was one of a group of twenty-two unmarried servants, and having completed his four-year indenture he sold his thirty-acre land entitlement and worked for a further five years on a farm before using his capital to set himself up as a tailor in Perth Amboy. Three years later he also had a farm of his own. Although East New Jersey did not remain a Scottish colony for long (the Scots proprietors handed over their control in 1702) the enthusiastic Scottish interest meant that actual involvement with the colony lasted much longer.

Even in the early 1600s, James VI was considering another, drastic, way of boosting the level of migration to America. Troubled by rowdies on the Scottish border, he considered shipping mischief-makers *en masse* to Virginia. Details are available on these highly-organised projects, but it's equally certain that in the first half of the seventeenth century Scots families and individuals were drifting across the Atlantic. As early as 1635, we have reports of a Strang family from Orkney who settled in the vicinity of the pioneering English colony of Jamestown, Virginia (established 1607). Beyond the mid-1600s, reports become more frequent. John MacCoon, born in Aberdeenshire, was to be found at Westerly, Rhode Island in 1669, according to his descendants. He married first in Scotland then again in America, and his children married into the family of Thomas Hazard, a founder of Newport, Rhode Island. By this time it seems likely that there were several thousand Scots settlers in New England alone. However, a large proportion of the Scots in America were there against their will—these were transported prisoners, the first large shipments beginning when the Scots found themselves pitted against Oliver Cromwell.

In August 1648, a Scots army was cut to pieces at Preston and within a month POWs were on their way to the colonies. On 3 September 1650, the Scots were defeated again at Dunbar and over 1,000 prisoners were ordered to America. Exactly a year later came the defeat at Worcester, and while most prisoners on this occasion went to the gold mines of Guinea in West Africa, a shipload of Scots reached Boston (MA) on *The John and Sara*.

In 1665, with Charles II on the throne, the Scots parliament took a lead from England and were shipping beggars, gypsies and thieves to America. The following year, Covenanters were among the prisoners, the start of an export that ran into the thousands. The scale of this operation is indicated by the loss of the merchant ship *Crown* in a storm off Orkney in 1679. From its cargo of 257 prisoners, 200 were drowned. These were the defeated men of Bothwell Brig. Some of these unwilling settlers eventually found their way home, but many stayed and some prospered. Their value to the colonial economy can be assessed by the fact that, in 1663, the English government prohibited exports from Scotland to English settlements in America. These 'servants' were specifically excluded.

ONWARD AND OUTWARD

As we've seen, Scots were present in North America from the very earliest days of settlement, but it wasn't until about a century after the founding of Jamestown (VA) that they began to arrive in sufficient numbers to develop a distinctive community life, including their own schools and churches.

Many of the Scottish settlers of the early 1700s came with the promise of free acres, especially if they were prepared to occupy the wilderness areas, as a barrier against the Indians and the threatened encroachment of the French. In Scotland, as land 'improvement' gained pace and clearances began in the mid-1700s, as the population grew with increasing threat of famine, the drift to the towns and eventually across the Atlantic gained momentum. Independence, the prospect of ownership rather than being a slave tied to the land was very enticing, and the problems to be encountered in the New World—getting produce to market, hostile Indians, disease and the rigours of the climate—were all part of a hazy future.

It would seem that few Scots left for America yearning for democracy. They simply sought to escape from the authority of government or its taxes, rural poverty and uncertainty. By the end of the century, however, they were also fleeing the threat of social upheaval, even revolution. Berthoff, in *British Immigrants in Industrial America* says:

> . . . there have been nearly as many personal motives for emigrating as there have been emigrants. Throughout three centuries, however, humdrum economic forces have probably moved most of the venturers.

And so the great tide of immigration began to flow. The criminals and POWs, the religious refugees and the beggars, were joined by earnest, hopeful families, by poor but ambitious Scots lads prepared to work for years as indentured servants to secure a foothold in America, and pious young men from Scottish universities bringing their skills in religion, medicine and teaching to the wild frontier.

By the time Dr Samuel Johnson and James Boswell were on their famous tour of the Hebrides in 1773, migration was at its height and they experienced the 'epidemick of wandering' at first hand, Boswell reporting:

> One morning I walked out and saw the ship 'Margaret of Clyde' fairly pass by with a number of emigrants on board. It was a kind of melancholy sight.

Patterns of settlement show that Scots generally chose areas which bore closest resemblance to their home ground. Highland farmers and soldiers (possibly as many as 12,000 who had fought for Britain in the French and Indian War 1756–63), picked the upland areas of places like New York state while Lowlanders made for the tidewater states where the sea, as it had done at home, dominated day-to-day life.

Despite the failure at Port Royal, the Carolinas still attracted Scots. Highlanders established settlements on the Cape Fear River (NC) as early as 1729, and there was a scattering of Jacobite refugees in the aftermath of the 1715 uprising. Neill MacNeill of Jura brought over a party of more than 350 folk from Argyllshire in 1739, the family names including McLachlan, Stewart, McDougall and MacBrayne.

Cross Creek, now Fayetteville (NC), was the focus of these Highland settlements, and the area remained popular with Highlanders for many years. Even as late as 1884, descendants of the pre-revolutionary Highlanders living in an area still known then as the 'Scotch Settlements' welcomed 300 poor crofters from Skye. In the summer of 1770 alone, fifty-four vessels carrying 1,200 immigrants had left the Highlands and islands and by the outbreak of the Revolutionary War five years later, some 12,000 Highlanders were said to have settled at Cape Fear.

In 1772, the great Macdonald exodus began and continued until the outbreak of the war. As far back as 1753, Cumberland County (named after the 'Butcher' of Culloden, it was an ironic place for so many Jacobites to end up) had 1,000 Scotsmen capable of bearing arms, and most of them were Macdonalds. Large communities of Ulster Scots were found in Orange, Rowan and Mecklenburg counties. Other Highland Scots with early land grants in this district included James Innes from Caithness, Hugh Campbell and William Forbes, in 1732.

Scots Presbyterian colonies sprang up in Virginia and Maryland where, at Paxutent, a church was in existence in 1704. A number of prominent Fife families were among the congregation. Elsewhere in these areas, little pockets of Scots were to be found, for example in the tobacco towns of Alexandria and Dumfries (VA).

Pennsylvania was a target for many of Scots blood, particularly the Ulster Scots and in Philadelphia there was a Presbyterian church in 1698. By 1720, these settlers had drifted steadily inland to reach the Susquehanna River; three years later, they were on the site of present-day Harrisburg. Between 1730 and 1745, they were settled in the Cumberland Valley and the push was inexorably westwards. Bernard Bailyn has described this great migration in his book, *Voyagers to the West*:

> It began with the movement to the frontiers of isolated family and community groups moving here and there along a thousand-mile perimeter in search of new locations—a few hundred isolated clusters of people, at first, pulling loaded carts and sledges and driving wagons along Indian paths across the foothills and through gaps in the first mountain barriers to the west.

Mule teams negotiate fifteen-foot high snowdrifts on the summit of the Sierra Nevadas above Lake Valley in 1866. (Library of Congress, Neg. No. USZ62–20358)

Between the years 1730 to 1775, Ulster Scots and Scots immigration into Pennsylvania often exceeded 10,000 people in a year. In 1736, it is recorded that there were 1,000 Ulster-Scots families waiting at Belfast for ships to take them to America. The stream of immigration flowed south into Virginia, the Carolinas, Georgia, Kentucky, Tennessee and west across the Allegheny Mountains into the vast territory of the Ohio.

By the start of the Revolutionary War, the Scots seemed to be everywhere along the rapidly expanding frontier and it is widely accepted that 'the majority of hardy settlers and pioneers of the Great Middle West were of Scottish birth or descent'.


INTO THE WILDERNESS
Some groups moving into the wilderness would make use of the great river network to float their rafts to their destinations. Nashville, Tennessee received the bulk of its first settlers in this manner. In 1734, Robert Harper, an Ulster Scot came to the junction of the Potomac and Shenandoah Rivers and there established a ferry, in his own name, which was to have historic importance in the opening-up of the American interior.

Many Highlanders also found a new home in Georgia, where an immigrant company started New Inverness in the Darien district. Scots on this Georgia frontier—many of them from the Clan Mackintosh and 'men of good character'—were a buffer against the Indians and Spanish, and were found principally in the Attahama Valley. Fort St Andrews sprouted on the frontier, and Governor Oglethorpe once paid the settlers a visit wearing full Highland dress.

'Loyal Protestant Highlanders' were sought for the vast area between the Hudson River and the Great Lakes in New York state. The contingent of pioneers there included many Scots and Ulster-Scots families brought to the valley of the Susquehanna by John Lindesay, 'a Scots gentleman', who, with three associates in 1738, obtained a tract of 8,000 acres in Cherry Valley, Otsego County. Sadly, on 11 October 1778 the entire settlement was destroyed and thirty-two residents were killed, others being taken as prisoners by loyalists and Indians.

Scots settlers were also found in Putnam and Dutchess counties in New York, and in 1738 an Islay man, Captain Lachlan Campbell, took eighty-three families from his neighbourhood to 47,000 acres of grant land on the borders of Lake George. Ballston in Saratoga County was settled in 1770 by a colony of Presbyterians, a mix of Scots and Ulster Scots. The first Presbyterian church in Albany was organised in 1760 by Scots who had settled there, and John More and his wife, Betty Taylor More, natives of Rothiemurchus, Inverness-shire, settled in the western Catskills, on the site of the present-day community of Roxbury (NY) in 1773.

Not all of these immigrants came by the direct route from Scotland.

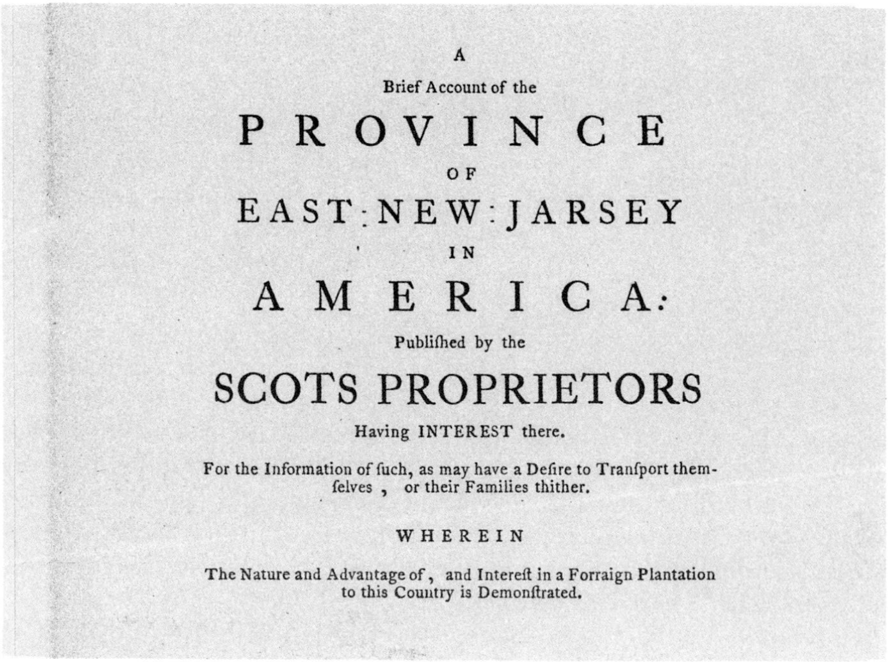

A
Brief Account of the

# PROVINCE

OF

# EAST:NEW:JARSEY

IN

# AMERICA:

Publifhed by the

# SCOTS PROPRIETORS

Having INTEREST there.

For the Information of fuch, as may have a Defire to Tranfport them-
felves , or their Families thither.

WHEREIN

The Nature and Advantage of , and Intereft in a Forraign Plantation
to this Country is Demonftrated.

Title page of a broadsheet designed to encourage settlers and issued in Scotland in 1683 by the proprietors of the Scots colony of East New Jersey. (New Jersey Historical Society)

Alexander Bissett Munro, born in Inverness in December 1793, left at the age of fourteen for the West Indies. He eventually owned a coffee and cotton plantation, and developed trading links with Boston (MA) and an important merchant of that city, Solomon Dockendorff. Accompanying Solomon's ship back to Boston on one occasion, he met the merchant's stunningly beautiful sister twenty-year-old Jane, and was smitten. Returning to the Caribbean, he sold out and came to America to marry Jane and settle in Round Pond, Maine, where he became district postmaster. His descendants are still in the area.

And still the POWs arrived by the shipload. Jacobite prisoners taken at Preston in Lancashire were sent to Maryland in the summer of 1717 in the ships *Friendship* and *God Speed*, and sold as servants. The names on the list of prisoners includes MacQueen, Garden, Wilson, Sinclair, Grant, Spark, Spalding, Webster and Robertson. In 1747, another shipload of Jacobites taken in the '45 were sent to Maryland in the ship *Johnson* of Liverpool. These followers of Bonnie Prince Charlie and the Stuart cause included names found on a certified list in the public records at Annapolis (MD)—Claperton, Melvil, Murdock, Duddoch, MacCallum and Arbuthnott.

It's difficult now to envisage the scale of this vast migration from a nation as small as Scotland. Some idea of the traumatic effect may, however, be grasped from the stark fact that on a single June day in 1773 between 700 and 800 people are said to have left Stornoway's crescent beach and single pier of loose stones. That same month, from the same port, a further 800 left for North Carolina. Lewis may have lost as many as 30,000 people in the 1760s and 70s. Although Greenock was the main port of departure, one-off sailings took place from obscure corners of the west coast of Scotland, like Gigha and Lochbroom.

FOLLOWING THE IRON HORSE

At the beginning of the Revolutionary War, when immigration slowed almost to a stop, there were reckoned to be nearly seventy communities of Scots and Ulster Scots in New England, including Maine, New Hampshire, Vermont, Massachusetts and Connecticut. In New York, there were between thirty and forty; fifty to sixty in New Jersey; more than 130 in Pennsylvania and Delaware; more than 100 in Virginia, Maryland and eastern Tennessee, fifty in North Carolina and seventy in South Carolina and Georgia—some 500 Scots settlements in all. Estimates of how many people this represents vary from 500,000 to over 1,000,000.

Immigration to the United States was banned at the outbreak of the Revolutionary War because the British government felt that Scots might become too easily disaffected and choose the independence line. There was also a fear of losing skilled workers.

Just before and after 1800, the United States started to expand rapidly, well beyond the confines of the original thirteen colonies, and the population of states like Ohio and Indiana began to increase dramatically. A major contribution to this 'second immigration' away from the old habitations along the east coast was made by the Scots. This was to be pioneering (in the sense that it has been broadly understood), the creation of agricultural land out of the forest.

From North Carolina the Scots moved into Mississippi and Tennessee. They were also in the vanguard further north as first Illinois, then Ohio, then Indiana and Michigan felt the tread of the settler. By the mid-1800s, for example, there were reckoned to be 5,000 Scots in Illinois. Among the founders of Chicago John Kinzie (1763–1828) from the Clan Mackenzie, whose family had originally come to Canada, and Alexander White, a native of Elgin (1814–1872), were prominent.

Samuel Muir is recorded as one of the earliest immigrants to Iowa. A graduate of Edinburgh University, he was a 'Scotchman to the core'. He was also to prove himself a tenacious frontiersman.

In a thousand little communities across the Midwest it's possible to trace the contributions of nineteenth-century Scots through local histories and popular biographies. Nobles County, for example, is in the south-west corner of Minnesota, running along the northern boundary of Iowa and only thirty miles from the eastern boundary of South Dakota. James Baird, a native of Dumfriess-shire, was born in 1843 and was a shepherd until he came to America at the age of forty. He spent his first winter working on the construction of the Northern Pacific Railroad. Reaching Nobles County, he took up farming and returned to his native skills in raising thoroughbred Shropshire sheep.

Edinburgh was the birthplace of Robert Bird, born on New Year's Eve 1836, who came to America at the age of fifteen and spent nine hard months as a teamster with the Union Army during the Civil War. After an adventurous career, which took him as far as Alaska to trade with the Indians, he settled in Minnesota in 1872, the first year of general occupation in Nobles County.

Appropriately, James Greig, who came to America as a teenager, was born on Columbus Day, 12 October 1850. Nobles County was empty when he came to file a land claim. This turned into a full-scale adventure. When James and his companions were caught in a blizzard they drew their wagons together, and while the storm raged for two days they were buried under a huge drift. They eventually dug themselves out but the Scotsman, thinking the weather in Minnesota too severe, shelved his plans for six years before returning for good to the county.

William Thom, born in Aberdeen in 1834, went to work on his uncle's Wisconsin farm after arriving in America but moved on to Minnesota and married sixteen-year-old Elizabeth Mitchell, also a native of Aberdeen who had crossed to the United States on the same ship. Shortly after the first train trundled into Nobles County, the Thoms settled there and raised a family of eleven children.

Despite being on the breadline during the grasshopper plagues of the 1870s, the homesteaders persevered and William and Elizabeth eventually came to own 1,500 acres. Like many of their compatriots they were staunch church-goers, and William was a founder of the First National Bank of Rushmore of which he became president. These were just some of the Nobles County Scots. Even in this far-flung corner they were busying themselves building a new life—new Americans but forever Scots.

States such as Minnesota and neighbouring North Dakota, which share a border with Canada, received a heavy immigration of folk of Scots blood from the north as the nineteenth century progressed. For many the first stopping-off point was Brandon, on the Canadian side of the border.

In August 1882, James Bruce and John F. Sinclair decided to head south across the trackless prairie and the unguarded 49th parallel to the town of Bottineau (ND). Both were to become important figures in the new town. The following year another Scot, John McIntosh, made the trek in an ox-drawn wagon loaded with his plough, bedding and household utensils. His notebook gives an indication of the steady stream of Scots now heading south from Manitoba when he writes that during one night fifteen caravans on the way from Brandon to Bottineau passed his campsite.

The target of all these settlers seems to have been more space and to provide their children with the opportunity of becoming landowners. One of them, William Stewart, set off for the Dakotas with the intention of buying enough property so that there would be 'room for them [his children] to own homes of their own'. It's worth pointing out that by 1900 the Stewarts of two generations owned 1,920 acres of Dakota territory.

The strong Scottish character of the town of Bottineau is again reflected in the names listed in the public records—McBain, Coulthard, McKay, Ferguson, McArthur, Dinwoodie and McKinnon. These Scots, who trekked the eighty miles from Brandon to Bottineau, were to witness a profound change in their community in later years, with a large influx of Scandinavians.

Even in the early years of the nineteenth century the Far West attracted a few Scots pioneers, but the real growth of the Scots population on the west coast only took place after 1848 and the discovery of gold in California, when 80,000 fortune hunters are estimated to have swamped the state.

Back east, as the century progressed a profound change was occuring in the shape of the US economy. The Civil War had acted as a catalyst, encouraging the transfer of resources from the commercial to the industrial sector, which had been showing signs of growth. America's industrial revolution was under way, and here again the Scots were prominent.

As pioneers poured further west in ever increasing numbers from about 1850, it seemed the Scots had the requirements for success: resourcefulness and boundless energy. Hundreds of towns were started, beginning simply as tented villages with lumber buildings springing up and carts quickly rutting the 'streets'. However, many stagnated or simply vanished. Mistakes aplenty were made, and the biggest gamble was trying to anticipate development plans for the rail network as the iron horse lumbered westwards. Many nascent towns were left stranded when the railroad failed to adopt the anticipated route.

Frontier towns were often ramshackle, tinderbox cities. Devastating fires were commonplace and communities built in the high valleys could be affected by snowstorms, with drifts reaching up to the eaves. People who flocked to these new communities—as well as the farmers, miners and railroad men—were the folk of the service industries such as barbers, bartenders, blacksmiths, grocers and, of course, saloon girls.

Pioneers called their wagons 'prairie schooners' and sometimes, with seams caulked and wheels removed, they did indeed float across swollen rivers. Plodding oxen were preferred to horses for the Great Trek. Settlement on the vast grasslands did not really get under way until after 1850. Unquestionably the best-organised large-scale journey west took place in the 1840s when the Mormons, with Scots among their ranks, anxious to be left alone to fulfil their dream of establishing a Kingdom of God on earth, headed for Utah.

Further south, the drift inland (which began in the eighteenth century and gained pace in the 1800s), can be traced in the census returns of various communities along the immigration pathways. In places such as Fort Payne, Alabama, pioneer families settling or passing through included Campbells, MacFarlands, McPhersons and McCartneys. The first Campbell associated with this town was a government agent with instructions to arrange the removal of the local Indians to the Oklahoma reservations, along the 'Trail of Tears'. The native American had by this time become an inconvenience.

As they moved from the east-coast states into the interior of Kentucky and Tennessee, Missouri and Nebraska, these Scots took with them their

This spectacular photograph of the Central Pacific Railroad as it cut through the Rocky Mountains was taken in the 1860s. Hundreds of Scots engineers and railwaymen were involved in the westward expansion of the railroads. (Library of Congress, Neg. No. USZ62–50744)

traditions and folk music. The path leads even further south, from the Appalachian Mountains into Mississippi and Louisiana, where Cajun music has been traced to Scots as well as French roots.

Although most attention was focused on the opening-up of the West, many more Scots were arriving to live and work in the growing cities of the East, their education and technical skills giving them key roles in the American economy. Thus, the industrial worker was added to the long list of immigrant categories from Lowland farmer to indentured Highlander, from the radicals of the 1790s to the Chartists of the 1840s, from Covenanter prisoners to goldminers. By the end of the nineteenth century, Scots could be found in every state of the Union, thinly spread in many places but active beyond their numbers. Larger communities had blossomed in Illinois, Ohio, Minnesota, Wisconsin and the Dakotas, with a large concentration around Seattle in Washington, on the west coast. Even at this later date, the families who made the Atlantic crossing still retained the spirit of those first settlers.

One elderly Scot interviewed during the years of the Depression in New England spoke of his journey to America, made with the twentieth century just around the corner. The family travelled third class to New York by steamer, loaded down with packets in string bags containing crockery and bric-a-brac. The old man, then a schoolboy, had charge of two large white 'cheena' cats wrapped in copies of *The Glasgow Herald*. They survived the journey without a nick. Amazingly, the only recommendation for their life in the New World had been a postcard from 'Seaside Park, Bridgeport, Connecticut', where a Scots friend had settled. They found their way out to Bridgeport from New York but it was left to the local priest, who came across them wandering the streets, to arrange their first night's accommodation.

THE NAMING GAME

In the eighteenth century the impact of the Scots had been principally in medicine, education and religion and, to a certain extent, in commerce. By the middle of the following century, as industrial America began to emerge, a new breed of Scots made its mark. No longer was it only the farmers, craftsmen and professional people of the colonial period who were in demand but all down the eastern seaboard Scots tradesmen were to be found in the factories and workplaces. Early documents connected with Scots settlement in America are few and far between, but one of the most intriguing is a list of prisoners, Covenanters from the Battle of Dunbar (1650), the bulk of whom put in a period of enforced labour before making a home for themselves in America. Among them we find individuals with curious-sounding names such as Archbell, Dugle, Gualter, Luddle, Macwater, Meeme, Pardoe, Rupton and Toish. Here is a phenomenon which, three and a half centuries on, confirms that countless Americans with variations of these and other odd, outlandish names are in reality descendants of those Scots POWs whose designations were so difficult for clerks to cope with that they were arbitrarily changed.

There are also lists of Scots prisoners sent to America after the Battle of Worcester in 1651, in which the same philological problem is encountered. Many puzzles arise from the efforts of impatient and indifferent seventeenth-century quill pen-pushers to spell out family or clan names, often of Gaelic origin, spoken in a dialect that simply defied reproduction in English. Most of the Scots were unable to write, English may have been their second language, and as a result their names over the years since that initial fabrication underwent curious transformations. It may be that colonial bureaucrats have a lot to answer for in submerging the Scots identity.

The Massachusetts Historical Society offers some examples of how these clerical alterations wrought fundamental changes. Most importantly, the prefix 'Mac' was frequently dropped and the remaining part of the name anglicised in a convenient, phonetic substitute. Examples cited by the Society include MacLothan/Claflin; MacFasset/Fassett; MacGowan/Magoon; Saint Clair/Sinkler; Forbes/Farrabas; Graham/Grimes; Farquharson/Farfasson; Jamieson/Jimson; Campbell/Cammell; McMaster/Macknester—and the origins of Muckstore could keep us guessing for hours.

Shipping clerks and officialdom generally manhandled Scots names, altering and shortening them until they were almost unrecognisable; historic, centuries-old clan titles disappeared at a stroke of the pen. The Society study of this peculiar chapter in American-Scots history observes:

> Few would suspect that a family bearing the cognomen of Tosh . . . were once possessors of the old Highland name MacIntosh. The typical Highland prenom Angus was written 'Anguish' which might be considered a true description of the state of the clerk after struggling with the rolling b-r-r-r-r of these clansmen.

Of the many millions of Americans who can claim (even much diluted) Scots blood, only a minority are able to trace their ancestors by name back beyond the turmoil of the Revolutionary War. Donald Duncan of Athena (OR), a retired lawyer, is one of this select group, his great-great-great-great grandfather John Duncan having arrived in Maryland from Glasgow sometime before the Revolution and achieving the status of a 'farmer of substance'.

Having an easily identifiable Scots name could lead to all sorts of problems. When American-Scots sailor, James M'Lean, was en route to the West Indies in 1796 from mainland USA, his ship was wrecked in a storm and he was picked up by a British merchantman which took him to London. He made a voyage working as crew to earn some cash for his return and in 1800 set off for Boston (MA) and home. His vessel was intercepted, however, and M'Lean 'accused of being a native-born Scot' and therefore subject to service in His Majesty's Navy. At first he refused to do the work assigned to him and got twenty-four lashes for his obstinacy; two years later he was put in irons when he tried to escape. Eventually, in 1805, he did manage to get away but coming back to New England on a French vessel they were boarded by a British frigate, and James was pressed into service for another six years. He got home, at last, in October 1814 . . . a transatlantic crossing which had taken eighteen years.

To keep memories of the homeland alive, Scots named features of the new landscape after the once-familiar sights of home. Daniel Pennie, born in Kinross-shire in 1832, went first of all to Illinois then moved on to Minnesota. Settling down to farm in Pope County, Daniel, a mason to trade, named the township Leven in honour of his beloved Loch Leven. Recognised as one of the founding fathers in this quarter of Minnesota, he took the lead in public activities in his new home but openly expressed his continuing love for Scotland.

For over twenty years Daniel was a contributor of poetry and prose to the local papers, and had the distinction of being the Minnesotan correspondent of *The Kinross-shire Advertiser*. His poetry betrays the ambivalence felt by so many Scots over settling in the New World, despite all its promise. 'The Exile's Dream of Lochleven' opens:

As lately I strayed through the forest shade—
When glories of summer were dying
And the autumn breeze through the leafless trees
Her last sad requiem sighing
While over my soul a strange sadness stole:
For beauties that fade I was grieven'
Like a sprite astray I was borne away
to thy pebbled shores—Lochleven.

But it wasn't simply in community names that recollections of Scotland could be found. In many Scots outposts in the Midwest, men went by the names of their farms, as they had in Scotland. In Tama County (IA), the Dunbartonshire and Ayrshire heritage of the farmers was immediately apparent—Kilpatrick, Renton, Boghead, Craigbrae, Pinmore, Drumgrier or Dangart. Farmers were known to their neighbours as Renton, or Drumgrier, or a hundred other echoes of home.

Such strong Scottish links are to be found right across the country. There are thirteen little Scotlands in the United States, and eight Scotias. Caledonias are common, Glencoes abound, several Scottsvilles are to be found, Argyles aplenty and Dundee was always popular. County names in particular took on a distinctly Scottish flavour, and in Texas the list includes: Anderson, Armstrong, Austin, Bowie, Brewster, Caldwell, Cameron, Cochran, Dallas, Dawson, Gillespie, Hamilton, Henderson, Houston, Hutchinson, McCulloch, Mitchell, Robertson, Sterling, Williamson, Wilson and Young. In Illinois, at least twenty-five counties bear Scottish names, and more than a hundred

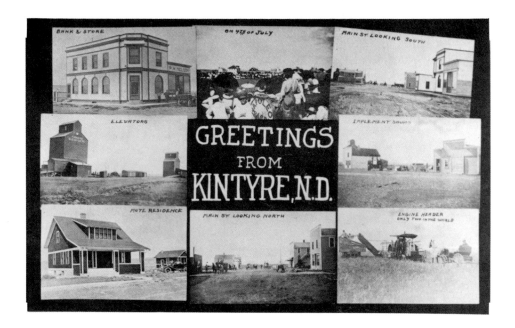

North Dakota's Kintyre was founded by the Campbell family, and this postcard showing the sights around town is thought to date from around 1911. (Leora Dickson and Betty Kuipers)

townships, such as Elgin, Dundee and Inverness, bear silent testimony to the great tide of Scottish founders.

This, however, was never a one-way traffic. It is thought that between 1820 and 1940 as many as 800,000 Scots entered the United States but perhaps a third of these folk returned home, either having made their fortune or, more often, having become disillusioned with 'The Promised Land'. Certainly by the late 1800s, there was hardly a clachan or city street which did not know of the United States through letters from Yankee sons, daughters, uncles or cousins.

Into the 1900s, and the unique Scottish influence was on the wane. New machinery meant that the special skills of the Scots were less in demand and as a distinct group they began to fade into the background. After World War I the end of significant movement from Scotland to America was in sight. There was a brief revival in 1923 and 24, when years of American prosperity contrasting with depression in the old country did bring a swarm of Scots from Clydeside and the Highlands but America seemed, somehow, less appealing. The late 1920s saw more bureaucratic red tape to negotiate, and as we've already noted, the 30s and 40s brought depression then war. With huge factories the norm, the entrepreneurial skills of the Scots had mainly become redundant.

Soon, second and third generation American Scots were bidding farewell to the close-knit Scottish communities where their folks had planted their roots and were branching out on their own. One wee lad summed it all up when, after a school history lesson on the Revolution, he reminded his father: 'You had the King's Army and we were only a lot of farmers, but we thrashed you!' Young people were beginning to think themselves American.

## Lexington & Concord 1775 by Sandham
# US Bicentennial IOcents

A skirmish at Lexington, just outside Boston (MA), is the event commemorated by this stamp. Scots fought on both sides in this exchange, which saw the first shots of the Revolutionary War. (United States Postal Service)

*Chapter 3*

# CUDDIES, COOS AND COYOTES

WHAT WAS LIFE LIKE in the 1700s, for those thousands of hardy Highlanders and Ulster Scots who ventured out along the trails up and over the Appalachian Mountains in search of a place to build their log cabins and put down roots? Always hard, occasionally brutal, would seem to be the general concensus. Everything was brought by pack-horse: there were no trails suitable for wagons. Bare essentials included weapons, food (although to a great extent the travellers lived off the land), pots and pans, simple clothes, a little seed-corn, an axe, a saw and, of course, the family bible.

Streams had to be waded or swum on the horses' backs, mountains climbed and forests negotiated, before a fertile spot was selected. Can you imagine the profound sense of joy and relief when work began to erect a home at last? Isolation bred a hardy, self-reliant people. In the first half of the eighteenth century there was no Indian menace, the local tribes sensing no threat, at this stage, to their traditional hunting grounds.

A good spring near the cabin was essential, and a spot sheltered by the forest or surrounding hills was preferred. Logs were usually cut 18 feet in length, allowing for an overlap which made the principal living area 16 feet long. A rough chimney at one end, made of rock and daubed with clay, provided the cooking and heating facilities. The window would be heavily shuttered and the door made of solid boards. Often the floor would be bare earth. Construction work was normally done by groups of neighbours and the occasion was always followed by a traditional house-warming.

Corn and potatoes were staples of the diet, and sometimes wild game might be the only source of food for weeks on end. Hunting expeditions were frequent, often by torchlight, the sparkling eyes of the wild creature betraying it in the darkness. Occasionally a fire was built into one end of a canoe as it went downstream revealing the eyes of the deer, which was gunned down from the boat.

Clothing for men was normally animal skins, mocassins were stuffed with moss in winter to keep feet dry, while women wore a rough, coarse cloth called linsey, a mix of flax and wool. Normally the woman was the tailor and the man the shoemaker. Hewn wooden plates were the order of the day.

Young folk made their own amusement. Boys staged races, both on foot and on horseback, and at mixed parties there was dancing and a few tears

33

as the old Scots ballads were sung. A marriage, of course, was a cause for general celebration with the ceremony being performed usually after the noon meal, giving the rest of the day and night for dancing which only slowed at first light of dawn. The bride and groom on this night of nights had to make do with the spartan comforts of the loft as their honeymoon suite.

For the Scots who planned their future on the land, that great army of agricultural immigrants who found a new home along the creeks of the east coast, amid the dense forest on the Alleghenies or the seemingly endless rolling prairies, arriving in America was a time of powerful and often mixed emotions. Over two centuries, despite the trials and tribulations which certainly lay ahead, the new arrivals were mostly filled with hope for the future, and a quiet confidence that they could secure a better life. Rancher and cattleman John Clay, in his book *My Life on the Range* spoke more emotionally than most of finding his promised land. He was in Nebraska in the late 1800s, preparing to leave for Cheyenne (WY):

> I woke up one morning at North Platte . . . to taste on the platform of the depot that champagne air, otherwise known as the Lure of the West . . . there was a freedom, a romance, a sort of mystic halo hanging over those green, grass swelling divides that impregnated, grafted into your system . . . far off heather hills lay 5000 miles away.

Equally, within a few weeks the newcomers might find themselves victims of drought, wild animals, bitterly cold winters, tornados, plagues of insects, Indian attacks, illness, flood and subsequent crop failure. In 1888, a blizzard of unprecedented ferocity overtook the Midwest. It was called 'The Schoolchildrens' Blizzard' because it occurred during school hours. Hundreds of people caught out in the open perished in the white-out, some only a few steps from the safety of their cabins.

One immigrant from Ayrshire to the American Midwest, who went on to become a prominent citizen, was seen shortly after his arrival, sitting in misery with his head in his hands lamenting 'Why, oh why, Lord, did I ever come to this country?' Like the Israelites of the Bible, the Scottish tribes, the Caledonian pioneers could, after a year or two in America, fairly claim: 'We are here, we are safe, but the Lord has brought us through fire and water.'

What did most of these early immigrants leave behind? Not a great deal, if we are to believe the account of the Rev. William Robb, which gives us one of the best portraits of agricultural conditions in Scotland during the mid-1700s. In his report for the First Statistical Account, published in 1793, the Rev. Robb tells us that houses were miserable hovels made from stone and turf, filled with choking smoke. In his Tongland parish in Kirkcudbright people slept on heather or straw on the floor, with their cattle beside them. There were no horse-drawn vehicles, few of his parishioners could read, and it was traditional that men changed their plaid shirts twice yearly.

Sheep-wagon in Wyoming with shepherd and collie. Such all-purpose wagons were designed by American-Scots blacksmith from Rawlings, James Candlish, for use on the summer pastures. (American Heritage Center, University of Wyoming W.B.D. Gray Collection (1053))

Shoes were worn only to church and food was 'brose, pottage, oatmeal, flummery and boiled greens'. Despite this tough lifestyle, the Rev. Robb is able to confirm that his flock (both men and women) were 'robust and healthy and subject to few diseases. They were strangers to every disease of a nervous nature.' They were fit and ready to struggle for a better deal on the other side of the Atlantic.

Further north in the Highlands and Islands conditions can have been no better, and in many instances much worse. Before the union of the Scottish and English parliaments in 1707, Scots agricultural methods had been primitive, with low wages and generally miserable living conditions. Improvements—enclosing fields, tree planting and drainage—were underway by the 1720s, and people were slowly being pushed off the land. From 1740 onwards a drift began, at first to the towns then onward to America. This was accentuated by the collapse of the clans, the increasing population and the clearances; the emptying of the glens and straths of people to make way for sheep, which got underway in earnest in the 1770s and 1780s, lasted well into the 1800s.

In all instances, whether we're talking about Highlander, Lowlander or Borderer, we can see that people sailed to America with two main goals—to take a share in the 'unlimited acres', to be lord of their own lands and to try to hold on to a rural way of life which seemed to be fast slipping away. As ever, the economic argument was the most telling: land was attractively priced in America and readily available. For many, the Atlantic crossing seemed the obvious escape route from servitude.

For the vast majority of these eighteenth-century immigrants farming was the only way of life they knew, and this was largely the case into the next century. Louie Attebery, in his study of the Scottish contribution to Idaho's livestock industry, has noted:

> It's almost as if the generations of cattle tending had caused the inter-dependence of cattle and man to become internalised.

FARMERS ON THE FRONTIER

Although in the 1700s the majority of immigrants ended up on the frontier, some, who were luckier or better placed financially, could have fertile lands, orchards, barns and stone-built houses near the large coastal towns like Boston, Philadelphia or Charleston. For the frontier settlers farms might vary in size from 100 to 300 acres. First task was to clear the ground, a process which could take years. Log cabins and rough shelter for the animals were constructed and gradually improved.

In those early days primitive tools and farming methods predominated. Harrows, for example, were often simply thorn-bushes and the main crop would be corn rather than wheat. Harvesting was a long and laborious business using a scythe, and the best workmen, toiling from sunrise to sunset, could clear up to two acres daily. Due to improper housing and feeding, animals were often stunted, hardly fit for ploughing and a gallon of milk daily from a cow was considered a good average. Distance from markets was always a problem and a class of specialist drovers, possibly already with experience of the drove roads of Scotland, arose.

Into the 1800s, we find Scots farming communities developing across the sweep of westward expansion. By 1820 there were little enclaves at Caledonia, Scottsville and LeRoy in western New York state, and a group of Kintyre families was thriving at Argyle (IL) from 1830 onwards; elsewhere in Illinois, Scots were found in Will, Boone and Lasalle counties; in Wisconsin they were at Janesville and Portage City; and in the northern part of Tama County, Iowa, even in Walton County, Florida.

The difficulties of clearing woodland had been the lot of the Scots settlers for more than a century but by the 1830s many people were looking to the prairies for a more rewarding farming experience. Letters home spoke of countryside as 'beautiful and parklike', with trees arranged in clumps as if by the hand of man. After the American Civil War (1861–65) railroads and land speculators recruited many Scots for all parts of the West, including the

Great Plains which had been ignored by the passing wagon trains earlier in the century as unpromising and inhospitable.

Typical of the farmers who were encouraged to come to America during this period was Robert Firth, born in Orkney in 1830, who like so many of his fellow Orcadians joined the Hudson's Bay Company as a teenager. After working for the HBC at Victoria, he was transferred to the San Juan Islands in the disputed waters south of Vancouver Island. Here he raised sheep and cattle, supplying the company's outposts and Vancouver itself. After San Juan was awarded to the United States the company turned the land over to Firth, who homesteaded there and became an American citizen. His farm became known as Bellevue, and he remained there until his death in 1903.

The biggest incentive to the new Scots arrivals to take out American citizenship was the Homestead Act of 1862, which allowed any twenty-one year-old family head to claim 160 acres of public land for a twenty-four dollar registration fee. After six months, the land could be purchased outright for a dollar twenty-five an acre, a godsend for the brave pioneers—the only proviso, you had to be an American citizen.

Scots families of the East Fork of the Wind River in Wyoming around 1908, when sheep rearing was at its peak. (W.L. Duncan)

Cheap passages and guidance in the selection of farms in Iowa, Minnesota, Kansas, the Dakotas and Oregon, were offered by agencies who turned up at fairs and markets throughout Scotland. Crooks abounded in this open market free-for-all, one swindler making tempting offers of land around non-existent Texas towns such as Glasgow, Manchester, Birmingham and Brighton.

Cattle-ranching and sheep-rearing on the wide open spaces saw the Scots come into their element, but this way of life did not appeal only to the ordinary farmer: it also attracted the young Scottish gentry. The younger son of the Earl of Airlie raised cattle and horses on Colorado land given to him by his father, and John Sutherland Sinclair, who immigrated in 1875 at the age of seventeen, unexpectedly inherited the title of Seventh Earl of Caithness in 1891. By this time he was already farming 'an enormous acreage' in North Dakota, where he ran a successful dairy operation near Lakota. Few of his farming neighbours were aware that he was a Scots peer with a castle and seat in the House of Lords. Though during the next twenty years he often visited Britain and voted as a Scottish peer, he preferred to live near the source of his fortune and finally retired incognito to Los Angeles (CA).

Life for these farming settlers of the late 1700s and 1800s could be cruel. As they moved ever westward through the forests and out on to the rolling plains, generation after generation, many heartaches lay ahead. In his book *The British and Irish in Oklahoma*, Patrick Blessing tries to imagine the tough existence faced by these Scottish newcomers on reaching the grasslands:

> In the early years they lived in tents, sod huts or makeshift houses built
> of local materials. They worried about crops, weather and money and
> most of all their children who died at an alarming rate.

Tales of homesickness are often encountered among the older Scots; grandpa or grandma would often sit by the fire reminiscing on their youth in a Highland glen or Border farm. For the younger generations, however, there was only one certainty in life, as they took on the daunting task of building a new home on the prairies—each day would be filled with unremitting toil. One Iowa settler, talking about his neighbour, joked:

> He disna' work a' nicht ... When he gets through wi' his chores at
> twelve o'clock he just leans up against a tree, takes a wee nap, an' then
> goes on again.

By the 1800s these agricultural immigrants often acted as hosts to relatives from Scotland, particularly if the visitors were young and able to help around the farms. Nephews and nieces from the old country often found accommodation with their uncles. As you might expect, it was the folk from farming backgrounds who fared best; many who came from the cities and towns, with the intention of making a living off the land found, according to

Charlotte Erickson, that independent farming was not the idyllic and secure life they had imagined.

Not surprisingly then, by the late 1800s, as more and more capital became necessary to make a reality of the dream of land-ownership, fewer of the less well-off immigrants from Scotland attempted it. Many who had hoped to save enough from work in the cities of the East never made it to the country, and many who got a start found themselves ruined and returned to the growing urban centres. Evolution in action, only the most able survived and by the turn of the century most people coming to America from Scotland were determined to make a success of city life, having abandoned all thought of a future in agriculture.

Yet from time to time we encounter Scots who were peculiarly suited to farming and who found success in this later period in America. Willie Watt was born in the parish of Skene in Aberdeenshire in 1909, and was raised on a farm where Clydesdale horses did the heavy work, and beef cattle, sheep and grain were the main interests. Even from childhood he had the ambition to go abroad, according to his biography written by his wife Ayesha which appeared in *The Golden Heritage* of Thomas County (KS). Because friends had gone to America, he decided to apply to immigrate. Tradesmen and professionals were put on a quota at that time and occasionally had to wait years, but agricultural workers were allowed to come without delay. Willie was seventeen when he made his application, which required his parents consent and signature; it was also necessary to have a recommendation from a schoolmaster, minister and justice of the peace. On 1 April 1927 he sailed from Southampton on *The Berengaria*, a German ship, for New York. From there he made his way to Detroit (MI), where he worked in a lumber yard and on a golf course. By 1928 he was back in the farming environment he loved, working with shorthorn cattle at Grain Valley (MO). He came to Thomas County in 1929 to work with Hereford show cattle and received his naturalisation papers in November, 1932. He married, had three children and became a recognised expert on the Hereford breed, moving around the United States before finally settling in Kansas.

FLOODING THE UPCOUNTRY

Upper New York state was the scene of several Scottish agricultural settlement ventures in the second half of the eighteenth century. Best known is that organised by William Johnson, an Ulster Scot who for thirty years controlled a vast area of the wilderness, established peaceful relations with the Indians, set up trading posts and encouraged settlement. Johnson lived like a medieval baron at the impressive Johnson Hall near the Mohawk River and, while it was in the 1760s that the bulk of the Scots arrived, his most significant link, in the autumn of 1773, was with a relatively well-off group of Highlanders who had crossed the Atlantic on *The Pearl* having embarked at Fort William. Although mainly from the neighbouring glens—the name MacDonnell figures prominently among them—they were joined by a group of Lowland Scots.

Their journey was achieved in good time but was marred by the death of twenty-five children from smallpox. The group travelled north and struck a deal with Johnson, most settling between the Susquehanna and Delaware Rivers in wooded, hilly country, not unlike parts of their beloved western Highlands. After a year, these frontiers-folk were reportedly doing well, and a steady stream of fellow Highlanders arrived at New York before heading upstate to join their countrymen. This was a section of the Scots who, on the outbreak of the Revolutionary War, refused to be recruited as patriots. As life became more uncomfortable, they abandoned their homesteads and headed north for Canada.

John Cumming, a native of Strathspey, led another expedition to America in 1774 with 172 passengers on board the *George* of Greenock, mostly from his own district. He found a 1,000-acre site on land south of Albany, on the Hudson River, and named the settlement Oswald Field. With many of his kinsfolk around him, Cumming (according to Bernard Bailyn) soon established himself as a respected member of the local gentry. However, the revolution brought disaster.

Moderate in his approach Cumming may have been, but he was quickly identified as a leader of the loyalists and advised his people to flee while they could. He was officially classed as a 'dangerous person to the libertys of America' and jailed. Eventually, he and his family and a few friends from Oswald Field were able to leave New York for Britain, but only three days out to sea the boat sank, the passengers were saved but the cargo lost. Although his colony flourished, the tenants at Oswald Field were unsettled and asked the American authorities to be allowed to return to Scotland, not understanding the conflict in the midst of which they found themselves. Refused their request, these people were slowly absorbed into the communities of upper New York and Oswald Field soon became a memory.

Many of the Scots who settled on the expanding frontier in the immediate post-revolutionary period bought a tract of land called a 'tomahawk claim'. Such a man was Edinburgh-born John Campbell, a farmer, who followed the practice of the time by taking possession of all the land he could afford to have surveyed. He then indicated the extent of his claim by blazing trees around the perimeter or cutting his name on the bark of trees. This technique had no legal validity, but was widely accepted by the men of the frontier as establishing priority when applications were made for warrants. The Campbell family records speak of constant strife with hostile Indians, the settlers retreating regularly into their blockhouses. On one occasion, Mrs Campbell and her child narrowly escaped marauding Indians by hiding in the vegetable patch.

It's remarkable how often a Scottish heritage could be submerged in the vast tide of immigrants which swept westwards. Huston Horn, an American writer on the pioneers, tells the story of John Minto, a miner from

Newcastle who, the night before the wagon-train departure from Missouri on the great trek, sang his companions to sleep with

> Will ye go lassie?
> Go to the Braes of Balquhidder,
> Where the blaeberries grow,
> 'Mang the bonnie Highland heather.

This adventurous young man had clearly more than a little Scots blood in his veins, and on closer enquiry we discover that he was the grandson of a Scots Borders family who immigrated to Pittsburgh (PA) in 1840. John was steeped in Scottish tradition. His gruelling journey west took place in 1844, and as the party began to suffer he and two companions headed north to the Willamette Valley, floating 200 miles down the Columbia River on a raft where, at Oregon City, they were given supplies by Dr John McLoughlin, then returned to aid the wagon-train. John settled near Salem (OR), where he was a leading pioneer-farmer helping to organise the region's first Farmers' Club. He worked hard to promote immigration to the area and assisted in locating a suitable route for the Oregon Pacific Railroad. He died in 1915.

## THE CARDROSS DON

An intriguing tale of early California concerns Don Hugo Reid (son of a Cardross, Dunbartonshire shopkeeper), who was destined to become one of the most influential men on the west coast, gentleman rancher, politician and friend to the Indian. Jilted by his first love while studying at Cambridge, he set sail for America, spending six years in Mexico before visiting California. He had no doubt this was the place for him, and by 1834 he was in business in Los Angeles selling everything from silk to sugar, coffee to window glass. At that time, Los Angeles was merely a collection of scattered adobe houses and dusty streets, with a population of some 1,500, lying on a flat plain some distance inland and under the control of Mexico. It lacked a hotel and school although it had a jail and church.

Hugo met and fell in love with an Indian girl called Dona Victoria, by coincidence the same name as the girl who had spurned him in Scotland. They were married despite the opposition of friends and accusations that he had become a 'squaw man'. He had the last laugh, however, inheriting two farms from his father-in-law.

Cultivating vines and raising cattle occupied more of his time and a house was built at Santa Anita, looking out over the San Gabriel Valley. In addition, he bought a boat, *The Esmerelda* and traded up and down the coast as far as the Sandwich Islands (Hawaii), until accusations of smuggling clouded this side of the business and he concentrated on farming.

By this time, the Scotsman was established as a hacendado—a man of

The great city of Los Angeles as it was in the mid-1800s when Hugo Reid, a gentleman rancher from Cardross, Dunbartonshire, was one of California's most influential men. (California State Library)

position and influence. Surprisingly, another resident of early Los Angeles, Jim McKinley, also came from the village of Cardross. He was a regular visitor at the Reid home and used to bring the children presents, once kitting them out as 'kilties', having sent back their measurements to Scotland. These children were educated by their father, who gave them daily lessons in French, English, Spanish, arithmetic and geography.

Hugo Reid's concern for the once-noble Indian tribes, who now worked the land virtually as slaves, was deeply felt and in later life he catalogued the history, folklore and condition of the Californian Indian in a series of newspaper articles.

The war which saw California freed from Mexican domination began in 1846, and Hugo, having his property confiscated, turned his attention to the other great mid-century sensation, the California Gold Rush. The centre of prosperity switched from Los Angeles to Yerba Buena (San Francisco), and Reid and McKinley went into partnership in a dry-goods store supplying the vast army of prospectors in and around Monterey. Reid was elected to a convention which was to decide the future shape of California within the United States and served on the crucial Boundary Commission. He also helped frame the state laws and education system, as well as detailing the rights of women, Negroes and Indians; at the first constitutional legislature of California in 1849 he pushed through far-reaching laws to protect the Indians.

Meanwhile his Monterey business had failed and Hugo returned south a tired, sickly man. The Don who once farmed thousands of acres of vines and wheat, and owned vast herds of cattle, was left with 188 acres. However, Hugo Reid is recognised as one of the founding fathers of modern California.

BRIDGE ACROSS THE ATLANTIC

Kincardineshire has a unique link with one of the most spectacular natural wonders in North America—the Tonto Natural Bridge, a limestone span in northern Arizona which is 183 feet high over a 400-foot long tunnel, the largest natural travertine arch in the world.

When Scots seafarer-turned-prospector, David Gowan, entered the sheltered Pine Valley in 1877 he was almost certainly the first white civilian to have set eyes on the marvellous bridge. However, Gowan, known throughout the region as 'Uncle Davy', had more on his mind than the splendour of the location—he was being pursued by Apaches. He decided to go through the tunnel and, spotting a ledge high up on the side of the cavern, scrambled up the slippery slope. For three days he hid from the Indians until they gave up the hunt.

Emerging, Davy was so taken with this unusual spot that he decided to claim squatter's rights on the bridge and the surrounding acres, and soon had a homestead built and a farming operation under way. It's said that the seed of the wild filaree was first brought to Arizona on the wool of the sheep Davy imported to his farm at Tonto Bridge. At first he spent a considerable time dodging the Apaches, but eventually they accepted that he was here to stay and left him alone. In time, Davy became restless again, he had that urge to move on, but although he was anxious to resume his prospecting he was reluctant to abandon his bridge.

Davy's nephew, Andrew Ogilvie from Gourdon, near Inverbervie, was born in 1878 and joined the Navy at the age of fifteen. Having served four years, he jumped ship at New York and headed west to join his uncle, who also had been a sailor, serving on a slave ship before the Civil War.

Andrew was given the chance to run the farm but turned it down. Davy then sent for another of his Scottish nephews, David Gowan Goodfellow, who not only jumped at the opportunity to homestead but brought along his entire family on the epic journey, along with almost all their household items, including a pump organ.

The Goodfellow family and their worldly goods arrived by train at Flagstaff (AZ), and there everything was loaded into a wagon and hauled to the valley. After six days on the road they found themselves at the lip of a deep canyon, looking down on a tiny cabin far below. Somehow they got the wagonload of furniture, including the organ, down the three miles of incredibly steep, rugged trail. Mrs Goodfellow was moved to comment:

> I fervently wished that I had never come to Arizona. I honestly believed
> that I would never reach the cabin alive if I ever started over the

precipice and I was sure if I ever did get there that I would never be able to climb out again.

It seems that as the family waited at the top of the canyon, preparing to make the perilous descent, nerves became a bit strained. The three children, David, Harry and Lillias, were scolded by their mother for running around. But David Goodfellow, elated at having reached his goal, would hear none of it:

> Ah! Mither, mither, let the bairns move aboot a bit. They've been sitting on their little ausses for the last three weeks.

Of course, they did reach their goal safely; and in the years that followed, David Goodfellow improved the road that had caused so much anxiety, ploughed and planted fields, set out orchards and put livestock out to grass.

The Goodfellows also built a two-storey lodge and began to encourage tourists to visit the natural bridge. Today the graceful ten-room lodge still stands in Pine Valley, and the area boasts a spring-fed swimming pool, hiking trails and a campground. The old pedal organ remains one of the lodge's prize possessions.

In 1991, the Tonto Bridge and the surrounding area became Arizona's twenty-sixth state park, and the staff tell visitors that the spirit of David Gowan still walks the trails of Pine Valley which he knew so well and the halls of the old lodge.

## CALEDONIAN FLOCKMASTERS

> In Scotland when I brought down my flock people would say, 'Here comes the noble shepherd and his flock.' Out West people say, 'Here comes that damned sheepherder and his bunch of woolies.

This tale of wounded pride was related by an old Scots shepherd who had settled in the foothills of the Rockies. In his biography of Robert Taylor, the sheep king of Nebraska, Robert Perry talks in more detail of the deep-seated bias which had developed in American culture against sheep and shepherds:

> Cowboys, those darlings of the movie houses and art galleries despised shepherds and when Americans embraced the myth of the cowboy, they embraced his prejudices along with his virtues.

Consequently, this makes the career of Robert Taylor, born near Hawick in Roxburghshire, all the more remarkable. He built a vast livestock empire from a few hundred sheep. The Taylor family were prosperous farmers, but in 1865 at the age of eighteen Robert went to America and stayed for a time with his maternal grandparents in Pennsylvania. Determined to see more of the country, he made his way to California with his worldly goods carried in a belt around his waist.

Kincardineshire-born Davie Gowan and his family, who were the first to settle at the spectacular Tonto Natural Bridge in Arizona. (Arizona Historical Society Library) *right* Robert Taylor—'Sheep King of Nebraska'. (Stuhr Museum of the Prairie Pioneer, Nebraska)

Robert found a job shearing sheep and by the 1870s had struck out on his own, buying 600 sheep and paying back the loan within three years. In the following decade he headed for Wyoming (where he served twice in the State Senate) and finally in 1890 settled in Hall County, near Grand Island, Nebraska. By 1913, he owned nearly 75,000 acres and his stock comprised 65,000 range sheep, 3,000 steers, 700 cows and 400 horses. In addition, he had breeding stock which included 340 Aberdeen Angus cows and 250 Shire and Clydesdale horses. The historian of the American sheep industry, Edward Wentworth, made this assessment of the contribution of the boy from the Borders:

> The constructive influence possible for one man to wield in the industry is exemplified by a Scotsman Robert Taylor who strove more than any other single man, by personal precept and practice, to increase the numbers and quality of Wyoming sheep.

Less spectacular, but just as effective, were the other Scots shepherds who made their mark on the developing West. Ayrshire shepherd, John Murdoch, felt the call of the Mormon Church in 1851 and his arrival in Utah (with his collie) immediately had the Latter Day Saints' woollen industry up and running.

In the late 1800s the Scots sheepmen found themselves in conflict with

45

farmers and ranchers. 'Deadlines' were proclaimed by the cattlemen, across which the shepherds passed at their own risk. Violence and damage to property was reported in Washington and Oregon in the Pacific Northwest, where Scots shepherds—many drifting down from Canada—had congregated. A letter to *The Portland Oregonian* from the 'Crook County Sheep Shooters Association' boasted of thousands of animals killed during the recent 'sheep shooting season'. Sheep-poisoning was reported and herder's tents were burned down. But some sheep-raisers refused to recognise the titles of the cattlemen, continued to hide from summonses and kept well out of range of the rancher's gun. Dr Alexander McGregor of Washington, who has studied these conflicts, notes that veteran Scots sheepman, Doug McAllister, told his herders there was no such thing as a fence.

Football was the unlikely foundation for one of the most extensive and successful sheep outfits in Wyoming controlled by W.A. (Scotty) McKay, born in Renton, Dunbartonshire, in 1867. Scotty served his apprenticeship as a carpenter and worked in the famous Denny Brothers shipyard in Dumbarton. But even as a boy he had shown skill in athletics and gained 'no little fame' as a footballer for Renton, the now defunct team from the Vale of Leven, who were once world champions. His career blossomed and he went south to join Wolverhampton Wanderers, where he was a star player and was paid a handsome salary.

In 1893 he sailed from Glasgow to New York, and because he had friends in Rawlins (WY) he headed west and resumed work as a carpenter, joining the Union Pacific Railroad to repair locomotives in the days when many sections of the iron horse were still made of wood. By 1904, the sheep business occupied most of his time. Scotty had invested savings made from his football career to launch himself as a shepherd.

Through the thinly populated states of Wyoming and Montana we find the legacy of generations of Scots sheep farmers. Fremont County (WY), and particularly the Wind River Basin, were favoured by Scots to the extent that the East Fork of the Wind River became known as 'Little Scotland'. The Duncan family, from Maybole in Ayrshire, came to the area in the 1880s, and by 1907 four brothers—Tom, Bill, James and Gavin—were fixtures in 'Little Scotland', and the district soon became a stopping-off place for many young Scots who eventually established themselves in the region. The Macfie brothers, William and Alexander, from Lower Ettrick Farm in Bute, both became prosperous sheep farmers after arriving in Fremont County in the first years of this century, and in the town of Lander alone the roll of Scots settlers included Alex Greig from Kincardineshire, McDonalds, Jimmy Frazier, Alex Gillis, Findlays, Finlaysons, Murray and Brodies.

Annie Jean Anesi of Lander, whose parents came from Dyce in Aberdeenshire in the 1920s, has many fond memories of the great days of the Scots shepherds. She recalls living in a sheep-wagon and sleeping in a tepee as the family followed the sheep from the lower, winter range to the summer pastures. By today's standards, says Annie Jean, they lived crudely:

Two of Robert Taylor's four children: Mary (b.1897) and Bruce (b.1899), complete with man-sized sporran and miniature bagpipes. (Stuhr Museum of the Prairie Pioneer, Nebraska)

47

We bathed in a round tub once weekly and mother heated water on a small sheepwagon stove stoked with sagebrush.

At the 1927 dedication of a statue to Robert Burns at Cheyenne (WY), Governor Frank Emerson thanked the Scottish nation for the gift of its people who had 'an important part in the building of Wyoming, especially among our flockmasters'.

In southern Idaho, sheepmen with Scottish backgrounds were plentiful. Remembered are the stories of Andy Little, who landed in Boise with only his collie and a suit of clothes and built a vastly successful sheep farm; and of Finlay Mackenzie, 'King of the Scotchmen' in Owyhee County, running 40,000 sheep. James Laidlaw of Wood River—who helped many young Scots to settle in America—left Scotland, he told his family, because he detested cutting turnip tops for sheep feed, while his partner Robert Brockie's motive for immigration was equally bizarre—to avoid milking cows.

In the 1800s, by the time a boy was in his teens, he would be expected to be a full working hand around the Scots farms, as Clarence Watson recalls in his family history of life in the early Midwest. Farm work was hard labour in those days, everything being done by hand. Boys walked behind the ploughs and hay was pitched on to wagons and off on to haystacks. Neighbours helped each other out with threshing, with twenty to twenty-five men representing perhaps a dozen farms working until all the grain was threshed. Whenever a pig or 'hog' was butchered, the Scots boys waited around to claim the pig bladder as a football.

Mechanisation spread through the region towards the end of the nineteenth century, and the Scots were able to show other immigrant groups how to get best value from the new-fangled equipment. In Scotland township, Day County, South Dakota, they gave themselves steady employment and cut bills by operating a community threshing machine. The farmers lived up to their canny reputation by investing jointly in a horse-powered machine which operated for almost twenty years. The Scots started at one end of their four-mile settlement, threshed a little on each farm until they reached the other end, then turned back to finish. Since the machine was small, threshing sometimes lasted until December, but their Scandinavian, German, Irish and English neighbours admired their regularity, efficiency and, most of all, their co-operation.

The reputation of the Scot for economic farm-management preceded them to the United States, and the Americans often enjoyed a joke at their expense. One Scots farmer, who instead of feeding grain to his cow had taken to giving her sawdust, is said to have remarked when the beast collapsed:

She was jist gettin' used to it when the auld fool layed doon and died.

As in Day County, the Scots were often in the innovative vanguard. As a gangly lad, John Johnston roamed the hills of Galloway tending sheep. He always gave his grandfather credit for passing on his farming knowledge, and one of the old man's favourite pieces of homespun philosophy was 'Verily, a' the airth needs draining.' This phrase made a deep impression on young John and was to lead to him making an important contribution to the development of agriculture in the States. Coming to New York with his wife in 1821, John bought a run-down 112-acre farm on the east shore of Seneca Lake. Remembering that tiles were used for draining in Scotland, he sent to his homeland for a pattern and had tiles made locally by hand, commencing drainage work in 1836. He was soon a target for the ridicule of his worldly-wise neighbours. They mocked:

John Johnston is gone crazy—he's burying crockery in the ground!

By 1856 he had laid fifty-two miles of tiles and eventually, as his crops grew bigger and stronger, the critics were silenced. He also started to use lime and plaster, surface application of manure, oil meal for feeding cattle and sheep, and earlier cutting of hay, being among the first farmers on the eastern seaboard to adopt these revolutionary techniques. His farm became a pilgrimage centre for agriculturalists from all over the United States.

William Gilchrist, born in Dalry in Ayrshire in 1852, was a mining engineer to trade but like so many folk from an industrial background he ended up working the land in his new home. The first years of farm life for William and Janet Gilchrist and their ten children in their Kansas sod house must have typified the adventure undertaken by thousands of Scots families at this time. Eventually, William Gilchrist would serve as a probate judge, church elder and county commissioner but in those first pioneering years their lot was simply hard work, and plenty of it.

Many individuals contributed to the agricultural development of the prairies but none more so than a lad from Liddesdale without whom, it could be argued, the grasslands might never have been tamed. James Oliver (1823–1908) immigrated with his family first of all to New York then South Bend (IN), where he was responsible for the development of one of the biggest plough-manufacturing plants in the country, covering sixty-two acres, employing 2,000 men and manufacturing 200,000 ploughs. This success story followed a series of setbacks which might have broken a lesser man, notably a series of disastrous fires. James Oliver earns the label of 'inventor' for discovering a process to prevent castings cooling too quickly, and a superior plough was the result. South Bend benefitted from the presence of James Oliver in many ways. As well as his huge factory, he built the Oliver Hotel, the City Hall and an opera house.

THE RARE BREED

On the Great Plains the range-cattle industry of the 1870s and 80s promised quick profits for Scots investors and also brought many to a new home in the West. Claims for the industry were often over-optimistic, however, investors being assured that 'cattle raising in the Western States of America is at the present time the most lucrative enterprise in the world'. Some promotional brochures promised profits of thirty-five or forty percent on investment in Wyoming cattle ranches. Small investors by the thousand—bank clerks, accountants, merchants, ministers and teachers—poured their money into the various ventures. Completion of the transcontinental railroads and the invention of refrigeration had encouraged this interest in American cattle, and companies were often based in Glasgow, Edinburgh and Dundee. It is estimated that in 1884 some thirty British syndicates, the principals being Scots, owned 20,000,000 acres of range from Texas and New Mexico to Wyoming. Several of these companies sent out Scots managers and herdsmen.

Spread out across the Great Plains, where land was cheap (even free) some of these ranches extended to a million acres. Even though by 1890 200,000 head of American cattle were sent to Britain each year, there were constant problems with Indians, rustlers, fluctuating prices and extraordinary contrasts of weather. Elinore Stewart, a woman rancher in Wyoming, summarised the less obvious problems:

Seated centre among his family on the porch of their Indiana mansion, 'Copshaholm', James Oliver, born in Newcastleton in Liddesdale. Oliver developed one of America's largest plough-manufacturing concerns and had interests in business, farming and real estate. (Northern Indiana Historical Society)

Persons afraid of coyotes, work and loneliness had better leave ranching alone.

Along with other cattle companies, the Scots were guilty of over-expansion and failure to manage the grasslands properly. The distance separating the boards from their area of operation didn't help, and the time-lag in decision making was often crucial. By the mid-1880s many outfits had folded. However, the famous Swan Land and Cattle Company, sold in Edinburgh in 1882 by American-Scot Alexander Swan, remained in Scottish hands until 1925, when control was transferred to the American board of directors; but most other companies had gone under by 1895.

Colin and Brewster Cameron's struggles to establish themselves on a vast tract of land in southern Arizona well illustrate the problems faced by the enterprising Scots ranchers in the Wild West. The brothers named their property Lochiel, after the Cameron homeland in Scotland, but the boundaries of the old land grant had never been properly determined and for ten years the brothers fought, both in and out of court, to protect their property. Scarcely a day passed when they weren't threatened with death by squatters, and even after gaining title they still had swarms of border badmen and rustlers to contend with. However, they developed a prize-winning herd of Herefords, built two beautiful homes—one in the San Rafael Valley, called Lochiel, and the other in Tucson, called Lochaber—and in 1896 Brewster was able to make an emotional return trip to Scotland.

During this period, the most significant area for ranch development was probably in the Texas Panhandle. In Collingsworth County, the Rocking Chair Ranch ( some 150,000 acres) was sold in London to a company in which a Scot, Sir Dudley Coutts Marjoribanks, 1st Baron Tweedsmouth, was primary stockholder. He died soon after and his son, Edward was named manager; in 1887 his brother-in-law John Gordon, 7th Earl of Aberdeen, acquired a half-share. He was grandson of the Prime Minister and married to Penny Churchill, daughter of the 7th Duke of Marlborough.

Not surprisingly, locals dubbed the outfit 'Nobility's Ranch', and the first hamlet on ranch property was called Aberdeen. The British peers owned the Rocking Chair for only a few years and lost a considerable sum in the undertaking. When the operation began, they had almost 15,000 head of cattle and when it was sold only 4,000 could be found. Archibald, Edward's young brother, had been appointed to run the ranch and this proved a disastrous move. Local legend dubbed him a gross incompetent, who is said to have haughtily called his cowboys 'cow servants'.

In addition, Archie appointed one of the former owners as ranch foreman and he proceeded to steal thousands of head of cattle on the sly. Even when a Scots accountant was brought across the Atlantic to conduct a 'talley' of the Rocking Chair cattle, this foreman moved the beasts to the location of the next day's count to help boost the total. This cover-up failed when the wily Scots money man dabbed each cow with red paint. The foreman went to jail and Tweedmouth sold out. It is thought that the Rocking Chair was the inspiration for James Michiner's 'Crown Vee' ranch in his blockbuster novel, *Centennial*.

Perhaps the most famous Scottish undertaking in Texas (and certainly the largest) was the Matador Ranch, established in the early 1880s by the Matador Land and Cattle Company of Dundee, covering 300,000 acres of Motley County. Manager of this outfit was the former bank clerk and law apprentice from Tain in Ross-shire, Murdo Mackenzie, who was described by President Theodore Roosevelt as the most influential of western cattlemen and appointed by him to the National Commission for Conservation of Natural Resources.

Mackenzie, born in 1850, left Tain's Royal Academy in 1867, and while working as an insurance agent was 'headhunted' by an Edinburgh syndicate to take charge of the Prairie Cattle Company Ltd, which has been described as the 'mother of the British cattle companies', with interests in Texas, New Mexico and Colorado. For five years, based in Colorado, he managed the 'Prairie' but left after being criticised by a shareholder and took over at the Matador. By 1910, Mackenzie had expanded the operations of the ranch as far north as Montana, South Dakota and Wyoming, and was eventually elected president of the American Cattleman's Association. The Matador remained a working cattle ranch until 1955 when the company, still with its headquarters in Dundee, sold the Texas operation in three lots.

Other Texan-Scots ranchers included Ewan Cameron, the first of his clan in the Lone Star State, who hired young men to gather-in cattle abandoned during the Texas Revolution, and W.K. Bell, sheriff in the lawless Palo Pinto County before buying up cattle, fencing them in, and cultivating one of the finest herds in the region. Jesse Chisholm founded the famous trail in his name, which ran from Kansas to Oklahoma and was extended into Texas. In St Louis (MO) in November 1884, the Scot, Colonel Robert D. Hunter, was instrumental in organising and promoting the National Convention of Cattlemen. Thirteen hundred delegates, 'bronzed cattlemen' from thirty-four states and territories, gathered to give the steadily growing industry a strong political voice.

Long after the trapping expeditions and the gold and silver strikes were history, the strong economic base created in the West by these Scots ranchers persisted. The influence of the Scots in the American cattle industry was not overlooked by Hollywood. Many movies featuring cattle-ranching were made, the most notable probably being *The Rare Breed* with James Stewart and Maureen O'Hara, which dealt with the introduction of Hereford cattle to the Western Plains.

GUTHRIE'S INCREDIBLE BIRTH

University of Edinburgh graduate, William Guthrie, immigrated to Indiana in the early 1800s, but it is his son John who lives on in the history of the West, in connection with the mad dash to settle Oklahoma Indian territory

Cowboys from the Dundee-based Matador Land and Cattle Company, which occupied hundreds of thousands of acres of Texas, pictured at the chuckwagon. (Panhandle-Plains Historical Museum, Texas)

on 22 April 1889, the scramble that went down in frontier legend as the Great Land Race.

John was educated in Indiana, and taught school before becoming a lawyer. After serving in the Civil War, he moved to Topeka (KS), where he became associated with the Midland Road, a railroad then under construction. The Midland Road became an integral part of the famous Atcheson, Topeka and Santa Fe railroad, and Guthrie became lawyer-director for the organisation. A rail line was constructed through Indian territory to the Gulf of Mexico in 1876–77, and over subsequent years the directors successfully agitated for the opening up of the so-called 'Unassigned Lands' to homestead settlement.

At that time, Guthrie (named after him) was hardly more than a watering stop on the Santa Fe line. It was nevertheless designated as the site of the land office where claims for homesteads could be filed. In a matter of a few hours on the big day it became a town of 15,000 souls, as the noon deadline passed and Guthrie was hit by a noisy, excited tidal wave of humanity.

Judge Guthrie was one of those who attempted to claim a town lot as a 'sooner', having been in place before the starting gun, but it seems he quickly abandoned his interest. Guthrie died in Topeka in 1906 and is thought never to have returned to the town which bore his name. Today, Guthrie is the administrative seat of Logan County, the town having a population of 12,000.

In the thrusting, go-ahead atmosphere of the pioneer West, many places underwent what can best be described as an identity crisis, altering their names without a qualm to suit changing circumstances. The Campbell family organised a huge sheep and cattle ranch, as well as the town of Kintyre (ND), some twelve miles south-east of the state capital of Bismarck. Because of this Scots family's strong influence the town then became known as Campbell, but was officially renamed Kintyre as a lasting tribute to the Campbell's Scottish home.

### GEORGE GRANT'S 'LITTLE ENGLAND'

As a crofter's son in Banffshire in the early 1800s, George Grant was always on the lookout for odd jobs. Business acumen was in his nature and he was soon on his way to success in London, where he pulled off one of the coups of the century by cornering the market in black crêpe days before Prince Albert's death.

By the late 1860s, after a spectacular but exhausting career as a silk

Guthrie (OK), a town with strong Scottish connections, which sprang up in a matter of hours when the Indian lands were opened for settlement in what became known as 'The Great Land Race'. This is the town within a day or two of the opening on 22 April 1889. (Western History Collections, University of Oklahoma Library)

merchant, he was looking for a country estate for his retirement and during a trip to America came across a pamphlet praising the fertile soils of Kansas as better than the 'Nile or Shenandoah'. After a site visit in October 1872, he decided to found a colony. Organising teams of lawyers in London and Edinburgh, Grant let it be known that he was after men of substance—this was to be no escape to prosperity for the poor and downtrodden. His target: small farmers with sufficient capital to buy their own section of land, and the well-to-do younger sons of British nobility, who he knew would be attracted by the splendid hunting on offer. Within three months he had sold almost 60,000 acres, promising to supply the young aristocrats with seed to plant and thoroughbred cattle to rear.

On 17 May 1873, the first group of colonists arrived—thirty men and women. Grant had decided that the settlement was to be called Victoria in honour of his Queen, and it seems Her Majesty did take a personal interest in the venture because on board the same ship as the immigrants were several Aberdeen Angus cattle and a shorthorn bull, all thoroughbreds and some from the Queen's own herd at Windsor. It is said that these were the first black cattle to reach the US.

The Kansas Pacific Railroad constructed an impressive hotel-depot out on the plains, which became known as The Victoria Manor and served as headquarters for the colony. Grant himself lived there for a year. It was torn down in 1927.

Visiting dignitaries were very taken with the colony and even invested some of their own cash in the enterprise, and for four or five years there was a great deal of activity, the population probably peaking at around 250. The city plan included financial districts, civic buildings and housing; Grant began buying in prize stock, and soon the cattle and sheep were winning prizes as far away as St Louis and Denver.

Many fine houses were built, including a three-storey mansion belonging to Walter Maxwell, son of Lord Herries, which included a rooftop viewing balcony where the panorama of the Kansas countryside unfolded . . . beyond the tennis court. Maxwell set out 100 fruit trees, and to keep them from being destroyed by insects he imported forty British sparrows. Grant himself had a villa built on his own land surrounded by fruit trees and with flagpoles out front, on which he flew Scottish or American flags or the Union Jack depending on his mood and the occasion. The Grant house also included a 400-quart wine cellar—no pioneers sod houses these.

Grant was a great publicist, and for a time it seemed that the colony was set to prosper. However, according to Marjorie Raish in her profile of the Victoria experiment, there were never enough bona fide farmers and too many settlers described as 'playboys, remittance men with allowances who had come solely for the hunting'. This was probably due to the fact that genuine Scots farmers had been deterred by adverse publicity in Scotland, resulting from bickering among the promoters of the scheme. By the mid-1870s it had become largely a colony of the landed gentry.

They had even organised a hunt club with the regulation high boots and red coats. Queen Victoria sent out pheasants and a hunting dog. In addition, Grant helped organise a cricket club and sponsored dog and horse racing.

George Grant died suddenly in April 1878, and while some newspapers made optimistic noises about the future of the colony, it was soon clear that it was a terminal case. One reporter suggested that 'business was at a standstill here except for the coroner'. People began to drift away, many heading home, others moving within the United States. Today Victoria is a community of some 1,200 folk of Russian-German origin, grouped around the magnificent Cathedral of the Plains. George Grant's remarkable colony is all but forgotten.

## Chapter 4

# BLAZING A QUIET TRAIL

S CARCELY HAD THE CAMPFIRES of the first explorers of America cooled than the Scots were on the trail, ready to lead the way in land clearance for farming, opening fur-trading routes, seeing the potential of the rolling plains for cattle-ranching or exploiting the mineral-mining possibilities of the great mountain ranges. Historical accounts suggest that only a few Scots figured in the earliest journeys of exploration across America—but they were certainly there in numbers, waiting in the wings, for the start of the vital development phase.

Many of these Scots were to settle the frontier areas in the 1700s and the first half of the nineteenth century but are now forgotten, anonymous pioneers who cut down the forests, ploughed the land, raised their families and crops and died in obscurity. Not until local newspapers begin to appear, and folk begin to note the family pedigree and township and county biographies are written do the principal characters in this drama really begin to flesh out. Men like Jimmy Douglass, born on-board ship in the early 1800s as his family immigrated from Scotland. He chose the wilds of Arizona as his home, and for years contested with the Apaches in the Santa Cruz Valley for the right to farm there. Although his Sopori ranch was often under attack in the 1850s, he ranged herds of fat cattle in his pastures, raised grain and vegetables and kept flocks of poultry. There were women like Eliza Mann, who left Carroll County (AR) for the West with her daughters in a covered wagon and told in her journal how the womenfolk cut fence posts, raised cattle and crops, carded, spun and made cloth, milked and churned butter, moulded candles and made their own furniture.

Sifting the histories of the Midwest states, the names of Scots settlers who pushed the frontiers out into the backcountry begin to occur again and again. Major Christopher Clark, a Missouri pioneer, was one of six sons of Catherine Horn, a native-born Scot, and James Clark, probably an Ulster Scot. In 1799, Major Clark took his family to what is now Lincoln County (MO), where he helped establish the first settlement in the region after an epic journey in a keel boat down the Kentucky and Ohio Rivers, then up the Mississippi and Missouri.

Among Scottish trail-blazers, we find Christopher 'Kit' Carson (1809–1868), trader, guide, Indian agent and soldier, who was born into an

Ulster-Scots family in Madison County (KY). He received no formal education and after his father was killed by falling timber when Carson was nine, he later abandoned his job as an apprentice saddlemaker and headed off into the woodlands, where he learned to live off the land—and to survive in the Indian territories. He made his base in the Taos district of New Mexico, trapped in California and as far north as Montana, where he met other noted mountain men, several sharing a Scottish heritage. In 1836, he married an Arapahoe Indian and served as guide on three of John C. Fremont's expeditions across the Rocky Mountains. His knowledge of Indian culture and language was legendary, but he remained illiterate all his life and (as an Indian agent) had to dictate his reports to a colleague.

One of Colorado's pioneers, and a friend of Carson, was John McBroom, still fondly remembered by the people of the Rocky Mountain state. His parents were Scots and, like Carson, he was born in Kentucky, in 1822. While fighting for the United States against Mexico, he learned several Indian languages and became a scout. Moving to Colorado with his horse, dog and muzzle-loading rifle, he built a log cabin to the south of what is now Denver. His home became a familiar stopping-off place for Indians, trappers and pioneers including semi-legendary figures from the American West, such as Carson, Jim Baker and Dick Wooten. McBroom and his wife brought up six children in a single-room cabin, which has been preserved at the Littleton Historical Museum in the southern suburbs of Denver.

These Scots pioneers in the North West and the desert states were a tough breed—many of them, particularly in the empty lands of the West were also loners in life and death, even into the twentieth century. David Gowan from Kincardineshire, 'Uncle Davey' to his acquaintances in the Tonto region of Arizona, mined and farmed before he finally settled, in the autumn of his life in 1916, in the Deer Creek Canyon in the Mazatzal Mountains. He built a small cabin, cleared the land, dug an irrigation ditch and raised a vegetable garden. Thus Davey continued to live among the mountains he knew and loved, until one morning in 1924 he started to walk to the nearest town only to die beside the trail. He is buried in a grove of sycamore trees at the mouth of his beloved Deer Creek Canyon.

William Clark (1770–1838) was a Virginian-born soldier and explorer with a Scots background who, in 1803, joined Meriwether Lewis in command of a government-sponsored expedition in search of a land route to the Pacific. Three years of travelling took them up the Missouri River, across the continental divide and down the Columbia River to the sea. Clark devoted his efforts to map-making and the study of natural history in these totally unexplored regions. Later, he was Superintendent for Indian Affairs in Louisiana and established the first US outpost in what is now Wisconsin.

PASS THE BURGUNDY

But not all these early explorations were a case of gritting the teeth and staring death in the face on an hourly basis, challenging nature and the native Indians at every turn. Witness one of the early attempts to explore the great Shenandoah Valley, down which countless thousands of Scots and Ulster Scots would join the great inland trek.

The man behind this venture was Alexander Spotswood. Scion of an old and illustrious Scots family, he had been appointed lieutenant-governor of Virginia in 1710, a post he was to hold for twelve years. He was widely regarded as one of the ablest and most popular representatives of the British Crown authorities in the colonies, and is considered to have been the main driving force behind the growth of the tobacco industry, which became the foundation of Virginia's wealth.

In 1716 a sort of 'dress parade expedition' set out from Williamsburg, with the governor and his staff starting the journey in carriages and later exchanging them for horses. They were on top of the Blue Ridge Mountains by 6 September. Moving down into the Shenandoah Valley, John Fontaine, a member of the party, noted in his journal:

> We had a great dinner and after it we got the men together and loaded all of their firearms . . . we drank the King's health in champagne and fired a volley; the Princess' health in Burgundy and fired a volley and in claret and fired a volley.

These gentlemen were clearly not on a temperance march and not prepared to leave their little luxuries behind. The expedition, we learn, carried red and white wine, 'Esqubaugh', brandy shrub, rum, champain, casory, punch water, cider, etc. It is perhaps surprising that anything positive was reported from this Shenandoah expedition, but later Spotswood was convinced he had found the river which flowed northwards into the Great Lakes.

Scots could be found everywhere across the expanding nation as the years passed. The first governor of Wyoming, American-Scot John A. Campbell, an Ohio-born brigadier-general from the Civil War, selected Cheyenne as the state capital and immediately launched into a series of far-sighted legislative measures, particularly in relation to women's rights. Wyoming enacted women's suffrage in 1869, to the amazement of the rest of the United States, the first woman to vote being seventy-year-old Louisa Ann Swain who cast her vote on the way home from shopping in Laramie the following year.

But as well as providing the personalities to push through new laws, the Scots and Ulster Scots on the frontier were also in the vanguard of less weighty developments. Entertainment was much sought after by the hardy miners, trappers and farmers who poured into the rapidly growing towns in the West. At the cattle centre of Dodge City (KS), Professor James McDaniel became one of the West's famed saloon impressarios. Fined for having 'obscene and lascivious' pictures in his stereoscope machine, he was constantly producing new ideas to draw in the crowds. His most famous stunt was a challenge to a Mr Clark to walk back and forwards along a narrow platform above the bar for sixty hours without a break.

Oregon City in 1857. This community, founded by Dr John McLoughlin, attracted many Scots to the Pacific Northwest. (Oregon Historical Society)

This packed them into his saloon. Other attractions offered by the Prof. included 'dwarves, giants, exotic and dangerous animals'.

As more and more Scots, many of them single men, poured into the eastern seaports, the stories of their struggles against hardship began to take on epic proportions. The account of Brechin-born David O'Neil's arrival in Boston is typical. A joiner to trade, he arrived in Massachusetts in 1870 and (according to his diary and cash account) his only possessions were his tools and fifteen cents (a record low in the hard-up stakes). But David knew how to scale the heights, as he became New York's most renowned builder of staircases.

James Christie is remembered as the explorer of the Olympic Peninsula in Washington state. Born in Morayshire in 1851, he was a true adventurer although his ninety-one years took him into the age of rocket technology. He arrived in North America at the age of twenty initially joining the Canadian Mounted Police for special service, which included a meeting with Sitting Bull when the Sioux fled north after the Little Big Horn. Three years adventuring in the Arctic, prospecting as he went, saw him appointed as leader of the Seattle Press expedition into the Olympic wilderness for six months of exploration in 1889.

In 1860, during an expedition in the depths of Wyoming, the famous

James Christie, looking every inch a mountain man, led the Seattle Press Expedition into the Olympic Peninsula towards the end of last century. Born in Moray, he also met with the legendary Sioux war-chief, Sitting Bull. (Special Collections Division, University of Washington Libraries, Neg. No. 2765)

explorer Sir Richard Burton came across one of Scotland's less refined exports in the shape of David Lewis, who ran the Ham's Fork stage station. Sir Richard described the squalor and filth as the ultimate in Western discomfort:

> The shanty was made of dry-stone piled against a dwarf cliff to save backwall and ignored doors or windows. The flies—unequivocal sign of unclean living!—darkened the table and everything upon it.

The broken furniture consisted of wagon parts and the floor was filthy but, according to Burton, the reason was obvious. Lewis had *two* Irish wives, and the house was full of 'noisy and rampageous childer'. Sir Richard found Davie civil and intelligent, though a 'noted dawdler as that rare phenomenon, a Scotch idler, generally is'.

## A SOCIAL CONSCIENCE

We also find Scots blazing a quiet trail in more productive areas of American life. As well as industry, science, religion and education (examined elsewhere), the Scots figure prominently in the social field. Robert Owen's model village at New Lanark on the Clyde attracted many American philanthropists and entrepreneurs, and was the inspiration for a number of industrial and educational experiments Stateside. Owen went on to supervise his model settlement at New Harmony (IN), acquired in 1824, where he was assisted by his Glasgow-born son, Robert Dale Owen. Although the little community soon foundered, it served as a source of hope and inspiration for working-class radicals on America's eastern seaboard.

Similarly, the Chartist movement brought ambitious projects. From Mauchline in Ayrshire, John Alexander (1808–1872) went to Texas but failed to get the Cabot community off the ground. There was more success for the village of Glasgow (WI), immigrants coming mid-century, mainly from west central Scotland. They were reported to be happy and prosperous, keeping the Sabbath 'and anything else they could lay their hands on', according to one cynical commentator.

Temperance colonies and co-operative enterprises were the fashion during the mid to late 1800s, and many efforts were made to recruit Scots for what were often very questionable immigration schemes. One of the better-known involved Kilmarnock-born minister the Rev. John Kerr, Independent Congregational minister at Forres, in Moray, who was a leading temperance figure. In 1871, he resigned his charge and along with James Miller, editor and publisher of *The Forres Gazette*, another temperance supporter, he started to promote a colony in Minnesota. After a lengthy tour of the area, he returned and began to lecture on the benefits of immigration. He secured a tract of land of some 300 square miles but the colony was not a spectacular success.

Although many Scots with high social ideals found only disappointment in America instead of the fresh start they had hoped for, one early settler had a profound influence on the American way of life right into the present day. James Alexander left Edinburgh in 1695 and rose to become attorney-general of Pennsylvania. In 1735 he defended a printer named Zenger on charges of libel against the royal governor. Zenger had accused the governor of rigging elections and this was considered a libel against the King himself. Despite official threats and a bitterly unfriendly court, Alexander argued the case with such passionate eloquence that he persuaded the jury on an acquittal. Thus he pioneered freedom of the press and free speech, so highly valued in America today. Alexander's trail-blazing undoubtedly led to America's important tradition of investigative journalism as well as inviting sordid and sleazy reporting and regular intrusion of privacy.

Robert Hunter (1872–1942), born at Terre Haute (IN), was the son of a wealthy Scots businessman and became a noted social reformer working with charitable organisations in Chicago, and writing with great feeling and insight about slum conditions. Isabella Graham would be described by older biographical dictionaries simply as a philanthropist. She was much more. Born in Lanarkshire in 1742, she grew up and received her education in Elderslie, Renfrewshire, where she is thought to have heard the Rev. John Witherspoon, East Lothian clergyman and signatory to the Declaration of Independence, preach. In 1789, on his advice, she came to New York where she started a 'Penny Society', creating a pioneering sick fund for the poor. By the end of the eighteenth century, she had given up teaching to concentrate full-time on charitable work and established the first orphanage in the United States in 1807.

## TRANSYLVANIA: A TOOTHLESS EMPIRE

On the eve of the Revolutionary War an attempt was made to create a fourteenth colony in America called Transylvania (the land on the other side of the woods), the name chosen by a company with a strong Scottish involvement. When Richard Henderson, a Virginian born in 1735 of Ulster-Scots parentage, heard the first accounts from Daniel Boone of the rich territory beyond the westernmost settlement of the colonies at Fort Watauga, he was fired with the ambition to found an empire in the West.

Boone was sent back to negotiate an enormous land purchase in present-day Kentucky from the Cherokees and, as the deal took shape, nine partners had joined the enterprise. They included native-born Scots William Johnston and James Hogg. In 1773, Hogg decided to leave the north of Scotland, hired a ship and sold enough passages (at six pounds for adults and three for children) to allow him to bring his own family across the Atlantic free of charge. He had five children under the age of eight. For health reasons, the youngest daughter Robina was left in Scotland and became a friend of her cousin, Sir Walter Scott.

Hogg arrived on the Eno River in North Carolina in 1774, just in time to join Richard Henderson's Utopian scheme. Great feasts were organised by the company to persuade the Indians to part with their rights to the traditional hunting grounds, but the company machine was already in action, advertising land at twenty shillings for 100 acres to each immigrant who could raise a crop before 1 September 1775. As negotiations began at Fort Watauga (in present-day Tennessee), Boone took thirty men and started to hack a trail across the mountains, so confident were they of success. This was to be the famous Wilderness Road, the main land route into Kentucky.

Finally, the Transylvania Company bought all the land from the Kentucky River to the headwaters of the Cumberland from the Cherokees. Whether the Indians had sole right to this land was always a matter of dispute, but $50,000 was paid in goods and cash for an estimated twenty *million* acres. The first capital was established at Otter's Creek and in honour of the backwoodsman—again with a Scottish heritage—it was named Boonesburgh.

All along, the company's plan had been to establish a fourteenth American colony under the 'eminent domain' of George III; but the day before Henderson reached Boonesburgh the events at Lexington and Concord took place and the Revolutionary War was underway. Hogg, who had been sent as a delegate to the Continental Congress, arrived too late to be accepted although many saw the value of Transylvania as a buffer to the West. However, a growing number of settlers seemed to want to remain part of Virginia. In addition, the Henderson purchase had been declared illegal by the Crown.

On 7 August 1776 the new legislature of Virginia, which acted in the light of the Declaration of Independence, set up the western territories as the County of Kentucky and Henderson's proprietory government of Transylvania ceased to exist. Although the company went on to found other communities in the purchase, such as Henderson (KY), where descendants of those Scots partners still live, the great adventure was over.

The role of the Scots in the early development of Georgia and West Florida was a crucial one and can be traced to two significant historical events an ocean apart—the defeat and collapse of the clans after Culloden (1746) and the Revolutionary War. Highlanders made prisoner during the '45 Uprising were taken south and held in barges off Portsmouth before being transported, starting in 1748, to the colonies in North America. David Patillo, an expert on the Scots contribution in Florida, has described how they arrived in Georgia shackled together and, being political prisoners, were simply dumped.

During the Revolutionary War, Scottish regiments of the British Army marching through Georgia—to and from Pensacola, the British HQ on the Gulf of Mexico—came across family and clansmen from these transportations thirty years earlier, scattered across Georgia. As time passed, ordinary Scots soldiers were mustered out and re-joined these American 'clans'. Junior officers, Scots among them, were offered sizeable grants of land in West Florida as an inducement to stay and settle the region.

For instance, Lieutenant John Mackintosh, described as a 'hereditary clan leader', took advantage of the Crown offer in 1775. He in turn persuaded other Scots clansmen (including members of the Dunbar, Dunlap and Dungervin families) to join him in the enterprise. They selected lands along the Amasura River (now known by its Indian name, Withlacochee) about twenty-five miles south of Cedar Key, having done survey work which convinced them of the advantages offered by the river and the fertile land through which it flowed. The scheme was not for a town but for a group of crofts based on the style of settlement they had left behind in Scotland. David Patillo outlines the life they planned:

> They would work independently, cutting timber and logging, clearing land for planting, sowing and harvesting, raising horses, cattle and poultry, building boats and rafts, hunting, fishing and trapping, weaving and sewing, carving and making furniture.

Traces of those Scots are hard to find in the Withlacochee Valley today, but the main town tells almost the whole story—it is called Inverness.

## LORDS OF THE LAKES AND FORESTS

The first American town to be incorporated in the West was Oregon City, creation of Dr John McLoughlin, grandson of a Scots-Irish marriage, the white-haired, hawk-nosed entrepreneur who for twenty years helped direct the operations of the Hudson's Bay Company in the Columbia River area of the Pacific Northwest. For practically half a century the British-controlled HBC, covering a vast area from Alaska to northern California, employed many Scots, notably from Orkney. In the autumn of 1842, McLoughlin hired a pioneer named Sidney Moss to mark off a site beside the Fall of the Willamette River—Moss got the job because he had a pocket compass. The first surveyor lost his equipment on the difficult journey west and used a sixty-six foot length of rope which shrank in dry weather and stretched in wet. As a result, the first town in the West was also the oddest shaped.

Quebec-born Dr McLoughlin had, under the guidance of his grandparents, been educated for the medical profession at Edinburgh University—but the man who became known as 'The Father of Oregon' was soon in charge at Fort Vancouver, in what is now the state of Washington. Quickly he developed a sizeable little community with its own farm, shipyard and sawmill; but he is best remembered for the hospitality offered to fellow Scots and for his generous and humane treatment of settlers who arrived along The Oregon Trail, often destitute after their epic journey. His job was to maximise the HBC fur-trade profits, and his kindness towards the settlers often brought him into conflict with the company. He kept American traders at bay by undercutting them and kept a peace of sorts with the Indian tribes. However, he encouraged missionaries and this again was in direct conflict with HBC policy.

Almost inevitably, in 1846, the year that the 49th parallel was decided on as the US-Canadian border, he left the HBC amid growing criticism and directed his attention toward the founding of Oregon City, south of Portland in present-day Oregon. His claim to the land deal was contested, however, and it was not until five years after his death in 1857 that his family received title to the property.

McLoughlin was a memorable personality, standing six foot and four inches, with a dignified air of command and an imperial nose. He was called White Eagle by the Indians because of his silvery locks and, like so many other traders, he married a half-breed Indian woman and they had four children. Although the majority of the traders, like McLoughlin, took Indian wives, it was the fur trade which brought the first Scotswomen to the west coast, some of the Scots returning to the old country to marry.

The sleek fur of the river-dwelling beaver was prized in Europe for gentlemen's hats and while big money could be made, the life could also be a perilous one—working daily in freezing water, constantly threatened by Indians, wild animals, and even wilder weather.

Throughout the first thirty or forty years after the Revolutionary War, as the United States struggled to establish her borders, Scots fur traders and hunters, well-tuned to the politics of the Indian territories, played important roles. Many of the Scots mountain men who later acted as scouts for army and civilian expeditions into the West began their careers in the early 1800s as fur traders and trappers.

In the area where the city of St Paul (MN) now stands, Robert Dickson (1765–1823), the red-haired son of a Dumfries merchant, had great influence with the Sioux, marrying a chief's daughter called To-To-Win and controlling fur posts from the St Paul district through many hundreds of miles to the north and west. During the war of 1812 between Britain and the youthful United States, his clout with the Indians was regarded as crucial by both sides.

Danger was ever-present for these hard men of the rivers and mountains, or lords of the lakes and forests, as Washington Irving described them. Donald McTavish came to Oregon from Scotland in 1814 aboard the vessel *Isaac Todd*, as chief factor for the North-West Company at Astoria. On a return trip to Scotland, he and four others drowned when their boat overturned in the Columbia River only a few miles from their base. Charles McKay, a native of Sutherland, explored northern Utah in 1825 during a trapping expedition, and is said to have sighted the Great Salt Lake. His adventure paved the way for colonisation of the Great Basin by later pioneers, notably Mormons.

When Greenock-born Ramsay Crooks reached St Louis (MO) in the early 1800s as a teenager, the town had already become the national centre for the fur trade and by 1870, 1,341 residents listed Scotland as their birthplace. Forming a partnership with fellow Scot Robert McClellan, he set off for the Upper Missouri in 1806 with a party of eighty men, establishing a trading post near Calhoun in present-day Nebraska. By 1811, he had joined John

Jacob Astor and led an expedition through the little-known Snake River country, suffering 'great privations' which ruined his health.

Crooks' status in the fur trade grew, and by 1817 he was general manager of the American Fur Company, marrying into a prestigious St Louis family. A physically slight individual, he was remembered principally for his unswerving honesty in a business which had a well-oiled dirty tricks department and where guns mostly did the talking. He was, however, relentless in his quest for success and chronicled his enterprises in a splendid series of letters. In his old age he loved to regale guests with tales of adventure, but geographers remember his for him involvement in the controversy over the famous 'South Pass' through the Rockies, Crooks claiming, probably correctly, that his fellow Scot Robert Stuart had crossed it twelve years before the much-trumpeted Ashley party in 1824. Crooks is said to have made a tremendous impression on Indians he encountered during his years in the wilderness and one chief, Black Hawk, declared

Sir William Dunbar, Morayshire-born scientist, explorer and plantation owner. (Monroe-Ouachita Bicentennial Commission) *right* Dr John McLoughlin, Edinburgh-educated and from a Scottish background, was one of the great figures in the development of the Pacific Northwest in the first half of the nineteenth century. He is widely known as 'The Father of Oregon'. (Oregon Historical Society)

that the man from Greenock was the 'best paleface friend the red man ever had'.

Born at Kildonan in Sutherland, James Mackay (1759–1822) reached North America in 1776, first of all joining fur traders on their treks around the Great Lakes and as far west as the Rockies. He then moved south to Louisiana, where his talents quickly recommended themselves to the ruling Spanish authorities. In 1795, he led an expedition to explore the country bordering the Missouri River and across to the Pacific. Another target of the party was to erect a chain of forts and Mackay managed to negotiate a peace between the Spanish and Indian chiefs, as well as taking possession of a British fort. The Scotsman was appointed commander of a settlement on the Missouri and given a major land grant. Even the transfer of Upper Louisiana to the United States in 1804 did not phase him, and he continued in public service as a member of the Missouri Territory Legislature.

Donald Mackenzie, Scots-born fur trader (1783–1851), was a cousin of the explorer of north-western Canada, Alexander Mackenzie. Donald entered the North American fur trade around 1800, and within a decade was a partner with Astor in the Pacific Fur Company, his voyages taking him to the Willamette, Columbia and Snake Rivers. A huge man, over 300 lbs in weight, he was nicknamed 'Perpetual Motion'. Physically and mentally suited to the rigours of the wilderness, he developed a remarkable understanding of the Indians and found time to father thirteen children. His ascension of the Snake River through Hell's Canyon is still remembered as one of the great feats of early exploration in North America.

Yet another of the Mackenzie clan who made his reputation in the fur trade was Kenneth Mackenzie, born in Ross and Cromarty in 1797, a man who was eventually to be known as 'King of the Missouri'. He immigrated in 1818, again on the recommendation of Alexander Mackenzie, and within a few years (based in St Louis) was organising seasoned traders on behalf of the Columbia Fur Company over an enormous territory, from the headwaters of the Mississippi east to the Great Lakes and west to the Missouri. Amalgamation in 1827 with the rival American Fur Company saw Mackenzie take control of the Upper Missouri section and carry on business in areas where hostile Indians had forced out other (less resilient) traders.

Building up forts and trading posts, he lived like 'a monarch in his own domain'. Indeed from Fort Union he ruled as 'Emperor Mackenzie' at the same time loved and feared by his own men and the Indians alike. An odd incident saw him catapulted into the limelight in 1834, when he built a distillery at Fort Union. This threatened the company's charter and forced him to leave the country for a time, his 'royal remit' not extending to granting himself distilling licences. His time abroad was well spent. In Germany, he learned the art of wine-making and imported fine wines to America for the rest of his life; Fort Union would surely have made a lovely name for a medium dry sherry. Mackenzie died in 1861.

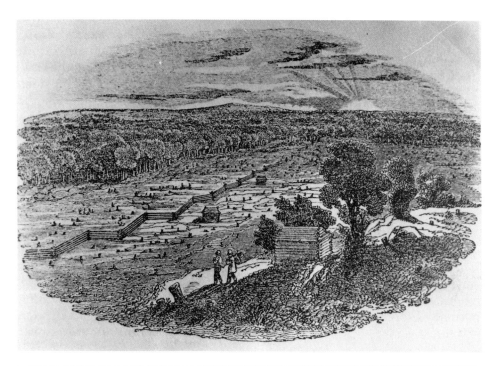

'Clearing the Forest' and 'Backwoods Log House', as illustrated in *The Emigrant's Guide to the Western States of America* (1852) written by John Regan, brought up at Whitletts, near Ayr. (Illinois State Historical Library)

Very positive views of the mobile western frontier were contained in *The Emigrant's Guide*, a remarkable travel book cum settler's manual written by John Regan, who was brought up at Whitletts near Ayr and settled in Illinois, where he became a newspaperman. After marrying, John had left Scotland at the age of twenty-three, in 1842, but was to travel back and forwards regularly; two of his four children were born in the homeland.

The village in Illinois where Regan settled was called Virgil but no longer exists, the broken-down schoolhouse the only remnant of the once-thriving community. There Regan built a log cabin, raised crops, worked as a harvest-hand, taught school and travelled extensively in Western Illinois. He returned to Scotland to write and publish his guide in 1847 and, back in America, he moved to Knoxville (IL), bought the local paper, *The Knoxville Journal*, and always found himself at the centre of local controversy. His guide was filled with practical advice but it also, according to Professor John Hallwas of Western Illinois University, contributed significantly to American literature, with its detailed descriptions of the local landscape, homesteads and communities, vivid character sketches and a delightful portrait of the author as an immigrant. For example, Regan's description of a forest glade:

> The woodpecker taps upon the limb—the bluebird flits from tree to tree, the dew trickles and frogs in distant ponds hold loud concert.

Regan was entranced by the region and could never understand Charles Dickens's 'moody, crabby and lack-lustre' account of the famed Illinois prairies. The Scot urged his countrymen and women to settle the Midwest, citing the town of Ellisville as being full to overflowing with 'enterprise, activity and resolution'.

How did these Scots families find their way to their new homes in America blazing their own private trail? The saga of the McMillans from Campbeltown, Argyll, is typical. John McMillan, born New Year's Day 1794, chose, 'for freedom of religion', to immigrate to the United States with his five sons and three daughters, not knowing where they would settle but putting his family in God's care for the journey. It took them six weeks to reach New York in a sailing ship, then they journeyed across Pennsylvania to Pittsburgh from where they came down the Ohio River to Cincinatti. There they met by chance James Clark from McDonough County (IL), who was attending a meeting of the National Synod of the Presbyterian Church. Clark told John McMillan of the wonderful prairie lands, and such an impression was formed that John took his family on down the Ohio. They halted at Sharp's Landing, the site of Beardstown (IL), and purchased 640 acres of land (appropriately) in 'Scotland' township. The McMillan dynasty in Illinois had been founded.

When American Scots started to move west in the mid-1800s, they often did so as family groups. Such was the experience of the Buchanan 'clan' whose antecedents first came from Stirlingshire in the early 1700s to what became Buchanan County (VA). By the middle of the nineteenth century, a branch of the family had reached the Springfield district (IL) and were ready to take the next big step—to Kansas.

Mattie Ellen Buchanan Brooks, writing about their great adventure in the 1920s, recalled that the convoy consisted of nine covered wagons and a herd of twenty-one horses and mules. Each wagon carried exactly 1000 lbs of provisions, bedding and clothing. Mattie noted everyone's name, twenty-one persons in all, 'big and little, old and young'. The party set off on 1 March 1867 and reached St Louis on the Missouri twelve days later, boarding the steamboat *Isabella* for the week-long journey to Kansas City. They landed there in a snowstorm, reloaded the wagons, and set off for Fort Scott (KS). Many years later, Mattie saw the movie *The Covered Wagon* and was struck by the similarities with her own adventure:

> The overland part of this trip was one of almost continual hardship
> ... it was almost a wilderness ... food and fuel were scarce—mud
> everywhere. I now sometimes wonder how we got through such an
> experience and came out alive, whole and well.

It's difficult to imagine the daunting yet challenging prospect which immigration meant for Scots: it tested their ingenuity and stamina to the full and even into the twentieth century could be spiced with real adventure. James Ford and his wife Agnes, from Roxburghshire, began to make plans to move to America in 1874, packing their possessions into large wooden trunks. With their three children, they set sail on a 'very rough journey' which lasted fourteen days. James helped the crew in a variety of ways, nailing down timbers to keep boxes and trunks from sliding back and forward across the ship and threatening its stability. Arriving in New York, they travelled by train into Adams County (IA), literally the end of the line for the railroad, and James had to help passengers and crew turn the engine at the start of her return leg to the coast.

The Fords, like so many others, had relatives to reach and it took an act of unexpected kindness to set them on the right road in the New World. A farmer learning of their need unloaded his timber-wagon and took them and their possessions to be reunited with their family. Even the last leg of this journey was not without incident. At the ominously named Mount Etna the river was in spate, and they only crossed with difficulty. But this 'first obliging' in their new home was never forgotten by the Fords.

Sacrifices made by the Scots pioneers were many. James Maclure and his family travelled west from Indiana in 1855 by covered wagon. In Kansas, James helped found Junction City and worked as quartermaster in nearby Fort Riley, home of the famous 7th Cavalry. Mrs Maclure had a lonely existence, telling her descendants that in the early days she had gone for eighteen months without seeing another woman. As a pioneer resident, and because of her work in developing the community of Junction City, she was chosen by novelist Margaret Hill McCarter as one of the 100 best-known pioneer women. Before coming to Kansas, Mrs Maclure had been educated in the East and among her accomplishments was the piano; unable to bring her beloved instrument out West, she marked the keys on the kitchen table and practised there—silently—each night.

Davenport (IA), on the Upper Rapids of the Mississippi, claims Dundee-born James MacKintosh as one of its founding fathers. Although he became a bookseller and binder in Canada after immigrating as a teenager in 1817, the adventurous spirit of his grandfather who fought at Culloden took him on to America. In 1835, he crossed the Mississippi at night to the thriving city of Keokuk (IA). He swam Flint Hill Creek through floating ice because there were no ferries or bridges, and roamed the as yet unpeopled prairies (as historian Bill Roba suggests) 'with the howling wolves as his only night-time companions'.

Within a year he had become among the first residents of Davenport, opening a dry-goods store on the riverfront and continuing his exploration of the prairie land to the west of the river. His dangerous treks gave him first option on prime land bought from the local Sauk Indians. MacKintosh became a leading businessman, served on the first jury empanelled in the state and, reverting to his original trade, was Iowa's first official bookbinder. He was killed in the Civil War.

## DISASTER AT MOSQUITO INLET

By the 1760s, Florida was the target for large-scale British attempts at settlement and it has to be admitted that the most catastrophic of these— the shipping of hundreds of Italians, Greeks and Minorcans—was the work of Scots doctor, Andrew Turnbull. For many years Turnbull, a long-time resident of Izmir in Turkey believed that East Europeans, anxious to escape civil and religious oppression, would gladly immigrate to America for a small plot of land where they could grow familiar semi-tropical crops.

A graduate of Edinburgh University, Turnbull was a physician and naturalist and quickly won official backing for his Florida settlement. By 1766, he and his family were in Florida, where he selected a spot about seventy-five miles south of St Augustine on the east coast—a district known rather worryingly as Mosquito Inlet. Leaving workmen to erect crude huts on the site, he set off for Europe and for ten months sailed the Mediterranean gathering recruits for his community. They included Italian labourers, Greek political refugees and residents of Minorca, where there was a famine. When the little fleet sailed out into the Atlantic on 17 April 1768, there were nearly 1,500 people in the expedition. Bernard Bailyn in his account of the project says

> It was a polyglot population of refugees from persecution, misery and starvation, unaware of the reality of the land they would inhabit.

Pioneer families halt in Wyoming to pose briefly for the photographer. In the days of the Oregon Trail guns were always close to hand, and many Scottish families found their way West on such expeditions. (Denver Public Library, Western History Department)

As was normal, some ten percent of the passengers died during the three-month crossing; and when they found that their first task was to clear the swampy lowlands, snake-infested and alive with insects, the immigrants began to sense the hardship that faced them. Driven on by the overseers, resentment built up and despite progress with clearance and construction work, there were revolts and an appalling death-rate. Over 300 people died within the first six months. According to Bailyn, this period saw Turnbull's greatest crimes:

> The enterprising doctor, faced with mounting costs and the prospect of catastrophic failure that would ruin him and his partners, drove the workers like animals.

Enforcing his own criminal code, workers were chained to logs, flogged and starved. It seems likely that some were beaten to death. Two years after its foundation, New Smyrna (named in honour of Turnbull's Greek wife) had lost half its population. With the outbreak of the Revolutionary War, civil order broke down and the remnants of the Mediterranean immigrants fled north. Hounded on all sides by creditors and political enemies, Turnbull retired north also, to Charleston (SC), where he became a respected physician and founder of the state's Medical Society. The memories of Mosquito Inlet haunted him for the rest of his life.

## Chapter 5

# CAMPED BESIDE A GOOD THING

IN THE WAKE OF THE BLOODBATH that was the American Civil War (1861–65) something remarkable began to happen to the United States. Beneath the surface froth of politics, the nation was changing from the domain of the small manufacturer producing for local consumption to a land of highly organised business and industry. It was in many ways a revolution as significant as the struggle to be free from British rule less than a century before. The changes had been maturing for decades but were now obvious in the growth of the soon-to-be densely populated eastern cities, the armies of immigrants flooding the ports, the bonanza farms and cattle ranges of the West, the El Dorados of gold and silver and the increasingly far-flung network of railroads. According to the writer John Leane, this was the era of the banking tycoon, manufacturing mogul, mining king, railroad-builder, oil baron and iron and steelmaster. As economic growing pains were felt across the land, and the polished rail lines reached the west coast, the 1890 census was to note that the frontier had ended as a dynamic factor in American life. Entrepreneurs flourished, including significant members of native-born and American Scots.

The Scotsman's favourite prayer, according to the Americans, ran something like this: 'O Lord, we do not ask you to give us wealth, just show us where it is!' A former premier of Canada, Sir Wilfrid Laurier, went a step further declaring: 'Wherever there's a good thing you'll find a Scotchman camped beside it'. Such was the impression made by these immigrants on the developing economy of the United States, a story of energy, initiative, integrity and, of course, opportunism. The high priority given to education and improvement and the hard slog that had been life in the old country combined to equip them better than most to exploit the many opportunities presented by the New World. For example, by the 1890s banking and merchant houses across the country were filled with Scots, the management boards of the major banks often containing one or more Scotsmen. Behind the counters in isolated trading posts, frontier town stores and small banks, the Scots were found.

At this time an increasing number of skilled labourers from Scotland, many of them single men 'on the tramp', wandering from job to job, began to arrive. Prior to the war, the bulk of Scots immigrants had come in family groups with agricultural backgrounds and specific settlement targets in mind, clustering together in clearly defined communities. The industrial immigrant was a different, more mobile kind of creature. Industrial workers as a group seem, perhaps naturally, to have taken a greater interest in political matters than did their agricultural counterparts. British immigrants actively developed the labour movement in the States and brought many of the guiding principles of British trade unionism into play.

Business acumen among the Scots was apparent from the earliest days. Soon after the Union of 1707 with England had been ratified, Glasgow's mercantile trade, which had hitherto been stifled in the English-dominated market across the Atlantic, began to flourish, tobacco from Maryland and Virginia providing the basis for this new prosperity.

Cotton-mill employees from the Clyde Valley were among the first industrial workers to make the transatlantic crossing, as the process in the old country became more mechanised. In the first years of the nineteenth century, a colony of Renfrewshire weavers had already settled in New York city. These industrious and orderly people stayed in Greenwich Village, in a quiet spot off a country lane which, in tribute to their home, they called Paisley Place.

However, ambitious young men from south-west Scotland also made their mark. On the Potomac River, south of Washington DC, stand Alexandria and Dumfries, two modern communities still intimately linked with Scotland and proud of their heritage.

John Graham (1718–1787) was born in Perthshire and died at his Graham Park plantation in Dumfries (VA). He grew up, however, in Dumfries-shire, Scotland, where he made the acquaintance of other youngsters such as John Dalton, William Ramsay and John Carlyle, who were all to forge new lives for themselves in Virginia. Around 1739, Graham immigrated to Prince William County in Virginia, purchasing land at Quantico Creek—from this tract the first sixty acres of the town of Dumfries was surveyed. His companions from Scotland were to move upriver when the harbour at Dumfries silted up, and the site they chose is now Alexandria. Graham nevertheless remained faithful to the original location, shipping tobacco and trading in the necessities of life from London and Glasgow. When he succeeded his father-in-law as county clerk, his position as a gentleman in Virginia's aristocracy was assured, and by 1756 his plantation was a thriving, self-sufficient colonial organisation with its own tradesmen—the whole system rooted, of course, on slave and indentured labour.

Graham's friend John Carlyle is thought to have been born in 1720 at Annan, in Dumfries-shire, and immigrated to the eastern seaboard where he was a factor for a Whitehaven merchant. By 1749, Carlyle had set up his own mercantile business, bought hundreds of acres, and was an original trustee of the town of Alexandria. His operation included trade with the West Indies, export of grain, beef and lumber in exchange for rum, sugar and slaves.

The town was named after Scots merchant John Alexander, and the co-founder with Carlyle was William Ramsay. Alexandria is best known as the home town of George Washington, and this fact goes a long way to explaining the first president's affection for the Scots.

Carlyle's beautiful riverside home, overlooking the Potomac, was built in 1752 and was considered one of the finest houses in Virginia, having been inspired (it is thought) by Craigiehall near Edinburgh. Ramsay's house has an interesting history, since it is said to have stood originally thirty miles downstream when the Scots first clustered around Dumfries, and was barged upriver to be re-sited when Ramsay left to settle in Alexandria. Only five doors from the Carlyle mansion, one assumes the Scots 'mafia' liked to stick together.

## THE SECOND AMERICAN REVOLUTION

One enthusiastic advocate of American independence, who had roots in the west of Scotland, was Thomas Leiper (1745–1825), a tobacco merchant from Strathaven, Lanarkshire, and educated in Glasgow and Edinburgh for the Kirk. He went first to Maryland then to Philadelphia, where he worked for his cousin, a tobacco exporter; eventually he set up on his own to become one of the city's leading businessmen, amassing a personal fortune and opening warehouses all over Pennsylvania.

Before the Declaration of Independence, Leiper launched a fund for open resistance to the Crown to which he personally contributed large sums. He was an original member of the Philadelphia City Cavalry and took part in the battles of Trenton, Princeton, Brandywine and Germantown. Re-entering business, his attention turned to experimental railroads and he set up a track for horse-drawn coaches in Philadelphia, building a working transport system from his quarries in 1810.

Speculators flourished in the aftermath of the Revolutionary War, but few as spectacularly as Fifer James Swan (1754–1830), who immigrated to Boston (MA) as a boy and became a counting-house clerk. He associated with the radically patriotic youth of the city and became a member of 'The Sons of Liberty', participating at the Boston Tea Party in 1773, and wounded twice at Bunker Hill. By the end of the war, he was a major and rose to the rank of colonel.

Having married into money, Swan bought up a number of confiscated Loyalist properties and was involved in land speculation in Pennsylvania, Kentucky and Virginia; in 1786 he purchased a group of islands off the coast of Maine, the largest of which bears his name. Swan went to France in 1787 and, assisted by his friend Lafayette, gained several lucrative military contracts and control of the US war debt to France. He secured the job of agent of the French republic and outsmarted his banking competitors with a scheme to commute the debt. Travelling back and forth between France and America, he launched a series of mercantile ventures but sadly died in a debtor's prison in Paris.

Fifer James Swan, who took part in the Boston Tea Party, painted here by another Scot, Gilbert Stuart. (Swan Collection Bequest of Elizabeth Howard Bartol, Museum of Fine Arts, Boston.) *right* Group of employees at the giant Santa Fe railroad workshops in Topeka (KS) c.1900, including James Duncan Wallace, born in Edinburgh but brought up and educated in Arbroath. He is smoking a pipe and resting his foot on the stepladder. (Douglass W. Wallace)

George Smith (1806–1899), banker and financier, was born in the parish of Old Deer, in Scotland's north-east, and by 1834 was in Chicago where he made his fortune in real estate speculation in the 'wild lands'. Founding figure of the Chicago Marine and Fire Insurance Company in 1836, he returned to Scotland the following year to organise the Scottish Illinois Land Investment Company. But back in the Windy City he found that the Illinois legislature had supressed the banking operations of his Chicago Corporation.

Following a series of financial crashes, tremendous mistrust of banks prevailed and private banks were effectively outlawed. Undaunted, Smith decided to move to Wisconsin, where he began another bank with a charter stating that the corporation could receive money on deposit and offer loans at specific rates of interest. He told his lawyer: 'get me a charter with a franchise as like a bank as you can, but call it what you will'. Thus the famous Wisconsin Marine and Fire Insurance Company—a bank in all but name—was chartered on 28 February 1839. Smith made Alexander Mitchell from Ellon, in Aberdeenshire, secretary of the company and they carried out banking business right from the start, with Mitchell soon becoming head of the organisation.

Throughout the 1840s, the territorial legislature tried unsuccessfully to cancel the company's charter. Wisconsin became a state in 1848, and in 1853 the WF&M became a state bank. In 1854, Smith sold out to Mitchell and went to Georgia and obtained a charter for a bank at Atlanta, then still a rather remote location. Later, Smith invested in the Rock Island, Northwestern and St Paul railroads. Estimates of his eventual fortune ran as high as 100,000,000 dollars. His contribution to the development of the West was immense, with his bank standing as a firm economic institution. It is certain that the development of Wisconsin and Illinois in the 1840s would have been much slower without George Smith's money and foresight. He never married and spent his final years in the UK, between Scotland and the Reform Club in London where he died.

Alexander Mitchell's career was, if anything, even more sensational than Smith's. He is catalogued as a banker, financier and railroad-builder, born in Aberdeenshire in 1817, the son of a struggling farmer. 'I intend to be a laird one day', the short, stocky boy told his sister. However, he decided at an early age that farming wasn't for him and went to work in a bank at Peterhead, where his canny grasp of financial matters soon drew him to George Smith's attention. When Mitchell was only twenty-one he arrived in Milwaukee (WI), his task to start the bank in what was still a frontier town. More like a naïve schoolboy than a young businessman, he carried with him a frayed carpet-bag stuffed with 50,000 dollars of George Smith's money.

The young Alexander faced many crises, the most dramatic being in 1849 when a group of Chicago and Detroit bankers, jealous of his success, tried to break the company. Collecting 100,000 dollars in the bank's notes, they presented the certificates for redemption. At the same time their paid agents circulated Milwaukee telling people that Smith's bank in Chicago, the source of Mitchell's cash, had failed. Mitchell sent the fastest riders he could find to Chicago, and before he had exhausted his own stock, gold had begun to flow from the Illinois metropolis—the quick-witted lad from Ellon was soon claiming victory.

THE MOBILE HOME

Many Scottish newcomers to America, particularly in the 1800s, became successful merchants and traders in branches of business for which they had trained in the old country. For instance, young men who had learned the drapery trade in Glasgow would eventually set up their own stores right across America. During the 1880s and 1890s, these expanded into the modern style of department store where young Scots immigrants who knew or wanted to learn the business could always find a berth.

William Donaldson (1849–97) was born at Milnathort in Kinross-shire, and immigrated to Rhode Island after serving an apprenticeship in the 'dry

Donaldson's Glass Block in Minneapolis (MN). This trendsetting department store brought fame and fortune to William Donaldson, who was born in Milnathort, Kinross-shire, in 1849. (Minnesota Historical Society)

goods' business. He then moved to St Paul (MN) in 1881 and began his merchant's business with almost immediate success. He built a vast, trendsetting five-storey department store in the twin city of Minneapolis and had buyers all over the United States and Europe. The store employed 900 people, and Donaldson was joined in partnership by his brother, Lawrence.

While the last three decades of the nineteenth century saw substantial immigration by Scots to America, it was also the period when a large number of Scottish investment companies were set up in the mad scramble to develop and exploit the West. Firms based in Aberdeen, Dundee, Edinburgh and Glasgow encouraged home-based, middle-class Scots—doctors, bank clerks, accountants and lawyers—to risk their savings in ventures which opened up land for railroads, farming, mining, forestry and ranching right along the rapidly expanding frontier. Many of these projects were to founder through lack of proper local control, market fluctuations, transportation difficulties, occasional fraud and new laws on land—a few (for example, the Arizona Copper Company) went on to great success.

Taking an average Midwest state such as Minnesota, we find at least five

Scots corporations entering the area's investment field after 1873. They were the Scottish-American Mortgage Company, the Dundee Mortgage and Trust Investment Company, the Edinburgh American Land Mortgage Company, the Oregon Mortgage Company and the American Land Colonisation Company. As in the rest of the United States, local agents (many with Scots backgrounds) were appointed. Most of the interest centred on the fertile areas of south-western Minnesota where, for example, the Scottish-American retained a local man at Sleepy Eye, in Brown County, and the Dundee-based investment company bought, improved and named the towns of Airlie and Dundee in Nobles County.

In his detailed financial study of the involvement of these Scots companies in America, W. Turrentine Jackson, Professor of History at the University of California, comes to the conclusion that there is evidence in this American adventure that seriously questions any assumption that the average Scot is inherently canny in money matters. He argues that

> A nation of four million people who plunged approximately twenty millions sterling into western lands, railroads, mines, ranches and forests within a three-year period must certainly have impaired its reputation for cannyness.

The son of a St Andrews golf club manufacturer, James Forgan (1852–1924), was destined to become one of the most influential figures in American banking and finance in the early years of this century. Making his way to the States in 1885 via Canada, he settled in Chicago (IL) and was president of the First National Bank and Treasury Secretary under McKinley. He made the First National into arguably the most powerful bank in the West, and if there ever was a man caught up in his work, it was James Forgan. He once admitted:

> My life has been absorbed in, and my energy concentrated on the growth and development of the banks which have so commanded my services that my life story has been practically inseparable from theirs.

At the other end of the scale, the acumen of the Scots saw them moving into positions of authority in many smaller banking operations throughout the heartland. At Macomb (IL), three Forfarshire brothers—John, James and Andrew Binnie—set up the Citizens National Bank on the town square, opening for business on 1 January 1890. The family had moved to Illinois in mid-century, settling in the Caledonian enclave of Scotland township. John Binnie, the bank's president from opening day until 1927, took a special interest in providing loans to help farmers starting on the prairies or to get them through hard times.

Real estate dealing has been big business in New York for well over three centuries, but it's worth noting that one of the early players there was a Scotsman, Archibald Kennedy (1685–1763), who is said to have hailed from Wigtownshire. He was a British colonial official and, like so many of his contemporaries down the eastern seaboard, was involved in land speculation. He bought Bedlow's Island in New York harbour for a hundred pounds in 1746 and sold it twelve years later for a thousand, the island being required as a quarantine station. Another famous transaction was his purchase of Number One Broadway, where he built a splendid mansion house. Kennedy might also be fairly described as a prophet of the Revolution, having warned that Americans could not be kept dependent by being kept poor, and that 'one country could not continue its subjection to another simply because their grandmothers were acquainted'.

Throughout the Old West Scots popped up in the most unlikely places, and one of the most colourful was surely Jedburgh-born Robert Robison, who chose Dodge City (KS) as his home in the New World. Known throughout the district as 'Old Scotty', he was a cabinet-maker who had immigrated first of all to Canada in the 1870s.

When the family moved into Dodge City, Scotty painted buggies and wagons in the ornate decorations of the day before opening up his own hardware store. In his later years, he would sit on the shady side of the store and sing himself to sleep with his old Scots songs. Every woman, young or old and including his wife, he called 'Bonnie Jean'. Throughout his life he maintained strict Calvinist views about gambling and dancing, once walking out of a concert when a popular dance tune was featured. A close friend of the eccentric, compatriot politician 'Sockless' Jerry Simpson, Scotty would sit in Simpson's audience and shout encouragement: 'Gie 'em hell, Jerry! Gie 'em hell!'

Scotty almost became the most famous face in the United States when the huge American Tobacco Company got their hands on an atmospheric photograph of the old man sporting his splendid sideburns, sitting day-dreaming, clay-pipe in hand. They wanted to use it in a national advertising campaign, but after consultations with the family it was decided that coast-to-coast fame was not what Scotty would have wanted.

OILING THE WHEELS OF INDUSTRY

There is ample evidence that, even from the earliest pioneering days, Scots aptitude for science, engineering, invention and improvisation saw them in the frontline of technological innovation. In shipbuilding, for example, Henry Eckford (1775–1832) gave New York a reputation as the best builder of wooden ships in the world during his lifetime, while in 1845, Donald Mackay, of Scots descent from Tain, Ross and Cromarty, established the shipyards in east Boston and was renowned as a builder of splendid clipper ships. George Dickie of Arbroath made his mark in California as a noted designer of marine engines and as a builder of steel ships, while Angus Macpherson (1812–76), born at Cluny, Inverness-shire, built the famous frigate *Ironsides*.

When ship-building developed on the Clyde in the 1860s, skilled ironship-workers soon began to drift to America. In San Francisco in 1905 it was said that in one yard there was hardly an employee from

Robbie Robison, Jedburgh-born Dodge City storekeeper. This photograph almost catapulted him to national fame when the American Tobacco Company wanted to use it in a major advertising campaign. (Kansas Heritage Center, Dodge City)

Heavy engineering—the lifeblood of Clydeside in the 1800s—is the theme of this monument to Glasgow-born locomotive and shipbuilder, Peter Donahue, in Market Street, San Francisco. The photograph was taken within hours of the devastating earthquake and fire of 1906. (San Francisco Public Library)

yardboss to workman who didn't speak with a Scots accent. Throughout the closing years of the nineteenth century, Scots machinists, turners and filers brought their skills to America, boasting of what had been achieved on the Clyde.

Elsewhere in heavy engineering, Peter Cooper built the first railroad locomotive in the United States, one of many Scots builders and operators active in the blossoming of the rail network. To Major-General Craig McCallum (1815–1878), born in Renfrewshire, goes the credit for the efficacy of the federal rail system during the Civil War, a vital factor in the eventual victory. Although Scots were to be found in almost every railroad operation, the Pennsylvania line had particularly strong Caledonian connections, pioneering managers having names such as Pitcairn, Carnegie, Scott, McCulloch and McCrae.

Arbroath-born Peter Wilson brought his skills in the manufacture of linen from Dundee to Philadelphia (PA) during the American industrial revolution and he was also a pioneer in the jute trade, importing the first load of East Indian jute. To the inventive mind of two Scots was due the success of the New England shoe industry. The sole-stitching machine invented by Gordon McKay and the pegging and stitching machines for sewing uppers of Duncan H. Campbell, born in Greenock in 1827, revolutionised the industry.

Hosiery and silk industries also brought Scots to America, Paterson (NJ) being an important centre. Lace-makers went to America from Ayrshire, and thread-making was an exclusive province of the British, and especially the Scots. The Clark company of Paisley introduced machine-making of cotton thread to Newark (NJ) during the 1850s, most of their employees coming from Renfrewshire; the Glasgow Linen Company had an almost entirely Scottish workforce at their plant at Grafton (MA) in the 1880s; J & P Coats of Paisley operated a large mill at Pawtucket (RI), and the Kerr Thread Company pulled up its roots and moved its plant to Fall River (MA) after 1890. Wages paid at Clark's and Coats's American factories were almost double those paid in Scotland, so the attractions of the Stateside workplace soon filtered back to the old country.

Inventors of Scots descent take credit for the telegraph (variously attributed to Charles Morrison, Joseph Henry or Samuel Morse); the steamboat (William Henry, Robert Rumsey and Robert Fulton); and the telephone (Alexander Graham Bell and improved by Elish Gray). Beside these captains of invention stand a great army of Scots innovators whose less spectacular efforts nevertheless helped change the shape of the American economy.

It was in the iron and steel industries that the Scottish input was perhaps at its most effective. The principal Scot we associate with the industry is, of course, Andrew Carnegie; but the Chisholm brothers, William and Henry, from Lochgelly in Fife, also pioneered many steel processes in the States. They settled in Cleveland (OH) in 1852, and William developed machinery for manufacturing steel shovels. Long-time head of the Union Steel Company of Cleveland, Henry was the first to introduce steel-making to the city and has been called the 'Father of Cleveland'.

One famous Kentucky industry—the manufacture of illicit liquor or 'moonshine'—owed its birth to an Ulster-Scots revolt. Congress had levied a tax on whisky, but the tough-minded, independent frontiersfolk of western Pennsylvania had never paid a tax on whisky and were not about to start, even though George Washington sent an army against them. The whisky-makers simply made a strategic retreat, many of them settling in the backwoods of what is now Kentucky. The 1794 Whisky Rebellion saw neither a drop of blood nor whisky spilled.

The arrival at Boston (MA) of the sailing ship *Unity* from London late in 1650, with 150 Covenanter prisoners from the Battle of Dunbar earlier in the year, provides the first glimpse of Scots involvement in early cottage industry. The majority of these men would serve lengthy sentences cutting wood or collecting bog-ore for the iron company at Lynn, but in the case of one Scots prisoner there is an intriguing story to tell.

In the mid-1600s the new community of Springfield (MA) had built a smiddy at a colony on the banks of the Connecticut River. All the early pioneers were farmers, and there was a constant demand for horses to be shod and ploughs and domestic instruments to be sharpened. They appealed urgently for a smith. Among the prisoners who had been working at the Saugus ironworks at Lynn was John Stewart, who had been blacksmith to his regiment at Dunbar. He was the answer to Springfield's prayer, and when his trade became known he was bound out to serve leading landowner, John Pynchon, for a period of eight years. By 1659, Stewart's former master had sold him a house in Springfield, with a street frontage and an orchard, for a sum of ten pounds. At the same time, a vote in the town gave him the smiddy in perpetuity. But times were still difficult, and Stewart's first home was burned to the ground in an Indian raid.

Throughout his life John boasted that he had seen service in five battles under the Marquis of Montrose and 'suffered many dangerous wounds'. He married Sarah Stiles of Windsor (MA), and although they had no children, he was able to pass on his blacksmith's skills to his foster-son. Some town records describe Stewart as a valuable and esteemed member of the community, but elsewhere we get hints that he did not always abide by the moral standards of the Puritan townsfolk. Jailed for a short term in 1670 for stabbing a man in a quarrel, in 1662 he was fined twenty-five shillings for allowing his home to be used for a card school.

In his book, *Labour in a New Land*, Stephen Innes mentions several other Scots (most probably POWs) resident in Springfield at this time. There was antagonism towards them because it was felt that, having been forced to America, they had no real commitment to the community. They were 'wordly and contentious', according to court records, and tolerated only because of their value to the local economy. Innes notes:

> All of them appeared before the magistrate at one time or another on charges varying from attempted murder to drunkenness, card playing and slander. The Scots tested the limits of social tolerance in early Springfield and sometimes the equanimity of their fellow villagers as well.

Considerable numbers of Scots who came to America in the mid-to-late 1800s were skilled industrial craftsmen. Interestingly, during this period a steady movement of a section of these folk from factories and engineering works on to the land can be traced. This is well illustrated by the life of James Duncan Wallace, born in Edinburgh in 1849 but brought up and educated in Arbroath. The boy spent his youth swimming, playing marbles and raising pigeons and was a good scholar. However, he chose to learn the machinist's trade in the rail workshops of Glasgow and Dundee rather than undertake an academic career.

In 1871, Wallace set sail for America and by way of Illinois and Missouri (where he married) finally reached Topeka (KS) and got a job in the vast Santa Fe Railroad workshops. He and his wife opened a boarding-house near the works and raised their family, but in 1898 he traded the boarding house for a farm six miles east of town, consisting of two old, stone houses under an ancient, isolated oak tree, which gave the farm its name—Lone Oak. The 1905 Kansas census tells of the value of the swap. The farm was 160 acres, with the building and land valued at 10,000 dollars; 60 acres in corn, 10 acres in sorghum; 3 acres millet; 2 acres Kaffer corn; 300 bushels of corn on hand; 140 lbs of butter made by the family; 20 dollars value of poultry products; 610 dollars in slaughtered animals; 500 dollars in wood sold; 6 horses; 6 milk cows, 31 other cattle and a dog.

James's family consisted of four daughters and two sons. For a time he continued to work at the Santa Fe, coming out to the farm at weekends; thus the Wallace children—whose descendants still play an active role in the community life of Topeka and treasure their Scots background—had both a rural upbringing and a skilled working-class background. This achievement, it could be argued, was the goal for many of the Scots immigrant families who moved initially to an urban environment, but had their sights set firmly on the countryside. This trend lasted until farm prices rose, forcing all but the most affluent to settle for city life.

CAMERON'S MARVELLOUS FIRE-ENGINE

The industrial revolution was slow in coming to the American South, where the economy was based on slave labour, and Scots expertise and engineering talents were not always welcome. This phenomenon is illustrated by the experience of Archibald Cameron and his famous fire engine, which helped save the city of Charleston (SC) from destruction.

Archie Cameron was born at Lismore, Argyllshire, in June 1813, and moved to Glasgow as a child. A machinist to trade, he went to America in 1842 and a few years later made his home in Charleston, starting a machine shop called the Phoenix Iron Works. Among the heavy equipment made there was steam engines, a number of which were designed for fire-fighting. But even as the Civil War began, the local authority was reluctant to bring the new-fangled engine into use, despite its obvious fire-fighting potential.

The lobby against it was headed by the fire chief, J.N. Nathans, and was successful in preventing the passage of a bill in the legislature granting a charter to the Charleston Fire Engine Co to introduce its use in the Volunteer Fire Department. Nathans and the Board of Firemasters argued that it would destroy the *esprit de corps* among the volunteers. However, as more and more men signed up for the Confederate Army, pressure grew for introduction of Cameron's machine.

On 11 December 1861, its big moment came when a Negro's campfire got out of control and flames quickly spread through the town. The volunteer crews fought gallantly against the inferno but houses, churches, meeting halls, a library, art gallery, gasworks and even the fire-engine houses were engulfed. The hand-pumps simply could not cope with the volume of work—then someone remembered the fire engine. It was pulled out and fired up and, according to one commentator, exhausted firemen admired its efficiency in pumping water to check the fire. The fire had a strong hold, however, and during the night scores of important buildings were destroyed, most notably the cathedral, the golden cross falling 300 feet from the spire to the roadway. The flames cut a swathe of destruction a mile long by 250 yards wide through the town.

At its first meeting after the Great Fire, the city council under its Provost, Charles MacBeth, announced that Cameron's fire-engine had proved itself and was thereafter a vital part of the fire-fighting force. Even the diehard

The photographer attracts a posse of boys on their way home from school as he captures the panorama of Andrew Carnegie's vast Homestead Steel Works at Pittsburgh (PA) c.1903. (Library of Congress, Neg. No. USZ62–34842)

opponents who had witnessed its performance at the height of the blaze had to agree.

## IN SEARCH OF THE 'BAG O'SILLER'

It is early in the eighteenth century before indications of a nascent American mining industry can be traced in the historical records. In 1709, the first mining company charter in America was granted by the Connecticut General Assembly for a copper mine at Simsbury.

Development of railroads and industry generally in the mid-1800s provided a great impetus for increased coal production. Scots miners, who excelled in the use of the pick in confined spaces, were skilled at shoring-up mine ceilings and had talents in detecting deadly damp fumes, were in great demand. During the Scottish economic depressions of the 1860s, thousands of miners left the Scottish coalfields: on his travels after the Civil War, Alexander Macdonald, the British miners' union leader, found 7,000 of his brother Scots miners in Maryland, 3,000 in Pennsylvania, 2,000 in Illinois and 'large colonies' in Ohio. The miners often crossed and re-crossed the Atlantic, streaming into Glasgow for passage when news came of good times in the American industry.

Scots miners, quarrymen and stone-masons attracted to America during the 1880s often arrived with the intention of undertaking a short, lucrative stint and returning home 'wi' a guid bag o' siller', while others made the commitment for life. Communities of Scots miners sprang up everywhere, from the cities like Pittsburgh (PA) to colonies like Braidwood (IL) where Lanarkshire miners congregated; other locations, like the quaintly-named What Cheer (IA) also had their Scots contingent.

New England granite was worked by the Scots, especially after an American tariff in the 1860s disrupted the granite industry in Aberdeen. Masons established Scots enclaves at places like Quincy and Ware (MA), Vinalhaven and Rockland (ME) and Concord (NH). Grey granite around St Cloud, Rockville and Cold Springs (MN), and sandstone in northern Ohio proved a draw, and Scots were employed in working the stone for some of the most impressive public buildings, monuments and memorials in the country.

In *The Boston Scotsman* in 1906, an article highlighted the particular Scots skills in the manufacture of granite tombstones. In Quincy, for example:

> If the native population had a feeling that the Scots are born into the world in a pall of gloom and have the blood frozen about their hearts, they are bound to be excused, for none of them ever saw a Scotsman enter their city who did not directly seek employment at the tombstone trade.

Scots foremen in the quarries dotted around the New England landscape were a tough breed. At Barre (VT) a particularly formidable overseer discovered two of his workers had damaged a block of granite, pressing

Granite Quarry, Salt Lake City (UT). Scots worked here cutting the massive blocks of stone for the Mormon Temple. (Denver Public Library)

ahead with the job rather than waiting for the boss to return. He found them measuring the depth of the fracture with a square and rule and, realising what had happened, seized the square and threw it across the yard. When one of the workers protested about this violent behaviour the foreman responded:

Ye bugger, I should ca' ye baith after't for knockin' in sic a hole!

Such brainstorms were generally short lived and although many men were 'sacked' on the spot by Scots supervisors, they found that before they could get their kit together they were directed to resume work as if nothing had happened. The employers and foremen demanded high standards of themselves and would accept nothing less from their employees.

In Utah the Mormon convert, John Sharp, born in Clackmannanshire in 1820 immigrated in 1848 and reached Salt Lake City, taking on the job of superintendent at the quarry where the massive granite blocks for the Mormon Temple were being excavated and cut. John, who was to become a bishop in the Mormon Church, had been pulling sledges at the coal-face at the age of eight. The work in the Utah granite quarries was, as always, hard and dangerous. Another Mormon immigrant, Thomas Campbell from Bo'ness, was crushed at the Temple quarry, leaving him paralysed and bed-ridden for the rest of his life.

In the pioneer mining camps of the Old West, Scots regularly feature. In Idaho, Caribou Jack, half Indian and half Scot, was mining at Rocky Bar in 1861. A recent ethnic study conducted in Idaho mentions Reuben McGregor, a mining engineer in Elk City, who was renowned for wearing his Clan MacGregor tartan trousers around town. Then there was the roving Scots prospector, Jackson McCracken, who travelled through the Indian nations in the mid-1800s, mining and looking for precious metals. He traded and sometimes fought the local tribes before finally striking pay-dirt in the Big Sandy Valley in Arizona (not, as far as I can discover, named after a burly Highlander). Around his McCracken mine a town grew, and by the time he sold his share Jackson was a rich man and got himself elected to the territorial legislature. His firm belief was that the man who raised the most points of order and complaints during the law-making session was performing the greatest service for his nation. His interjections were legendary, and he gained the nickname of 'Objection McCracken'.

IN A CABIN, BY A CANYON

Self-confessed wanderer, Alex McKay, was born in Perth in 1841 and arrived in America at the end of the Civil War. Sheep-rearing was the first work Alex took on, in California, and hereabouts fate took a hand when a riverboat on which he was travelling stuck on a sandbar in Arizona. Alex ended up in Tucson, at the start of a career which would secure him a reputation as one of the most famous prospectors in the Old West.

Setting off into the rugged mountains in 1878 for a lonely spot called Oracle, he rode one burro and had his mining gear and supplies packed on another. After a brief but friendly encounter with local Indians, he discovered the Christmas gold mine (named after its day of discovery), and a week later he found another mine which he called the New Year. The town of Oracle was born.

During the next year, Alex built Oracle's first house—a one-room adobe dwelling—and gradually other folk, getting word of the strikes, began to arrive in search of gold, silver and lead. The community's future received another boost when an all-important stagecoach run began from Tucson to nearby American Flag. Remarkably his career went full circle when, in the 1880s, he added sheep-farming to his mining interests. And fate was to play a part yet again. One afternoon, working at the Christmas mine, Alex and his partners tapped into an underground stream. Water came up so fast that they were forced to abandon the mine, but Alex laid four and a half miles of pipe down the parched mountainside, built a rock corral and house down on the mesa, and with unlimited supplies of water he began his sheep ranch. Here, wild animals were a constant problem: a nosy old bear would

Quijotoa's Star Hotel in Arizona c.1884. This mining town was founded by wandering Perth-born prospector Alex McKay. (Arizona Historical Society Library)

wander down from the hills to the farm building, and mountain lions would occasionally take fully-grown sheep over the corral wall while badgers went after the lambs. Alex McKay recalled in later years how Indians and wild animals were plentiful around Oracle; a pet bull snake that had the freedom of the house was killed by an over-excited visitor at the front door.

The Peer and Peerless mines, discovered by McKay in 1883, brought the Quijotoa district to life. This strike came when his companions gave up on a particularly steep and exhausting rock climb after a long day's prospecting in the hills. Alex pressed on, and within a few yards chanced upon a silver-rich outcrop of rock. This discovery saw Quijotoa grow from a few tents to a 'camp' of over 3,000 people, with its own churches, hotel, gambling houses and even a newspaper called *The Silver Bullion*. Eventually, Alex McKay sold out to the famous Comstock Company of Nevada for a modest 30,000 dollars.

Perhaps the most sensational episode in a life packed with incident came when the Scotsman was in his eighty-fifth year. He was arrested when police raided his home in Tucson in 1926 and found three gallons of bootleg corn whisky. Along with forty other prohibition violators, old Alex was jailed by the district judge. However, two months later, President Calvin Coolidge wired the local sheriff with a presidential pardon for the prospector because of his services to the economic development of Arizona and his prospecting exploits. It was the first such pardon in connection with national prohibition. *The Citizen*, the local Tucson newspaper, seemed to think that Alex had been in failing health during the last few days of his imprisonment. The journal tells us:

> Each evening as the sun lowered itself back of the Tucson mountains, the picturesque old miner with tottering steps would go to one of the barred windows and with a longing look would watch the sunset that once stilled his shovel and pick in the days when he led prospecting trips into nearly every known mining district around Tucson.

The prison 'ordeal' does not seem to have weakened the tough Scot . . . he lived to be ninety-five.

### QUEEN OF THE COMSTOCK

The great California Gold Rush of 1849 barely lasted a decade but it brought as many as 100,000 fortune seekers to the Far West, including many thousands with Scots or Ulster-Scots connections. They came from all over the world to the western slopes of the Sierras, risking the perilous overland journey from the East or the equally hazardous sea trip round Cape Horn to San Francisco, or a trek across Panama for a sea journey north.

Stories had filtered East which suggested that gold was lying around waiting to be picked up. One unambitious soul is reported to have declared meekly that he had no lust for gold and would happily settle for a 'hatful a day'. It may not have been so readily available, but there are some remarkable tales of discovery nonetheless. One of the many Ulster Scots who backpacked into the goldfields literally stumbled into the folklore of the 'forty-niners'. The man, by the name of McKnight, set off in pursuit of a runaway cow in Grass Valley and stubbed his toe on an outcrop of quartz which he then discovered to be studded with gold.

The conversion of a Scots lass to the Mormon faith in 1842 seems a most unlikely route to a fortune and into the folklore of the American mining industry. Women, who were found in the mining camps of the Sierras in the 1850s, frequently got the profits from rich mines as they plied the oldest profession in the streets and saloons; but it was only very rarely that women operated or owned a mine.

Eilley Bowers—self-styled Queen of the Comstock—came into possession of a piece of fabulously rich silver lode in Nevada soon after its discovery, in the most unusual of circumstances. She came from a humble Scots background, but by the mid-1840s she was at the Mormon colony of Nauvoo (IL). She married a church elder when she was sixteen, a man more than thirty years older than herself, and together they journeyed to the Mormon capital of Salt Lake City, possibly in the vast exodus organised by the religion's leader, Brigham Young. In Utah, when Eilley's husband began to build his harem (as was permitted by the Mormon religion), Eilley divorced him and married again, soon moving away to the Carson Valley near the (as yet undiscovered) Comstock lode.

Again she was divorced and this time, to earn a crust, she began to wash

Eilley Orrum Bowers, a Mormon Scotswoman who struck it rich in silver and became one of the celebrities at the famous Nevada Comstock lode. (Nevada Historical Society)

93

clothes and cook for miners in nearby Gold Canyon. In exchange for an unpaid bill for board and lodging she accepted a ten-foot claim which turned out to be a section of a silver-rich vein. It was the best deal she was likely to strike in this or a dozen lifetimes. Another of her lodgers, Sandy Bowers, held an adjacent claim. Marriage seemed a logical sort of partnership, and shortly afterwards their joint claim was yielding 50,000 dollars annually.

Eilley may have seen her fortune in the stars because she was a very superstitious individual and often consulted her crystal ball, which she called her 'peepstone'. And when it came to spending her fortune Eilley did it in style, building a 300,000-dollar mansion ten miles from Comstock, resplendent with lace curtains, Venetian mirrors, a grand balcony and even a fountain playing the rough garden carved out of the semi-desert.

Her most outrageous project was to pay a visit on Queen Victoria, whom she now regarded as her equal. In London in 1862, Eilley was dismayed when the American ambassador refused to arrange an audience. To soothe her despair, Eilley went on a shopping spree in London and Paris, the scale of which staggered even the high-spending society folk of Europe. In her baggage on her return journey was a clipping of ivy from the wall of Westminster Abbey, which she planted beside her mansion at Washoe Meadows and told folk was a gift from her friend, the Queen.

In the 1860s, Eilley's claim was worked out, Sandy died, and the Queen of the Comstock left for the California coast where she gained a wide reputation as a fortune-teller. But another Comstock was not in Eilley's stars.

For every successful prospector in the Old West there were a thousand who netted only a handful of colourful experiences, tales for re-telling over a glass of whisky in the autumn of their lives. Such a one was James 'Scotty' Philip, born at the farm of Auchness, near Dallas, Morayshire, on 30 April 1858. Within a few months of meeting up with his relatives at Victoria (KS), James was on his way to join hundreds of adventurers in the Black Hills of Dakota. Gold had been found.

These rolling hills, sacred to the Sioux Indians, were witnessing a bizarre game of hide-and-seek in the year 1875. The Indians were resolutely defending the last remnants of their natural heritage from the gold-seeking hordes, while the US Cavalry, who had been responsible for alerting the public to the gold in the first place, were under orders to maintain the sanctity of Indian rights and were evicting the would-be gold-diggers.

In a series of letters to his family, young James recounted the excitement, frustration, promise and eventual bitter disappointment in this great adventure, his quest for gold. In one letter James reveals that 1,500 people were now in the Hills and a town named Custer had been platted (laid out). It was named after the Cavalry general soon to be killed at the Battle of the Little Big Horn and who led the expedition which first reported gold. James also discloses a growing sense of his Americanisation:

I do not like the British Government and will always be an American. The people are generous to a fault, respecting all men for their worth, not their birth.

By the summer of 1876 the Hills were overrun and James, with his partner, had sunk a hole ten feet by six. But things were not going well. Although he thought the place beautiful, he records:

July 21—I have not 50 cents although it would save my life.
July 22—Still draining (after hitting water); no signs of pay dirt.
July 24—Still nothing. The young fellow who works with me is going back disheartened, but I mean to stay yet. I have 100lb of flour and will work until that is done.

The spring of 1877 saw James Philip leave the Black Hills with many of his youthful, romantic notions erased. However, he had been steeled to the hard realities of life in the West and it was to stand him in good stead as we find elsewhere.

The Bowers' splendidly out-of-place mansion in the midst of the Nevada wilderness, constructed with the money from her famous Comstock claim. (Nevada Historical Society)

~ *Chapter 6* ~

# GOOD GUYS, BAD GUYS AND
# MAD GUYS

N EXT TIME YOU'RE WATCHING one of those scratchy, black-and-white
Westerns from the early 1930s look very carefully at the whooping
redskins on their wild-eyed mustangs as they come tumbling out of the
screen towards you; beneath the war paint you might just catch a glimpse
of some rugged and distinctly Scottish features. One of the Indian warriors
is almost certainly 'Pee Wee' McDougall, former Sheriff of Fremont County
(WY) but born and raised within sight of Edinburgh Castle.

Alexander Campbell McDougall was born in 1914 and immigrated with
his parents and sisters to the United States in the 1920s, part of that last great
exodus of Scots to North America. John and Margaret McDougall arrived in
the town of Lander (WY), where there was already a substantial colony of
Scots sheepmen. His father worked as a shop assistant before buying his
own store in the neighbouring town of Dubois.

Early on in his school days, Alex gained the nickname of 'Pee Wee',
possibly because he was on the small side before he started to grow at High
School and became a formidable quarterback in the school football team. His
nickname stuck, as did his alternative title, 'The Oatmeal Savage', so-given
(it seems) because he could never tuck away enough of the traditional Scots
belt-tightener.

In his teens, Pee Wee swiftly gained a reputation for his skilled horsemanship and as a result he and his pals secured jobs as extras in several
Westerns filmed in the area. On one occasion they were called in to a movie
being filmed up at Jackson, near the border with Idaho. The film-makers
decided that they needed many hundreds of Indians, so white boys who
could ride were bussed to the location to supplement the numbers. Pee Wee
recalled:

> We'd get sponged down in the Snake River—My God, it was cold!—then
> they'd paint us with mud and calcimine for scenes when we attacked the
> covered wagons.

It appears that the genuine Indians got the best deal, being paid five dollars
daily plus board, while the white boys got four dollars a day and their free
transport. Another of Pee Wee's memories of those exciting days was of

Pee Wee McDougall, Sheriff of Fremont Country (WY) and anonymous film star in Westerns of the 1930s. (The McDougall Family)

the wild horses the producer had shipped in from all across the Midwest; half of them, he recalled, had not been properly broken-in. The boys from Lander did not always treat the film business as seriously as they should. Cameras were placed in holes under fallen logs so that they could film the flying hooves and, just for the hell of it, Alex and his pals would put on a spurt and

> ... ride around them and then outrun the chiefs. They'd yell to stop the cameras. We got ten dollars for taking a spill and after a day of falling naked in the sagebrush we were skinned from the ears down.

A Tim McCoy extravaganza called *War Paint* was filmed near Lander, and Pee Wee drove a herd of pinto ponies to the set each day along with the wagon for McCoy and his leading lady, Dorothy Sebastian—'I just loved her; I was so jealous of McCoy', he recalled.

After his schooling was over Pee Wee helped construct a dam and then in 1939 eloped with his wife-to-be, Gladys. Their first two children were born while he was in the Cavalry, the Lander unit of the National Guard. While stationed at Fort Lewis in Washington, Pee Wee made the national headlines when, in a challenge to prove he was the most skilled cowboy around (on machine or horse) he and a friend entered a local rodeo and roped calves from a jeep.

In 1950, friends from all over Fremont County persuaded him to run for Sheriff and, although unsuccessful, he was eventually elected in 1952. He was instrumental in setting up the Sheriff's posse—a trained horseback search and rescue unit to go to the aid of people lost in the mountains. Shoot-outs, even in the post-war years, were not infrequent and he was regularly called on to track down moonshiners. He was also responsible for ridding the county of organised prostitution, which was run by a crime syndicate under the formidable Ace Boggs. Perhaps his most unusual problem was policing a 2000-strong national gathering of the Rainbow Family, a naturist group. There were twice as many sightseers as there were participants. Pee Wee, who retired as Sheriff in 1979, wanted his deputies to be rugged and ready to tackle anything—he was that way himself.

From a Sheriff's office in the heart of Wyoming to the United States Supreme Court, or from the deck of a privateer to the opulence of the French Court at Versailles, we can trace Scots contributions in the making—and breaking—of the laws and principles which were to shape American democracy.

There is every reason to be proud of the earliest influence of the Scots in the judiciary, for example; their efforts in this field were in many ways as significant as those in education and the church. It has even been suggested that the distinct character of American jurisprudence is down to the sterling work of men of Scots blood at bench and bar. The evidence certainly seems to bear this out.

The United States Supreme Court, as first organised by George Washington, had four Associate Justices and three were of the same roots: James Wilson of Pennsylvania and John Blair of Virginia were Scots, and John Rutledge of South Carolina was an Ulster Scot. Of the fifty judges in the Supreme Court in the century after the Revolutionary War, there were no less than fifteen who were Scottish by birth or descent. They included Andrew Kirkpatrick (1756–1831), Chief Justice of New Jersey for twenty-one years, descended from the Dumfriesshire Kirkpatricks; the splendidly-named Eugenius Aristides Nisbet (1803–1871), Chief Justice of Georgia, descended from Murdoch Nisbet, a Lollard immigrant from Kyle; Chief Justice of Delaware, William Killen (1722–1805), born of Ulster-Scots parents; Alexander Addison (1759–1807), born in Scotland, became President Judge of the Fifth Judicial District of Pennsylvania under the Constitution of 1770. The impressive list goes on and on.

While recognising the great achievements of these courtroom clansmen, it is important to understand that there is another side to the coin; their efforts are balanced and occasionally overshadowed by the nasty exploits of 'scoundrels and ne'er-do-wells' among the Scottish immigrant tribes. And there are plenty to choose from.

Scots were in the front line when 'Lynch Law' (named after a seventeenth-century farmer from Virginia noted for his ice-cool impartiality in legal matters in the days before organised law enforcement) was properly inaugurated in America by the citizens of Harrisburg (PA). The first six victims of this particular style of mob justice are said to have been Iroquois Indians, one of whom was recognised by the angry townspeople as being a member of a raiding party who had killed a woman. The year was 1763. Attacking the Indian settlement, the mob murdered six Indians and fourteen others fled to Lancaster where they sought sanctuary in the jail. To compound their crime, fifty members of the community marched to Lancaster from Paxtang (now called Harrisburg), broke into the jail and killed every Indian they could find.

## LAW OF THE JUNGLE IN LOUISIANA

In seeking our number one villain—godfather in our gallery of American-Scots rogues—we have a bewildering selection, ranging from conmen through pirates, to bigots with pointed hoods. In making my own nomination of gambler, financial wizard, founder of the Bank of France and general smooth operator, John Law of Lauriston, (1671–1729), one of the guidelines for this enquiry into the story of the Scots in America is shattered. As far as can be established, Law, born in Edinburgh, never set foot on the continent of America. However, the activities of this brilliant Scots speculator and money-juggler so profoundly affected the early development of the southern United States that it would be foolish not to include the story which still forms an important part of basic regional history for thousands of school-children in the states of Louisiana and Mississippi.

Law arrived in France after having killed a man called Beau Wilson in a

London duel. The Scotsman quickly expanded his sphere of influence across the Channel, soon having the Regent of Louis XV, the Duke of Orleans, in his pocket. Law sought and was given approval for a bold colonisation scheme to enrich the French Treasury—and himself—by exploiting the vast, little-known territory along the great Mississippi River. Often called the first modern financial speculator, Law is remembered in France as the man who inflated the Mississippi bubble with a scheme which he innocuously termed the 'System' but which burst with the ruination of thousands and left many more stranded on the other side of the Atlantic, abandoned to build a new life in the most unpromising of locations.

His Company of the West virtually owned the Mississippi Valley and all the trading rights therein. To make the company pay, he knew he had to settle and develop the valley wilderness. However, since the establishment of the original French colony on the Gulf Coast, only a few immigrants had arrived and most had remained in the relative security of the district around New Orleans. To bring the colonisation scheme to life, Law devised a remarkably sophisticated public relations campaign. He launched an attractive seal for the Company of the West depicting a river god leaning on a horn of plenty from which gold coins cascaded. The handbills which attracted legions of would-be settlers spoke of gold, precious stones, valuable metals, furs and extraordinarily fertile lands. The reality was very different, as the writer on the Deep South, Hodding Carter, has explained:

> Had we been impoverished and adventurous Frenchmen or Germans in the year 1720 we would have blessed the name of John Law who promised a rich life in the New World. Had we followed from Europe to America the golden Will o' the Wisp which he created we would have come to curse him. That is if we survived the plagues, famines and neglect that were the almost universal lot of those heading for France's Louisiana colony.

By their thousands, desperate Europeans, especially peasants from the small, war-weary German states sought escape on John Law's ships . . . and by the thousand they died of disease in the French ports, in overcrowded ships, on the sand coast of the Gulf or fever-wracked on the tangled banks of the Mississippi.

Ambitiously, Law had schemed to substitute his company for the French Treasury, lending money to the government, selling stock to the public and collecting all taxes and revenues for a fee. His 'System' failed amid frenzied public speculation in the stock of his companies, and in the public commotion which followed, Law's house was torched and he was forced to flee the country.

Despite this financial disaster, Louisiana built a new beginning on the shaky foundations of Law's great lie. The area began to grow and slowly prosper under France, until 1765, then under Spain. Returned to France in 1802, Napoleon sold it almost immediately to the infant United States for

15,000,000 dollars—four cents an acre. Those who stayed knew Law had deceived them but they still believed that a cornucopia could be theirs. Hodding Carter again:

> Today Louisiana is a land of farms, forests and industry. Millions of descendants of those first settlers have made the State into a horn of plenty through ingenuity and skill.

John Law, for centuries a bogey-man to the folk of the Deep South, is remembered today not with affection but perhaps with greater under-standing. His fantasy has been brought to life by the descendants of the very people he conned.

BUSY MAKING HISTORY

In Will Oury, whose grandmother proudly claimed descent from the Scots patriot, William Wallace, we have the Scots schizophrenic, the lawman and villain rolled into one, serving on one hand with distinction as a Texas Ranger and Sheriff of Pima County (AZ) but also considered as the instigator, and certainly a participant in, the infamous Camp Grant Massacre in April 1871.

The execution of Captain Ewen Cameron on 25 April 1843 by the Mexicans during the Texas Revolution. Born in the Highlands, he was shot for leading an unsuccessful escape attempt, and Cameron Country (TX) is named in his honour.
(Institute of Texan Cultures, San Antonio)

The Ourys arrived in the colonies from Scotland before the Revolutionary War and made their home in Pennsylvania. Will Oury's grandfather, George, a drummer in the Revolutionary Army, moved on to Virginia, then Missouri, where Will was born and from where, as a teenager, he struck out on his own. Tales of adventure and wealth drew him to Texas, where he took a hand in the Texas Revolution against Mexican rule and as a member of Will Travis's band—along with Jim Bowie and Davy Crockett—was at the Alamo. When the final slaughter took place, Oury was away from the scene delivering despatches.

He was, however, one of 160 Texans captured at the Battle of Mier, after which the Mexican General Santa Ana ordered that every tenth prisoner was to be executed. Their lot was decided by drawing beans and those who picked a black bean were shot. Oury was one of the lucky ones.

After an unsuccessful stint hunting gold in California, during which he married, Oury found himself in Arizona, where he established a farm on the Santa Cruz. Although troubled by Indian raids, he gave as good as he got, on one occasion taking off after a war party and killing three of the Indians. Among his more notorious acts was the killing of Benito Flournoy in a duel—muzzle-loading muskets at fifty paces. This was no dandified, symbolic exchange of shots to retrieve honour. Coffins were carried to the field of combat, which later became known as Elysian Grove.

Unquestionably the grimmest tragedy associated with Will Oury was the Camp Grant incident. There may have been public outrage over this massacre but Oury seemed unashamed and even read a paper to the Pioneers Historical Society 'with gusto and pride' outlining the events. In February 1871 a group of 150 Apaches came to Camp Grant and asked the commandant if they could cultivate their ancestral plots in the Aravaipa Valley. This was agreed to, but when a series of murderous raids took place in the Santa Cruz Valley near Tucson (AZ) it was widely held that the renegades came from the Aravaipa settlement.

When in April a band of Indians raided San Xavier, killing a man and driving off stock, Oury organised a retaliatory attack, surprised the Apaches at sunrise and massacred 108 men, women and children—only eight of the victims were male adults.

Many settlers in Arizona felt the act was justified and certainly Oury never expressed any remorse. Described as a man of 'force and fire', he was apparently well-schooled in the 'virtues' of the pioneer—drinking, gambling and profanity. Yet he seems to have been held in the highest esteem by his contemporaries—even after selling off 105 muskets and 18,000 rounds of ammunition in Sonora for his own profit, although they had been given to him by the Arizona territorial authorities to distribute among the settlers for protection against hostile Apaches.

In the 1880s, when he was asked why he hadn't written a history of Arizona, Oury reportedly said: 'Because I'm too busy making it'.

Another American-Scots view of the Camp Grant Massacre comes from Andrew Hays Cargill, who was auditing books at the fort when the Indians came down from the hills to say they were tired of war. Cargill, whose family arrived in the colonies from Scotland in the 1720s, also witnessed Apaches handing in rifles, guns, bows and arrows before being issued with rations. On the day of the slaughter, Andrew recalled that a strange quietness was reported around the Indian camp three miles from the fort:

> We mounted at once and rode down and found women, children and one very old fellow killed. No live Indians about. We knew at once it had been done by parties from Tucson.

When the Indian chiefs came into the fort they were reassured that the government would treat the incident as murder. However, from bitter experience the Indians had every reason to be sceptical and their chief, Eskimenzin, declared:

> I do not expect to see any of them punished; for they will never punish a white man for killing an Indian.

After the grand jury had been drawn, Andrew Cargill was appointed Secretary. Feeling was running so strongly against the prosecution in Tucson that it took Cargill many hours to persuade the jury to proceed with the indictment; after the citizens found out the hard line being taken by Cargill, he was burned in effigy in the street. Eventually the case went ahead against Oury, four other white men and a group of Mexicans. All admitted their involvement but argued that it had been justified killing, since the Indians had murdered a man near the reservation. The jury acquitted the men 'amid great hurrahs'. Old Eskimenzin was proved correct.

KINDHEARTED CARMICHAEL

During the last years of the eighteenth century, members of the Carmichael family started to arrive in numbers in the Carolinas, settling on the north side of the Little Pee Dee River. Perhaps the most famous of these Scots was Neill Carmichael, the son of one of the immigrant couples and known throughout Marion County as Sheriff Carmichael. Born in 1797, he lived to be eighty-six and according to local biographies was a 'universally loved' character.

He was twice elected sheriff of the district, his first four-year term from 1841 to 45. During this period there was a deep financial depression throughout the South and most folk around the Pee Dee were in debt. Money could not be raised, property had little value and generally the people were very distressed. Fortunately for the debtors of Marion County, there was a kind-hearted man wearing the Sheriff's badge and he refused to enforce collections by levy or by sale of property during this troubled period. The money sharks, therefore, sought an order against Carmichael for failing to collect what they regarded as their just entitlements, and the outcome was that the Sheriff ended up behind bars in his own jail.

As his biographer, W.W. Sellers, wrote in 1902, Carmichael became a 'martyr to the kindness of his heart, the leniency of his office'. He was in jail for about twenty months from 1842 to 43, with his family occupying the apartments provided for the jailer's family. Carmichael moved his papers, books and personal effects into his cell and attended to his business as though he had remained in his office at the court-house.

Effectively, as he took money in and paid it out, he remained in the post of sheriff, although deprived of his liberty. During this bizarre episode, his oldest son, A.B. Carmichael, was born in the jail and had a remarkable tale to tell his own grandchildren in years to come. The incarceration led Neill Carmichael to achieve the status of local folk-hero and he will, according to his biographer, 'live in the hearts of the people for all time to come'.

Throughout the 1800s and into the 1900s, the reputation of lawyers with a Scots heritage was second to none. From the highest tribunals in the land to the rough and ready, out-of-the-way court-house, their debating skills and sharpness was legendary. Typical of this breed was William Henry Malcolm (b. 1881), the son of a Glasgow couple, who put himself through colleges in Virginia and Indiana in the early years of this century by working as a mine foreman.

Willie Malcolm was described as a 'fierce debater' but kind, resourceful and opinionated. He is generally accepted as one of the best criminal lawyers West Virginia has ever seen and was the typical wee Scot: five foot five in his stocking soles, he strode around the courtroom like a giant and he maintained this impressive style when he was appointed a judge.

On one memorable occasion, he was defending a well-known bootlegger accused of making moonshine. Willie was later to deny any involvement in the strange scene that unfolded, but it was Malcolm who asked the judge to make sure that the sealed jars which had been seized by the Sheriff and presented in evidence actually contained liquor. What the judge found, instead of whisky, was pure water. How this remarkable feat had been achieved was never revealed—but this indomitable lawyer was never short of a bottle of whisky thereafter, according to his descendants. A bronze plaque commemorates this 'bonnie fechter' in the Mercer County Court-house.

BUSINESS—FUNNY AND OTHERWISE

The history of big business in the United States will always reserve a special place for the famous Dunfermline-born philanthropist, Andrew Carnegie (1835–1919). He left Scotland for America with his family in 1848, and began to make money after persuading his father to mortgage the family home to buy shares. Carnegie seemingly had a Midas touch, enjoying spectacular success in steel, railroads and shipping, but he got rid of his wealth almost as quickly as he created it, endowing thousands of libraries and educational trusts on both sides of the Atlantic. While Carnegie can be said to illustrate Scots business acumen in its most flattering light, a wily compatriot was showing that there was a more dubious side to the nation's stereotypical flair for all things financial.

'Some folk hae mair money than sense.' This piece of homespun philosophy was adopted by Scots actor-turned-conman, Arthur Fergusson, who went on to prove the maxim in the homeland of enterprise and initiative, the United States. Fergusson had observed in the early 1920s that Americans had the annoying habit of wanting to buy up everything they clapped eyes on; in addition, he reckoned they had cornered the market in wide-eyed gullibility. After playing the stage role of an American taken in by a confidence trickster, a daring scheme recommended itself to Fergusson. He went into the monument-selling business.

And the Scotsman didn't begin with half-measures. His first 'sale' was Nelson's Column, which he flogged to a tourist from Iowa for a knock-down price, telling the visitor that he was a government official and that the column had to be disposed of to help repay Britain's First World War debt to the USA. When the American went to a demolition firm (cheekily recommended by Fergusson), presumably with the intention of having the column re-erected in his backyard in Des Moines, the hoax was unveiled. The conman, however, was long gone.

Fired by this success, Fergusson swiftly sold off Buckingham Palace and Big Ben before deciding that the United States was the place for him; after all, it was filled with Americans all desperate, he believed, to part with their cash. He immigrated in 1925 and lost no time in getting into action, renting out the White House to a Texan cattleman for 100,000 dollars. He had almost persuaded an Australian that the Statue of Liberty would look good at the entrance to Sydney Harbour when he foolishly allowed himself to be photographed in front of the monument, was recognised, and the game was up.

Having served five years, he was able to retire to California to live out his life in comparative luxury on the income from these and a hundred other scams. If anyone proved that all the world's a stage, then it was that mere player, Arthur Fergusson.

JUSTICE JIM

When émigré Scot, Jimmie Crain, finally settled on the lower reaches of the Yellowstone River in Montana, he had spent most of his life west of the auburn waters of the River Missouri and was reckoned a dead shot with the rifle, an ardent lover of whisky and an expert at draw poker. As his biographer caustically observes: 'Apart from these skills he had no religious accomplishments worth speaking of.'

Ranching and farming became his life after building his steading in 1877, and he was always full of praise for his adopted home, even writing to the local paper in his later years, praising his neighbours as good settlers and waxing poetic on the remarkable fertility of the valley. He described the well-watered rolling prairie beyond the two-mile wide stand of timber by the river as the best stock country in the world. Jimmie Crain grew crops of corn, wheat, oats, vegetables, watermelons, canteloupe and tomatoes. Five kinds of grass, some green all winter, were also found.

A community twelve miles south of Sidney (MT) has been named after this Scottish adventurer, but it was in his earlier years on the wild frontier that, almost by chance, he found himself elected to the post of Justice of the Peace. Lone Tree, in the beautiful valley of the River Platte, 131 miles west of Omaha (NE), was a township of half a dozen hastily constructed houses. The public perception of Jimmie Crain at this time was of an 'eccentric, time-beaten frontiersman, unpolished, uneducated and ungodly'. However, when JP Bill Bennett was gunned down in an argument during a card game, the roughnecks (for a laugh, it's said) elected Jimmie to the post. But our Scotsman took his role very seriously, combing his hair at least once a week and conducting himself with as much dignity as he could muster.

A few days after his installation, a young couple appeared and asked to be married. Jimmie—who had never seen a marriage ceremony per-formed—was nevertheless determined that it should be conducted with all the proper procedures. Having asked if 'any o' you knows any cause why they shouldn't make the play, you want to squeal at this stage or corral yer jaws on the subject furevermore', no objections were raised and Jimmie continued:

> Do you an' each other of you solemnly sw'ar that you will marry each other in the presence of this court; that you will do the squar' thing by each other; that you will give everybody else the go-by; an' cling to each other through life until death calls upon you to cash in yer earthly checks . . .

And so the ceremony continued with Jimmie improvising brilliantly. The couple swore their oath and Jimmie, sweating profusely with his exertions, rounded things off in style:

> Then I James Crain, Justice of the Peace, announce you as husband and wife now and furevermore, world without end, amen; an' if the style don't suit you, you have the legal right to appeal to the supreme court in Omaha anytime within the next 60 days. Now light out, an' me an' the boys'll go and drink yer health.

An odd ceremony and no mistake; but according to reports, the couple walked away hand in hand perfectly satisfied with the performance of Justice Jim.

A classic example of the eccentric but tremendously gifted inventor—that was how neighbours in Fresno County (CA) regarded Jim Porteous, an East

Lothian lad who served his time in his father's wheelwright's workshop in Haddington. Born in 1848, he arrived in the fertile county of Fresno in 1877, having decided to try his luck in the United States and, like his father, he set up a blacksmith and wagon-making business.

Essentially it was as an inventor that James Porteous should be remembered today, although you would be hard put to find many in the district who could detail his contribution to agriculture, immense though it was. Perhaps his greatest invention was the Fresno 'scraper', a dirt scraper which made land-levelling, ditch-digging and road-building easier and quicker. The device was exported to South America, India, the Orient, South Africa, Australia and Europe. He worked on other devices for improving agricultural practices and built a five-gang vineyard plough, a raisin-grader, a raisin and fig-press and a cultivator.

When he was in the midst of invention he became totally engrossed, eating and sleeping when the mood took him and occasionally missing out on social engagements. Having been included in a friend's wedding plans, as best man, Porteous was busily working in his shop on the day of the wedding and had to be reminded of the event ten minutes before the ceremony. According to Maria Ortiz, archivist at the Fresno Historical Society, the wedding took place without the best man and the wedding party stormed the Porteous place to tell him what they thought of him only to find, to their amazement, that he was asleep in bed. Once awake, he explained that he was changing for the wedding when an idea for a new centrifugal pump occurred to him and the wedding was forgotten. Finishing the design, he had gone to bed to sleep.

James, who married and had six children, continued throughout his life to be fascinated by technical developments and became a camera buff and owner of the first electric car in Fresno. Porteous, an absent-minded but brilliant man, is rightly called the county's 'forgotten pioneer'.

MORE THAN A SOCIAL CLUB

The Ku-Klux Klan started off as a social club and ended up as one of the most sinister organisations the United States has seen. Founded at Pulaski (TN) in 1866 by a group of ex-Confederate Army veterans of Scottish descent, the aim was simply to 'have fun, make mischief and play pranks in public'. The officers called their organisation the Ku-Klux from the Greek for circle and Klan was added in recognition of their Caledonian ancestry.

As Scots writer Archie McKerracher has noted, they rode out one night covered in bed sheets as a joke and found that superstitious former slaves thought the ghosts of the Confederate dead had returned to harass them. This sparked the notion of a secret society which would inspire fear among lawless, freed slaves. The history books tell us that the night-riders began by breaking up prayer meetings and issuing death threats, but were soon actually involved in murder and rape. With the law enforcement agencies

The Ku-Klux Klan, founded as a social club by young American-Scots Confederate cavalry officers after the Civil War, experienced a resurgence following the First World War. Thousands of KKK members marched down Pennsylvania Avenue in Washington DC in 1925. (Library of Congress, Neg. No. F81-36635)

helpless, it was left to a congressional committee in 1871 to force the disbandment of the order.

There was a major revival in the fortunes of the Klan in the aftermath of the First World War and in the wake of D.W. Griffith's epic film *The Birth of a Nation*, which in 1915 portrayed KKK members as defenders of the old values of the South. At this time membership of the Klan may have been as high as 6,000,000 but various internal squabbles, allegations of involvement in organised crime and official condemnation had its effect. The movement today, with its headquarters in Baton Rouge (LA), has around 15,000 members.

Oaths and rituals used by the Klansmen were adapted from ceremonies of the secret Society of the Horseman's Word which flourished in north-east Scotland between 1830 and 1930 and which is still said to be found in parts of Scotland today. Their procedures were taken to America by nineteenth-century agricultural immigrants and new members underwent initiation rituals almost identical to those required of Scottish ploughboys.

The influence of the Klan spread. In North Carolina, with its strong Scottish links, Klansmen wore horned hoods and, says Archie McKerracher,

> . . . forced terrified blacks to shake the skeletal hand of the Auld Chiel, as many an equally terrified loon had done in a Kincardineshire bothy.

Their cause in recent years was not helped by a well-publicised incident in which, during one of the spasmodic revivals of cross-burning (taken from the traditional Highland call-to-arms), night forays and whippings, a group of Klansmen in North Carolina set out to 'discipline' some Red Indians but found the native Americans more than ready for a fight and were sent away bruised and bloodied.

### THE UNDERGROUND RAILROAD

The anti-slavery movement which led to the American Civil War (1861–65) can fairly be said to have begun amongst Scottish Covenanters (largely in South Carolina and eastern Tennessee) twenty or thirty years before there was any organised opposition to slavery, even in the north. The Rev. Dr Alexander McLeod hesitated to accept a call to the Covenanter congregation in Chambers Street, New York, because some members of the congregation kept slaves. Hearing of this reluctance, the Presbytery immediately ordered that 'no slaveholder should be retained in their communion'. This took place in November 1800.

By 1815, Covenanters, Methodists and Quakers of eastern Tennessee had eighteen emancipation societies, and by 1826 it was reckoned there were over 140 such groups in the United States, the vast majority, perhaps suprisingly, found in the South. It's worth noting that the leading Covenanter anti-slavery leader, John Rankin, thought it safer in 1820 to make abolition speeches in Kentucky or Tennessee than in the northern states.

Ulster Scots, although they were to play their part in the abolition movement, were, at least in early years of settlement, great advocates of the slavery system. Josiah Moffat, in his study of the Ulster Scots in the Piedmont area of the Carolinas, comments:

> Those sturdy individualists, staunch defenders of personal liberty and the God-given right of all men to 'life, liberty and the pursuit of happiness' had modified their views to the extent of excluding the Negro from this divinely arranged scheme of things.

Ulster Scots became convinced, like the majority of whites in the South, that the blacks were not only an inferior race but doomed, as the sons of Ham upon whom his father Noah pronounced the curse of perpetual servitude, to be nothing more than hewers of wood and drawers of water to the end of time. At least one doctor of divinity even wrote a book in which he triumphantly proved, to the satisfaction of his limited circle of believers at least, that the Negro had no soul.

It has to be accepted that prejudice amongst the Scots and Ulster Scots persisted long after the supposed emancipation of the Civil War.

For many it took years to accept the negro folk as their equals. *The Granite Cutters Journal* reported in 1885 how a young Scot working in the granite quarries of Pennsylvania point-blank 'refused to be bossed by a nigger'.

The Rev. George Miller was born in the Chester district of South Carolina into an Ulster-Scots family proud of their Presbyterian heritage. The year was 1834 and his family were members of the Associate Scotch Presbyterian Church, which by this time took a strong stance against slavery, despite having thousands of members in the southern states. No one owning slaves was permitted to be a church member and, as attitudes hardened among the pro-slavery southerners, many of the liberal families sold up and moved north.

After a circuit-rider (a travelling preacher) from the synod who had taken on the perilous task of visiting their churches in Virginia and the Carolinas was tarred and feathered, the Rev. Miller's father, Robert Hyndman Miller, decided to prosecute the parties in the civil courts. Only a few weeks later, however, as he was delivering baled cotton he was waylaid by a gang, knocked from his horse and beaten unconscious. It took him months to recover full fitness and in that time he ordered a brace of pistols and a dirk, warning that the next time he was waylaid somebody would die. The Rev. Miller's oldest brother, Josiah, went north at the age of eighteen, studied law, then opened a newspaper office in Kansas, publishing from a sod house in the town of Lawrence. His anti-slavery stance saw his press and office burned down by border raiders from Missouri. Despite being rescued at the last minute from a mock trial which could have ended in his summary execution, he braved it out in Kansas.

There is additional early evidence that at least elements of the American-Scots community were uncomfortable about the slave trade.

In North Carolina, James McKay, who descended from the Cromartie family of Orkney, left money in his will for his slaves to go back to Africa if they wished. Some apparently did so. In the same state, James Elliott (b.1730) of Pasquotank County was a successful farmer from a line of early Scots immigrants to the colonies. He held a number of slaves but family histories tell us that, as a member of the Society of Friends (Quakers) and 'an upright man of moral character', he became convinced the practice was wrong and, yielding to his conscience, freed his slaves. The economic repercussions of this brave gesture are not recorded.

Despite these examples, it does seem that planters and traders of Scots origins were among the most enthusiastic users and abusers of slave labour, particularly during the eighteenth century. On his first Florida planta-tion—New Richmond—Morayshire-born Sir William Dunbar, scientist and explorer, used slaves from the Caribbean to wrest his plantation from the wilderness. Bernard Bailyn has observed that Dunbar's estate was really a work camp cum agricultural factory, with its owner strangely insensitive to the suffering of those who served him.

In his journals for 1776, Dunbar records details of a slave 'uprising'. A ringleader, bound hand and foot, was taken by boat to be identified by informers but threw himself overboard and was drowned. Dunbar could not fathom this despair. When he recaptured two runaways and condemned them to 500 lashes each and to carry a chain and log fixed to their ankles, he wrote:

> For why do they run away? They are well cloathed, work easy, and have all kinds of plantation produce at no allowance.

The Scotsman had an underground cell which he called the Bastille, and his records are filled with incidents which merited confinement. When a slave called Bessy got into a fight with another slave, and bit off part of his ear, they were both thrown into the punishment cell. Another slave girl, convicted of killing a white, had her hand cut off before being executed. To be fair to Dunbar, his regime was possibly less rigid than many down the east coast.

Callander-born Robert Stuart, a leading fur trader who in his later years was Superintendent of Indian Affairs in Michigan, had a stance on slavery which was very common in the years leading up to the Civil War. He opposed outright abolition but was a friend and helper of runaway slaves. Some anti-slavery supporters were not so restrained or discreet. 'Jimmy the Jayhawker' or James Montgomery (1814–1871) claimed he was the great-grandson of a Highland chieftain who had immigrated in the 1700s. Settling in Kansas, Jimmy declared himself to be passionately against slavery and organised a group which used extreme violence to drive pro-slavery advocates from the district. He made several attempts to destroy Fort Scott, where a pro-slavery judge pursued an open policy of discrimination. During the Civil War he earned a reputation for 'jayhawking' or plundering, and made several raids into Georgia and Florida destroying Confederate property and liberating slaves. Fearless in combat, it seems his military tactics were non-existent.

The Underground Railroad—a secret network of safe houses which helped some 50,000 slaves escape north between 1830 and 1860—included the homes of a number of American Scots. John Ritchie, who came from a family of Indiana Scots, arrived in Kansas as the violent debate over the 'Free-State' issue, slavery or non-slavery, was raging in the 1850s. Mary Ritchie Jarboe, in a recent profile, described him as a 'philanthropist, generous to a fault, Ultra-Abolitionist, women's rights man, friend and champion of the poor, Friend of God and lover of freedom, admirer of John Brown'. In fact, the famous abolitionist Brown (whose soul still marches on, according to the song) visited the Ritchie home in Topeka, which was attacked by pro-slavery elements in search of runaway slaves. In a eulogy following his death, *The Topeka Commonwealth* remembered:

> John Ritchie was a staunch friend of the negro and used to say that no less than 100,000 dollars worth of runaway slaves passed through his place.

Captain William Kidd was a Scots sea commander who settled in New York and became an almost-legendary figure following his daring exploits on the high seas. Certainly the most celebrated pirate in English literature, he was born, as far as can be established, in Greenock around the year 1650, the son of a Calvinist preacher.

Going to sea, probably while still in his teens, he swiftly gained the reputation for almost reckless courage and first appears in America in 1691 as a respected gentleman and merchant in New York, the Colonial Assembly voting him its thanks for 'services to the commerce of the colony'. Then the governor of New York recruited him on a roving, world-wide commission to clear the trade routes of pirates and to act against the French. He was given a ship of thirty guns for this formidable task.

Apparently the incident which saw him embark on a career of piracy, so the story goes, happened when Kidd refused to allow an attack on a Dutch ship. This provoked a minor mutiny, which Kidd quelled by striking one of his gunners on the head with a bucket; the seaman died and from then on the captain was outside the law. Having seen the possibilities of plunder, Kidd launched into a spectacular career as the archetypal, cutlass-between-the-teeth pirate chief, filling the adventure books with his exploits and exotic tales of treasures left scattered around the oceans of the world.

In an era when there were many wild men at sea, the pirate-chaser turned pirate was the wildest. Although he must have known that word of his adventures would have reached America, he sailed into Boston where he was arrested and sent to England. On 23 May 1701, he was hanged at Execution Dock in London but even his death was filled with drama. As he hung from the gibbet, the rope broke and he fell to the ground; the gallows collapsed in this incident, so he was hanged finally from a nearby tree. His only son is said to have been killed at the Battle of Sheriffmuir near Dunblane in 1715, during the Jacobite Uprising.

America became the home for the fascinating James Tytler (1747–1805) when he fled Edinburgh amid accusations of sedition after publishing a *Manifesto of the People's Wrongs*. While in the debtor's sanctuary at Holyrood he had written and published many books and made large contributions to the second and third editions of Encyclopedia Britannica. Tytler was a man of many talents: a true eccentric, he even made a pioneering flight in a gas balloon over the walls of Holyrood. His short journey ended messily when he crash-landed in a dung-heap. Tytler lived out his life in Salem (MA).

Also in Massachusetts we find Peter Mackintosh, a Boston blacksmith who was a ringleader in the riots against the British government in 1765; and Daniel Malcolm, a Boston merchant who was prominent among the mob in 1768. Thomas Gallagher, born in Glasgow in 1851, worked as a child in a city foundry. Immigrating to America in his mid-twenties, he became a doctor in Brooklyn (NY) . . . and a member of the Fenian movement. Coming to Britain on a bombing campaign in 1883, he was arrested and imprisoned until 1896 when he emerged insane and died in a lunatic asylum.

WORLD'S FIRST PRIVATE EYE

Perhaps the most startling allegation made against the Glaswegian radical and refugee, Allan Pinkerton, who established the world's first detective agency after immigrating to the United States, was that he prolonged the bloody American Civil War by up to three years.

Critics of the unscrupulous ex-Chartist barrel-maker say that while he was in charge of Federal spying activities, gross overestimates of Southern strength by Pinkerton and his agents made President Abraham Lincoln's military advisers overcautious, when the War might have been brought to a speedy conclusion as early as the spring of 1862.

Pinkerton, the son of a Glasgow policeman, was very active in the mid-1800s in the west of Scotland promoting workers' rights but, like many other radicals, was forced to flee eventually to North America. He settled in Dundee (IL) and began to take an interest in crime detection, acting in the first instance as a police informer and devising a series of ingenious schemes including, according to some sources, the pioneering undercover procedure of sitting inside barrels listening to criminals' conversations. In 1857 he set up his agency in Chicago, but it only took off after he persuaded railway companies that he and his teams could halt widespread theft on the great network of railroads which was snaking across America.

Ironically, bearing in mind his radical background, some of his greatest successes came in strike-breaking activities. He was involved in an infamous strike-breaking episode at Carnegie's giant Homestead steel works in Pittsburgh in 1892. While Carnegie was on holiday in Scotland, his partner, Henry Frick, brought in armed Pinkerton agents to subdue the strikers. In a pitched battle in the shadow of the steelmill chimneys ten people were killed.

Out West, Pinkerton and his detectives did a lot of hard riding after outlaws but their success was minimal. And as writer of Western history James Callaghan, has pointed out, they often took the law into their own hands; for example, posters were seen all around Chicago after the Great Fire threatening looters with death—all completely unauthorised.

> There was also a shameful vigilante attack on the home of Jesse James's mother. A grenade was thrown into her house and Jesse's mother lost her arm. Her 14-year-old son was killed. Jesse James spent three months in Chicago intending to assassinate Pinkerton after that raid.

Pinkerton also took credit for getting Abraham Lincoln safely to Washington in the face of a murder plot, but he was posted missing when the President was gunned down at the Ford Theatre in Washington in April 1865.

While Pinkerton is seen in many quarters as an unmitigated villain, pro-Pinkerton historians point to the trendsetting aspects of his detective

Friday, 3 October 1862. President Abraham Lincoln poses with Glasgow-born
detective, Allan Pinkerton, and Major General John A. McClernand on the battlefield
of Antietam (MD). Photograph by Alexander Gardner, a pioneering American
photographer born in Paisley. (Abraham Lincoln Museum, Harrogate (TN))

agency, which introduced modern and innovative methods of catching criminals, including detailed records and a photographic 'rogues' gallery'. The agency's communication network was said to be more efficient than those of state and federal governments.

Peter Chisholm, Deputy Sheriff of Oakland (MD) last century, had been given the task of escorting a citizen and fellow American Scot, a Mr Totten, to the insane asylum. Local histories are filled with rich men who go crazy and Oakland was no exception. Mr Totten's behaviour had become steadily more and more worrying. When it came to the point that he would appear on his porch shouting obscenities and waving a butcher's knife at passers-by, the community decided it was time to act. Papers were prepared to have him admitted to care, and Peter Chisholm was delegated the sad task of taking him there by train.

Along the way, Mr Totten, who seemed very quiet, waited until Peter dozed off then picked his pocket and removed the official documents. When they arrived at the asylum, Mr Totten calmly informed the staff that he was Deputy Sheriff and that Peter was the insane Mr Totten, handing over the purloined papers to prove his point. The result was that Peter was locked up, Mr Totten came home on the next train, and it took the sheriff three days to get Peter released from the asylum.

The murder of Andy Hall, a Borders-born messenger with Wells Fargo, caused outrage in his adopted state of Arizona. Andy had come to the West as a boy and gained a reputation as an Indian-fighter and explorer. He was with the Powell Expedition of 1869, which explored the Colorado River and Grand Canyon. One overcast, sultry Sunday in August 1882, Andy was escorting a mule-train carrying among other things, a 5,000-dollar payroll for the Mackmorris mine, near the town of Globe. Shots rang out and the mules, including the animal carrying the payroll, bolted.

Sending his companions on to Globe to collect a posse, Andy, who had seen the thieves Grimes and Hawley break open the moneybox after shooting the mule, tracked the bandits into the hills. Keeping at a safe distance, he was unable to prevent them shooting a prospector, Doc Vail, and stealing his horses. Doc Vail was to die shortly after the posse reached him, guided by a trail left by Andy Hall, but not before he gave a good description of his attackers.

Eventually catching up with the men, Andy tried a bold ruse. He indicated that he thought the payroll caravan had been attacked by Indians and said they should all get back into Globe before the Indians struck again. Whether they believed the story or not, Grimes and Hawley went along with Andy in the direction of town until, at the top of a rise, they shot him in the back and pumped him full of bullets as he lay on the ground.

The sequel to the killings was even more dramatic. The younger of the two bandits, Fate Grimes, was a dancing master and remarkably small footprints had been noticed near the murder scenes. When confronted, Grimes confessed all and Hawley followed suit. Then there was a dispute between the US marshall and the local sheriff, who wanted to keep the men in town to face the murder charges while the marshall was more concerned about the robbing of the mail and wanted the men taken to the state capital. The mob, in the two days since the murders, had been seething with excitement. The fact that there were two men in custody having confessed to the killings and the possibility that they might be taken out of the county convinced them that a lynching was the only solution.

Late on the Wednesday night, the sheriff persuaded the crowd to at least allow a hearing. The town judge held 'court' in a local hall. The place was full-to-overflowing, and when the magistrate bound the two men over for further examination, the mob took control.

At 2 a.m., by the eerie light of blazing beer-barrels, the two men were hanged from a sycamore in front of the St Elmo saloon. The burly Hawley, asked if he wished to pray, answered: 'What the hell do I care for the hereafter. It's this damned mob I want rid of.' *The Arizona Weekly Enterprise* showed the affection which was felt for the murdered Scots messenger in his obituary:

> No sadder news ever shocked a community or fired a people with righteous indignation than the intelligence of Andrew Hall's murder. The indignant grief which burns today in many hearts, the sorrow and tears of those whose hand will never press his again and who will ever miss him, speak eloquently of our loss.

GUN LAW ON THE PECOS

Appointed by the Scottish Mortgage and Land Investment Company to look after their interests in New Mexico, native Scot, Thomas S. Carson, did not expect that his first major run-in would be with a rancher of the same blood—the formidable William Henry McBroom. Although born in Canada, McBroom's mother was Scots, formerly Eliza Rock, and his father was an Ulster Scot. He came first of all to New Mexico as a government surveyor and over a period of years undertook nine major surveys, amassing the (for the time) princely sum of over 40,000 dollars, which enabled him to buy his way into ranching.

Carson, on the other hand, had arrived in New Mexico after a four-year career as a tea-planter in India and a stint as a rancher in Arizona. He joined the company at a time when it was keen to enlarge its holding, and he was active in acquiring several herds and ranches for the organisation. The take-over of Henry McBroom's operation at the Coniva ranch, some thirty-five miles south-west of Tucumcari, was to give the company its new headquarters—but McBroom did not go down without a fight.

Early in 1890, as the spring round-up began along the Pecos River, Carson was told that McBroom had a large loan with the company but had paid no interest for years, and that the organisation had decided to foreclose and take possession. He was instructed to take over 'in any way that his wits might suggest'. Finding the McBroom outfit, Carson explained his business, saying he had come to take McBroom's saddle-horses and showing the official papers. When the cowhands threatened him, Carson withdrew and wrote an affadavit explaining how force had been used to prevent him carrying out his job. This seemed to satisfy the company lawyers and they told him to adopt similar techniques in the future.

McBroom, having heard of Carson's campaign, began calling him 'that damned Scotsman' and their face-to-face encounter was not long delayed. Carson came across 200 of McBroom's stockhorses and claimed them for the company. That night, while camped near the McBroom steading, the rancher himself appeared, shotgun in hand and with his wife clinging to his coat tails. In his autobiography, Carson admitted:

> No doubt he meant to shoot, but I was quite ready for him and put a bold face on it. Things looked nasty indeed and I was determined to fire should he once raise his gun. Perhaps this boldness made him think a bit.

The men parted company, but Carson—moving along the Pecos—saw that McBroom was gathering steers and bulls of all ages, presumably with the intention of driving them into Texas where he would be untroubled by the Scottish company and its persistent agent. However, when the break came Carson was ready and (with a lawman) was soon in pursuit. They caught up with the herd seven or eight miles from the Texas border. McBroom's foreman had made a major blunder by watering the cattle, making it impossible to drive them forward at speed. A slow walk was the most the herd could manage. The distraught McBroom was not with them but was found on the prairie nearby 'prostrated by the sun'.

Even after he 'threw up the sponge' and agreed to turn the property over, McBroom was still a formidable adversary. Finding Carson branding horses to which McBroom still had a claim, the rancher levelled his shotgun and said he would kill him if he proceeded further. 'I never saw a man who looked so angry and mean', reported Carson. Sensibly, he backed off.

But this remarkable Caledonian confrontation was not over. McBroom successfully sued the Scottish Mortgage and Land Investment Company for charging too high a rate of interest on the loan, and Carson's true colours were shown when he started ranching for himself at the arid and oddly-named spot called Running Water Draw. He bragged about having enclosed public land illegally and boasted that the county assessor didn't even know of his existence and that for a period of eight years he hadn't paid a cent's rental on his ranch. Hard citizens both on the New Mexican frontier.

For a family of Scots rogues, you don't have to look much further than the McClures of Indiana. Reminiscences over these American Scots focus on their twin interests—horse-racing and gambling. The story of the McClures, who arrived from Scotland in the mid-1700s and settled in Richmond (VA), moving to Indiana via South Carolina and Ohio, reads like a romantic novel of the early West filled with love tangles and dark intrigue.

In the mid-1800s they created close to their house a race-track where regular meetings were held, bringing folk from all over the state and some of the finest horses in the 'heartland' to compete. The McClures' philosophy was 'win at any cost' and their home boasted a second-floor gambling room. There, particularly on race days, big-money poker games took place, as well as substantial gambles on the horses.

Determined to win, Mrs McClure (so it's said) sat in a room where she could see the finish of the races and by some means managed to let her husband, Robert, in the gambling room know the outcome so that he could place a bet before the official result had reached the gamblers.

They are also alleged to have tampered with the horses, filling their guests with drink then arranging for the grooms to tire the horses out on the track while their owners lay in a stupor in the house. They even went as far as stealing horses that they particularly fancied, hiding them in a cave down by the river and blaming rustlers. Among their other 'hobbies' the family turned out counterfeit coins which were hidden in different parts of the estate.

Dave McClure, described by local historians as a bully and 'mean as hell' managed to force the beautiful Nancy Baxter to marry him by threatening to kill her lover, a Virginia gentleman called Jack Dew who came regularly to the race meetings. It's said McClure kept the girl like a pirate's coveted treasure, dressing her up and showing her off. Eventually he left her and she died quite young, buried in an unmarked grave on the McClures' Wabash County estate. She was wearing the wedding dress intended for her wedding to Jack Dew.

Dave McClure met a villain's end in rather bizarre circumstances. On the estate there was a fish pond, and on one occasion McClure found a gypsy woman there who was nursing a very sickly child. She had just drawn a pail of water when McClure arrived and, swearing loudly, ordered her to empty it. The woman raised her arms and began a tirade which included a curse on the house and a warning to McClure that his skin would fall from his bones. The curse was laughed off and forgotten . . . at least for a while.

During the 1870s the McClures left Indiana for Little Rock (AR). Dave was drifting downriver with a hunting party in canoes when he saw an Indian squaw on a rock, spearing fish. Laughing, he shot her. The woman somehow managed to stumble back to her camp and soon the Indians overtook the hunters. They staked Dave to the ground and skinned him alive. A gypsy prophecy fulfilled?

LAIRD OF THE WEST
Natural historians of Scots descent, many of them children of the Enlightenment, played an important role in classifying trees, plants and insect life

Sir William Drummond Stewart, a Perthshire-born adventurer and aristocrat, was instrumental in leading expeditions through the wilds of the American West. His passion was natural history, and he transported a marvellous variety of American flora and fauna to his Scottish estates. (George Forbes/Lang Syne Publishers)

from about 1740 onwards. Many of these people were doctors, who as an adjunct to health care studied their new environment. Outstanding among them were Cadwallader Colden in New York state, William Douglas in Boston (MA), John Lining, Lionel Chalmers and Alexander Garden (these three working chiefly in Charleston (SC)), and Alexander Hamilton in Annapolis (MD).

Moving towards the mid-1800s, ordinary Scots, who up until then had been concerned with more simple, down-to-earth matters like staying alive, began to take an interest in their natural surroundings. Methods of study varied. John Regan, author of *The Emigrant's Guide*, was content to write at length about the natural beauties of his new home while Sir William Drummond Stewart, who spent much of the 1830s trekking across the Rockies, did not rest easy until he had filled the grounds of his ancestral seat at Murthly in Perthshire with plants, birds and animals plucked from their America setting.

The sort of marvellous Garden of Eden in which amateur botanists, biologists and zoologists found themselves is well illustrated by excerpts from Regan's writing of the 1850s. Take for example his description of the first sight of the prairies in Illinois:

> Before us lay one vast plane of verdure and flowers, without house or home, or anything to break in upon the uniformity of the scene, except the shadow of a passing cloud. To the right and left long points of timber, like capes and headlands, stretched in the blue distance, the light breeze of the morning brushing along the young grass and the blue and pink flowers—the strong sunlight pouring down everywhere.

Regan remarked on the all-pervading silence and the elation engendered by the whole scene. Of course, he was writing to try to encourage Scots to desert the harsh agrarian conditions in the homeland for the agricultural potential of the Midwest; but for those interested in the study of the natural world, it must truly have seemed that he had stumbled into some sort of paradise on earth. Regan reached the Spoon River:

> The scenery was beyond description beautiful, being now in half-leaf the majestic forest had a particularly pleasing aspect ... young and tender grass of brightest green, with yellow mosses ... the cheerful booming of the grouse in the upper lands, the strings of geese and cranes on their northern migration to the [Great] Lakes.

Simply viewing these wonders was not sufficient for Sir William, the Perthshire aristocrat, who went to America in 1832 after his elder brother inherited the family estates. Subsequently, Sir William made a series of epic trips through the West, attending fur-traders meetings, gaining the reputation as a marksman with the long rifle, and encountering legendary figures of the frontier such as Jim Bridger. In his absence he was to fall heir to the Perthshire estates.

When he travelled in the West, Stewart proceeded in style, carrying in his extravagant baggage (among other luxuries) a vast, crimson tent in which he held court like some conquering warlord. All in all, this veteran of Waterloo was hardly the buckskin-clad mountain man. He made the acquaintance of the American artist, Alfred Jacob Miller, who joined an expedition to record the fast-disappearing Indian civilisations.

Despite some nasty encounters with the native Americans, Sir William continued to praise the grandeur of the tribal tradition. On one occasion, left in charge of the encampment, Stewart was dismayed to see a party of renegade Crow Indians ride in. The expedition was outnumbered four to one, and Stewart's guides told him that the medicine man with the Indians was predicting a great victory—providing they did not strike the first blow. The only hope of survival for the white men was to ignore whatever provocation was put their way. Tomahawks were brandished in their faces, insults shouted, but the men remained unmoved, silent in the face of this abuse. Eventually the Indians moved off, having stolen almost everything of value in the camp, but leaving Stewart and company with their scalps.

On a return visit to Scotland, Sir William brought back two Indians and a half-breed servant called Antoine (who became a bit of a local celebrity, albeit with an overfondness for drink) and had boxes of plants, seeds and other souvenirs shipped to the old country. Seedling trees were planted in the grounds of Murthly Castle and a paddock filled with deer, bison and western game birds. This menagerie proved a great attraction for crowds of curious Scots who had only heard of American wildlife through letters from their immigrant relatives.

In 1843, on his last expedition to the Rocky Mountains, Sir William took with him a distinguished company of botanists including Dr Charles Mersch, F.G.L. Luders, A.G. Geyers and the Scot, Alexander Gordon. It was perhaps the best equipped such group ever to venture into the Great Divide, a pioneering expedition in every sense.

Porter and Davenport, in their biography of Stewart, say that around this time botanists the world over were deeply interested in the wealth of new plants that were thought to be awaiting discovery in the Far West:

> In taking these highly trained men with him Sir William performed a valuable service to the science of botany.

Highly trained they may have been, but Gordon for one was a constant headache for the expedition leader. As they left Fort Laramie and moved along the Platte River in what is now the heart of Wyoming, Gordon became more and more entranced by the wealth of flora they found around them, many plants (as expected) completely new to science. Porter and Davenport tell us:

> Discarding both caution and common sense in his frenzied botanizing, Gordon abandoned his horse and walked all the rest of the way, scarcely lifting his eyes from the ground, fearful that he might miss something.

The Scot wandered miles from the wagon-train, unheeding of warnings issued by Stewart. Only 'by the greatest good luck' did he escape being killed or captured by a wandering band of Indians.

### SAVIOUR OF THE BUFFALO

The last major buffalo hunt on the American plains is said to have taken place on the Grand River (SD) in 1881. By the turn of the century practically all the bison in existence were a few head on the Goodnight Ranch in Texas; a similar number on the 101 Ranch in Oklahoma; a small transplanted herd in Massachusetts which never thrived, a herd in Montana, and a herd owned by Pete Dupree, who had taken part in that last great hunting expedition. Millions of these creatures had once roamed the plains, hunted by the Indian. However, it was the greed of the white man, with his long rifle, which pushed the magnificent creatures almost to the edge of extinction.

When Morayshire-born rancher and adventurer, James 'Scotty' Philip, who came originally to the Victoria colony in Kansas in 1874, learned of

Morayshire-born James 'Scotty' Philip as portrayed on the lid of a tobacco tin. An adventurer and rancher, he helped save the North American buffalo from extinction. (South Dakota State Historical Society)

Dupree's death he bought his herd, determined that the buffalo should be preserved.

The first problem was the roving character of the animal. No one had told them about fences, yet for their own welfare they had to be confined. Extra-strong barbed wire and sturdy posts were used to fence in a large pasture at Scotty's ranch, near Pierre (SD). Cattle round-ups often brought in a few stray head of buffalo, and they were added to the herd in the fenced pasture, quickly bringing the total in the first years of this century up to eighty three. All mixed bloods, or cattalo as they had been styled, were sold and only the pure-blooded animals were retained. From these came a large herd which at one time numbered as many as 900 beasts.

In 1906, the National Congress passed an act allowing an area of 3,500 acres on the west bank of the Missouri River to be withdrawn from public access and rented exclusively to Scotty for pasturing native buffalo. This park was to become one of the biggest tourist attractions in the West. Shrewd Scot that he was, James Philip was able to combine the noble aim of preserving the buffalo with earning a few bob through selling specimens to parks and museums, and offering buffalo flesh as a holiday season novelty meat.

The buffalo would never again roam the plains in the vast herds which are said to have stretched to the horizon; but thanks to the far-seeing Scot from Dallas in Moray, neither were they to go the way of the dinosaur.

## Chapter 7

# CLANNISH – WHIT US?

Leafing through the pages which outline the remarkable story of tenacious Scots settlers constructing new and purposeful lives for themselves in the colonies and the United States, you are from time to time confronted with a perplexing contradiction. On one hand, the Scots are widely congratulated by commentators on their gregarious and sociable approach to living in America, while on the other they are accused of being tight-knit and clannish. Something odd here surely? Just how well and how quickly did the Scots actually adjust to their adopted home? Examining the different waves of settlement, it becomes clear that the immigrants' approach to the job of peopling America depended very much on the circumstances of their arrival. Some, chased or banished from their homes, were cautious and uncertain; many eagerly seeking a fresh start were open and keen to adapt, while others were decidedly insular, probably much as they had been in Scotland.

Obviously, for the earliest immigrants the decision to cross the Atlantic was usually irrevocable—there was no turning back. In such stressful, unfamiliar and challenging circumstances, it's hardly surprising that most of these first arrivals should cling stubbornly to the old ways. In any case for many there was no choice, no opportunity to mingle except with kith and kin or the 'heathen Indian'.

But this cagey approach among Scots agricultural settlers seems to have persisted for almost the entire span of immigration. In the parish of Tranquillity (IA), peopled by many Scots families, notably from Ayrshire, the writer Janette Stevenson Murray noted as late as the 1880s that immigrant children intermarried with other Scots family groups and nearly all had settled on adjoining farms in the same agricultural community. She observed:

> Thus it was that the Tranquillity people were bound into a homogenous group by the three strong ties of race, religion and family. No wonder that outsiders spoke of these people as the clannish Scots of Tranquillity.

So it seems that native-born Scots agricultural immigrants did stand aloof. Only gradually, as the generations passed, did they become more American than Scots, retaining an interest—though perhaps in a misty-eyed sort of way—in their Scottish heritage but with the Stars and Stripes firmly engraved on their hearts.

Later industrial immigrants, often single men, seem to have been much more mobile, adaptable and outward-looking. They too enjoyed social evenings with the local Burns club or St Andrews Society but also mixed more enthusiastically with the Americans around them, probably unaffected by two of the limiting factors mentioned by Janette Murray—religion and family. They did, however, take every opportunity to boast of their Scottishness.

Young single Scots who left their homeland for the American frontier found themselves, as often as not, marrying a Scottish partner. William Guthrie was born in Perth in 1795, the son of wealthy parents. Soon after graduating from Edinburgh University he found, on the death of his father, that the law of primogeniture left his older brother in charge and young William out in the cold. Stung, according to his biography, by a 'sense of outraged justice', like so many other young Scots in similar circumstances, he turned his back on his homeland and sailed for America, coming to rest around 1825 in Switzerland County (IN), where he began farming.

Here he met an Ayrshire lass, Margaret Japp, born in 1812 on the Banks of the Doon, who had come to America with her foster-parents after being orphaned. William and Maggie married in 1828 and, moving to the wilderness area south of what is now the town of Logansport (IN), they began to carve a living out of the forest. In their new home by the shores of Rock Creek, William Guthrie spent the rest of his life—a life given over to 'subduing the forest' and raising a family of thirteen children.

In the state of Colorado, this clinging together of Scots immigrants was quite marked. A Caledonian Club was formed in 1880, and St Andrews Day and 'Bobby Burns' Day were celebrated enthusiastically. This is what the reporter from *The Denver Republican* had to say about the Caledonian Club Ball on 1 December 1882:

> If any people know how to enjoy themselves it's the Scotch. Of course, they are somewhat clannish but a people coming from a country so rich in historical reminiscences have a right to be.

The reporter added that the Scots seemed to hold to the customs of their country with the tenacity characteristic of their race. By the mid-twentieth century, however, a quite contradictory view is expressed in a study published by the Colorado Department of Education, which says that Scots, whether they came with money to invest in cattle ranching or as humble miners, had 'become totally Americanised' and made their mark as leaders in the state history and community life.

A SHIELD AND COMFORT

As the farming Scots settled into their new life in America, shielded by their traditional family ties, religion and pastimes, many also found it difficult to make that final, symbolic break with the old country. American citizenship, which was necessary to buy farmland, included an oath relinquishing allegiance to Queen and country. A member of the ill-starred Furness colony in Minnesota, talking about the process of repeating the oath, recalled feeling as if he was 'selling me queen and country for 80 acres of land'. His companion, also a Scot, agreed it had been a difficult decision—'I meant to be a guid American citizen but I must say that in the meantime the old love was stronger than the new.' From the records of the Furness colony we learn that, despite their apprehension, these men and their families stayed on in Minnesota.

Anger occasionally surfaced in connection with the naturalisation issue, and one old Scot flung his certificate on the clerk's desk shouting:

> Take this paper, I do not want it, for I am sick of the corruption and favouritism shown everywhere. I don't want to be a citizen in a land where there is no justice.

For these older folk the transition was difficult, and they enjoyed nothing better than getting together with their cronies 'fur a crack' about the good times in Scotland. Correspondingly, for the younger Scots not set in the ways of the old country there were opportunities galore. Whereas in Scotland circumstances of birth often determined status in life and social behaviour, America was without such strict divisions and the individual had the chance to become whatever they wished without regard to social norms, providing they carried a large slice of luck and were prepared to work until they dropped. A challenging, even frightening prospect.

Originally, Scots societies were established in America to help destitute immigrants from the old country stranded in eastern seaports. This move was prompted by anxieties among Scots merchants that the poverty-stricken arrivals would damage Scotland's good name. Boston (MA) was the location of the first of these—the Scots Charitable Society—founded in 1657 specifically to ease the plight of the Cromwellian prisoners. Over the next two centuries others sprang up along the Atlantic seaboard, at places like Philadelphia (PA), New York (NY), Charleston (SC), and Savannah (GA)—really wherever the need was felt. These charitable societies, which usually took the name of St Andrew, were the only permanent American-Scots organisations up until the mid-1800s.

At the first meeting of the St Andrews Society of Battle Creek (MI) on 21 October 1887 there were songs including 'The Emigrant's Farewell' and 'Think of your head in the Morning'. The President, Mr Duff, pointed out that Scots societies had been springing up all over the United States and it was the bound duty of members to recruit expatriate Scots wherever they were found. Dishes 'peculiar to the Scotch' (according to the local paper) followed, then there was dancing until 2 a.m.

The thought that such organisations might become discriminatory and prejudiced against other ethnic groups was laughed out of court by the Scots, one authority wryly commenting: 'Most of the Black people in our group have more Celtic blood than I do.'

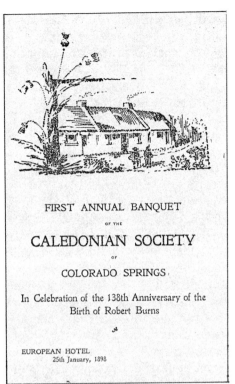

FIRST ANNUAL BANQUET

OF THE

CALEDONIAN SOCIETY

OF

COLORADO SPRINGS,

In Celebration of the 138th Anniversary of the
Birth of Robert Burns

EUROPEAN HOTEL
25th January, 1898

Clannish—whit, us? Segregated parking at the Illinois Saint Andrew Society
Highland Games. (Illinois Saint Andrew Society.) *right* America's first Burns
Club was founded in New York in 1847. Colorado Springs Caledonian Society
held their first Burns Night in 1898. (Colorado Springs Pioneers Museum)

Boston was also the location of the first Caledonian Club, founded in 1853,
and the first Burns Club has been traced to New York in 1847. But interest
in celebrating the Scottish heritage soon spread from the urban areas to the
far-flung corners of the great nation.

Among the Rocky Mountains, at the small town of Kalispell (MT), the
Caledonian Club met in 1892 to celebrate Burns's birthday and one of the
toasts was 'Our Adopted Country'. The response came from a local attorney,
Scott Sanford, who indicated many of the reasons why the Scots had become
the invisible race in America, assimilated to a greater degree than perhaps
any other group.

> Scotland sends out to America no anarchists, no men who plot to
> take the lives of others and the country which receives her sons and
> daughters receives a benefit thereby.

He then toasted the 'braw lads of Bonnie Scotland' (missing out the bonnie
lassies, apparently) and it took the toastmaster, Big Jock Wilson, several
minutes to hush the storm of applause.

Further south it didn't take the small contingent of Mormon Scots long to impress their culture on Utah. As early as 1852, according to Professor Fred Buchanan of the University of Utah, William C. Dunbar donned his kilt at the New Year's party and sang 'Alister McAllister', a Scots comedy song. The kilt was often seen at social events and Robert Young, a native of Kirkintilloch and for many years President of the Salt Lake Temple, dressed in his Highland garb and danced the sword-dance at Scottish gatherings.

It has also been said that the Scots were the most parochial of incomers. Certainly in the 1800s natives of Lewis and Skye, Caithness, Orkney and Shetland, Aberdeen, Dundee and Glasgow belonged to their own local societies in Chicago, New York and Boston. Border clubs in Boston and Philadelphia arranged the celebration of the Hawick Common Riding, and the Shetland Benevolent Association of Chicago staged their version of the Up-Helly Aa fire festival. Other events regularly marked included the births of Sir Walter Scott and James Hogg, the Ettrick shepherd-poet, and the Battle of Bannockburn.

In contrast to the strictly closed-shop Scottish societies, the Burns Clubs were open to all, and some (according to Berthoff) included very few Scots. The nature of the charitable societies also changed over the years, and the celebration of the great events on the Scottish calender became as much a reason for their existence as their humanitarian undertakings.

Last century in Tacoma (WA) there was a Cronies Club which was typical of the less formal Scottish gatherings. Its members included James Neil, a printer from Glasgow; David Healy, a tea importer from Ayrshire; Robert MacQuarrie, a lumber-mill owner; and Francis Cameron from Strathspey, an industrial broker.

Women are conspicuous by their absence from many of the earlier organisations, but by 1892 we can trace the first stirrings of the independent female among the ranks of the Scottish immigrants. James Alexander Milne, born at Skilmafilly Farm, near Drumwhindie, Aberdeenshire, in 1862, was a builder and joiner who worked mainly in Massachusetts before sailing back to Scotland in 1892 to marry his sweetheart, Jemima Shearer of Brankston, Kennethmont. They returned to America, and after working briefly at Poughkeepsie (NY) they put down roots at Pittsfield (MA). They had a successful marriage and eight children. The Milne family say that James was a taciturn man but Jemima gave him food for thought one evening as he sat reading his paper by the fire. Without lifting his head he told her to switch on the light but must have been stunned when the defiant reply came: 'We're in America noo, Jamie, switch it on yourself.'

Fraternal orders were set up, the first lodge of the Order of Scottish Clans being located at St Louis (MO) in 1878. The Clans were often totally unconnected with the names and tartans they adopted (unlike their twentieth-century counterparts, the Clan Societies and Family Groups) but nevertheless they proved very popular. At the outbreak of World War I there were 160 lodges affiliated and some 16,000 members. The old traditions still

Get-together of the Caledonian Society of Cavalier County (ND) c.1896. Assimilation note: gents in the front row are wearing trousers beneath their kilts. (State Historical Society of North Dakota)

held sway, however. And there was a scandal in Boston when a lady turned up for the annual Highland Games in a kilt. Orange Lodges and Masonic Lodges flourished in tandem with the strictly Scottish groups.

Highland Gatherings were a feature of the Scottish social calendar in the United States in the 1800s, as they are today with over a hundred Gatherings staged nationwide annually. Royal birthdays, funerals and anniversaries were all marked and New York City Scots joined a forty-eight hour party to celebrate Queen Victoria's marriage in 1840.

BLA' AWA DUNCAN!

In a thousand communities across the United States in the nineteenth century every opportunity was taken by the immigrants—homesick or otherwise—to enact the Scots pageant at big Caledonian feast-days. Witness the steadily growing Scots colony in the milltown of Fitchburg (MA) in the year 1890, as described by Doris Kirkpatrick in her book, *Around the World in Fitchburg*. As many as 1,500 people crowded into the city hall on 25 January to applaud their Scots neighbours as they danced and sang in celebration of Rabbie's birthday, certainly in Fitchburg the most popular holiday of the year for Scots. An expectant murmur stirred the crowd as the first lively strains of the bagpipe pierced the air. The scene unfolds:

> Kilts swirled and feet flashed in step as attentive Fitchburgers watched 70 Scots couples promenade in the Grand March led by champion Duncan McLean blowing his bagpipes. Gentlemen in knee-length tartans proudly escorted bonnie ladies in long flowing white dresses draped with plaid shoulder sashes.

By the early years of the twentieth century Burns celebrations were less widespread. In Wyoming, Mary Gilchrist—seeing the decline in Burns Day observances—decided in 1927 that a memorial to him in a public place in Cheyenne would 'exert a tendency to direct thought in the community to the wholesome consideration of his sweet, gentle philosophy'. She gave 20,000 dollars for the raising of a statue.

Today, according to Willis Cunning of Iowa, head of the Clan Cunning in the United States, there are families who still maintain Scots traditions like eating porridge despite seven or more generations in America since immigration; reasons for maintaining these traditions are often obscure. On the other hand, he also suggests another, very practical explanation as to why, in some cases, the Scots heritage did often seem to have faded into the background, even to have been forgotten:

> Scots pioneers strongly influenced important American institutions— education, frontier place naming, the churches, capital formation and industry but they were often too preoccupied, working flat-out to make a nation, to dwell on their heritage.

Hardworking, even stubborn the Scots may have been in their determination to carve a new life for themselves; but the occasional accusation that they were dour is less easy to sustain. One history of Massachusetts suggests that the Scots reminded their new-found American compatriots that laughter and joy of life was no crime; and it is certain that the Scots' and Ulster-Scots' love of poetry and music brightened the air of many grey, industrial towns in the East, bunkhouses in the West and the mining camps of Colorado and California.

TRUE LOVE WAYS

The names of the McDonald and Johnson families are forever linked romantically in the annals of the state of Georgia through a story which reaches back to the great exodus from the Western Isles of Scotland in the second half of the eighteenth century. From Skye in 1776, a boatload of immigrants sailed for Wilmington (NC) and into the tumult of the Revolutionary War. Two children—Donald McDonald, aged six, and four-year-old Catherine Johnson belonged to families among these adventurers, and their relationship was to span almost a century.

According to tradition handed down in the families, the children laughed their way through the hardships of the long voyage and shared with their parents the joy of eventually landing in the 'beautiful, heaven-blessed' country of which they had dreamed. Soon, however, they were experiencing the privations of the pioneer's life, particularly at this time when the young nation was struggling to secure its freedom. While other settler families went their own way from Wilmington, the McDonalds and the Johnsons seem to have stuck by each other and are found moving through the Carolinas before crossing the Savannah River to make a home in Elbert County (GA).

Over the years, childhood companionship changed to love for Donald and Catherine as they grew together in the little company. They married and were eventually to have five children. Donald, however, was determined to find the best possible location for permanent settlement, and went on horseback to South Georgia, taking a pine tree seedling in his saddlebag which he planted at the chosen site. Then, as a family group, they came south to the spot in Banks County, four miles south of Homer, on the Grove River. Although their house has long since gone, oral tradition tells of their log cabin with a rock chimney at one end and the date 1828 chiselled in the masonry. The kitchen, which stood a few feet from the 'big' house, was built of logs in the round, with a rock chimney and a fireplace big enough to cook for the extended family who might gather there.

Donald's obituary summarises his story: 'Departed this life (March 28, 1863), Donald McDonald, born and raised in Scotland, aged 93 years and 9 months. He had been for over 60 years an exemplary member of the Presbyterian Church, a kind and indulgent father and affectionate husband.' He was buried in the little tree-shaded cemetery near his home. The neat gravestones of Donald and Catherine, are still carefully tended by the people of Banks County and the occasional visiting descendant.

THE SOUGH O' HAME

Nostalgia for the old country was easily touched off. In 1904, when Scot John Hogben visited Pittsburgh (PA), he met a group of his former countrymen and was touched to see eyes glitter over songs that had 'the sough o' hame', and to find that after half a century Scotland was still the land of dreams, even if the steel corner of Pennsylvania was the land of dollars. These emotions could occasionally provoke quite aggressive pro-Scottish, almost jingoistic, outbursts. One traveller recalled meeting in an out-of-the-way Nevada town a Scot who regarded America as another Scotland, and, listing the Scots who had helped shape the United States, he thumped the table with his fist declaring triumphantly that America would have been a 'poor show' without the Scots. Little wonder then that the Yankee impression of the emotions felt by the immigrant Scots for their homeland could sometimes be overstated. A biographical record from 1895 of the Scots in Bureau, Marshall and Putnam Counties in Illinois waxes eloquent:

> Far from the land of his birth the true Scotchman never forgets and
> often sighs for his blue-clad hills, beautiful lakes and heavy forests . . .
> while he may discard the Highland garb for the more modern garment
> his heart will thrill at the sound of the bagpipe . . . however staid he
> may be he will dance with you the Highland Fling.

Following the trauma of immigration, once settled in their backwoods home
many Scots chose to stay put, never venturing far from their own fireside.
'Uncle Tom' Pennie, whose parents hailed from Kinross, lived a solitary life
in central Minnesota for more than half a century. An intriguing article in
*The Minneapolis Journal* of 1912 tells of Tom's first visit to the big city:

> Bachelor, hunter, chicken raiser and lover of dumb animals he has lived,
> as lived the pioneers in the new country.

Three features of life bothered him in Minneapolis—the speed of the cars,
the fact that his feet hurt on the hard pavements, and the refusal of
the shops to accept the metal tokens he used to buy goods at his local
dry-goods store.

It must be remembered that in relation to other ethnic groups, such as
the English and Germans, the Scots were few in number and thinly spread
across the vast continent. Therefore, when Scot met fellow Scot, particularly
in the depths of the wilderness, it was a time for rejoicing and the pooling
of emotions and memories.

William Drummond Stewart, the Scots aristocrat from Murthly in Perthshire who spent much of the 1830s with fur-trading expeditions in the
Rockies, met one of the legends of the Far West, Dr John McLoughlin,
head factor of the Hudson's Bay Company and 'king' of a huge tract of
land in Oregon. Arriving with his party at Fort Vancouver on the Columbia
River in present-day Washington state, Stewart was amazed to be greeted
by the sound of bagpipes. Outside the wooden stockade which fringed
the settlement stood the piper in full Highland dress of the Royal Stewart
tartan and McLoughlin, with his distinctive shock of white hair, led the
reception committee. At the gates of the stockade stood two sentries dressed
in Scots uniform, and as Porter and Davenport suggest in their biography
of Stewart:

> As he stepped inside Dr. McLoughlin's home Stewart might also have
> imagined himself in a Scottish castle. Thick rugs covered the floor, oil
> paintings and engravings of hunting scenes in the Highlands hung on
> the walls.

Although John McLoughlin had been born in Canada, he was of a Scots
line and his affection for Scotland was unbounded. The fact that his
hero was Napoleon and that Stewart had fought at Waterloo as a young
officer cemented their relationship. Many Scots adventurers in the Pacific
Northwest were gratefully to share in the good doctor's hospitality.

The town of Biddeford in Maine has many connections with the old country. In the 1700s as many as thirty Ulster-Scots families arrived bringing, according to the local author Roy Fairfield, the white potato and the Presbyterian faith.

During the Civil War, and again in the 1880s, groups of Glasgow girls were encouraged to come to the mills of Biddeford because of their fine work on ginghams. Most of the girls stayed in lodging houses and attended the Congregational church, which sponsored Scotch suppers and entertainments. In 1892 the immigrants formed themselves into the Order of the Scottish Thistle for 'mutual benefit and social intercourse', meeting every Tuesday and opening their doors to their American friends on Saturday nights. Although the girls worked long and hard at the spindles, they are said always to have found time for parlour games or folk-dancing and relished special delights such as a visit to town from Barnum and Bailey's Circus in 1882.

The waterfront area of town was, as always, a district of crime and deliquency and of all the places frowned on by the Biddeford upper classes, 'Scotland' took first place. According to town histories, a Scots

PORTLAND CALEDONIAN CLUB. 1896.

This unusual 'team' photo of the Caledonian Club of Portland (OR) c.1896 comprises individual portraits stuck on to a scenic backdrop. (Oregon Historical Society)

immigrant erected five houses in Bacon Court in the 1840s and this cluster of homes, with a water pump in the middle, was designed to recreate the atmosphere of country life in Scotland. The builder felt the representation accurate enough to name the hamlet after his homeland. Rents for these two-family wooden dwellings in the Saco district of town were always low, and as a result it attracted some of the community's weirdest characters. Roy Fairfield explains that when police were not checking out 'red-light' reports, they were breaking up a fight in one of the apartments.

'Scotland's' most notorious lady was 'Red-Eyed Ellen', possibly also a Scots exile. Young lads enjoyed tapping on her window and Ellen, thinking she had a customer, would appear seductively at the front door to a chorus of wolf-whistles. One commentator wrote of the area's almost mystical resilience:

> This hamlet has withstood all attempts at betterment and seems likely to weather many more storms. It seems to be immune from all the ills that have beset other localities . . .

Most of the houses in 'Scotland' were simply 'bed-bug incubators', he suggested, and were so foul that nothing good had lived in them for years. One wit thought the town could make some cash out of this squalor by charging a ten-cent admission fee to a tall building overlooking the district, where folk would get a grandstand view of 'Scotland' and all its seedy goings-on.

For the straggling procession of Scots families, arrival in the prairie lands of the Midwest was often the culmination of years of struggle, as important an event as the memorable day when, bewildered and more than a little scared, they, their parents or their grandparents, first set foot in America. One writer described the scene as a Scots family from Connecticut arrived late one November afternoon at Wolf Creek, Tama County (IA). Through snowflakes and gathering gloom:

> Heading the caravan and driving two yoke of oxen was the eldest son, in like occupation followed another, then came the father with the younger son, each driving a team of horses; mixed in with various loads were the mother, younger children and the household effects. It was like the arrival of a Scotch clan.

Robert Young wrote back to Ayrshire from the same area, describing conditions on the frontier. In a letter dated 1860 he explained that people were living in hastily-erected houses, and though he looked forward to his family joining him he cautioned that, in his view at least, not as much could be grown as in Scotland—that year (which was above average) wheat was running at fifteen to thirty bushels an acre and Indian corn, forty bushels. The following year he was trying to reassure them about the Civil War:

> I'm glad to hear you have decided to come out on the prairies. You need not be afraid of the Secession movement . . . The Western people treat the matter pretty coolly. The thing will blow over in a little while. The

people here hate slavery as they do in Britain. It is evident that they can't get along in the same union, the fire eaters of the South and the people of the North.

Returning to more practical matters, Robert informed his relatives that he had secured an old log-house for them, it's 'dismal appearance' no great disadvantage because in summer you could live in any kind of house. The railroad had reached to within eighteen miles of the settlement and he reminded them that in the census of 1850 only two white men were recorded in Tama County. Now there was a county town (Toledo) with two newspapers.

> This is a fine country but there is a good deal of hard work for immigrants until they get things fixed; then they can live like kings.

Even a century earlier, this slow yet steady progress west of the Scots tribes can be tracked. It was during a punitive expedition in 1779 against the Seneca Indians—who had been assisting the British during the Revolutionary War—that the potential for settlement in western New York was first realised. Amongst the many pioneers who headed upstate from the Atlantic coast towards the Great Lakes were parties of Scots, many of the families finding a home at Scottsville, a community south of the Lake Ontario port of Rochester (NY).

First person on record as owning land in this district was a Scot, Ebenezer Allan, who built his log-cabin on the north bank of Oatka Creek in 1786, having obtained title to the land from the Senecas. From New Hampshire came Isaac Scott, after whom the town is named—the year, 1790. According to local histories, the house he built on the south side of Main Street was kept as a 'place of entertainment' by Scott, and afterwards by his son, Jacob. Isaac and his wife are buried in the local cemetery.

The bulk of the 'Scotch settlers' (as they became known) began to arrive

Scots of all ages turned out for the annual gathering of Clan Stewart of Duluth (MN), held at Fond Du Lac on Lake Superior in the 1920s. (Minnesota Historical Society)

from 1799, and the advance party included the McNaughton, McLaren, Campbell and McVean families. In common with so many of the Scots who were members of the Kirk, this group had been issued with testimonials before they left Scotland. Perthshire was the home ground of John McNaughton, and his certificate read:

> This do certify that the bearer, John M'Naughton and his spouse Margaret M'Dermid, are natives of this parish of Killin and lived therein mostly from their infancy; and always behaved in their single and married state virtuously, honestly and unoffensively; free from all public scandal known to us.

The certificate is signed by Hugh M'Dougal (minister), James M'Nabb (elder) and James McGibbon (parish clerk). There is also a trio of interesting witnesses—Charles Campbell (Esq. of Lock Dorcht), Francis M'Nabb (Chief of M'Nabbs) and John Robson (baron, bailie to the Earl of Breadalbane). Despite this splendid reference, Mrs McNaughton was to remark that ten years passed on the frontier before she had the opportunity to attend a religious service.

DINNA BE FEART, THE LORD IS WI' YE

Alexander Ferguson was born in Stirling in 1833 and was left an orphan at the age of eight. Almost immediately he was apprenticed as a bobbin boy in a local mill, and over the next few years was thoroughly schooled in the woollen industry. In 1855, he went into partnership and opened a mill in Galashiels but within three years had moved to a new mill and a new life in Philadelphia (PA).

When the Civil War stopped shipments of wool to the United States, he returned to the Borders, to Hawick, where he worked in the Laidlaw Mills and met and married Bessie Linton. Already recognised as an expert in the industry, and with a growing demand for woollen cloth in America, he was hired by a group of mill-owners to set up plants in the state of Maine. On the completion of each mill he returned to Hawick, to his growing family which now consisted of three sons and a daughter. Finally, persuaded by his friend and fellow Scot, John Cowan, owner of a mill named after him at Lewiston (ME), the Fergusons decided to immigrate.

Alexander was already established in the States, so when his family made the Atlantic crossing they were not required to enter through Ellis Island, the immigration station in New York harbour which was the landfall for many hundreds of thousands of newcomers. The Fergusons docked at the Battery on Manhattan.

John, the eldest son, recalled his disappointment with the first sight of America from the ship's deck. The streets, far from being paved with gold, were dirt-tracks; broken-down fences and shacks covered the land now occupied by Wall Street. However, his greatest disappointment came when he saw his father standing on the quay. He burst out crying and shouted, in a broad Hawick accent: 'Faither, ye are wearing the same suit ye had on at hame!' John had imagined that his father should be sporting a swallow-tail coat and top-hat—marks of a successful businessman.

After settling in their new home at Lewiston, the children amused their Yankee neighbours with their Scottish accent. Despite the fact that there were hundreds of Scots in the neighbourhood, the brogue still drew attention. One of the Ferguson boys, Jim, told of a school-teacher who would regularly ask where Jim's father was just to hear the lilting reply: 'Ma faither's gane ti the mull.' Another son, Robert, remembered reciting bible verses in Sunday School. His classmates loved young Bob's rendering of a particular verse: 'Dinna be feart, the Lord is wi' ye.' Oddly, when the family returned to visit Hawick their old friends were just as amused to hear them talk in their newly-acquired Yankee accents.

Among the Mormons in Utah, the immigrant Scots were mainly Low-landers speaking what was (for non-Scots) a confusing mixture of English and Lallans. James Henderson complained that he had difficulty making Americans understand his Glasgow brogue, sprinkled as it was with rolling 'r's, glottal stops and broad 'a's. It could present serious problems. The theatre critic of *The Daily Union Vedette* in 1863 bemoaned David McKenzie's accent as the fisherman in the play, *Warlock in the Glen*.

> We have no doubt that his accent was Scotch all over and was rendered in the most natural way. Yet if he had given us a little more English idiom ... we think the audience would have been better able to appreciate and understand the good things, which we have no doubt old Andrews said.

It was a source of some pride that Scots could lapse into their 'plain, good Scotch' with ease, but the attempts of some folk to convince others they were Yankee through and through by way of their accent angered a contributor to *The Scottish-American Journal* in 1866. The behaviour of a section of his fellow Scots clearly infuriated him. Apparently they

> ... nibbled their words, to try to smooth down the rough Doric of their northern tongue and to lisp or sniffle out the natural speech with which the Creator had endowed them. They would just as soon have people believe that they had been born this side of the Atlantic and that their grandfather had signed the Declaration of Independence as that they came direct from Drumclog with the parish minister's certificate that their luckie-daddy was ruling elder for 40 years.

By contrast, a few years later it was noticed that ladies in particular were contemptuous of the American twang, and spoke as if they had 'newly come from Paisley or Hawick, the Carse of Gowrie, or the windings of the silvery Forth'.

## TARGET BLUE EARTH

Having already followed the progress of the Scots into the Midwest in a general way, it's useful to examine the manner in which particular districts in this vast region were peopled. Every area had its own distinctive pattern of settlement, but the mid-nineteenth-century movement west is perhaps typified by Scots arrivals in Minnesota.

New York, in 1854, saw the first attempt to attract the Scots in numbers with a newspaper advert offering opportunities to people who wanted to own farms in the West. Scores of Scots families signed up, and with a promise of 160 acres each and access to a township, they left for Blue Earth County in southern Minnesota. On arrival, however, they found a shortage of claims, so lots were drawn and many left disillusioned. Despite this early disappointment, a steady stream of Scots began to arrive. The first settlers had called themselves the Mapleton colony and soon two stores were up and running, both under the control of Scots.

In this district, as elsewhere, the Scots quickly organised themselves—a Burns Club was founded in Sterling township in 1866 for 'social, moral, intellectual and physical improvement', and for benevolent purposes. For its first thirty years, meetings were held in members' houses before they moved to the grand setting of the Mapleton Opera House.

Some of the Mapleton colony who had been unable to obtain claims moved into neighbouring Fariboult County, and further west the Scots populations of Lyon and Nobles Counties expanded, the development of the railroad in the 1870s providing, as elsewhere, a tremendous boost to the ease of access for immigrants. Ulster Scots communities flourished in Hennepin and Todd Counties. Like so many ethnic groups, the Scots and Ulster Scots normally made the journey west in stages, moving from the east-coast states and stopping over for months or even years in Illinois and Ohio.

The town in Minnesota where the Scots had perhaps their greatest impact was Duluth, an important seaport on Lake Superior. They founded banks, became wholesalers of grocery and fishing produce, organisers of the Chamber of Commerce and the Duluth Board of Trade and promoters of the Duluth Life Saving Station (forerunner of the coastguard). Scots designed and built railroads, grain elevators, office blocks, churches and houses; they developed iron-ore mines and shipping on the Great Lakes, and one of these men, Alexander McDougall, invented the famous whale-back ore carrier.

William McEwen, the son of an immigrant Scot, was editor of *The Labor World*, based in Duluth, and was active in the labour movement for forty years. The Scots were staunch supporters of the two Presbyterian churches in town during the second half of the nineteenth century.

Scottish associations in urban Minnesota flourished. The St Andrews Society of St Paul appeared in 1859 when a constitution was drafted providing (as we've seen elsewhere) for needy Scots immigrants and their children, and continued on and off ever since. Other organisations in St Paul included the Caledonian Club, the Order of Scottish Clans and country dance groups. Duluth quickly followed the Twin Cities (Minneapolis and St Paul) in setting up a branch of the St Andrews Society and Caledonian

Club. The idea of forming a permanent group in Duluth led to the receipt of a charter for Clan Stewart 50 of the Order of Scottish Clans.

One of the annual highlights for this group was its summer picnic to Fond du Lac, when upwards of 1,000 people would march behind a dozen pipers who led them to a boat which ferried them along Lake Superior to the picnic site. There followed a day of Highland Games, dancing and bagpipe-playing.

A Lewis Society was founded in Duluth in 1911 by several natives of the Isle of Lewis. Gaelic speakers, they made a conscious effort to maintain the traditions of the Outer Hebrides. Unfortunately, by 1955 this group had shut up shop.

Not every venture in Minnesota proved a success for the Scots. When a joint party of English and Scots settlers came to Furness, in Wadena County, the two factions found it impossible to agree on how to divide the land. The Scots pulled out and began homesteading further west in Otter Tail County. However, it wasn't only the Scots who found the English difficult to get along with.

When American Scot, Robert Coulter, struck out for a new life in the wilds of western Minnesota, which was then a trackless wilderness, he arrived at the town of Winona in 1866 with only a two-dollar bill in his pocket—and that proved to be counterfeit.

At the beginning of this century, Bob told a newspaper reporter of his epic and arduous journey to his new home in Polk County, which borders on the Red River. He worked in the timber trade for two or three years before deciding to set out with two Scots families—the Flemings and the McVettys—in search of a hospitable section of wilderness suitable for settlement. Mile after mile they travelled north along the line of the Red River without coming across any sign of habitation until they found a 'sort of tavern' in what is now Grand Forks County (ND).

The partners in this wayside inn (described by Bob Coulter as more of a dugout) were William Budge, a well-known businessman and politician, and George Winship, the editor of *The Grand Forks Herald*. Spartan though the surroundings were, the Scots travellers welcomed the chance to rest up, feed their horses and take refreshment.

It was here that Budge put a self-important Englishman in his place with a put down that lives on in the folklore of the Red River Valley, particularly among the Scots. The English 'guest' was taking dinner at the shanty and Bill Budge was officiating as cook. The menu consisted of huge pancakes fried in a long-handled skillet. Looking with disgust at the 'not over-clean mess' which was being concocted, the English traveller asked if that was all they were to get to eat. 'Why, no,' said Budge, who then took the man by the arm and, leading him to the haystack at the front door, suggested: 'Just you help yourself!'

When Bob Coulter finally arrived at his chosen land, his earthly possessions in the livestock line were an ox team and a cow. During his first year as one of the pioneer settlers of Polk County, he made most of his money with guns and traps. However, careful husbandry of 300 acres saw him end his days comfortably in the vicinity of the Red River Valley.

MAKING YOUR OWN LUCK

Persistence, initiative and a lot of luck were required to make a go of the new life in America. One of the most successful trading operations in the rapidly developing West was created by Ardrossan-born Fred Drummond, who immigrated to America in 1884 as a young man. Fred's story has come to symbolise, at least for the folk in Oklahoma, the 'optimistic, implusive era' in the state's history, when risk-taking was a way of life.

Fred arrived in America with dreams of becoming a ranch king but had to bounce back when he went into an abortive Texas cattle venture with his brother, George. It collapsed, like so many others, for lack of capital and know-how. After working as a clerk in St Louis (MO), he moved to the Osage Indian reservation in Oklahoma, where he was a licensed government trader and operated a sort of frontier supermarket selling everything from groceries to coffins. After marrying, he set up his own trading business in Hominy and expanded into banking, real estate and ranching. The splendid three-storey Drummond home in Hominy has been lovingly restored during the past ten years.

One writer has described the house as a symbol of the Scotsman's 'prosperity and a dream achieved'—a sure sign that, despite the hardships, a good life was to be had on the frontier. It's said that when Fred died in August 1913 the line of buggies and wagons reached for a mile from the cemetery and more Indians attended than had ever been seen before in that district at the funeral of a white man.

Native cunning, never lacking among the Scots, became finely honed in the new American environment. Tradition in South Carolina has it that, around the time of the outbreak of the Revolutionary War, an old man, Ian McRae, left Skye for America with his nine sons. From this impressive outfit large numbers of people in both North and South Carolina claim descent. In the midst of the war, a band of loyalists crept up on the home of one of the sons (who had joined the patriots' side), leaving the family no time to flee or hide their valuables. The family history relates that

> One of the women placed the silver spoons in her dress bosom and conscious that she was observed seized a hank of thread and stuffed that in after the spoons.

When one of the intruders asked what she had hidden she drew out the yarn and hurled it in his face, saying: 'I think you might allow a poor woman to keep her own thread.' Stunned, the loyalist threw it back, telling her to keep it and enquiring no further about the contents of her cleavage. The spoons have become treasured family heirlooms, their legend passed down through the generations with the silver ware.

Fred Drummond from Ardrossan. He is bearded and standing between two Indians at the main door outside his trading post in Hominy (OK) c.1905. (Oklahoma Historical Society)

With Scots families eventually dispersing across the wide nation, chances of a get-together were limited to occasions such as marriages, christenings and, inevitably, funerals. When his doctor realised that Malcolm McGregor, a pioneer prospector of the great silver camp at Georgetown (NM), was on his last legs in 1908, the call went out to his family. A telegram went to his daughter, Eva, in Honolulu, where she was a teacher; to his daughters, Elsa and Ena in Nova Scotia, and his brothers, Alexander in California, and Archie, who was only a few hours away. Archie was first at his bedside. Alex and his wife boarded a train in San Francisco and covered the last fifty miles by wagon across a searingly hot desert in under six hours, arriving in time to say their farewells to Malcolm. The Canadian daughters arrived the next day.

THE IRISH STEW MURDER

As immigrants from all over the world flooded into the United States from the mid-1800s onward, it was inevitable that such a gathering of ethnic groups would give rise to conflict.

In the tough mining camps of Nevada, for example, misunderstanding in language, differences in social habits and economic competition led to discrimination . . . and violence. The Chinese, who carried out menial tasks such as digging irrigation ditches and canals and laying rails, were often under attack when they drifted around seeking more lucrative work. Everywhere conflict was found, as French Canadians tried to expel the Chinese from the lumber trade and the Irish attacked them when they tried to enter the mines; Scots and Basques refused to herd sheep with the Orientals. Resentment and fear of Southern Europeans spilled over into bloodshed in 1907 when three Greeks were killed. The Irish fought the Cornish while the Celtic countries got together to fight the English.

Paradoxically, amid all this racial strife our most dramatic story from Nevada in the 1870s concerns that long-established Scottish tradition of fighting among ourselves. John McCallum and his friend and fellow Scot, John Murphy, were to die because they couldn't agree on how to make an Irish stew.

In May 1874 the two men were employed by a fluming company near Lake Tahoe. Although both were born in Scotland, Murphy, not surprisingly, had Irish parents and insisted that McCallum learn to make the stew properly. According to the Nevada Historical Society, McCallum belittled the diet of the Emerald Isle and, while drunk, seriously injured his friend in a fight. Murphy walked fourteen miles to Carson City to see a doctor and returned to the mountains a few days later to even the score. For nearly a week Murphy tracked McCallum through much of western Nevada and finally overtook him again in Carson City, chasing his countryman down alleyways before gunning him down in front of the post office. Murphy's trial took several months, his execution being postponed three times, but he was finally strung up at high noon on 29 December 1874.

Murphy's life story must have been typical of the wandering Scots prospector in those unruly days. He did not know where he was born but ran away to sea, arriving in California in 1849 at the height of the Gold Rush, working first as a miner, then as a boxing-booth fighter, finally enlisting in the Army. He deserted in 1860 and made his way to the Comstock, where, resuming his career as a pugilist, he became widely known in Virginia City and Aurora. Both Murphy and his manager were involved in shooting affrays with Cornishmen and Manxmen.

During the late 1860s he became a cook but devoted most of his time to 'anti-Christian spiritualism'. Although completely illiterate, he could draw in the crowds when he communed with the spirits. From the gallows he was to deliver a final hour and a half long sermon. This is the Historical Society's assessment of Murphy: 'John Murphy was a braggart, a drunk, a pugilist, a swordsman, a preacher, and a classic example of the undisciplined and emotionally disturbed immigrant who, with an attractive vulgarity and an openness to pain, created a grave and disturbing element on the Nevada frontier.' What a testimonial!

Drink was a major element in this tragic story and is encountered more than occasionally in the sagas of the Scots settlers. On the famous McGregor sheep farms in Washington in the Pacific Northwest, Jock Macrae had left his law office job in Scotland to pan for gold and tend livestock before settling down as the McGregor's sheep foreman, holding the post for forty-seven years.

*The Shepherd's Journal*, a Chicago newspaper credited him with the technique of curing lupin-poisoned sheep by giving them a dram. As agricultural experts puzzled over this phenomenon, sheep-owners had visions of their shepherds demanding rations of medicinal whisky. Anticipating this, the McGregors laced their whisky with ammonia—the shepherds hated it but the sheep are said to have lapped it up.

Jock Macrae was not so self-sacrificing as to give all his whisky away to the woolly ones. He enjoyed a drink himself and in 1915, in trying to explain reports that he had been drunk for a week, wrote to his employer:

> I admit I got full in Spokane . . . Well you know me well enough that when things beat me I fly to drink . . . John, don't think for one moment that I'll neglect my business . . . I don't say I'm an angel. If I was I wouldn't be here; I'd be up above along with the rest of 'em. You can depend on the sheep being cared for.

Chapter 8

# MUSKET, MAINSAIL AND
# MAGIC BUNNET

NO BETTER EXAMPLE EXISTS of the Scottish military tradition exported to America (via Ulster) than the legendary 'Fighting McCooks' of Ohio. Just two families, descended from immigrant Ulster Scot, George McCook, produced a fighting progeny that will probably never be equalled under any flag, anywhere in the world. Old George's two sons, Major Daniel and Dr John McCook, had nine sons and five sons respectively, and around the years of the Civil War (1861–65) all of them served either in the Union army or navy, all but one being a commanding officer. Among their military colleagues they were distinguished as coming from 'the Tribe of Dan' or 'the Tribe of John'.

By the time the first American colonies had established strong roots in the late 1600s, warfare had become almost second nature to the Scots, fixed in the national psyche as a result of centuries of strife with 'the Auld Enemy' to the south and bloodthirsty internal family, clan or religious struggles. In addition, for those Scots undergoing the Ulster experience, conflict was becoming a way of life.

Descendants of Bruce's pikemen from Bannockburn or Wallace's wild raiders were on the quays to join the armada which sailed for the sunset from the mid-1600s onwards, and they went to the New World with a reputation as fierce and uncompromising warriors. Sir David Stewart of Garth, one of Wellington's generals and, interestingly, an opponent of immigration, knew more about the Scots fighting man than anyone of his generation and believed that his soldiers made such formidable adversaries because they considered courage as the most honourable virtue, cowardice the most disgraceful failing.

In the earliest days of settlement there was little trouble from the native Americans along the frontier who saw the newcomers as a novelty rather than a threat. However, as more and more white men flooded into the colonies and pressure for land pushed the Indians further and further back from their traditional hunting grounds, conflict became inevitable and the combat skills of the Scots were soon in demand.

After a century of skirmishing and jockeying for position by the colonial powers in the backwoods of North America, the 1750s brought to the

144

continent the first war that approached the conventional European model. The French and Indian, or the Seven Years War as it is also known, is said to have been precipitated by the military probings of Robert Dinwiddie, who was born in 1693 at Germiston on the outskirts of Glasgow from a family originating in south-west Scotland.

In the first half of the eighteenth century, Britain's colonies down the east coast of America felt constantly under threat from French expansion further west. Efforts to create a 'New France' by linking the French-Canadian territories in the North with Louisiana down a broad corridor traced by the Ohio and Missouri rivers were a source of constant anxiety to the British government.

Dinwiddie, a famed colonial administrator who learned the merchant's trade, became surveyor-general for Virginia and then assumed the mantle of lieutenant-governor. He saw the vast Ohio region as vital to the security and future development of British North America. Determined that the French would never succeed in their link-up, he began to make the British presence felt. Young George Washington was sent into the territory to stymie the ambitious French, and the construction was undertaken of a fort on the site of present-day Pittsburgh (PA). Efforts to establish a

'The Fighting McCooks' of Ohio. This Ulster-Scots family produced a military progeny probably unequalled anywhere in the world. (Ohio Historical Society)

strong British presence were plagued with difficulties, but the French and Indian War was to see the final downfall of plans to create the 'New France'.

### TERRIBLE TICONDEROGA

Scottish interest in this war must centre on the disastrous assault on Fort Ticonderoga, one of the bloodiest episodes in British military history. Banffshire-born Lord James Abercrombie (1706–81) assumed command of all British forces in North America after a bullet from a French patrol killed Lord Howe. Abercrombie was in charge at Ticonderoga, and afterwards his medical officer noted in his diary that he

> . . . returns to Europe as little regretted as any man that ever left America. He had no resolution, no will of his own, was bullied into favours he bestowed, made few friends thereby, created some enemies and in short fell into universal contempt.

In July 1758, a British force set off for Lake George to attack French forts in the disputed border country. Among the British were 1,000 men of the Black Watch. It was decided to attack Ticonderoga first because it lay on a supply route, and although the French had created a barrier of felled trees and branches on the narrow neck of land leading to the peninsula, with a high wooden breastwork beyond, Abercrombie decided on an all-out frontal attack. During the battle French regulars were kept in reserve for most of the day, sharpshooters and Indians manning the stockades as wave after wave of British soldiers were mown down, caught in the tangled traps and picked off as they struggled to break free.

Eventually, the 42nd Black Watch were sent into the deadly pincers, where they drew their swords and hacked their way out of the traps, some even fighting their way into the French lines. In the face of such devastating fire-power this was an astonishing breakthrough, but Abercrombie had no reinforcements to consolidate this valiant action, so the 42nd fought their way back, dragging their wounded and under fire continuously in the brushwood maze. Twenty-four officers were killed and one estimate put the Scots dead and wounded at 600—roughly twice the total of 7th Cavalrymen killed at Custer's Little Big Horn 118 years later.

A chilling legend attaches itself to the conflict at Ticonderoga. One of the Black Watch officers was Duncan Campbell of Inverewe, a kinsman to the Duke of Argyll. As the British forces retreated from the slaughter, he received a slight arm wound, infection set in and the arm was amputated. He died nine days later.

This fulfilled a prophecy which Campbell had spoken of for years. Back in Scotland, after his cousin was knifed to death Campbell unwittingly gave sanctuary to his killer. The spectre of his slaughtered relative had appeared and said they would meet again at Ticonderoga. Years passed and, the name meaning nothing to him, Campbell grew convinced that the ghostly prediction had been simply the product of his troubled mind. It was only as the British forces prepared for the assault on Fort Carillon, now in Essex County (NY) that Campbell discovered to his horror that the Indian name for the marshy peninsula was Ticonderoga. On the eve of battle, Campbell told his commanding officer that his cousin's ghost had appeared again. He knew he was about to die.

An interesting sideline to the story is that this infamous battle, in all its gory detail, was seen by three independent witnesses in the sky above Inveraray Castle, Argyll, at the very hour of the bloody conflict thousands of miles away. Some Scottish societies in the United States and Canada still observe 8 July as Ticonderoga Day.

Militia units, who needed no convincing that attack was the best form of defence, were in existence very early in the frontier settlement. Outfits like the 'Rangers', for example, a group of tough and highly mobile Ulster Scots formed before the Revolutionary War to defend pioneers in the western reaches of Pennsylvania against Indian attack. Hard men were needed. Men like James Gibson, born in County Tyrone in 1740, and instantly recognised in the blockhouses and stockades along the wilderness frontier by his constant companion, a huge bloodhound that had been trained to track Indians. Gibson was a natural leader and was often at odds with the pacifist Quakers of Philadelphia over their softly-softly approach to Indian atrocities. Such men were to play a vital role for the Patriots with the outbreak of the Revolutionary War.

When the thirteen colonies finally decided to make their break from Britain in 1775, concluding that they could no longer bear taxation without representation, the Scottish contribution in the ranks of the revolutionary high command was nothing short of spectacular. Of George Washington's major-generals, Henry Knox (MA), William Alexander (NJ), Alexander MacDougall (NY) and Arthur St Clair (PA) were all Scots. Caledonian blood has also been identified in five of his twenty-two brigadier-generals—William Irvine (PA), Lachlan McIntosh (GA), John Paterson (MA), Charles Scott (VA) and John Stark (NH). Over twenty generals of the war are also known to have had Scottish origins.

St Clair (1736–1818) was born in Thurso, Caithness, studied at Edinburgh University and, after trying the medical profession, he left for the army. Coming to America in 1758, he served with General Wolfe at Quebec and after marrying in 1764 settled at Bedford (PA), where he used inherited money to buy tracts of land, making him the colony's largest landowner west of the Allegheny Mountains. He became an ardent Patriot, rising through the ranks to major-general after the Battle of Princeton in 1777. He is remembered for his reaction to the news of the Declaration of Independence: 'God save the free and independent States of America.'

Spending almost his entire fortune in raising volunteers and aiding Washington, St Clair was president of the Continental Congress in 1787, and from 1788 to 1802 was the first Governor of the Northwest Territory, although his opposition to the entrance of Ohio into the Union saw him replaced.

The parish of Kildalton in Islay was the native heath of Alexander MacDougall, who was born in 1732 and left Scotland as a child with his parents as members of Lachlan Campbell's group of colonists who established a settlement at Fort Edward (NY). When this ambitious venture failed the family moved to New York City, where Alexander's father secured a job as a milkman.

Young Alexander had a longing for the sea and became skipper of a privateer before settling in New York as a merchant. He was the author of pamphlets and broadsides that pushed public opinion towards separation from the old country, and he was a busy leader of 'The Sons of Liberty'. Unlike many of his Highland compatriots, he plumped squarely for independence, showing himself a formidable fighter and took part in the battles at White Plains and Germantown. His most important role was in the highlands of the Hudson Valley, control of which, Washington believed, would dictate the course of the war. His leader described him as a 'brave soldier and distinguished patriot', and a street in New York was named after him.

Major-General Alexander (1726–83) claimed to be the Earl of Stirling, and was one of Washington's most trusted aides. His family came from south-west Scotland, and as well as his military prowess (he took charge of the British surrender at Yorktown) he was an astronomer and mathematician. Henry Knox was born in Massachusetts in 1750, coming from Country Antrim stock, a descendant of the Ulster Scots we've already encountered founding Londonderry (NH) in 1718.

THE FIRST SHOT

There is also a strong and controversial Scottish involvement in the spark that lit the American Revolution, the skirmish at Lexington. John Pitcairn, a minister's son born at Dysart in Fife in 1722, has perhaps the briefest connection with America we'll encounter in these pages—a matter of a few months—but it is unquestionably among the most significant.

He was sent with the Royal Marines to Boston in the wake of the Tea Party, as war began to look inevitable. An uneasy peace persisted until 18 April 1775, when Major Pitcairn went with his troops to seize rebel stores at Concord. Earlier, he had attended a session with a fortune-teller and foolishly confided in her the plans for the campaign, which 'would make the Yankees pay for their Indian capers and tea-parties'. In turn, the woman predicted success for the British cause, sent him away happy and lost no time in letting the Sons of Liberty know what was afoot.

It was (therefore) a confident, perhaps over-confident, Pitcairn who pushed ahead of the main column to secure strategic bridges; he was also in command of the redcoats who came face to face with the Minute Men, a line of some seventy-five volunteers, in the historic encounter on

Postage stamp commemorating a key event in American history: the centenary of the siege of the Alamo, in which Scots played a significant role as the quest for Texan independence gained momentum. (United States Postal Service)

Lexington common. The official American version was that the British opened fire without warning, on Pitcairn's orders, but the Fifer always maintained that the American line let loose the first shots. After having eight men killed and ten wounded, the revolutionaries (for that is what they now were) fled.

In that little bunch of Patriots on the green were seven members of the Munroe clan, who had thrown in their lot with the new homeland. Ebenezer Munroe faced the volley of shot from the British lines, and as several of his comrades fell he sought shelter with the rest behind stone walls and in ditches. Though wounded in the elbow, Ebenezer stood his ground until he could return fire. To his cousin John, standing next in line, he hissed: 'I'll give them the guts o' my gun.' That exchange of shots was to echo round the world.

At Concord, the British found that the supplies had been spirited away and as Pitcairn and the other British officers tried to convince the townsfolk that they meant no harm, one of the citizen's gave the unanimous American response by landing a punch square on the Major's chin. This is ironic, since the histories record that Pitcairn was about the only British officer who had the trust and liking of the people of Boston and was from time to time called in to arbitrate in civil disputes. As far as we know, Pitcairn did not consult the spaewives again, which is just as well because his brief American adventure was almost at an end. Within a few weeks he had been killed at the Battle of Bunker Hill, leading an attack on a redoubt.

John Stark, born at the Ulster-Scots colony at Londonderry (NH), on hearing news of the skirmish at Lexington started out for Cambridge (MA) and hurriedly gathered 800 backwoodsmen. He marched them towards the sound of the guns at Bunker Hill above Boston, and it was there, facing the well-fed British troops, that he gave the still-remembered order—'Boys, aim at their waist bands.'

One of the most interesting of the brigadier-generals who served Washington was Lachlan McIntosh, born at Raits of Badenoch, Inverness-shire, in 1725. Immigrating to Georgia, he then secured a job as a clerk at Charleston (SC) in the late 1740s and reappears in Savannah (GA) in 1775 as the war alarms rang. Appointed as a colonel, his task was to forestall military activity based on the Great Lakes, and he built a fort named after himself on the Ohio River at present-day Beaver (PA). A bitter military rivalry saw him fight a duel with one of his comrades in 1777 and, although wounded, McIntosh managed to kill his adversary, being freed after trial. His career never recovered from this scandal and he was captured at Charleston in 1780.

KING'S MOUNTAIN—A SCOTS AFFAIR

Historians are unanimous that the Battle of King's Mountain on 7 October 1780 was a turning-point in the conflict. A rag-tag army of tough mountain men from the western reaches of the two Carolinas and Georgia defeated a Loyalist army on a mountain ridge in York County, South Carolina. The battle broke the momentum of the British advance, heartened the Patriots and gave them time to reorganise. It dismayed the Loyalists. One year and eleven days later, Cornwallis, supreme commander of the British forces, surrendered at Yorktown and the colonies had won their freedom.

The leaders of these two armies—Colonel William Campbell for the Patriots and Colonel Patrick Ferguson for the King's men—were both Scots and the armies, totalling 3,000 men, had sizeable Scottish contingents, perhaps as many as a third of those who took part in the battle.

Up until King's Mountain, Cornwallis had seemed invincible and it was left to the over-mountain men, who swarmed across the hills in their racoon hats and animal hides shouldering their antiquated muskets and flintlocks, to change the course of history. Aberdeenshire-born Colonel Ferguson, a brilliant young officer and aide to Cornwallis, had moved into the western districts of the Carolinas in search of supplies and to force the partisan groups deeper into the hills. An energetic and confident soldier, Ferguson was on a high and convinced that his success could finally secure victory for the Loyalist forces on all fronts. When he threatened to lay waste to the entire region, a general muster of mountain men was called by the

Americans at Sycamore Shoals (TN), and the fiery preacher, the Rev. Samuel Doak, took a service for the men and their families, urging them on to victory. Over 1,000 people set out on the long march.

Ferguson, it would appear, received news of this 'backwater army' but fatally underestimated the calibre of the opposition and, confident that he would be reinforced, chose King's Mountain to make his stand, declaring that 'God Almighty could not drive him from it.'

After the revolutionaries encircled the ridge, the smoke of battle soon filled the air as the mountain men charged, regrouped and charged again. Ferguson's command whistle could be heard from above mixing strangely with the Indian-style yelps of the revolutionaries. When all seemed lost, Ferguson and two fellow officers on horseback made a break for freedom but one of the American Scots, Robert Young, is given credit for shooting Ferguson from his saddle, the officer's foot catching in his stirrup. He was dragged around the ever-tightening circle of American fighters and the surrender was not long delayed.

Colonel Campbell, his arms eventually full, collected the swords of the surrendering British officers who refused to believe that this hatless, coatless man was the commanding officer of the victorious force. Ferguson was buried on the battlefield, now a national monument. American losses were said to be twenty-eight killed and sixty wounded. Out of a British force of 1,100, 150 were killed and as many wounded. Among the American dead we find such names as Blackburn, Laird, McCulloch, Paterson and Watson, all indicating their Scottish heritage.

A fascinating footnote to this battle is the story of how young Joseph Greer (whose father was born in Scotland) had fought in the battle and was despatched to carry news of the victory to congress assembled in Philadelphia (PA). Twenty years old and *seven* feet tall, Greer was armed with a musket and compass for the dangerous journey, and was selected because of his knowledge of the Indians and the fact that, despite his relative youth, he was an experienced backwoodsman who could plot his way through the forests and past Loyalist settlements. As he journeyed north, he had one or more horses shot from under him and much of the epic journey had to be covered on foot. He swam ice-covered streams and spent one night in a hollow log, hiding from a band of Indians who actually sat on the upturned tree as they discussed his whereabouts.

Arriving in Philadelphia, he was initially prevented from entering congress but the giant Scot forced his way in, strode down the aisle, and delivered his message to the astonished politicians. General George Washington observed: 'With soldiers like him, no wonder the frontiersmen won.' For his services, Joseph Greer was given a grant of land in what is now Lincoln County (TN), and the Greer Clan claims many of his descendants in the district.

Among the most famous segments of the Revolutionary Army was the 'Pennsylvania Line'—seven companies of this regiment were composed almost exclusively of Ulster Scots. Contemporary reports indicate that these fighters were excellent marksmen, frequently able to shoot far beyond the recognised range of the ordinary musket. Most of the men on the frontier had learned to use the rifle at an early age, and these skills with the long rifles had gained them much respect from the Indian tribes.

### THE UNSUNG HERO

Various towns and counties throughout the United States were named in honour of General Hugh Mercer (1725–77), a hero of the Revolution who was born in Aberdeen but is virtually unknown in Scotland and, more suprisingly, has been almost forgotten by the Americans themselves. Like so many other Scots, he could claim to be a close friend of Washington and was mortally wounded on the battlefield of Princeton (NJ).

The son of a Presbyterian minister, Mercer graduated at the age of nineteen from the medical school at Aberdeen University. During the '45 Uprising, he volunteered as assistant surgeon with the Jacobite Army, despite warnings from his father. After tending the wounded at Culloden, he went into hiding near his home town and in 1747 sailed from Leith to Pennsylvania. In Philadelphia, this healer with the military background did not feel at ease among the Quakers and moved west into the Allegheny Mountains, looking, according to his American biographer, Jack Scott

> ... for a bit of Scotland. Wherever Mercer went he was made most welcome because he set bones and ministered to the other injuries and ailments of the frontiersmen.

During the French and Indian War, Mercer achieved widespread (if temporary) fame. During a skirmish with Indians on his way to relieve Fort Shirley, he was left the only survivor of his company and hid in the woods to avoid capture. Having lost his horse to the Indians, and with an injured right arm and a sore heart at the loss of his comrades, he set off to walk 100 miles to the fort: he didn't even have a hunting knife. Living on wild berries, fruit, freshwater clams and raw rattlesnake, he completed the journey and soon found himself a celebrity, with stories of his ordeal carried in newspapers throughout the colonies.

When the Pennsylvania Assembly disbanded the Provincial Militia in 1760, the red-haired Mercer found himself a civilian again and opened a medical practice in Fredericksburg (VA), then a town of about 3,000 people. He married Isabella Gordon, his beautiful, unattached sister-in-law. His practice flourished, he invested in land, and in 1771 opened an apothecary's shop which still stands today. As war loomed, three regiments were formed in Virginia, Hugh Mercer being appointed Colonel of the Third Regiment, and in 1776 he was given charge of a Flying Camp (a mobile reserve army of 10,000 troops) and reported for duty the day before the Declaration of Independence.

There was never any doubt on which side Hugh Mercer would fight.

Hugh Mercer, born in Aberdeen, served as a general in the Revolutionary War and was killed at Princeton. Considered by many an unsung hero, his statue stands in Fredericksburg (VA), where he was an apothecary before the Revolution. (Department of Tourism, Fredericksburg (VA))

He told Dr Benjamin Rush that he would 'cross the mountains and live among the Indians rather than submit to the power of Great Britain'. His expertise led to several successes for the American Army before he was fatally wounded leading an attack on the British rear-guard at Princeton. Despite suffering a musket wound to the head, he fought on to taunts of 'Surrender, you rebel'. He was bayonetted several times and carried to a farm where he died nine days later. His funeral in Philadelphia was attended by 20,000 people, and the local St Andrews Society raised a monument. Military historian Douglas Freeman has said that, if he had lived, Mercer might have been Washington's 'peer or superior'.

ALL THE NICE GIRLS

It's a historical fact that Kirkcudbrightshire's famous son, the swashbuckling John Paul Jones (1747–92), Kirkbean's finest and founder of the United States Navy, secured most of his significant victories beneath the petticoats of the ladies of New Hampshire. Swiftly it should be explained that the young women of Portsmouth (NH) doted on Jones and banded together to sew an extra-special American flag from their undergarments: it flew proudly at the masthead during a series of historic naval encounters.

Considered by Americans to be the leading naval hero of the Revolutionary War, Jones took the fight to the British fleet in its own back yard and, in a sea battle off Flamborough Head in 1779, achieved a famous victory. At one point during the battle he was asked by the English commander if he was ready to surrender: 'I've just begun to fight' came the cocky and classic response . . . and he meant it.

As America strove for independence, Jones crossed the Atlantic to harry the British. Gradually, as news filtered back of his exploits, he was elevated to the status of folk hero. But like most superstars, Jones had a couple of skeletons rattling around in his cupboard. Soon after immigrating to America, he took command of a slave ship and made several runs to Africa. He gradually became disgusted by this trade in human flesh and left for more 'reputable and legitimate commerce'. Memories of sad journeys lived with him for the rest of his days.

In April 1778 he landed at St Mary's Isle on the Galloway coast, no distance at all from the house of his birth. His intention was to take the Earl of Selkirk hostage but he was told that the womenfolk were home alone; Jones was for returning to the ship but his followers were set on plunder. Leaving them to it, Jones insisted there should be no violence and the minimum of looting, but the ladies, fearing for their lives, handed over the family silver. This sordid episode of thieving badly dented his image as the Robin Hood of the high seas and, in an effort to retrieve the situation, he bought all the plate from his crew and in due course returned it to the family. In a sparkling career it was an incident that was never fully shrugged off.

Interestingly, the flag of America before 1776 had strong Scottish symbolism. It showed a rattlesnake with thirteen rattles to represent the colonies, and the motto—'Don't Tread on Me'—is clearly a poor imitation of the thistle and the motto, 'Wha' daur meddle wi' me?'

But many ordinary men with Scots roots are known to have served with American forces on sea as well as land. During the Revolutionary War, the muster books from various privateers fitting out along the New England coast contain many Scots names. Among thirty-two men on the sloop *Guildford* there was a lieutenant, William McQueen, gunner Timothy Andrews and pilot William Stuart; and on the frigate *Trumbull* a group of Scots 'of fair complexion' are to be found, including James Jeffrey, Robert Aitkins and John Brice—all listed as native-born Scots and, it's worth noting, none of them over five foot six inches in height. Bonnie wee fechters, indeed.

Alexander Murray (1755–1821) had a Jacobite grandfather who fled Scotland for the West Indies. By the age of eighteen, Murray had command of a vessel but his most notable achievements came while he commanded frigates in the Mediterranean. Among the other captains remembered for their services to the US Navy in its earliest days, we find the names of Stewart, Barron, McDonough, Buchanan and Perry—all either Scots or Ulster Scots.

Oliver Hazard Perry won a famous victory at Put-In Bay on Lake Erie during the war of 1812 between Great Britain and the youthful United States. His opposing commander that day was another Scot, Robert H. Barclay. This significant victory ended fears of a British invasion, and is said to have been the first time since it created a navy that Britain had lost an entire squadron. Thomas McDonough achieved an equally important success on Lake Champlain.

Franklin Buchanan (1800–74) was born in Baltimore (MD) of Scottish descent and organised the Naval Academy at Annapolis in 1845. Entering the Confederate Navy in 1861, he was given command of the famous ironclad *Merrimac*. Wounded the day before, he did not take part in the battle with *The Monitor*, a Civil War clash of metal sea monsters which opened a new chapter in world naval history. On board *The Monitor*, however, was Ericsson, its builder, whose mother was Scots; and in charge of her engines and turrets was Isaac Newton, a Scot with a famous name.

WHEN JOCKY COMES MARCHING HOME
Many thousands of Scots civilians, often newly-arrived immigrants, found themselves caught up in the bloody turmoil and confusion of the Civil War. Donald Manson, who was born in Thurso in 1839 and was to become one of New York's most famous carpenters and cabinet-makers, left Scotland just in time to answer Abraham Lincoln's first call for 75,000 men. He served for three years in the United States Navy, where most of his work was on board vessels blockading southern ports.

Alexander MacInnes, from Dufftown in Banffshire, went with his family to settle in Oakland (MD) while the conflict was at its height. Because

Maryland was a border state, there were spies for both sides operating in these rural communities. Alexander was still a British citizen, and when a Confederate raiding party from the Virginia Cavalry Regiment halted at his front gate he pointed to the Union Jack flying from the flagpole in the garden and declared confidently that he was a subject of the Queen. Then, in spirited but foolhardy outburst, he cursed the entire troop for rebelling against the organised government. The Confederate cavalrymen were stunned but the young lieutenant in charge took off his hat politely and explained that they had been briefed about the MacInneses political status.

According to MacInnes's descendant, John Grant, who still lives in Oakland, Alexander was impressed by the young officer and invited him to take tea on the front porch while the troopers sat on their horses in the roadway.

Andrew Cargill, descendant of three Scots brothers who came to America in 1725, recorded his experiences of blockade-running from Cuba. His strong Confederate sympathies forced him to leave school in New York early: 'It would have been very unpleasant for me to remain.' Anxious to fight for the Confederacy, he was ordered to North Carolina and secured passage from Havana on the blockade-runner *The Ptarmigan*, a three-funnel Clyde-built steamer. Loaded with arms and ammunition the ship was designated to bring out cotton. After a false start when they were chased back to port by two fast Federal patrol boats, they headed for Galveston in Texas but were caught in a fearful storm in the Gulf of Mexico. On the third day the captain told everyone to stay on deck because he feared *The Ptarmigan* might split in half.

Six miles from Galveston, in the half-dark with the fires banked and lights out, they crept towards the port. Suddenly a flare went up and they raced for safety. By the light of more flares they could see they were in the middle of a pack of US patrol boats, so close they could not fire until *The Ptarmigan* passed for fear of sinking each other. Andrew remembered:

> They put three shot in us—one knocked over two cases of rifles, one went through the paddlebox and out into the sea and the third shot off part of the starboard rail.

Having anchored in shallow water in the safety of the port, they learned that the fort had been making signals which had gone unseen urging the ship to drop anchor because there were mines ahead. Unwittingly—and at top speed—they had safely negotiated the minefield.

Among the most notable of these Civil War blockade-runners was Thurso-born sea captain James McKay, regarded as the founder of Tampa, Florida. Born in 1808, he had his master's certificate by the time he was twenty-five. Soon after, in Edinburgh, he met and fell in love with Matilda Alexander. Her mother was a wealthy widow and disapproved of the match because of James's dangerous occupation. Mother and daughter immigrated but James followed, and persistence paid off when they married. Some time later the whole family moved to Florida, and on this journey south the ship was wrecked on a reef—the tough Caithness sailor had to swim to rescue his wife, children . . . and mother-in-law.

Making Tampa his base, in 1846 he successfully invested in real estate and set up a general store selling everything from the proverbial needle to anchor. The sea was still in his blood, however, and he bought two schooners and began shipping cattle to Cuba, the first American entrepreneur to do so. His quick thinking and bravery during the war between the States allowed him regularly to break the blockade, and when his last ship was destroyed he became head of the Fifth Commissary District for the Confederate Army.

George Dewey (1837–1917) was a legendary naval officer who was quietly proud of his Scottish heritage. Born in Vermont, he led the squadron which entered Manila Bay on 1 May 1898 during the Spanish-American War. He sank or destroyed all ten ships of the Spanish fleet, his own vessels escaping unscathed. Only eight US seaman were injured and this victory, as well as demonstrating the superiority of US warships (his flagship *Olympia* had been built in San Francisco by Scot George Dickie) also earned for the United States the position of major Pacific power.

Some Scots found themselves in the navy very much against their wishes. William Scoon was born near Dumfries in 1776 and decided to take his chance in the New World in 1812, when Britain and the US were at war. He found a berth on an American vessel but was captured and pressed into British naval service. His escape was the stuff of story-books. After two years' service he managed to conceal himself in a coil of rope at New York harbour, where he remained with only a sea biscuit to eat until his ship sailed. By this time his wife, who had expected to be summoned to the States, had given him up for dead and remarried. William's story has a spectacularly successful ending: he settled in Washington County (NY), where he married Nancy Pratt and had ten children.

In the Civil War of 1861–65, Scotsmen served with distinction and in considerable numbers in the land armies on both sides. It has been calculated that at least 50,000 soldiers in the Union forces had been born in Scotland; and although figures for the South are more difficult to come by, it is certain that many thousands of native-born Scots stood in the ranks of the Confederacy.

The Highland Guard of Chicago (IL) was one of the first groups to answer Lincoln's call to arms in 1861. Its first commander, as was fitting, was a Scot, John McArthur (b.1826), a blacksmith and foundry master from Erskine in Renfrewshire, who came to the US in the 1850s and served with distinction at Fort Donelson, Shiloh, Vicksburg and Nashville. Before 1860, the Union Light Infantry of Charleston (SC) wore Cameron tartan trews. Another regiment of volunteers of Scots origin, the 79th Highlanders of New York, were originally, like their countrymen in Chicago, called the 'Highland Guard' with a uniform patterned on the Black Watch. Reorganised in 1861 at the outbreak of war, it held the record for 'fighting more battles and marching more miles' than any other New York regiment.

Its colonel during the early years was James Cameron, whose grandfather had fought at Culloden. James was killed at the first battle of Bull Run. Among the Scots officers of this regiment who are remembered were Glaswegian Colonel David Morrison (Cameron's successor), and Colonels Laing, Baird and Gair.

Of the four field commanders on the Union side, three—Scott, Grant and McClellan—were of Scottish descent, while in the Confederate high command General Robert E. Lee claimed that the blood of Bruce flowed through his veins. Stonewall Jackson, Johnstone and Stuart were all Scots.

Among the Civil War generals, Ulysses Grant claimed the longest Scots immigrant pedigree, with Scots blood on both sides of his family. He was the eighth lineal descendant of a Scot, Matthew Grant, who sailed with his wife and child from Plymouth among a party of 140 immigrants on *The Mary and John*. His destination was New England in the earliest days of settlement. In 1993, the United States consul general for Scotland, Bobette Orr, claimed descent from Grant through her grandmother.

Grant served on the western front in the early years of the war, his single most important success during that period being the taking of Vicksburg. Once in control of the Union armies further east, he launched attack after attack on General Lee, losing thousands of men in the process. Pressure to have him replaced was resisted by Lincoln, who felt that Grant was successfully harrying the Confederate forces. Grant justified the President's faith in him when he pushed Lee back to Richmond (VA), and then out-manoeuvred him to force a Confederate surrender at Appomattox Court House (VA) on 9 April 1865.

Ancestors of George Brinton McClellan came to America in the early 1700s from Scotland, and his great-grandfather served in the Revolutionary War. Such dynasties of fighting Scots, stretching from the formative years of the United States right through the Civil War to the industrial era and both World Wars, can be traced in many states.

McClellan entered West Point in 1842 and had command of the Army of the Potomac at the start of the Civil War. Lee was impressed by McClellan's military skills, praising him as the most efficient Union general he had encountered and their armies met in the peninsular campaign and at Antietam. In 1864, McClellan ran for president as a Democrat but was defeated by Lincoln.

General Winfield Hancock is remembered for his assured leadership at Gettysburg, and on the same battlefield General John F. Reynolds fell to a sniper's bullet—both men were from Scots stock. Irwin McDowell, given command of the Union army at the first Battle of Bull Run, failed through lack of experience of independent command to turn his forces who were retreating in confusion.

On the Confederate side, the family of Robert E. Lee were of Virginia

Ulysses Simpson Grant, eighteenth president of the United States, Civil War hero and descendant of an immigrant Scot who landed in New England in the mid-1600s. (United States Postal Service)

fighting stock and claimed 'good Scottish blood', while General Thomas Jackson, a veteran of the Mexican War and a lecturer at the Virginia Military Institute, gained the nickname 'Stonewall' for his dour and determined approach to warfare. With Lee he forged a formidable partnership, and they were able to inflict many reverses on the Union armies before the final surrender. Jackson was shot by one of his own men on 2 May 1863, while returning to his lines. It was a telling loss to the Confederate cause.

Other Southern generals with Scottish connections included Joseph Johnston, whose father served in the Revolutionary War, and General James 'Jeb' Stuart, who was Lee's eyes and ears, conducting a series of hazardous scouting expeditions.

Of the ordinary Scots soldier there are only sketchy paragraphs, dispersed through family histories and county biographies—stories of quiet dedication to the cause, unspectacular, reliable service. Western-history writer, James Callaghan, has identified this trait as making life difficult for the would-be chronicler of the fighting Scots:

There were not a lot of colourful anecdotes about them as there were with Irish and German officers. These are stark service records in many cases, but these speak volumes in terms of courage, dedication and professionalism.

However, family folklore abounds with simple, unadorned tales of the Scots in the Civil War. For example, while writer Frank Andrew Stone of the University of Connecticut was researching the service records of Connecticut men in the war between the States, he was excited to discover on the rolls the name of his great-grandfather. Hugh McBrayne had immigrated from Glasgow and settled at Middletown, serving as a private in Company A, Second Connecticut Volunteers, from May to August 1861. Company A had been recruited exclusively from Middletown and its surgeon was another American Scot, Dr Archibald T. Douglass. On 17 September 1862, while serving with the 14th Connecticut Volunteers, McBrayne was seriously wounded at Antietam (MD) and was discharged the following year. The family moved to New Britain (CT), so that Hugh's son Alexander could obtain better employment, but Hugh had been permanently disabled by his war wounds.

Another conflict in which the Scots played a role disproportionate to their small numbers was the Texan struggle for independence from Mexico. Sam Houston (1793–1863) was a soldier-statesman from Rockridge County (VA) who became the first president of the Republic of Texas. He was steeped in the Ulster-Scots traditions, and as a young man gave up the opportunity of clerking to live with the Cherokees. After the war of 1812, he remained in the army and helped with the sad removal of the Cherokees to Arkansas along 'the Trail of Tears'.

Studying law, he was elected to the House of Representatives and after being formally adopted into the Cherokee nation he made several trips to Washington to plead the Indian case. Sent to Texas by Andrew Jackson to negotiate with the Indian tribes, he became caught up in the growing agitation for Texan independence and led the forces which defeated the Mexican general Santa Ana at the Battle of San Jacinto in 1836, effectively gaining liberty for Texas. The same year he was elected president, and when Texas joined the Union in 1845, he served as senator.

The debt owed by Texas to the American Scots who fought and died at the Alamo is widely recognised, and the Saltire flies alongside flags of other nationals who died at San Antonio to help make Texas free. Jim Bowie (of Bowie-knife fame) and Davy Crockett, born in Tennessee (his Ulster-Scots father fought for the Patriots at King's Mountain), were among the garrison that died defending the mission station against Santa Ana. John McGregor, whose background in Scotland has been a source of debate among genealogists over the past couple of years, was unquestionably one of the characters of the thirteen-day siege. According to one of the women spared by the Mexicans, Suzanna Dickinson, McGregor competed with Davy Crockett in musical contests during the lulls between Mexican attacks. Davy played the fiddle and John the bagpipes, making what Suzanna described as a 'strange and dreadful sound'.

FORSYTH AND THE MAGIC BUNNET

The classic cavalry-Indian encounter—with the bluecoats heavily outnumbered and defending a low, scrub-covered island in a shallow river—has been portrayed in more than a few Westerns. Yet this stereotype is based on reality—the Battle of Beecher's Island—a clash which, as well as being one of the most publicised of the Indian wars, has as its principal character an American Scot from Illinois, George Forsyth.

Indians on the Great Plains, mainly Sioux and Cheyenne, had been staging more and more daring raids during the late 1860s; Forsyth came up with the audacious plan to hunt down the Indians and force a decisive fight by seeming to offer themselves up, almost as a sacrifice. On 16 September 1868, Forsyth and his party of fifty men rode out over the flood plain of the Arikaree River in eastern Colorado. His men, hardened frontiersmen and volunteers, were uneasy about the huge war party they were trailing which included the legendary Cheyenne warrior known to the soldiers as Roman Nose.

By first light, 600 Indians had encircled the cavalry party; but Forsyth had seen a sixty-yard long island in the middle of the river and ordered his men to dig in. The Indians charged again and again but were driven back by the raking fire from the repeating rifles.

Roman Nose entered the fray only reluctantly after being accused of cowardice. Initially, he would not join the fight because he had a sacred bunnet which he believed gave him protection from bullets but he had not completed his rituals properly on this occasion and joined the assault convinced he was going to die. The fearsome charge carried the screaming warriors splashing through the stream and on to the island when Roman Nose fell, a bullet in the small of his back.

For a week the cavalry unit was besieged on the island, named in honour of Forsyth's second-in-command, Frederick Beecher, killed in the early hours of the battle. Forsyth had also been wounded, but when his men refused to cut the bullet from his thigh because of its proximity to an artery, he cut it out himself, using an open razor. Scouts had been sent to summon help but by the time the relief column arrived, Forsyth and his men had been reduced to eating the festering flesh of the fallen horses. Just to consign the story firmly to cavalry legend, Forsyth is said to have been reading *Oliver Twist* when the relief column appeared on the horizon.

Another legendary couple from the US cavalry were Paisley buddie Thomas McGregor (b. 1837) and his wife, Jane—a more redoubtable pair in the annals of American military history, you're unlikely to find. Tam, power-packed and standing five foot six inches in his stocking-soles, came to New York at the age of sixteen and (like so many other adventurers) headed for California and the gold rush. However, after Indians surprised

General Thomas McGregor, a Paisley 'buddie', with his family on the porch of the CO's quarters at Fort Grant (AZ). (Arizona Historical Society Library)

his camp and killed his partner, he joined the cavalry and served in the Civil War under Grant and Sherman, being wounded twice.

At cavalry HQ at Carlisle (PA) he met and married Jane, a judge's daughter. What a team they were to make. Thomas was ordered to California again, in the aftermath of the war between the States, and then to Idaho—an overland trip which in those days could take six months. Mrs McGregor was accompanied by her mother and her two babies on this hazardous expedition, and there were numerous clashes with the Indians. The party was forced to sleep nightly behind barricades of flour-bags and grain. Mrs McGregor was described in newspaper tributes after her death as a 'pioneer character' who, on one occasion when the women were left on their own, had to fight off an Indian attack single-handed.

In Idaho, Arizona, Washington and Oregon, Thomas McGregor fought in various Indian campaigns and gained steady promotion, constantly encouraged by his wife. By the time he retired in 1901, he was a brigadier-general and had also fought in the Spanish-American war in Cuba and in the Philippines during the Boxer uprising. He was commended for bravery in the Tonto Basin Campaign of 1873 and ended up as commander at Fort Grant (AZ).

While they were stationed in Arizona, Thomas, due to force of circumstances, had to give command of a raw bunch of recruits to Mrs McGregor, who led them on a journey downriver from Yuma to Ehrenburg (AZ). Having no rations except raw sugar, beans and coffee, the men mutinied—but Jane proved more than a match for them, and gained control by turning hot steam on the rebellious young soldiers. After arriving in Edinburgh, she marched the boys 180 miles over the desert to Whipple Barracks. Although the couple had thirteen children, six died in infancy. One son, Rob Roy McGregor, became a cowboy in the wild Chiricahua Mountains.

In the modern era, one figure towers over the fighting Scots in America— General Douglas MacArthur. His grandfather was born in Glasgow in 1817, and immigrated with his widowed mother to Massachusetts. He settled in Milwaukee (WI) in mid-century and was governor of Wisconsin, as well as a justice of the Supreme Court. His father, Arthur MacArthur, was a general serving in the Union army in the Civil War and held the rank of colonel when he was scarcely out of his teens. Douglas MacArthur grew up, as a result, in a military environment, travelling around with his family before entering West Point and graduating first in his class in 1903. During World War I he became a brigadier-general and was wounded in action.

'I shall return', he memorably declared when the Japanese swept the Americans from the Philippines in 1942, and as senior army commander in the Pacific he began a step-by-step campaign to recapture key islands. As supreme commander of the forces of occupation after the Japanese surrender, MacArthur became virtually ruler of Japan and was given the task of helping to rebuild the shattered nation and to introduce a system of democracy.

Cowboy Rob Roy McGregor, son of a Paisley-born army general, pictured in the Chiricahua Mountains c.1892. (Arizona Historical Society Library)

## Chapter 9

# THE CHIEFTAIN'S EAGLE FEATHERS

I T NEVER WOULD HAVE HAPPENED IN BARRA. When Andrew McNeil's new Indian neighbours came calling and found they weren't welcome, they simply lifted his sturdy oak door clear off its pins, stepped inside and made themselves at home. A proud Gael, Andrew settled in New York state in the years before the Revolutionary War and in common with thousands of his countryfolk who made the Atlantic crossing he had a great deal to learn about the ways of the native American.

Arriving in Philadelphia (PA), Andrew—who was bilingual, having polished his English during a spell in west-central Scotland before immigrating—secured a job in New York at the farm of a French nobleman. Andrew was at home one day when a group of local Indians paid him a visit. The tradition was that it was always open house in the encampments, and the braves wandered casually into the McNeil house looking for the newcomer.

Thunderstruck by this bold behaviour, Andrew cursed them roundly in the Gaelic, ushered them roughly out the door and barred it behind them. Undaunted, the Indians removed the door and wandered in. All set for warfare, Andrew climbed to the loft for his broadsword which he'd brought all the way from Scotland, but bloodshed was avoided by the arrival of a neighbour who calmed the situation. At the end of the day, they all sat down together and smoked the pipe of peace.

The Scots were still learning about Indian behaviour a century later, judging by the story of Perth-born Alex McKay who, with a companion called Roark, was prospecting in the 1880s in the wild mountain country on the Arizona-Mexico border. One morning they reached the top of a high pass and directly in front of them, coming up from the other side, was a mounted band of Indians. Alex was convinced that his time was at hand and whispered to Roark: 'Right here, the jig's up.' They were so close, however, there was nothing for it but to continue on. To the amazement of the prospectors, the Indians trotted past, scarcely looking at the road they were on. A short distance further on, they met a company of troopers who had been looking for Indians: 'My God, man,' said Alex, 'we jist passed aboot a dozen.' The troopers laughed, explaining that the men they'd seen were Indian scouts, instantly recognisable because they wore white rags tied round their heads, whereas renegade Indians usually wore red. A lesson worth learning.

Alice 'Allie' Twist came from a Scots family who settled in Wisconsin in the mid-1800s and found that when it comes to sharing a social event with the Indians, it's as well to have a wide culinary taste. When her husband bought a farm including the site of an Indian village, the Twists decided to have a pow-wow with their neighbours to discuss ways of co-existing. When Chief Ah-ha-Chocher (known to the settlers as Artichoker) invited the immigrants to his camp, the main item on the menu was boiled prairie dog with beans.

Between 1607 and 1914 it is estimated that some 40,000,000 Europeans came to America. At first it seemed that the vast continent could absorb all the new tribes, that there was a better-than-even chance of peaceful co-existence with the native Indians. But within a few short decades of settlement the seeds that were to destroy the Indian nations were sown.

First of all, with the white man came his diseases—cholera and smallpox, ably assisted by scarlet fever, dysentery, venereal disease and alcoholism, which killed millions; then his prejudices against the social, cultural and religious traditions of the Indians surfaced; finally, and most tellingly, emerged his insatiable thirst for land, leading initially to conflict and by the late 1800s the complete subjugation of the tribes, hemmed in as they were on all sides by a strange, unfamiliar and grasping world.

The Scots, and particularly the Highlanders, traded with, fought, killed, and in turn were killed by the Red Indian, yet paradoxically they also achieved a surprisingly high degree of assimilation with the native tribes. One intriguing theory put forward to explain the Scots-Indian bond suggests that the two peoples had more in common than just the eagle feather symbol of power of the chieftain's head-dress.

Particularly in the south-eastern United States, where the Indians had a much longer contact with white settlers, similarities between the social and cultural structure of the Indian tribal hierarchy and the clan system enabled a natural coming-together in a way unmatched by any other immigrant group. Genealogists have studied this phenomenon, and historian William Lindsay McDonald of Florence (AL) notes the key roles played by Scots among the 'civilised' tribes of the south east.

McDonald cites the example of John Ross, chief of the Cherokee nation. His grandfather, John McDonald, was born at Inverness, Scotland, about 1747 and came to settle near the present site of Chattanooga (TN) where he married Ann Shorey, daughter of a Scotsman, William Shorey, and his Cherokee wife, Ghigooie. McDonald exerted an iron will over his family of Cherokees, particularly young John Ross. 'Old McDonald', as he was known, insisted that his descendants should be reared as Scots and not Indians, and as a child wee John would often beg his grandfather to allow him to wear Indian clothes rather than the Highland dress. William McDonald suggests that

> ... among the early migrants to America it was predominantly Scots who capitalised as influential men and leaders among the native Americans. I think it was their inherited background in the old Celtic clan system that gave them a natural advantage to assume leadership roles among the Indian tribes.

At the opposite corner of the country in the far north-west, among the Rockies, Hugh Munroe, born in 1798 into a Scots family, was to have a considerable influence upon the lives of the Blackfeet Indians in the area of Montana now designated as the vast and spectacular Glacier National Park. He came west in 1814 as a Hudson's Bay Company apprentice and arrived at Fort Bow on the Saskatchewan River expressing an interest in the Indians and a wish to learn their language. The company saw value in having a foot in the Indian camp and he joined the Piegan branch of the Blackfeet, with the commission to scout for beaver-trapping areas and to learn if any other American companies were working the Blackfeet territory.

Hugh was put under the care of Chief Lone Walker, whose daughter, Sinopah, he later married. He is thought to have seen the St Mary Lake on the eastern edge of the Rockies as early as 1814 or 1815, making him the first white man to wander its shores. He remained with the Blackfeet for the rest of his life, eventually becoming a free-trader and trapper. His frequent trips into the Glacier Park region, and his friendly and confident manner with the Indians, made him a crucial go-between in maintaining peace between the Indians and the white men. Munroe died in December 1892, at the age of ninety-four, and was buried at the Holy Family Mission on the Two Medicine River. He also assisted in various government expeditions which criss-crossed the mountains.

HOLDING BACK THE TIDE

Theodore Roosevelt once wrote that for a generation the Creeks had managed to hold their own against the encroachment of the white man better than any other native race. This was largely down to the 'consummate craft and cool, masterly diplomacy' of one man, Alexander McGillivray (b.1759), the son of a wealthy Scots trader and an Indian princess. As a Loyalist, his father fled to Scotland during the revolution. Alexander died young at thirty-four, and his funeral was attended by representatives from three important nations: Spain, Britain and the United States—at one time or another he had them all dancing to his tune. For many he was the greatest Indian diplomat of all time. Gene Burnett, in his book *Florida's Past*, says that McGillivray was deferred to by kings and fêted by George Washington, having shunned the tomahawk for the more subtle art of statesmanship.

After being sent as a teenage prince to the coast to receive an education in the classics, he became a chief, symbolic leader of more than 45,000 Creeks, Chickasaws, Choctaws and Seminoles in the south-east. Pensacola (FL) was then a bustling centre of the Indian trade, a trade which made a millionaire of another Scots trader and Loyalist, William Panton. McGillivray became

Alexander McGillivray, son of a Scots trader and an Indian princess, and the symbolic leader of 45,000 Creeks, Chicasaws, Choctaws and Seminoles in the south-eastern United States in the late 1700s. (Library of the University of South Florida)

his silent partner. The chief, an avid history buff and a remarkably fast learner, had already decided that the only way to protect his people was to be even smarter than the 'plotting whites'.

The chief sought and achieved British protection for the Creek nation, was appointed an honorary British colonel, and within a few months he had also signed a treaty with the Spanish. McGillivray initially spurned overtures from the Americans, saying they talked down to his people, but eventually George Washington persuaded him to come to New York where he stayed at the home of Ulster-Scots war secretary, Henry Knox, and a treaty was formally hammered out in 1790. The Creeks were to be protected jointly by the US and Spain; this treaty has been described as his 'masterwork'. Back in Florida his enemies launched a whispering campaign saying he had sold out the Creek lands, but McGillivray rejected this accusation.

Tall, with piercing eyes, the chief had been plagued by illness most of his life, not eased by his love of whisky, and he died at his partner Panton's home on 17 February 1793. In an obituary in *The Gentleman's Magazine* in London (in space normally reserved for royalty and nobility) he was hailed as a great statesman, who, with the vigour of his mind, overcame the disadvantages of an education had in the wilds of America. In the Creek language his name was 'Hoboi-Hilr-Miko'—Big Mac.

His partner, Panton, was born in Aberdeenshire in 1742 and immigrated to South Carolina before reaching Florida in the 1760s. He soon owned a chain of trading posts and although he was a Loyalist, he stayed on when the British abandoned east Florida. The Spanish realised that Panton and his Scots associates, John Leslie and Thomas Forbes, could supply the Indians of southern Georgia, Alabama and northern Florida with arms, and that these Indians could provide a barrier against American penetration.

By 1789, after moving to Pensacola, Panton, Leslie and Company had a complete monopoly over the Indian trade; but McGillivray's death four years later saw the end of their control of this side of the business. Panton died in 1801. Commenting on McGillivray's death, he confided:

> I advised him, I pushed him to be a great man. Spaniards and Americans felt his weight and this enabled him to haul me after him so as to establish this house with more solid privileges than without him I should have got.

There is another powerful connection between the Creeks and the Scots settlers in the south-eastern United States around this period in the shape of Chief William McIntosh (1775–1825). In his novel based on the life of McIntosh, author George Chapman describes the chief as a 'man between two worlds'.

During the early days of settlement in Georgia (and elsewhere), Highland Scots were asked to serve as a shield against Indian uprising. In the south they also provided a buffer against Spanish aggression. The founder of Savannah, James E. Oglethorpe, had among his officers a John McIntosh

Chief Waldo Emerson 'Dode' McIntosh, ninety-five year old grandson of an American Scot who married into the Creek nation. (The Herald Archives)

whose son, William, was to become a captain in the colonial army and who married a Creek Indian princess, Senoia Henneha. Their son William, the chief, was born in what is now Alabama.

This William McIntosh grew to be a powerful figure in the tribe, leading the Lower Creeks from the southern part of Georgia against the British in the war of 1812. Already, however, the Creek nation was split in its allegiance. While McIntosh managed to persuade the Creeks in the south to sign a treaty with the US government, their northern brothers were determined to retain control of their tribal lands and steadfastly refused to sign. They declared McIntosh a traitor and outlaw, and refused to recognise his authority. Nothing but vengeance would satisfy those Indians who felt they had been sold out, and they came to McIntosh's house on the east bank of the Chattahoochee, set it alight and butchered the chief. Histories will tell you that the fate of William McIntosh illustrates the all-too-frequent tragedy of the American half-breed in the nation's story, torn as they were between two cultures.

Described as a commanding, finely formed figure, McIntosh learned to speak and write English and was the first person to codify the Creek laws. He was cited by General Andrew Jackson for bravery at the Battle of Horseshoe Bend (in the war of 1812). A shrewd businessman, he owned a trading post, tavern, ferries and considerable land and livestock. He is known to have had at least three wives and as many as twelve children. It's also interesting to note that throughout his life he retained a fascination with Scotland. Once, while in his teens, he was on board a boat preparing to sail for Scotland and, along with his brother, was removed by his Indian uncles at the last minute.

The McIntosh link with the Creeks was not lost. In the late 1980s, Chief Waldo Emerson 'Dode' McIntosh, William's great-grandson, with Indian head-dress and tartan plaid was still attending Scottish festivals in his nineties, and freely admitting his love of all things Scottish—including the skirl of the pipes and drums.

Very often Scots who did not marry into the Indian nations, but who embraced Indian rights as a just cause, found themselves in deep water. Old-timer Alexander Arbuthnot, who traded with Indians in the Bahamas and Florida in the early 1800s, came from Scotland late in life hoping to give his family a fresh start. In the highly unstable and politically charged atmosphere of Florida—an area of contention between Britain, Spain and the United States—Arbuthnot became very sympathetic to the plight of the Indians, noting in his journal that they had been ill-treated by the English and robbed by the Americans. Creek Indian leaders asked him to plead their case for fairer treatment, and he did so in a series of letters over the period of a year. These epistles were to be his downfall.

Captured by American marines, he was taken to the Bahamas on the orders of the future Ulster-Scots president, Andrew Jackson, and accused of stirring up the Creek nation against the United States and assisting the enemy. On the morning of 29 April 1818, he was hanged from the yard-arm of his own schooner, *The Chance*. Doubts have been expressed over the justice of his execution, and Dr James Covington of Florida University has concluded that the court martial and verdict were illegal, since an American court martial could not try a civilian.

There are many examples of Scots like Arbuthnot, who identified with the Indian struggle to maintain their identity—fur trader Robert Stuart from Callander, in Perthshire, was superintendent of Indian affairs in Michigan in the 1840s, and was (according to G.F. Black) a 'staunch advocate of justice for native Americans'. John Harris (1716–91), an Ulster Scot, was founder of Harrisburg (PA) and, as the wild frontier's principal storekeeper, built the first ferry used to cross the Susquehanna River. Fair dealing gained him the trust of the Indians, and many important councils were held at his home, which still stands today. Pioneer missionary, John Fleming, born of Scots parents, began work among the Creek Indians at Fort Gibson in present-day Arkansas in 1832. His wife opened a school, and John was the first person to put the Creek language into writing—a particularly difficult task because of the numerous and puzzling combination of consonants. The government judged John's mission a failure, however, and closed it down; but he went on to work with the Wea Indians in Kansas, and the Chippewa and Ottawa tribes in Michigan.

Before we become overwhelmed with this idea that the Scots had some mystical bond with the red man, it should be understood that there is a much darker, more sinister side to this relationship. The Scots played their part over the centuries in harrying and hounding the Indian tribes; tit-for-tat atrocities and senseless slaughter permeate historical records of our involvement with the Indians.

The role of the Indian agent was a particularly difficult and dangerous calling in the early days. In the early 1700s, Scots-born Thomas Nairne seemed to have achieved some success in pacifying discontented tribes on the extreme southern edge of the Carolina settlement. He was seeking to expand British influence westwards but had the misfortune to be involved in parleys with the Yamasee Indians at Pocotaligo on 15 April 1715, when news of the outbreak of the Southern Indian War reached the conference. In the wrong place at decidedly the wrong time, Nairne was seized and died at the stake after being tortured for several days.

DEVIOUS IN DEATH

Montgomery's Highlanders were formed in 1757 and went to America to fight against the French in the Seven Years War during which both France and Britain ruthlessly used the Indian tribes against each other. The Highlanders patrolled in small, mobile units, criss-crossing the tricky terrain around the Great Lakes and skirmishing with Indians and French.

Several soldiers of the regiment fell into Indian hands, captured in an ambush. One of them, Allan Macpherson, witnessing numbers of his fellow

Crazy Horse, the dashing young Oglala Sioux war-chief who was bayoneted by a trooper after surrendering, was related through marriage to the Morayshire-born adventurer 'Scotty' Philip. (United States Postal Service)

prisoners dying under torture and preparations being made to start on him, signalled that he had something to communicate. An interpreter was brought, and Macpherson explained that if his life was spared he would communicate the secret of an extraordinary medicine, which, if applied to the skin, would deflect the strongest blow of a tomahawk: he offered himself for the experiment. Intrigued, the Indians agreed to his request and he was allowed under escort into the woods to collect plants which he then boiled into an ointment.

Macpherson rubbed his neck with the juice and lay his head on a log, inviting the strongest man to strike him. The Indian, levelling a blow with all his might, cut with such force that the head flew off a distance of several yards. The Indians were astounded at their own gullibility, and the skill with which the prisoner had avoided a lingering death. The story of Allan Macpherson became a legend in the Indian lodges.

A substantial number of the best-known Indian-fighters of the north-west territories (the vast area to the south of the Great Lakes) during the Revolutionary period had strong Scottish connections—Clark, McCulloch, the Lewises, McKee, Crawford, Patterson, Robertson, Johnston, Adams, Poe and Hardy. General Forbes, a founder of Pittsburgh; William Paterson, who gave his name to the community in New Jersey; Moses Cleveland, after whom Cleveland (OH) is named—all were from Scots stock. Ulster-Scot John Whistler (grandfather of the painter), was sent in 1803 to build Fort Dearborn, signalling the birth of Chicago. Daniel Boone (1735–1820), according to his biographers, almost single-handedly conquered the region comprising Kentucky, Tennessee and Missouri. He was the grandson of an Ulster Scot who landed at Philidelphia in 1717, an American 'Border Hero' who became the scourge of the Indian. Simon Kenton (1755–1836), Boone's companion on many of his most daring exploits in the untamed forest, was the son of a Scots mother and Ulster-Scots father. He served with George Clark and was one of the longest surviving of the early pioneers. Kenton County takes it name from this backwoodsman.

Three Lewises—Andrew, Colonel William and Charles—were all of Scottish descent, and distinguished themselves in the border-fighting against the Indian war parties on the frontiers of Virginia. Colonel William Crawford, a friend and associate of George Washington, was sent on frontier duty in Ohio in the closing days of the Revolutionary War, but was captured by Indians and burned to death—again, after torture. Robert Patterson also fought in many Indian campaigns but was luckier than Crawford. He survived to build the first house on the site of Lexington (KY), was owner of a third of Cincinatti (OH) when it was first laid out, and he built the first settlement at Dayton (OH).

General James Robertson (1742–1814), considered by most to be the founding father of Tennessee, was born in Virginia of Scots parents and accompanied Boone on his third expedition in 1759 beyond the Alleghenies. He founded the city of Nashville (TN), and a biographer has described his life as 'a bitter fight with the Indians'.

Even into the 1800s we encounter Scots who fully justified the confidence of officialdom that they would provide a solid buffer against the native tribes. Among the first of what Stephen Gredel termed a 'vigourous, sturdy and thrifty' group of Scots settlers who made Buffalo (NY) their home was David Rees, who set up his famous red-painted blacksmith's shop in the town's Washington Street in 1803. David was described by friends as an 'eccentric, quick-tempered Scotsman'. He was certainly no Indian-lover and tales of his violent clashes with Indians of the district live on in local folklore, as does the skill he brought from Scotland enabling him to forge broadaxes which were greatly admired in the new settlement.

Once a noted Indian chief called Red Jacket ordered a special tomahawk, but on seeing the finished product was very critical, eventually producing a wooden pattern for Rees to use as a model. When Red Jacket returned for his tomahawk, he took one look at it and threw it away in disgust. The Scotsman had made it exactly like the model, without a hole for the handle.

In 1815, Rees was involved in a stand-up fight when the Seneca chief, Young King, rode up, dismounted and attacked him 'without provocation'. Rees grabbed a scythe from a bystander and struck Young King, almost severing his arm, which was amputated the next day. Ironically, Young King was later to receive a government pension for 'brave services during the War of 1812, when he lost an arm'. The truth had been bent somewhat.

'FRIEND' OF THE CHEROKEES

By the late 1720s, young Sir Archibald Cuming was finding life as a lawyer in Edinburgh increasingly mundane and unrewarding. On a whim, he left litigation and legal briefs behind to join an expedition to America. His arrival in 1727 signalled a fundamental change of course for the mighty Cherokee nation.

An alliance had been agreed between the British government and the tribe in 1721, but it was Cuming who built on this with what one historian has described as 'an amazing stunt'. His critics say he took blatant advantage of the naïvety of the red men. An important council meeting attended by 300 chiefs was interrupted by Cuming, who entered the council hall with a gun and sword concealed under his long coat. Using a combination of veiled threats and eloquence, he forced all the headmen to kneel and pledge allegiance to George II. Cuming more or less forced all the white traders present to sign their names as witnesses to the event. Pat Alderman, in his book *The Overmountain Men*, assessed Cuming's action thus:

> ... he had no authority for this performance. He merely seized this course to gain prominence for himself. He dreamed of becoming important as the great benefactor of the red man. He made a Grand Tour of the Cherokee nation in an attempt to set up his kingdom.

Subsequent events suggest that this appraisal is spot-on. Determined to make the British government—and more importantly the King—aware of his achievement, Cuming devised a plan to take several young chiefs to London. Sailing from Charleston (SC) in the spring of 1730 were Oukounaco, Onokanowin, Kilonah, Clogoitah, Tiftowe, Oukahulah and Kitagista—and, of course, their mentor, Cuming.

Quite a stir was caused in London on the arrival of these colourful characters who were entertained by George II at the palace, where the Indians presented the King with their crown of possum fur, dyed red and decorated with scalps and eagle's tails. The Indians promised to support Britain in any future war and to trade only with the representatives of King George. In turn, the King paid their travelling and entertainment expenses during the stay. As reported in Brown's *Old Frontiers*, Oukahulah, spokesman for the group, made a splendidly moving speech of allegiance:

> We look upon King George as the Sun, and our Father, and upon ourselves as his children, for though you are white and we are red, our hands and hearts are joined together.

After a year the Indians returned home, loaded with honours and presents. The Scotsman Cuming remained behind because of financial problems. In Pat Alderman's estimation,

> The Cherokees had gained a Great White Father but had lost their freedom. The Indian was used by the English and it was the red man who had to pay.

Seven Cherokee Indian chiefs brought to London in 1730 to meet George II by Scots lawyer Sir Alexander Cuming, self-appointed head of the Cherokee nation. (The British Museum)

In the years before the Revolutionary War, Lord Dunmore, Governor of Virginia, writing to the British government about settlers' demands for more Indian land, caught the attitude of these frontiersmen towards the Indians who shared the forest:

> ... they do not conceive that the government has any right to forbid their taking possession of a vast tract of country ... which serves only as a shelter for a few scattered tribes of Indians ... whom they consider as little removed from the brute Creation.

TALES OF THE WILD FRONTIER

The increasing tension between settler and Indian often exploded into open warfare, and by selecting just three episodes from the dozens of recorded incidents involving Scots and Ulster Scots in the second half of the eighteenth century, we can gauge the climate of fear and violence which permeated life on the frontier.

### Slaughter at Draper's Meadow

James Patton, an Ulster Scot, set off in 1748 to explore south-west Virginia and land now in Tennessee. With him he took Thomas Inglis and his three sons, and Mrs Draper and her son and daughter. These hardy folk found a spot on the New River for their settlement and called it Draper's Meadow.

Inglis set up a ferry service, and the little community was soon joined by other Ulster-Scots families, including the Crocketts, Sayers, Cloyds, McGavocks and McCalls. The surrounding land was rich, the settlement prospered. Crops were good, marriages took place and children were born: the future seemed set fair. Even with news of an Indian uprising in the north in 1755, nobody was unduly concerned. Draper's Meadow seemed a world away from the troubles. However, one July afternoon, while most of the men were harvesting and the women were busy with household chores, a band of Indians attacked the cluster of cabins. James Patton was still at the Inglis house and seems to have given a good account of himself—two brawny Indians were found beside his body, cut down by his sword.

Mrs John Draper was wounded as she tried to escape with her baby, which was snatched from her arms and dashed against a log. Mrs Inglis was also captured and every cabin set alight. The ordeal for the women was just beginning. Mrs Inglis gave birth to a child three days after her capture but was forced to abandon the infant in making a break for freedom in Kentucky. Keeping to the river banks and living off berries and shrubs, she sheltered occasionally from the rain under fallen trees. After forty days in the wilderness she stumbled, half-starved and with her clothes in rags, into a clearing with a cabin. Remarkably she was only a few miles from her home.

## Morodock's Long Search

Filled with hope and expectation, Morodock Otis McKenzie (b. 1738) sailed from Glasgow to Virginia as a teenager. Like the Draper's Meadow folk, Morodock ended up on the New River at Wolf Creek in 1778. One morning, failing to hear the bells on his animals, Morodock thought the beasts must have wandered back to their old home on Walker's Creek, so he set off in pursuit with his eldest son, Isaac. In fact, the Indians had stolen the beasts and watched the men leave from close by the house.

Henley, the second eldest son, was working in the potato field near the McKenzie's cabin and as soon as the Indians thought the two older men were out of earshot, they killed him. They burst into the house and in the struggle the mother, two daughters and a baby were killed; ten-year-old Peggy and eight-year-old Betsy were taken captive and dragged off to Ohio.

Peggy was destined to be a captive for eighteen years. Their ordeal began when the sisters refused bread cut with the knife which had killed their mother. Eventually Peggy adapted to Indian life, learning the languages of the Shawnee and Delawares, having been adopted by their chief, Kootthumpum. While with the Delawares, she married a man called John Kinzie, a silversmith and fur trader who was actually the son of a British army surgeon, John McKenzie, a member of father Morodock's own clan.

After several fruitless trips north, Morodock eventually found Peggy in 1796 near Detroit, and she returned to the New River settlement with him. Betsy came back that same year, having also married a Scotsman called Clarke, by whom she had two children.

## Siege of the Blockhouse

In the late 1700s, news of Indian uprisings in the backwoods meant that families usually congregated at the nearest stockade and blockhouse. On this occasion, fifteen frontiersmen, their wives and children hurried to John Buchanan's station about four miles south of Nashville (TN). Within hours they were under siege by a party of 400 Cherokees and Creeks, who launched a barrage of fire against the timber keep and crept up to try to set the building alight. One Indian even managed to clamber on to the roof with a blazing torch before being shot.

The settlers kept up a steady fusillade, and by morning the raiders had drifted away. Miraculously, none of the pioneers within the stockade had been injured, but they emerged to find the timber ramparts riddled with musket balls. They also found evidence of heavy Indian casualties and, unfortunately, indications that two young men who had ventured out just before the siege to assess the strength of the war party had been killed. All that was ever found of the men was a mocassin and a handkerchief.

Stories of entire families wiped out in Indian attacks were common. The Clendennins (Glendennings when they left Scotland) crossed the Alleghenies in 1760 to settle in what is now West Virginia, establishing the most westerly outpost of 'civilisation' at this time. This was a danger zone and no mistake. Shawnee Indians annihilated the Clendennin clan in a brutal raid—the only survivor was the mother, who was taken captive.

The situation had deteriorated to such an extent that a natural death on the frontier caused more comment and interest among the settlers than did another Indian atrocity. This slaughter went on into the nineteenth century along the flexible frontier from Maine to Mexico.

A 'brave and adventurous spirit' is how the Texan histories describe Neil McLennan, who immigrated to North Carolina from the Scottish Highlands in 1801 at the age of twenty-four. Moving to Florida, he remained there for twenty years before his wanderlust was sparked again by tales of Texas. With his brothers and a few friends, he bought a schooner and sailed to the Brazos River in 1835, settling at Pond Creek, now Falls County.

While making fence rails, McLennan's brother, Laughlin, was 'shot full of arrows' during an attack; his wife and three small boys were hauled away as captives and the house was burned to the ground. Neil's other brother also died in a separate Indian ambush. The Scotsman's life was then dedicated to stamping out Indian uprisings and, after joining Erath Milam's County Company, he bought land on the south bank of the Bosque River, eight miles from Waco, in a county which now bears his name.

Bravery, self-assurance and resilience were all needed by the early Scottish pioneering families and often it was the womenfolk who were left, quite literally, holding the fort. John Anderson, who never lost his Scots brogue despite years in America, was born in August 1771, in a village on the outskirts of Glasgow. He arrived in the New World with his parents, and the hardships of frontier life were hammered home when his father was killed by Indians in Upper New York during the Revolutionary War. John, with his mother and sisters, was taken captive to Montreal.

In the 1790s, Anderson came to the Detroit area, where he succeeded as a trader in the Maumee region. He built a substantial trading post, established himself as a major figure in River Raisin politics, and was perhaps the first English-speaking settler in the area then called Frenchtown, now Monroe.

In August 1812, war with Great Britain forced him to flee the district because, as a colonel in the Michigan Territorial Militia, he was a target for vengeful Indians. He left the trading post in the care of his remarkable wife, Elizabeth. After the wholesale slaughter at the Battle of the River Raisin in January 1813, rampaging tribesmen in Monroe burst into the trading post and found Mrs Anderson, sitting on a chest containing the family savings and with her son, Alexander Duncan Anderson, then three-years-old, sitting on her knee. One Indian waved a tomahawk in her face and threatened to scalp her. Instead of shrinking back, Elizabeth defiantly opened the top button of her dress and invited the Indian to strike. A biography of the Anderson family written when memories of Indian atrocities were still fresh, saluted her heroism:

The red man appreciates and admires courage even in his bitterest enemy and the defiance of the white woman filled this savage with admiration. He put up his tomahawk, caught her by the hand and said: 'You brave squaw; me no kill you.'

## THE LATER INDIAN WARS

In 1838 in Ohio, James Forsyth, who was destined to play a controversial role in the concluding Indian wars, was born. As a major-general, he gained fame during the Civil War on the staff of another soldier with a Scots background, George McLellan. A series of successful actions saw him placed in command of a Cavalry brigade, and he joined the pursuit of the Army of Virginia which ended in Lee's surrender at Appomattox.

After the Civil War, the enemy was the Indian. Forsyth reported to Fort Riley in Kansas where, by 1887, he was commandant. Late in 1890, when the Sioux took to the warpath under Big Foot—Sitting Bull's warriors who had fought at the Little Big Horn in 1876 had joined Big Foot after their chief's death—it was James Forsyth who led out the Seventh Cavalry. On 28 December the troops found Big Foot's band at Wounded Knee Creek, in the Pine Ridge reservation of South Dakota.

Called on to surrender, the Sioux gave up some small arms but a search of the village uncovered another forty weapons. Egged on by a medicine man who harangued the warriors by insisting that their ghost shirts would save them from the soldiers' bullets, the tension began to rise. The battle, in which 200 Indians and forty Cavalrymen were killed, began when the medicine man tossed a handful of dirt in the air. Outnumbered, the Sioux fought ferociously, even the squaws beating bluecoats to the ground with clubs.

Throughout the United States there were cries of 'massacre' and 'vengeance for the Little Big Horn', and Forsyth was suspended from duty pending an investigation. It was said that Forsyth's men had been in positions where they shot each other and killed squaws and babies. However, Forsyth was completely cleared and restored to his command. This sequel to the Little Big Horn extinguished, once and for all, the fighting spirit of the Sioux nation.

Further south, in New Mexico, regular clashes had been taking place between Scots ranchers and roving bands of Indians. Many of them went unreported, but the more serious found their way—often in the briefest form—into the local paper. *The Grant County Herald* carried a despatch on 11 October 1879 telling of the fate of one American Scot in this out-of-the-way corner of the States. It simply read:

> The mail carrier reports this morning that R.D. McEvers and four men were killed by Indians yesterday. Also that McEvers' ranche, this side of Hillsboro, was destroyed.

General William Sherman once described Brigadier-General George Crook, an able military man descended from Scots and German ancestors, as

America's greatest Indian-fighter. He was a hard campaigner but also recognised as one of the most humane commanders during the Indian wars, risking his life on several occasions to see that the US lived up to its treaty obligations. Crook was born in 1828 in Ohio, and like Forsyth rose through the ranks in the Civil War. He served against Indians in Idaho (1866–72), in Arizona (1872–75) and crushed the great rising in Wyoming and Montana (1875–77).

When Crook arrived in Arizona in the aftermath of the Camp Grant Massacre, the settlers fully expected him to pursue a policy of exterminating the Apache tribe. However, he stunned them by expressing sympathy for Apache problems. Crook has been described as a strong, silent man with keen, blue-gray eyes (Apaches knew him as Grey Wolf). He stood over six foot, 'straight as a lance'. He closely questioned all his officers about local conditions before embarking on his campaign, and became skilled in sign language. Despite growing accusations that he was an 'Indian-lover', he pressed ahead and was successful in rooting out Geronimo from his mountain retreat. When Geronimo fled again, Crook's soft line was blamed and he was replaced. However, a junior officer paid tribute to him:

> There was never an officer in our military service so completely in accord with all the ideas, views and opinions of the savages who he had to fight to control.

Crook's policy that 'peace was best' was declared at every opportunity, and while he showed understanding and compassion for the plight of the native tribes, he was, paradoxically, one of the greatest scourges of the renegades.

As one by one the tribes bowed to the military superiority of the army and offered themselves up to dependency, sad tales aplenty emerged. Morayshire-born James 'Scotty' Philip—an adventurer and rancher who settled in Kansas in the late 1800s and was brother-in-law of the famous Oglala Sioux chief, Crazy Horse—told of the arrival at Fort Robinson of a band of 100 Cheyenne who wished to surrender. Scotty recalled:

> I doubt if 100 men could be found in the West who would be superior to that band of 100. They were kept around the fort for six months. At the end of that time they were broken in spirit and health. They could never be the same again . . . That's what happened to the Indian . . .

### APACHE ARCHIE

The Apache branch of the Clan MacIntosh was created by Archie McIntosh, one of the greatest Indian scouts of the Old West, who was born in Canada in 1834, the son of a Chippewa mother and a Scots father. Civilian scouts have become figures of excitement through their portrayal in Westerns, but Archie was a larger-than-life character. After two years' education in Scotland, he joined the Oregon cavalry and his service record tells us that

The tired and gaunt faces of these farming families from the Williamson and Riggs stations in Minnesota tell the story of the 1862 Sioux Uprising, which they are fleeing. The girl in centre foreground is wrapped in a tartan plaid. (Adrian J. Ebell, Minnesota Historical Society)

he was five foot eight inches in height, of dark complexion, with hazel eyes and black hair. We also learn that

> . . . near the North Fork of the John Day River, in the State of Oregon, 10th day of September, 1864, he incurred an injury to his right leg, knee and hip, caused by his horse falling on him while chasing an Indian to get a better shot at!

Archie distinguished himself in a series of campaigns against the Columbia River Indians and as his reputation grew he was offered a post with General George Crook. Among the tribesmen he was considered almost superhuman, and when he led a regiment thirty miles across the desert in a blinding blizzard, right to the gates of the fort, his white comrades dubbed him the 'bloodhound'. Archie admitted that the trick had been simply to keep the wind on his right cheek for nine long hours. He later agreed that

> If the wind had changed its direction ten degrees my goose would have been cooked.

After moving to Arizona, where he showed his talent for survival in wilderness by fighting in campaigns against the Tonto and San Carlos Apaches, Archie's fondness for the Indian home brews (tulapai and tizwin) saw him fall by the wayside. He even announced, optimistically, in *The Arizona Weekly Miner* in 1875, that he had sworn off drink for ten years. But brew got the better of him, and he ended up a sad old man separated from his Apache wife, Domingo, and his son, Donald.

Other MacIntoshes are to be found among the Indian nations and in the histories of the West. Daniel MacIntosh was yet another of the Scottish Creeks, and he led his followers into the Confederate Army in the Civil War. Lieutenant Donald MacIntosh, half-Scot and half-Iroquois, was killed with Custer at the Little Big Horn.

When Peter Campbell and his family left Scotland after the close of the Civil War to seek their fortune in Nebraska, hardships shared by so many of the Scottish agricultural immigrants to the West awaited. The family—father, mother, four sisters and three brothers—built a one-room house covered with sod and chinked with mud, some ten miles from the present-day town of Grand Island. The long, hard winter of 1865–66 took its toll. Mrs Campbell, though frail, had survived the exhausting journey but died while the valley of the River Platte was in the icy grip of winter.

By 1867, Peter had taken out his naturalisation papers, barns were built, the land ploughed and crops planted. Corn, wheat and oats were soon growing. The settlers were thinly spread along the valley in those pioneering days, no more than a dozen families in a ten-mile stretch. When the harvest began six miles from the Campbell homestead, Peter and his eldest son, J.R., went to help their neighbours. In J.R.'s account of that day he tells how, in mid-afternoon, a rider was seen coming full tilt along the valley:

> The reaper was still and golden sheaves were left unbound and all hurried to learn the oft-dreaded news—Indians had raided the valley.

The Campbells took to their horses, and at their nearest neighbour found the woman of the house lying dead on her doorstep, clasping her infant in her arms. A few feet away lay her fourteen-year-old son, shot through the thigh. At their own farm they found the house ransacked and partly demolished, the contents scattered around the yard—but there was no sign of the children. Two of Peter's nieces, aged seventeen and nineteen, and twin boys aged four had been carried away. The youngest girl, aged nine, had hidden in a grain field, and by crawling on her hands and knees for quarter of a mile, then running for four miles, she had raised the alarm.

A search of the neighbourhood revealed nothing, and most of the settlers decided to abandon this stretch of the valley, since the company of soldiers at Fort Kearney were scarcely able to protect the fort, let alone farms scattered along the valley.

However, the Campbells decided to stay put, in the hope that there might be word of the kidnapped youngsters. A further search ranging twenty-five miles round the homestead was undertaken, but still no sign. Then on 20 October news came from Grand Island that the boys and girls had been seen in the camp of a band of Oglala Sioux in south-eastern Colorado. The government is said to have paid 4,000 dollars for their release.

The first Scot on record in Colorado was Duncan Blair, a big, brawny Perthshire man said to have settled on the White River near Meeker in the mid-1850s, when legends like Carson, Wootton and Baker were the only white men in the mountains. He married a squaw who was related to the great Indian chief, Ouray, and Blair was considered a friend and counsellor of the tribes. The story of Blair and of his affection for the Indians, which even landed him in jail, is a romantic tale of the Old West. For decades he hunted, and was in turn hunted by renegade Ute war parties.

It was on one such expedition that he met his wife. Hearing cries and groans from the bottom of a deep arroyo near where he was camped, Duncan found an Indian girl and her horse lying in a heap, having apparently fallen into the canyon the previous day. The horse had been killed but the woman, knocked unconscious, was trapped by her fallen mount. He freed her and took her back to his isolated cabin, nursing her back to health.

In the spectacular Rocky Mountains of Montana lies McDonald's Lake. Duncan McDonald was from a Ross and Cromarty family, and was in charge of a Hudson's Bay trading post in the area in 1874 when he was asked to freight supplies to Canada. Hostile Indians forced him off his normal route and into unknown territory to the east. Accompanied by a group of Selish Indians, he came across the lake and camped overnight by its shores. While there, he carved his name on the bark of a birch. Previously the stretch of water had been known, as Terry Lake, but more and more people saw the carving on the tree and it became commonly known as McDonald's Lake— the name stuck. Duncan, a Montana legend, adopted the language, garb and manners of the Indians. Helen Sanders, in a profile, wrote:

> ... their picturesque paganism likewise found a responsive chord in his fancy ... he believed in the transmigration of the soul and was often heard to say that when death closed his mortal career he desired to become a wild white horse with free range over the boundless plains.

A SPRINT FOR LIFE

Pierce County in Washington, near the present-day city of Tacoma, was the site chosen by Scots shepherd Peter Smith and his wife, Martha, for their new home in the Pacific Northwest. They came overland in 1852–53 to Oregon Territory from Wisconsin, and Peter left his wife at Portland (OR) while he went north to stake his claim. On his return, he found his wife had presented him with a baby daughter, and Belle was the name they chose for her.

As soon as they reached, Pierce County, Peter began the task of clearing the land and building a house, helped by his neighbours. In the Smith family's dealings with the local Indians we learn most of their trail-blazing lifestyle. Martha Smith traded pieces of jewellery and clothing in exchange

Looking less than comfortable in his collar and tie is Duncan McDonald, a Montana pioneer from a Ross and Cromarty family who lived most of his life among the Indians and has a Rocky Mountain lake named after him. (National Park Service)

for dried fish, and the whole family began to learn the Chinook jargon. The Indians, according to Peter, were a friendly crew, and often enjoyed a meal at the Smith house.

In those early years, Peter became the guardian of an old Indian woman. Old Dotsie's husband had died of black smallpox, and because she had nursed him the tribe were in the act of burying her alive in her husband's grave when Peter happened along and told the Indians he would take care of her. She was with the family for several years and called herself 'Peter Smith's slave'.

The Puyallup and Nisqually Indian tribes were constantly at war, and in 1860 a warrior burst into the Smith home asking for a hiding place. His Puyallup pursuers soon arrived and demanded the boy for scalping. Quick thinking by Peter averted an immediate crisis. A champion runner in Scotland, Peter asked and was allowed to keep the boy for two weeks to coach him in running. The deal was that if, after this period, the boy could run faster than his enemies, the Puyallups would free him.

Peter then launched into an intensive training course, trying to give the young brave a good running action and teaching him to improve his breathing. On the appointed day there was a big turn-out of Puyallup tribesmen, all anticipating an easy scalping. The boy was given a 100-yard start, as per the agreement, and the others set off in pursuit. Peter's time with the lad had been well spent because the boy reached the top of Melville Springs Hill well ahead of his pursuers. The last Peter saw of his protégé was the Nisqually warrior turning to wave goodbye to his trainer.

Surely the most spectacular cinema portrayal of the unspoiled West in the late twentieth century is the Academy Award-winning *Dances with Wolves*. The central character is an army lieutenant who arranges to be posted to the Dakotas, where he hopes to see the frontier before it vanishes. Slowly drawn to the culture and traditions of the Sioux Indians, he shares the lives of the plains Indians and their fears over the coming of the white man. The strong Scottish connection with the native American is reflected in the name chosen by the writers for this lone adventurer—Lieutenant John Dunbar.

*Chapter 10* 

# SLUMBERERS – ONE PACE FORWARD!

S URVIVAL WAS UNQUESTIONABLY the priority for most Scots in the early days of American settlement. Getting through one day to the next without starving, being scalped, devoured by wild animals, eaten alive by insects, baked or frozen (depending on the season), or catching a selection of the mostly-fatal diseases that were widely found, was an achievement in its own right. Superfluous is the only way to describe 'artistic pastimes' such as painting, music, poetry or writing. Even in the coastal towns, culture was at a premium for many decades. But creativity had not been left in the old country—it was simply slumbering.

We know that folk skills such as dancing, singing, handicrafts and story-telling always formed a cornerstone of the settlers' lives. But some American historians, running the rule over various ethnic groups, would have us believe that beyond these basic accomplishments the Scots immigrants and their descendants were, on the whole, an uninspired bunch; hard-working, thrifty and tough certainly, but oh so serious, devoid of any spark of creativity, flair or imagination. This flawed assessment, can of course, be traced in part to that old Scots tradition of not making a fuss, of labouring quietly and purposefully, seeking no recognition save the knowledge that the job has been well done.

Mastery of the chessboard was the unlikely route to success for George Mackenzie (1837–91), who was born at Belfield House, North Kessock, Ross and Cromarty. Educated at Aberdeen, he completed army service then won a London chess tournament in 1862, beating Anderssen, Europe's foremost chess player of the time.

The following year Mackenzie immigrated, and after another brief stint in the army (this time in New York) he took the plunge and opted for the uncertainties of life as a professional chess player. This career was always precarious and he suffered difficult times financially. At chess tournaments he cut a striking figure: tall, with a Vandyke beard and a slouch-hat, looking for all the world, according to one acquaintance, 'like a typical Southern officer'. Sadly, he was found dead, apparently from pneumonia, in the Cooper Union Hotel in New York.

In Europe, the first American authors to be widely read were Washington Irving (1783–1859) and James Fenimore Cooper (1789–1851). Irving, the son of a Presbyterian family from the island of Shapinsay in Orkney, was born in New York and his best-known work is surely 'Rip Van Winkle'. Cooper, descended from a Scots Quaker family out of New Jersey, wrote most successfully about the sea and the Red Indian.

The first Scottish 'writer' who can be traced on the wild frontier was John Lawson (1658–1711), surveyor-general of North Carolina, who was born in Aberdeen. He first published the regularly-reprinted *A New Voyage to Carolina* in 1709, and was 'cruelly murdered' by Tuscarora Indians. New Jersey-born Gilbert Imlay, was a writer of Scots pedigree who flourished in the second half of the eighteenth century, and is reckoned to be Kentucky's first novelist of note, while Perthshire-born John Melish (1771–1822) was a pioneer United States travel writer.

Hugh Brackenridge was born in Campbeltown, Argyllshire, but settled in Pittsburgh (PA) about 1782; a judge of the Supreme Court, he was also a magazine editor and novelist. Anne M'Vicar Grant (1755–1838), born in Glasgow, is considered by many to be the first American woman author of note, her poems being praised by both Sir Walter Scott and Robert Southey. Horror merchant Edgar Allan Poe (1809–1849) claimed Scots descent, as did philosopher William and novelist Henry James, the brilliant Ulster-Scots brothers. Hermann Melville, creator of *Moby Dick*, was born in New York in 1819 and came from New England Scottish stock, his grandfather, Thomas, having had a hand in the Boston Tea Party.

Joel Chandler Harris, first person to write down Negro folk literature, had Scottish forebears. Born in 1848 in Georgia, he became a journalist and author, jotting down Negro plantation speech and publishing *The Tar Baby Story*, in 1879, the first of the Uncle Remus series which became extraordinarily popular throughout American society.

THE YEAST OF CREATIVITY

We can identify Scots poets aplenty. Edinburgh's William Lyle and David Gray both settled in New York state, at Rochester and Buffalo respectively; John Burt from Riccarton in Ayrshire made America his home, and in the twentieth century Archibald MacLeish, a Pulitzer Prize winner of Scots descent, was regarded as one of America's most noted poets and critics. One of the earliest Scots poets was David Bruce, who immigrated to Maryland in 1784 before settling in Pennsylvania, and whose work was widely read in newspapers of the day.

Hew Ainslie of Bargeny Mains, Ayrshire, was considered by many to be Kentucky's most influential poet of the nineteenth century. Like Burns (who lived only a few miles away), Ainslie showed an enthusiasm for poetry in his childhood, no doubt inspired, like the bard, by the beauty of the countryside, its ballads and folklore. He was educated at Ballantrae and Ayr, then studied law but found the routine boring.

While employed as a copyist in Register House, Edinburgh he was introduced to many of the leading literary figures of the early 1800s. Having married his cousin, Janet, in 1812 he set off, alone, for America in

N. E.                                                                    Numb. 17.

# The Boston News-Letter.

## Published by Authority.

From **Monday** April 17. to **Monday** April 24. 1704.

*London Flying-Post from Decemb. 21. to 4th. 1703.*

Letters from *Scotland* bring us the Copy of a Sheet lately Printed there, Intituled, *A seasonable Alarm for Scotland. In a Letter from a Gentleman in the City, to his Friend in the Country, concerning the present Danger of the Kingdom and of the Protestant Religion.*

This Letter takes Notice, That Papists swarm in that Nation, that they traffick more avowedly than formerly, and that of late many Scores of Priests & Jesuites are come thither from France, and gone to the North, to the Highlands & other places of the Country. That the Ministers of the Highlands and North gave in large Lists of them to the Committee of the General Assembly, to be laid before the Privy-Council.

It likewise observes, that a great Number of other ill-affected persons are come over from *France*, under pretence of accepting her Majesty's Gracious Indemnity ; but, in reality, to increase Divisions in the Nation, and to entertain a Correspondence with *France* : That their ill Intentions are evident from their talking big, their owning the Interest of the pretended King *James* VIII. their secret Cabals, and their buying up of Arms and Ammunition, wherever they can find them.

To this he adds the late Writings and Actings of some disaffected persons, many of whom are for that Pretender ; that several of them have declar'd they had rather embrace Popery than conform to the present Government ; that they refuse to pray for the Queen, but use the ambiguous word Soveraign, and some of them pray in express Words for the King and Royal Family ; and the charitable and generous Prince who has shew'd them so much Kindness. He likewise takes notice of Letters, not long ago found in Cypher, & directed to a Person lately come thither from St. *Germains*.

He says that the greatest Jacobites, who will not qualifie themselves by taking the Oaths to Her Majesty, do now with the Papists and their Companions from St. *Germains* set up for the Liberty of the Subject, contrary to their own Principles, but meerly to keep up a Division in the Nation. He adds, that they aggravate those things which the People complain of, as to *England's* refusing to allow them a freedom of Trade, &c. and do all they can to foment Divisions betwixt the Nations, & to obstruct a Redress of those things complain'd of.

The Jacobites, he says, do all they can to persuade the Nation that their pretended King is a Protestant in his Heart, tho' he dares not declare it, while under the Power of *France* ; that he is acquainted with the Mistakes of his Father's Government, will govern us more according to Law, and endear himself to his Subjects.

They magnifie the Strength of their own Party, and the Weakness and Divisions of the other, in order to facilitate and hasten their Undertaking ; they argue themselves out of their Fears, and into the highest assurance of accomplishing their purpose.

From all this he infers, That they have hopes of Assistance from *France*, otherwise they would be so impudent ; and he gives Reasons for this Apprehensions that the *French* King may send Troops thither this Winter, 1. Because the *English* & *Dutch* will not then be at Sea to oppose them. 2. He can then best spare them, the Season of Action beyond Sea being over. 3. The Expectation given him of a considerable number to joyn them, may incourage him to the undertaking with fewer Men, if he can but send over a sufficient number of Officers with Arms and Ammunition.

He endeavours in the rest of his Letters to answer the foolish Pretences of the Pretender's being a Protestant, and that he will govern us according to Law. He says, that being bred up in the Religion and Politicks of *France*, he is by Education a stated Enemy to our Liberty and Religion. That the Obligations which he and his Family owe to the *French* King, must necessarily make him to be wholly at his Devotion, and to follow his Example ; that if he sit upon the Throne, the three Nations must be oblig'd to pay the Debt which he owes the *French* King for the Education of himself, and for Entertaining his supposed Father and his Family. And since the King must restore him by his Troops, if ever he be restored, he will see to secure his own Debt, before those Troops leave *Britain*. The Pretender being a good Proficient in the *French* and *Romish* Schools, he will never think himself sufficiently aveng'd, but by the utter Ruine of his Protestant Subjects, both as Hereticks and Traitors. The late Queen, his pretended Mother, who in cold Blood when she was Queen of *Britain*, advis'd to turn the West of *Scotland* into a hunting Field, will be then for doing so by the greatest part of the Nation ; and, no doubt, is at Pains to have her pretended Son educated to her own Mind : Therefore, he says, it were a great Madness in the Nation to take a Prince bred up in the horrid School of ingratitude, Persecution and Cruelty, and filled with Rage and Envy. The *Jacobites*, he says, both in *Scotland* and at St. *Germains*, are impatient under their present Straits, and knowing their Circumstances cannot be much worse than they are, at present, are the more inclinable to the Undertaking. He adds, That the *French* King knows there cannot be a more effectual way for himself to arrive at the Universal Monarchy, and to ruine the Protestant Interest, than by setting up the Pretender upon the Throne of Great *Britain*, he will in all probability attempt it ; and tho' he should be persuaded that the Design would miscarry in the close, yet he cannot but reap some Advantage by imbroiling the three Nations.

From all this the Author concludes it to be the Interest of the Nation, to provide for self defence ; and says, that as many have already taken the Alarm, and are furnishing themselves with Arms and Ammunition, he hopes the Government will not only allow it, but encourage it, since the Nation ought all to appear as one Man in the Defence

America's first newspaper, *The Boston News-Letter*, was on the streets in April 1704 and was the brainchild of American Scot, John Campbell. News is dominated by the activities of the Jacobites. (The British Library)

1822. Three years passed as he unsuccessfully tried to make a go of farming before joining Robert Owen's experimental colony at New Harmony (IN). By the time he was reunited with his family, he had moved into the brewing business. Fire and flood put paid to his own ambitious enterprises, but Ainslie then began constructing breweries and distilleries for other people. He was learning to be a philosopher as well as a poet.

Throughout his busy commercial career he continued to write poetry, often in dialect. One biographer, damning with faint praise, said Ainslie wrote three or four 'very fair lyrics' and more than a hundred very indifferent ones. Probably best remembered for his 'Pilgrimage to the Land of Burns', first published in 1822, Hew came back to Scotland for a visit forty years later and was given a hero's welcome. In his later years he settled in Louisville (KY), where his tall frame and mop of tousled hair made him one of the town's best kent faces. He died in 1878.

THE AMAZING GORDON BENNETTS

The first newspaper published in America, *The Boston News-Letter*, was on the streets on 24 April 1704, the man behind this brave venture being American-Scot John Campbell (1653–1728). He was just the first in a long line of Scottish newspapermen who have shaped and informed public opinion in America for generations, a legacy which was carried into the 1990s by the Aberdeenshire Forbes family, the eponymous owners of one of America's most prestigious and successful magazines based in New York.

Keith, Banffshire, was the birthplace of James Gordon Bennett, a giant figure in the history of the American newspaper industry. He studied for the priesthood at Aberdeen, but his devotions did not match his interest in literature and in the spring of 1819 he left for America. Hard times awaited: later in life he would tell of avoiding starvation by finding a coin in the gutter.

In New York, Bennett started submitting articles to city newspapers and his work was noticed by the owner of *The Courier* in Charleston (SC). A visit to the South gave him a chance to see slavery in action, and he was always sympathetic to the Southern viewpoint thereafter. Bennett worked his way up the journalistic ladder, his big break coming in 1826 when the associate editor of *The New York Enquirer* fell in a duel, a not uncommon end for newsmen in those days. Working in New York and Washington, he soon gained a reputation for his perceptive sketches of leading American political figures.

As associate editor of *The Courier and Enquirer* in New York, Bennett brought the paper to life defending the right of the Press to report trials without permission of the courts, contending that newspapers were the 'living jury of the nation'. A failed attempt to publish *The New York Globe* was followed on 6 May 1835 by the publication of the first edition of *The New York Herald*. His office was in a cellar at 20 Wall Street, where a plank of wood across two flour barrels served as his editorial desk. He took on

J.J. Burke, a pioneer newspaper man of the American West, was born in Ayr in 1855. In the early years of this century, he and his son guided *The Transcript* in Norman (OK), which was noted for its outspoken editorials. The picture shows Burke in the caseroom in 1912. (Norman Transcript)

all the tasks connected with the paper, from tea boy to managing editor, and loved to describe himself as 'one poor man in a cellar against the world'. Disclaiming all political ties, the paper was an immediate success. Working a sixteen-hour day, Bennett's bold criticism of big business saw him assaulted more than once in the street. He told friends this must mean he was doing his job.

Bennett maintained a remarkable work schedule—he rose at five, writing his 'leaders, squibs and sketches' before breakfast; from nine till one he read newspapers and edited copy, wrote a column of news, received callers; he then went to Wall Street and wrote his money article, dined at four, read proofs, took in cash and adverts and was in bed by ten.

One critic, struggling to express his loathing of Bennett, described him as 'an obscene foreign vagabond, a pestilential scoundrel, ass, rogue, habitual liar, a loathsome and leprous slanderer and libeller'. Bennett loved it. The newspaper prospered and Bennett launched a series of campaigns for reporters to be allowed into the galleries of Congress.

To keep a step ahead of his rivals, he maintained a fleet of despatch boats up to 250 miles off the coast to intercept steamers from Europe and hasten news to shore. *The Herald* was also the first paper to make lavish use of the telegraph. Bennett once demanded that chapters from the Bible be filed to keep rivals off the line. During the Civil War the newspaper employed sixty-three war correspondents. Bennett died on 25 May 1872 and is buried in Greenwood Cemetery, Brooklyn (NY).

James Gordon Bennett Jr. (1841–1918) was educated in Europe, to avoid the daily verbal and physical attacks on his father. He served with the Federal Navy in the Civil War then moved with a 'fast set' of New York bachelors. It was young James who despatched Stanley on the trail of David Livingstone and financed a search for the North-West Passage. During a winter of economic panic (1873–74) *The Herald* opened soup kitchens for the poor in the slums of New York.

However, his increasingly eccentric behaviour forced several top newsmen to leave the paper. Once, on a whim, he decided to promote the first of his reporters he met on the street to city editor. As the orders became more outlandish, staff became more demoralised.

Due to be married to the daughter of a prominent Washington family, the engagement was called off in mysterious circumstances. His ex-fiance's brother attacked Bennett with a horsewhip outside the Union Club on Fifth Avenue, and a duel followed on the Delaware-Maryland border in which shots were exchanged harmlessly. Bennett loved yachting, introduced polo to Newport (RI) in the 1870s, encouraged aeroplane and balloon-racing, he loved dogs and owls and gave enormous tips. It is reckoned he spent 30,000,000 dollars from the earnings of *The Herald*.

Scots-interest newspapers flourished in the United States during the nineteenth century. According to Berthoff, from 1857 until 1919 the *Scottish-American Journal*—owned and edited for almost its entire span by Archibald M. Stewart—served as many as 15,000 subscribers. A New York rival, *The Scotsman*, (apparently combined with *The Caledonian Advertiser* in 1874) survived only from 1869 to 1886; and another weekly, John Adamson's *Boston Scotsman* from 1906 to 1914. A literary monthly, *The Caledonian*, appeared between 1901 and 1923. Today *The Highlander* and *The Scottish Banner* serve the vast American-Scots community.

Arguably Horace Greeley, another journalist with Scots roots, founder and editor of *New York Tribune*, was even more influential than the Bennetts. In a historic open-letter editorial to Abraham Lincoln in 1862, known as the 'Prayer to Twenty Millions', he asked the President to take a stand on slavery. Greeley ran unsuccessfully for president as a Democrat in 1872.

In the twentieth century among the Scots newsmen are Robert McCormick, publisher of *The Chicago Tribune*, and James 'Scotty' Reston, Pulitzer Prize-winning writer who was born in Scotland but made his name internationally with his syndicated *New York Times* column.

While Scotland can claim credit for cranking up the American newspaper industry, it must also, if reluctantly, lay claim to the infamous wordsmith who is said to have launched 'yellow journalism', the gutter press. James

Thompson Callender (d.1806), professional libeller and blackmailer, was an immigrant who took cash for persistently libelling the founding fathers of the United States—George Washington, Alexander Hamilton, John Adams and Thomas Jefferson. According to one historian, he was

> ... as destitute of principle as of money, his talents which were not despicable were ever up for sale. The question with him was never what he wrote but what he was to be paid for writing.

## EDITORIAL STRUGGLES

Dalkeith-born printer and publisher Robert Aitken (1734–1802) is first found in America at Philadelphia (PA), where he had set himself up as a bookseller. A few years later, he was publishing *The Pennsylvania Magazine* which had the illustrious radical Tom Paine among its contributors. Occasionally Paine (like so many gifted and temperamental columnists) was late with his copy, and Aitken found it necessary to seat him at a table with a supply of paper and brandy and insist that he stay put until the article was finished. By Whitelaw Reid's account, it seems that what Paine produced from 'the inspiration of brandy' was perfectly fit for publication without editing.

Among Aitken's other successes were engravings showing some of the first views of the Revolutionary War. He also printed the 'Aitken Bible', the first complete English Bible printed in America, this being made necessary when war halted the import of bibles from Britain. Despite official backing, this enterprise failed. Described as an 'industrious and frugal Scot' it is interesting that Aitken was succeeded in his business by his daughter Jane, who 'obtained much reputation by productions which issued from her press'.

In colonial days, Scots are found at the centre of newspaper development in the Carolinas, Virginia and Georgia. In the 1750s, James Robertson learned the trade of printer from his father in Edinburgh; still a teenager he then went to Boston where he and his brother Alexander started *The New York Chronicle*, which survived for a year. In 1771 his next enterprise was *The Albany Gazette*, also in New York state, and he had an interest in papers in Connecticut.

The Loyalist sympathies of the brothers Robertson were widely known and, as the revolution approached, their printing press and types were given to a friend who buried them on a farm outside Albany.

On the outbreak of hostilities in 1775, James moved back to New York where he published *The Royal American Gazette* and followed the British Army to Philadelphia in 1778, where he set up *The Royal Pennsylvania Gazette*. After the conflict most New York Loyalists moved to Canada, and in Nova Scotia James continued publishing *The Royal American Gazette* for a time before returning to his native city of Edinburgh, where he remained in printing until 1810—his life and business career had gone full circle.

Problems for editors in the Wild West were just as weighty. William Byers, Ohio-born into an American-Scots family who traced the arrival of their ancestors to before the Revolutionary War, was editor of the *Rocky Mountain News* in the booming frontier town of Denver (CO) in the mid-1850s. Editorial fearlessness in those lawless days could carry dire consequences. In his columns he regularly lambasted a group of outlaws who were threatening to take over the town from their base in the Criterion saloon. After one particularly pointed attack, two gang members burst into the office and dragged Willie off to the bar where (according to Francis Melrose) they threatened to 'stop his attacks by stopping his breath'. Escaping out the back door, Byers had just returned to the office when one of the outlaws galloped past the front door, firing shots wildly as he went. Two *News* reporters returned fire but no one was hit. From then on, according to Francis Melrose, rifles stood in readiness near the type cases, and it was said the canny Scot chose future employees partly on their journalistic skills and partly on the ability to shoot straight.

Out in the Midwest competition was fierce for the would-be newspaper editor/publisher. For instance, in the town of Aurora (MO)—which has several Scots and Ulster-Scots connections—there were, in the spring of 1899, three daily, three weekly and a monthly newspaper . . . this for a town with a population of a few thousand. Today, only *The Aurora Advertiser* survives. Newspapers were a high-risk business in those uncertain days, and many a Scots newspaperman could be found wandering from town to town. When threats became too menacing or creditors crowded the door, often the only answer was to load the printing press and type box on a wagon at dead of night and head off to try your luck in another county or state.

Yet still they came. Renton, Dunbartonshire, was the home ground of Andrew McLean, who arrived in the United States in 1863, having worked his passage on the barque *Agra* and immediately enlisted for war service. He is remembered as founder and editor of the influential *Brooklyn Citizen*, as a strong supporter of the Democratic cause and a brilliant after-dinner speaker. Robert Mackenzie, born in Dublin of Scots parents, had the distinction in 1834 of being the first, regular salaried correspondent of an American newspaper, *The New York Evening Star*.

THE COW CONTROVERSY

Immediately after the Civil War, New York swarmed with society folk determined to surround themselves with what they considered culture. In this frenzied atmosphere the indomitable Hart brothers, Scots-born painters-in-oil, flourished.

James McDougall Hart (1828–1901), the younger brother, was born at Kilmarnock, and when the family moved to New York state he was still a child. Serving his apprenticeship with a sign and banner painter at Albany (NY), he moved on to portrait work before setting off to study his craft in Europe. His speciality, his trademark almost, was to fill his wonderfully atmospheric landscapes with farmyard animals. He liked to include cattle especially, and New York society people liked to pride themselves on being able to distinguish between the different breeds in Hart's paintings. However, these skills did not impress everyone. His brother, William, was once moved to remark on hearing someone lavishing praise on James's brushwork: 'James, he's a fair mon, but he cannot paint a coo!'

James Hart is said to have loved the pastoral tranquility of south-eastern New York state and tried to encourage a love of the countryside in others, according to the *American Dictionary of Biography*. But this was a confusing period, and how much his clients valued the content and quality of his paintings, and how much simple possession of works of art mattered, we can only guess.

Brother William began his career in art by painting panels on coaches, and ended up as president of the Brooklyn Academy and the American Water Color Society. At the age of eighteen he was charging five dollars apiece for portraits painted in his father's woodshed. After a visit to Scotland, he opened a studio in New York. Sharing his brother's passion for the rural beauties of New York, he belonged to what has been called 'The Hudson River School'. Art experts of today will tell you that his style is notable for its minute attention to detail. He died in 1894.

Scotland can fairly claim the first painter of note in America in the shape of Edinburgh-born James Smibert (1684–1751), who immigrated in 1728 and settled at Boston where he specialised and achieved success as a portrait painter. Between 1725 and 1751 he painted many of New England's magistrates and ministers.

Among the Scots at Perth Amboy in East New Jersey was the painter, John Watson. Gilbert Stuart, born at Rhode Island in 1755, was the son of an immigrant from Perth and was the foremost American painter of the late eighteenth century. His portraits include Presidents Washington, Adams, Jefferson, Madison, Monroe, and John Quincy Adams, Kings George III and IV and Louis XVII of France. In 1772 he went to Scotland with his tutor Cosmo Alexander, also Scots born, but soon after Alexander died and young Stuart had to work his passage home.

Birds and seashells was the forte of engraver Alexander Lawson (1773–1846), who was born at the farm of Ravenstruthers in Lanarkshire. He began his career as a boy, using a penknife and smooth halfpenny, and went to the United States in 1794, again finding a base in Philadelphia. When fellow Scot Alexander Wilson showed interest in publishing a definitive book on American birdlife, Lawson offered to engrave the plates for less than a dollar a day, declaring it was all 'for the old country'. Wilson's classic work was issued in nine volumes and is still considered a masterpiece.

Paisley-born Walter Shirlaw, first president of the Society of American Artists, is remembered as the first American artist successfully to paint the nude. Sculptor John Crookshanks King, who hailed from Kilwinning in Ayrshire and died at Boston in 1882, produced a fine series of busts—among them Daniel Webster, John Quincy Adams and Ralph Waldo Emerson—which gave him the reputation for a time as America's most distinguished exponent of the fine chisel. Sculptors of Scots descent were involved in a variety of civic projects—statues, bronze doors and busts—from San Francisco to New York.

The late 1800s found William Keith wandering the high passes of the Rocky Mountains, completing a series of drawings of the route for the Northern Pacific Railroad, a far cry from his home ground in Old Meldrum, Aberdeenshire. He reached America in the mid-1800s and became entranced by the mountains and the sea. He began producing black and white sketches of the west coast and the Sierras before launching into spectacular landscapes. Like his countryman, the environmentalist John Muir, he was a passionate enthusiast for the natural world and the two men trekked together through the hills. Keith died in 1911 and his best paintings are probably of the giant redwood trees; there was scarcely a mountain range in California he hadn't trekked through, and even in his old age he made an annual trip to Yosemite from his Berkeley home.

EAVESDROPPING ON ULYSSES

East Lothian has produced many famous sons and daughters, but as far as American journalism is concerned, above them all stand John and William Swinton of Saltoun.

John had given thought to life in the church but left the seminary with the idea of going into newspaper journalism. He trekked around the Midwest gaining experience and, back in New York, casual contributions landed him a job on *The New York Times*. He held various senior editorial posts in the city and became interested in 'wage workers', even standing unsuccessfully for mayor as a candidate of the Industrial Political Party. He produced a brilliantly written four-page labour journal which never caught on, acted as correspondent for half a dozen European newspapers, and was a great friend of Karl Marx. A strong advocate of organisation for others, Swinton paradoxically was a bit of a loner, always denying that he was a socialist.

His brother William, war correspondent extraordinary, had also (somewhat oddly in the light of the career that stretched out in front of him) prepared for the ministry, but having taught in New York and North Carolina he landed a job with *The New York Times*. Swinton was a front-line correspondent in the Civil War and gained a reputation for his hard-hitting criticism of the Federal generals and their tactics. As a result, he was none too popular among the top brass and was

*By the Creek, Sonoma* by William Keith, from Old Meldrum, Aberdeenshire. The silvan glade which could easily be mistaken for Royal Deeside is, in fact, in California, where Keith settled. (The Corcoran Gallery of Art, Museum Purchase, Gallery Fund 11.11)

universally reckoned to be a 'tough operator' who sought to secure privileges with methods which, according to his critics, smacked of blackmail. He was prepared to do anything—legal or otherwise—to secure his story.

Early in the Virginia campaign of 1864, one of Ulysses Grant's staff officers hauled Swinton out of a cupboard where he was hiding and listening to a conversation between Grant and General George Meade. Not surprisingly the War Department's patience soon ran out and he was deprived of his correspondent's privileges—a very serious measure—and ordered away from the front line.

He wrote several books on the war and in 1869 became Professor of English at the University of California, but was again in conflict with authority and had to resign in 1874. He then turned to writing textbooks for geography students, spelling books, readers, grammars and histories, gaining a gold medal at the Paris Exposition of 1878 for his work. Swinton spent his last years in Brooklyn (NY). A hard worker, he was financially scatter-brained and had to dispose of valuable copyrights for a pittance to see his family through difficult times. He died in 1892.

KENNEDY ON THE FIDDLE

David Kennedy's prowess on the fiddle not only gained him many friends in Moore County (NC) but was also instrumental in helping the expansion of his famous gun-manufacturing business. The Kennedy family fled Scotland during the Jacobite troubles, and David's father had been a Revolutionary soldier and gun-maker who fashioned a 'Kennedy' rifle which helped the colonies gain independence.

Beginning his business in 1795 at a site which became known as Mechanics' Hill, David was soon employing seventy-five people. Various types of guns and swords were made in the factory, and the finer rifles are said to have been embellished with silver melted from silver dollars. Although he only played the fiddle at family get-togethers and dances, David was to find that his musical talent was of value in the commercial world when, weary of paying exhorbitant prices for gun locks which he imported from New York, he made a horseback journey to the 'Nawthern factory'.

Kennedy learned that the method used in making locks was a mysterious, closely-guarded secret. For a moment he was stumped, then he remembered his fiddle which he had brought with him. His knowledge of human nature and of the effect of his music on his Moore County neighbours sparked an ingenious idea. Over a period, he skilfully 'wrought heart-deep melodies on his violin' according to his biography and 'played his way into the confidence of the employees'. Disarmed by his nifty bow work and his Southern yarns, they allowed him inside the shop; that meant he was privy to the great secret and, with ears and eyes open widest, he observed the process.

When he returned to Mechanics' Hill, it was no longer necessary for David to import locks—he made his own. Kennedy rifles, with their handsome stocks, are much sought after by collectors.

This Scots love of music, which was brought across the Atlantic, was even to play a minor but dramatic role in the creation of the Mormon state of Utah. Professor Fred Buchanan of the University of Utah explains that in 1858 peace commissioners were negotiating with Brigham Young, the Mormon leader, regarding the positioning of Federal forces in Utah. During the meeting word was received that the army was on the move and Young, no doubt intending to impress the commissioners, called on David Dunbar, a Scots immigrant, to sing 'Zion', the lyrics of which include

> In thy mountain retreat
> God will strengthen thy feet;
> On the necks of thy foes
> thou shalt tread . . .

The commissioners were suitably influenced and after a few stormy sessions a deal was struck without bloodshed. 'Zion' was written in England in 1856 by Charles W. Penrose and originally sung to a Scottish tune 'O Minnie, O Minnie, Come o'er the Lea'.

Bill Duncan of Lander (WY) recalls that the arrival of a musician from the old country in the early years of this century was always a cause for celebration in the sheep-farming communities of Fremont County where so many Scots, particularly from Ayrshire, congregated.

When John Campbell arrived at 'Little Scotland' on the East Fork of the Wind River, he was able to provide dance music on his melodian for 'scotch quadrille, scottische, hiland fling and other folk dances'. The gatherings usually took place in homes that had room for two or three squares.

Best fiddler in the district in the first years of this century was generally reckoned to be Bill Robertson, famous for his eightsome reels. However, the musical skills of the Scots were not always welcome in Wyoming. After the McAuliffe Kiltie Band was formed at Rock Springs, one lady commented about her Scots neighbour:

> As soon as he has his meals he retires to his room and plays on his bagpipe, only he calls it his 'bugpeep'. It is 'The Campbells are Coming' without variation, at intervals all day long and from seven till eleven at night. Sometimes I wish they would make haste and get here!

Ambition is a marvellous motivator but it doesn't always lead in the anticipated direction. John McTammany, born in the beautiful Vale of Kelvin in the west end of Glasgow, only ever had one ambition as a child—to be an internationally-known concert pianist. McTammany is remembered, however, not for his skill on the keyboard but for a musical invention that gave pleasure to millions: the perforated music roll.

When John entered the shipyards as a youngster he still held the dream of concert hall fame, but hard labouring in the yards saw him quickly lose the flexibility in his hands. His father had immigrated to the United States and in 1862 the family were sent for. They settled at Uniontown (OH) and John immediately tested his inventor's skills, working first of all on improving harvesting equipment.

Serving with the Ohio Volunteers in the Civil War, McTammany was critically wounded at Chattanooga. During his convalescence at Nashville (TN), while visiting a pawn shop where musical instruments were held, he volunteered to repair a musical box and the idea of a musical instrument with depressions rather than pins and staples occurred to him. Back in Uniontown he taught music, played in a band and sold pianos and organs. But the lights burned late in the McTammany household as John worked to perfect the player and the machine to prepare the perforated sheets.

The musical profession, once it got wind of the invention, expressed opposition, fearing redundancy, but John saw his invention as simply complementing existing musical instruments. His failure to patent his invention led to heart-breaking times, and he lived in a garret in Boston (MA) until a buyer could be found for his 'organette'. He also invented a pioneering mechanical voting machine, but his ballot box, registering votes on a pneumatic principle never caught on.

Edinburgh-born soldier and songwriter, James Lorraine Geddes, was another Civil War veteran. Born in 1827, he served in the Punjab before settling at Vinton (OH). He enrolled as a private in the Union Army at the outbreak of war, rising to brigadier-general by the end of hostilities. Agriculture was his main interest in later years, but he penned the lyrics for several Civil War songs which, set to music, became extremely popular, including 'The Soldier's Battle Prayer' and 'The Stars and Stripes'.

Mansfield (CT) was the location of a four-storey factory which, when opened in 1893, was the largest in the world devoted exclusively to the manufacture of church organ pipes. Behind this venture was Fenelon McCollom, great-grandson of a Scots immigrant. Along with his father, Fenelon built their first pipe organ in a barn—but the young man was fired with the idea of his own factory. At the height of operations the plant used more than 400,000 feet of best Michigan pine annually.

From the bustle of New England we cross America to the panorama of huge mountains and glassy lakes found in the Flathead district of Montana. It was to this remote corner of the States that John L. McIntosh, son of Scots parents, brought the idea of an opera house among the hills. John sold bibles in North Dakota and worked in the logging business before opening a hardware shop in Demersville (MT). Here he brought to reality his ambitious plan for an opera house, completed in 1896. A frame building a hundred foot by fifty, it was dual purpose, one half being used as a public hall and the other as the opera house-cum-dance-hall. It was destined to become the social and entertainment centre for the entire Flathead Valley. In 1904, the partition was removed and the building made into a single auditorium with stage and gallery.

Many theatre companies added Demersville to their schedule, and among the early favourites was *Uncle Tom's Cabin*, which played to an audience of 1,132 with people packed into every available corner. Another success was *Little Lord Fauntleroy*. Politicians spoke at the McIntosh Opera House, and the versatile venue was used over the years for plays, musicals, wrestling matches, debates, basketball and graduations.

When Peter S. Smith from Inverurie, Aberdeenshire, made his home in Fitchburg (MA) in 1912, he brought with him his bagpipes and uniform from his days with the Gordon Highlanders. A baker to trade, he also brought a reputation as a piper of great ability and almost as soon as he arrived he was drafted as piper for Clan Leslie, one of the Order of Scottish Clans, which had been formed in 1895. Thereafter, no clan meeting was complete without the skirl of Peter's pipes.

In this thriving milltown there was no shortage of candidates for a pipe band. Peter taught a young journeyman plumber, Alex Wilson, to play bass drum, and Carl Ferguson to play snare drum. Three other members of the band needed no lessons: Alex Paul had piped in Aberdeen, William Logan was a proficient player and his brother, James, who had formerly played with the Buchanan Institute brass band in Glasgow, was second snare drum. These six formed the Fitchburg Pipe Band that made its début in 1915, when Scottish bands were still something of a rarity in the States. They selected the plaid of the Gordon Highlanders, and when they marched down Main Street it's said that every Fitchburger for blocks around turned out.

### THE LAUDER CONNECTION

Outside major city newspaper centres in America many journalists who cherished their Scottish roots achieved notable success. Frank P. Mac-Lennan, for forty-nine years editor and publisher of *The Topeka State Journal* in Kansas, would recall his childhood in Ohio when his mother would dress him up in the kilt. His father had been born in the early 1800s in Inverness, and young Frank was never allowed to forget his heritage. He

Frank P. MacLennan, Kansas newspaper editor and close friend of the Scots entertainer, Sir Harry Lauder (right). (Kansas State Historical Society) This comic singer, born in Portobello in 1870, was for some Scotland's greatest ambassador, while for others his caricature of the tight-fisted wee bachle is an image which the Scots are still trying to live down. His popularity was undeniable, however, and he filled theatres on both sides of the Atlantic. (The Herald Archive)

gained his newspaper experience doing odd jobs around various editorial offices, but still found time to gain a science degree from the University of Kansas and to work with a railroad survey team in western Kansas and Colorado.

MacLennan was a friend of the Scots legend of the first decades of the twentieth century, Sir Harry Lauder, who, with his crooked stick and tartan garb, came to personify Scotland—rightly or wrongly—for millions of Americans. Over the years MacLennan and Lauder became firm friends, culminating in a visit by the Scotsman in 1918 to address the Rotary Club in Topeka.

Proudly Frank told the gathering that Lauder's mother was a MacLennan, and put Sir Harry's success down to the fact that he was in the 'cheering-up business'. Some food for thought there for Lauder's critics.

MacLennan told the story of the night in New York when Lauder was to sing at the Manhattan Opera House. The newspaper editor was in the audience but *The Carpathia*, which was due to dock at eight that evening, was running late. Initially, no apology was made to the audience and vaudeville acts filled in. By ten o'clock the theatre manager *did* apologise, and added that Lauder's ship had been sighted from Fire Island and that the show would go on . . . eventually.

Theatres up and down Broadway had been emptying and word got round of this novel piece of drama. The crowd at the Opera House was larger by eleven-thirty than it had been at eight—even standing room was at a premium. At half past midnight it was announced that Sir Harry's ship had berthed and he was being whisked direct from the docks in a fast car. MacLennan recalled,

> At 1 a.m. Lauder walked out on stage, put his grip on the platform and began pulling off his gloves. The audience rose en masse and gave him an ovation.

Lauder sang into the wee sma' hours and delighted the audience.

On a hill in Topeka, MacLennan built his own 'laird castle' filled with the carved emblem of Scotland, the thistle. He dubbed it 'Cedar Crest' and it is now the official home of the governor of Kansas. Frank MacLennan, newspaperman and proud Scot, died in 1933.

NASSAU STREET'S ANTIQUARIAN

'Booklover' is scarcely an adequate title for William Gowans from Lanarkshire, who was educated in a parish school near the Falls of Clyde before immigrating with his family in 1821. At the age of twenty-five he went to New York and tried his hand at a dazzling variety of jobs—gardening, news-vending, stone-cutting, even acting. At length he set up a bookstall in Chatham Street, a row of shelves packed with books, protected at night (or when Gowans was at an auction) with shutters, an iron bar and padlock. During this Bohemian period, Gowans boarded for a time with the family of Edgar Allan Poe, whose Scots roots we've already noted. For the years up until his death in 1870, he was known to almost everyone in New York as the eccentric yet likeable 'Antiquarian of Nassau Street'.

Gowans made no pretence about it: he much preferred to buy books rather than sell, and if a customer complained that a book was too pricey his response was: 'We'll make it higher then!' He would then clamber up a ladder and place the book out of reach on a precipitous shelf. His books filled his Nassau Street store, first floor, basement and sub-cellar, and he would lead people through these literary catacombs by the light of a small whale-oil lamp. One visitor remarked:

> Books lay everywhere, in seemingly dire confusion, piled on tables and on the floor until they finally toppled over and the few narrow alleys became well nigh impassable.

Incredibly, his executors sold at auction 250,000 bound volumes. *Eight tons* of pamphlets and leaflets were sold as waste paper.

Auctioneer and bookseller, Robert Bell, was one of the most colourful characters of pre-revolutionary Philadelphia. Born in Glasgow in 1732, he served his apprenticeship as a bookbinder and arrived in America in 1768. In the city of brotherly love he bought and sold library collections and smaller lots of books. A stout, cheery Scot, he was apparently a hoot as an auctioneer, and for many in polite Philadelphia society a visit to one of Bob Bell's auctions was better than a night at the theatre.

Folk would turn up simply to watch his antics or listen to his patter. He would sit with a glass of beer at his side and drink comical toasts to the authors whose books were being sold. There were few writers about whom he was unable to produce a funny anecdote, and newspaper reports of the day suggested that he often had the audience rolling in the aisles.

Bell plied his trade up and down the colonial coast, and when the British occupied Philadelphia during the Revolutionary War he kept a circulating library which was popular among the British officers. Above all, however, he was the archetypal Scot, a hard-headed businessman—he charged a guinea deposit for each book.

Scots booksellers also played vital roles in the development of the West. Robert Clarke (1829–99), born in Annan, Dumfries-shire, is found in Cincinatti (OH) in 1840, where he opened a second-hand bookshop which soon became the unofficial rendezvous for the city's literati. Around his bookshelves the great debates of the time were aired.

Robert moved on, however, and purchased a publishing company which he soon moulded into one of the most powerful in the land. Early on he had decided to concentrate on the wide open spaces of the rapidly expanding West, and his was the first company to import large quantities of books to the Ohio Valley from Europe. Perhaps his single biggest service to the 'civilisation' of the West was in supplying almost every small-town judge and lawyer with their essential textbooks.

Cincinatti was the location of the first newspaper published in the vast territory north-west of the Ohio by American Scot, William Maxwell, and there was Scots input in the region's first religious newspaper.

To all the above mentioned must be added the great legion of talent in all sorts of unlikely areas. John Long, village stone-carver of Macomb (IL), was born in Glasgow in 1812. During the 1840s, he worked on the Mormon temple at Nauvoo before the historic trek to Utah. John—who died from injuries sustained in the war against Mexico—carved stones in the old Macomb cemetery in the town's Wigwam Hollow Road, which eerily echoed the old gravestones of Ayrshire or the Clyde Valley. His antiquated style, lettering and poetic epitaphs are regarded by academics as marking out an important European tradition transplanted to the Midwest. The stones are John Long's true memorial.

Duncan Phyfe, maker of exquisite furniture, from Loch Fannich in Ross and Cromarty, was said to be an equal of the best in the world in his craft during the first half of the nineteenth century. This immigrant is briefly described in a way which would fit so many Scots: 'a strict Calvinist, noted for his craftmanship'. Pottery, clock-making, wagon-building, stained glass and porcelain manufacture . . . all these skills claimed their share of American Scots.

Many internationally known showbusiness personalities have also claimed Scottish heritage over the years. Today Hollywood screen actors such as Clint Eastwood and Robert Redford have intimated that they have ties to Scotland, and in the past there are the likes of Hoagy Carmichael, the song-writer responsible for 'Lazybones' and 'Georgia on my Mind'; Isadora Duncan, born into an artistic San Francisco family, had a colourful life as an exotic dancer before being choked to death in Nice by a long scarf which caught in a car wheel; Stephen Foster, folk-song composer born in Pittsburgh in 1826, wrote 'O Susannah' which became the anthem of the California Gold Rush. He also wrote 'Jeanie with the Light Brown Hair'. All these people claimed a Scottish pedigree.

Actor Edwin Forrest, born in Philadelphia in 1806, who learned his trade with a frontier troupe and a circus before triumphing as Othello in New York in 1826, also boasted of his Scottishness. Dominating his career was a feud with the great Shakespearian actor, W.C. Macready. In 1845 in London, when many actors including Macready were out of work, Forrest was jeered by some of the audience as he played Macbeth. He was convinced Macready was behind the incident and retaliated by hissing Macready in Edinburgh, where he was appearing in Hamlet.

The feud reached its tragic climax in 1849. Macready was appearing at New York's Astor Place Opera House when crowds of Forrest's unruly fans attacked the theatre. Troops were called in and the riot resulted in twenty-two deaths, many injuries, and the complete wrecking of the theatre. Forrest was elsewhere but was said to have encouraged the affair, which later became known as the Astor Place Riot. For years afterwards,

Forrest filled theatres through his notoriety and gave speeches vindicating himself between acts. In later years he was considered as much a curiosity as a great actor.

We also remember Cissie Loftus, a Glasgow-born actress and impersonator, who made the switch from stage to screen; and Robert Bruce Mantell, born at the Wheatsheaf Inn in Irvine, who was regarded as perhaps America's most talented Shakespearian actor of the early twentieth century. Their successes were followed by other stage and screen stars such as Jack Buchanan and Deborah Kerr, both born in Helensburgh, Dunbartonshire and John Finlayson, classic, pop-eyed villain of early movies, who was born at Larbert, Stirlingshire.

Russell Smith's politically radical family left Glasgow in 1819 for Pittsburgh. While still a young man, Russell landed a job as a scene painter, his famous 'tent interior' for an Arabian fantasy so impressing theatre management that he was launched on a career which took him to Philadelphia, Boston, Baltimore and Washington. He produced spectacular panoramas, operatic scenery and backdrops, and was commissioned to paint the same for the Philadelphia Academy of Music when it was built in the mid-1850s.

It's perhaps appropriate that we should conclude this glimpse at the breadth of Scots artistic and literary achievement in America with a Glaswegian who, typical of his tribe, got on quietly with the job, content to remain quite literally behind the scenes.

*The Transcript*, one of Oklahoma's oldest surviving newspapers, had a home at the corner of West Main Street and Santa Fe Avenue in the town of Norman. Here the staff strike a casual pose. (Norman Transcript)

## Chapter 11

# RINGING THE CHANGES

S TRONG, HARD-WORKING, TENACIOUS, thrifty, quiet and undemonstra-
tive; clannish, argumentative, tight-fisted and dour—just a few of the
long list of adjectives applied to the Scots in America over the centuries.
Missing from this catalogue, however, is perhaps the single most important
feature in the make-up of these immigrants—versatility, the ability to
adjust to dramatically changed circumstances. The flexible Scot was truly
a remarkable phenomenon.

Tied to this adaptability, another odd contradiction is encountered in
the Scots psyche. Ever anxious to become responsible members of the
community, to serve church, school and government, it's also clear that
many still felt a curiosity, a febrile hankering to know what lay over the
hill. Ben Robertson, writing of the Scots and their descendants in South
Carolina, evocatively made the point:

> . . . then the old restlessness will stir again, like a wind rising and we
> have to travel. We are like that. High winds and lonesome sounds
> disturb us, something within us makes us go.

This Scottish ability to ring the changes when necessary is well illustrated
by an examination of the census records. In Wyoming in 1870, Scots found
employment in forty-five different occupations from jeweller to labourer.
Ten years later the variety had increased to eighty trades, ranging across
the employment spectrum from prostitute to nurse and from freighter to
'gentleman'.

As the American Scots began their westward trek in the mid-1800s, their
versatility was tested to the full. The Louthain family, who moved first from
Virginia to Ohio, took their chance in 1835 when the land agency opened up
some 1,250,000 acres of Indiana. Leannah, a daughter of this intrepid Scots
family, experienced this migration as a child and wrote:

> The country was not cleared and there were many Indians roaming
> about. It was necessary to build a fire in front of the house to keep
> wolves away at night. They howled all night and attacked young pigs
> and sheep.

Icy prairie winters also had to be faced. Janette Murray recalls a particularly
severe New Year's Day in the 1880s. In the clear, cold conditions several
oxen belonging to a neighbour got away from their shed and gathered in

the opposite corner of the yard, their tails to the icy blast. They were found there next morning, frozen stiff but still on their feet. On the other side of the coin, there were summer droughts so intense (according to the waggish Kansas Scots) that pebbles had to be thrown on to the byre roof to let the horses think it was raining and to keep them from being discouraged.

Factual Scottish evidence of the effect of a Kansas 'twister' is available. The Gilchrist family from Lanarkshire moved first of all to Illinois, then on to Sheridan County (KS). There were ten children in the family and Lorena Newland recalls the day a tornado skimmed their farm, pulling up two legs of their windmill and bending it over. They had a lucky escape, because as the tornado continued its path of destruction through the community it tore up the nearby Catholic church.

Safety in numbers seems to have been the motto of many of these immigrants to the prairies. In Cass, Miami, Howard and Tipton Counties in Indiana we find the number of children in Scots families on this frontier around 1850 often reaching double figures. Fourteen or fifteen children in the household was not exceptional and, predictably, the mortality rate was very high. One Scots mother from this area lost two of her children in the same year, one to a bolt of lightning and another to a prairie fire.

Having as many possible strings to the occupational bow does indeed seem to have been a key to success. Ecclefechan, Dumfries-shire-born William Harkness (b.1837), the son of a clergyman, was an astronomer but on immigrating to New York as a child he became first a journalist and homeopathic doctor; James Lawson, Glasgow-born in 1799 and a graduate of Glasgow University, was an author, editor, insurance expert and friend of Edgar Allan Poe.

John McArthur, born at Erskine, Renfrewshire, ran a boilermaking plant in Chicago, served in the Civil War and became the city's postmaster; David Meekison from Dundee settled at Napoleon (OH) and is remembered as a soldier, printer, banker and mayor; from Stirlingshire, James White settled in Indiana in the mid-1850s, where he was a calico-printer, soldier, tailor, ran a department store, manufactured wheels and managed a bank.

It would be equally wrong to think that every Scot wore his or her versatility like a badge. Many knew their trade through and through and stuck by it no matter how many job opportunities the New World offered. Such was the case of George Forbes, a coachman from Dornoch in Sutherland, who had driven the aristocracy of the county for years before moving with his family to Massachusetts in 1885. Here, he sought no new career nor tried to work the land, but found employment on familiar ground as coachman to Congressman George Weymouth. He cared for the Weymouth horses in a large barn behind the house, and when the era of the horse and coach passed into history he worked at the city stables, where the horses continued to supply the pulling power for the town's public works department.

American researchers unfortunately granted anonymity to a young

Ayrshire woman who immigrated from Scotland at the turn of this century, and whose story constitutes perhaps the most startling example of versatility (some would say shiftlessness) that we're likely to encounter.

The daughter of a gentleman farmer, she couldn't stand rural life and left home to work at the Coats threadmill at Paisley, then she went into domestic service and worked in a carpet factory, being sacked for asking for a pay rise. Hired in Scotland as a family cook, she immigrated with her employers to Canada before moving to the United States in the spring of 1924. In New York she waited on tables at a boys' school, then was a nanny to a wealthy family. Next came nursing, before working as a coffee girl in a restaurant. During the era of prohibition, she was a coat-check girl at the Cotton Club, then sold this profitable concession to become a housekeeper then a rooming-house manageress during the Depression. Settling eventually in Connecticut, she worked in a variety of factories but was laid off because of her union activities.

Short and stocky, blonde-haired and blue-eyed, with a generous laugh and a ready wit, the researcher's subject was found to have a tremendous appetite for life. Amazingly, when this interview was conducted by Frank Andrews Stone for his book, *Scots and Scotch-Irish in Connecticut*, the remarkable Scotswoman was only thirty-five years old!

JOCK-OF-ALL-TRADES

The eighteenth and early nineteenth-century Scots who found themselves carving a new life in the backwoods of America were, of necessity, multi-talented. Even if there had been tradesmen to employ, money was lacking to pay them. On the largely self-sufficient frontier farms, the first and second-generation pioneer was his or her own shoe-maker, blacksmith, tailor or carpenter. Everyone in the family had a role to play. Only when the frontier stage gradually ended do we find itinerant craftsmen and village specialists appearing on the scene. Principal home industries were spinning and weaving of flax, wool and hemp, the manufacture of shoes, hats, caps and bedding; milling, distilling, soap and candle-making; leather products, brooms, baskets and food processing such as pickling, preserving and making maple sugar.

Easily as many self-determined women were to be found in the ranks of the Caledonian immigrants. The story is told of Ulster-Scots lass, Polly Mulhollin, who arrived in America as an indentured servant. Once her years of service (usually five or seven) were complete, she donned a man's clothing and hiked into Burden's Grant in the Virginia interior to build log cabins. With every cabin erected, the pioneer was entitled to a parcel of land. When Benjamin Burden came in to make out the deeds for those who held cabin rights, he was stunned to find a substantial number of cabins in Polly's name.

When a Glasgow woman, Jessie Macmillan, decided that her future lay on a homestead in the remote Sacramento Mountains of New Mexico, the first

Jessie Macmillan outside her cabin in the mountains of New Mexico in the early years of this century. The cabin, Glen Eben, was named after her brother. Jessie, who grew up in Glasgow, is seen giving lessons to a neighbour's child, Tommy Prather, on the porch at Agua Chiquita c.1908. (Ray Buckner, Tularosa (NM))

item she purchased when she stepped off the steamer at New York was a beautiful long-barrelled Colt police revolver. Jessie was an independent sort of female, but even in the first few years of the twentieth century she wasn't going to take any chances. Stories of the Wild West and of the desperate characters who populated the empty acres were still widely heard in Britain. Born in Glasgow around 1870, Jessie lost her parents when she was very young; but the family were reasonably affluent, and she left her Kelvinside home for private schooling in Cumbria and Switzerland.

It was in these places that her skill in horsemanship developed and sparked the idea of a new life in the United States. She wrote unsuccessfully to the US consul, asking about land, but through her grandmother (who lived in Fife) Jessie was put in touch with a relative who had recently moved to a 160-acre homestead in New Mexico.

October 1903 and Jessie was on board *The Lusitania* as it sailed from Liverpool. After several weeks travelling Stateside, during which she saw her first real, live cowboy, she reached Alamogordo, in her words 'a wee railroad town'. She stayed in a rooming house and waited for a wagon to arrive from the Agua Chiquita valley with two of her neighbours, Will and Lila Buckner. They took Jessie up steep canyons and through dense forest to her future home, a 160-acre farm which she purchased for 300 dollars, two miles below 'Eagle', the farm belonging to her grandmother's cousin. A log house had been started and some fencing already done. She named her home 'Glen Eben', after her brother, Eben, who was still in Scotland.

Over the years, as Jessie got to know the mountains, she developed a sizeable homestead with several buildings and grew the first alfalfa crop in the district. Her relative, Ray Buckner, in a biography of the Glasgwegian homesteader, remembers that Jessie was perhaps not the typical settler:

> Her house was filled with interesting decor and furnishings including a grand piano.

She loved and took pride in her fine horses, making packs trips alone down to Alamogordo and horseback and wagon journeys further afield. While visiting Kansas, she met an Englishman and left her beloved 'Glen Eben' for ever to become his bride.

Ulysses S. Grant, frontier soldier, Civil War general and president of the United States, claimed direct descent from one of the earliest Scots settlers who arrived in Massachusetts in 1630. While serving as regimental quartermaster at Fort Vancouver in the Pacific Northwest in the 1850s, Grant showed much enterprise (in the old Scots style) but it was poorly rewarded. His first plan to ship ice to California soon melted away, a potato field he planted was flooded out, and a batch of chickens bound for San Francisco all died en route.

Under pressure from his superiors, he took to drink and resigned his commission. As they say, from the depths of despair there's only one way

Two descendants of the Scotch Grove pioneers are pictured with the quern stones which the Sutherland immigrants brought from Scotland to Canada then carried to Iowa. (People of Scotch Grove)

to go and that's up—within a few years Grant was Commander of the Union Army, and by 1868 he was President.

BEYOND THE RED RIVER

Among the many tales of the Highlanders and their adventures in the New World, none is more dramatic nor better illustrates the hardships they faced than the saga of the Red River settlement and the Scots who eventually found a home at Scotch Grove, Iowa. These pioneers refused to give up in the face of seemingly impossible odds.

During 1812 and 1813, with the Highland evictions at their height, tenants of the Duchess of Sutherland from Kildonan accepted an offer from the Earl of Selkirk to transport them to his new colony on the Red River—a huge tract of land comprising roughly what is now the Canadian province of Manitoba and the border country of North Dakota and Minnesota.

The immigrants walked into the middle of a dispute between Selkirk's Hudson's Bay Company and the rival North-West Company. The bulk of the party had arrived in the summer of 1814, after a year-long journey. Following a horrendous sea crossing from Stromness in Orkney, the pioneers were encouraged on the long march by a piper who 'skirled a pibroch' as they trudged westwards. Near the site of present-day Winnipeg, they were allocated their 100-acre lot and supplied with horses, guns, tools and seed.

Behind the scenes the North-West Company was at work, and some settlers were persuaded away to try their luck in Upper Canada while other kept the faith: 'We have eaten Selkirk's bread, we dwell on lands he bought. We stay here as long as he wishes and if we perish, we perish.' Eventually, the Red River immigrants were forced to flee and their cabins were burned by the North-West Company. They returned and rebuilt, but the worst was to come. During a clash with French-Indian half-breeds at Seven Oaks, the governor and twenty men were killed.

By 1821 the two companies had merged, and although it seemed after seven years of conflict that their troubles were over, the settlers were unhappy. Bleak, cold winters and grasshopper plagues made farming just as difficult as it had been in the valleys of Sutherland, and the promised church and school did not materialise.

Word reached the Red River colony of opportunities to buy cheap farms in the rich valley of the northern Mississippi in the States, and Alexander McClain got the job in 1835 of running the rule over this fertile, well-watered prairie land. After his positive report, a group consisting of John Sutherland (with his ten sons and two daughters), Alexander Sutherland, David McCoy, Joseph Brimner and McClain, set off with their families on the 1,000-mile trek to the 'new' promised land.

With their heavily laden, rough-and-ready wooden oxcarts, they crawled steadily south, circling the wagons at night to avoid Indian attack. They waded marshes, forded rivers and were constantly tormented under a burning sun by black flies, mosquitoes and gnats. Making about fifteen miles on an average day, they pressed on until the great prairie lay before them—the journey had taken four months. They picked their spot and Scotch Grove was born. Two more parties followed and suddenly life became more rewarding, as log cabins sprang up, fields were planted and at last the church and school, the cornerstones of any Scots immigrant community, were in place.

Today Scotch Grove is a quiet little community. In a nearby museum lie two heavy quern stones which the pioneers had brought across the Atlantic to the Red River from Sutherland, then carried all the way to Iowa. They serve as mute reminders of the grit, determination and confidence in the future of these displaced folk from Kildonan.

INTO THE VALLEY OF DEATH

It might be unfair to describe Alex Henry, a pioneer fruit-grower of Orange County (CA), as an eccentric; but this Leith-born lad, who proudly boasted of being present at the Charge of the Light Brigade at Balaclava, was a wee bit different. Even when he settled in America, his fighting spirit surfaced whenever he heard of Britain's military exploits. As an American citizen, he was rejected when he asked to fight in the Boer War and when, at the

Alex Henry's remarkable Californian home built 'in the Egyptian and Roman style' in 1905. (Anaheim Public Library)

age of almost eighty, he tried to sign up to help the US World War I effort, he was told: 'We can see the fighting devil in your eye but we are very sorry to state that you are too young to be accepted.'

As a teenager, Henry received his most serious injury at Sebastapol, where a Russian bullet passed through both his legs. He was taken to Florence Nightingale's field hospital at Scutari, where he made the acquaintance of the legendary 'Lady with the Lamp'.

There was nothing Alex liked better than to get dressed up in his full Scottish regalia and go into Anaheim, his adopted home. In 1901, at the helm of *The Ship of State*—the construction of which he had personally supervised—he stood in his sailor's outfit, leading Anaheim's fourth of July parade.

Alex was born at Leith in February 1837, his parents having come from Lerwick in the Shetland Islands. He liked to tell his Californian neighbours that his great-grandfather, Innes Henry, was chief of the clan and lord of the islands. Certainly there was a military background in the family, his maternal grandfather having been at Waterloo. When Alex was ten he was apprenticed to his brother, a ship owner, and in 1852 he joined the Royal Navy and served as a marine right through the Crimean War, having been wounded six times.

Leaving the RN he learned the carpenter's trade, and while serving in the merchant navy visited almost every important seaport in the world before eventually leaving ship at San Francisco in 1867 to become one of Anaheim's pioneers. He bought 220 acres of land on which he planted vines and for eight years maintained his own winery. In addition, he planted fruit trees; but when blight struck one vineyard after another in the mid-1880s he turned to growing oranges and walnuts, his orange brandy becoming famous.

He called his ranch 'Caledonia Grove', and in 1905 he built a remarkable 100,000-dollar pressed-steel house once described in a local paper as 'a novelty in Roman and Egyptian design'. A feature of the house was the gold lions sitting at the wide front steps, which were sculpted by Gutzon Borglum, who carved the faces of the presidents in the Black Hills of North Dakota. The old campaigner's 'tin house' was torn down in 1937 and a supermarket has been built on the site.

Alexander and his wife, Catherine, had four sons. Even in the autumn of his life Alex still enjoyed the splendour of the military pageant. On patriotic days he would bring along a little cannon which he made himself, set it up in the middle of a playing field and let rip with a series of thunderous salvos. Later, when he became less mobile, he would fire the cannon in his garden when it came round to the Fourth of July or Armistice Day. His son, George Henry, recalled the occasion when the old man set up the cannon in the backyard, rather too near the house, and blew out every window in the rear of the building. It's somehow appropriate that he should have settled in Anaheim, home of the first Disneyland.

David Crawford was a sixty-year-old Scot encountered by John Regan while compiling his *Emigrant's Guide* in Illinois. In Scotland it appears that Crawford's prospects had been very dim, his employers keeping him

> ... working in the dike sheugh till the day o' my daith, or if I wasna'
> able to work I might gang and beg.

The West beckoned in 1841 and David, from Ayrshire, found his life transformed. At Knoxville (IL) he worked in a brickyard, accepting part of his final pay for the season in bricks! He quickly discovered that they were a valuable commodity to barter on the frontier where money was scarce, and this prompted him to go into the brick-making business on his own account. Buying some land, he was soon the region's principal brick-maker selling at a thousand for five dollars and now able, in his own words, to feel security for the first time in his life:

> When I wanted a pickle flour, or a bit of pork, or maybe a wee hue tea
> and sugar, I just paid for it wi' bricks.

213

# A. Y. McDONALD'S

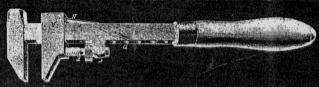

# PATENT SCREW WRENCH.

*(From the SCIENTIFIC AMERICAN, January 9th, 1864.)*

Upon examining the engraving it will be seen that the jaw A, has a spring B, fastened to its Back in such a way that it bears upon the shank of the wrench; this jaw is made larger than the exact size of the shank, so that by taking hold of the sliding block, C, it is lifted out of the holes, D, in the shank; in this block there is a short stout pin which just fits the holes and takes the strain thrown on the jaw, A, when the wrench is in use. There is also a small screw, E, which runs through the block, C, and works in a thread cut in the jaw, A. The manner of adjusting this tool and using it is readily apparent to every one; it is only necessary to throw the pin in the block, C, out of the holes by pressing on the bottom of the jaw, moving the same along to the size required; any inaccuracy may then be compensated for by the screw, E."

The advantages claimed for this Wrench over others are as follows:

1st. The facility with which the Sliding Jaw may be moved back or forward.

2nd. It can be opened A THIRD FARTHER than other Wrenches of the same size—consequently catching larger nuts and couplings.

3d. There is NO LONG SCREW, therefore NO LIABILITY TO GUM up, as is the case with other Wrenches, often rendering them very difficult to open and close. It is particularly adapted to the use of Plumbers and Machinists who work around Pumps, as a 12-inch Wrench can be opened 4 ¼ inches, which is more than is generally necessary to catch the largest size of Pump couplings.

Persons wishing to buy the entire Patent or take an interest in the Manufacture, can address the Patentee or his Agent,

## JOHN MORRISON,
### Dubuque, Iowa.

Advert from the *Scientific American* of January 1864 for McDonald's amazing screw wrench. (R.D. McDonald and the Center for Dubuque History)

Glasgow's Eglinton Street was where Andrew Young McDonald—the fighting plumber of Duboque (IA)—grew up. He was born in 1834 and served his apprenticeship with a local plumber. Orphaned at an early age, he went with an aunt to the United States in 1854 and after working in Cleveland (OH) and St Louis (MO), where he gained the reputation of a skilled plumber, he finally settled beside the Mississippi at Duboque, establishing a small plumber's business; and on 5 November 1860 he became a citizen of the United States.

The Civil War soon followed and he enlisted with the Union Army, in the First Iowa Infantry. His company, 'Governor's Greys', claimed to have been the first to answer Abe Lincoln's call-to-arms and they were soon in action. John M. Faley, in his history of the still-thriving McDonald company, records that Andrew was wounded during the Battle of Wilson's Creek (MO) in 1861 and lay on the battlefield for four days before being taken prisoner and held in a barn hospital for three months.

During these days of confinement there was an unusual encounter. One afternoon a fiery young Confederate lieutenant, booted and spurred, came swaggering into the barn cursing the 'damned Yankees' and threatening to shoot the prisoners. Andrew immediately recognised his voice and as he drew near raised himself up on one elbow, saying:

> Whit are ye talking aboot, Archie Ferguson? No Scotsman is coward enough to touch a wounded man!

The young soldier looked at Andrew and immediately recognised him as a former workmate from their St Louis days. He stuttered—'My God Mac, what are you doing here?' Andrew's response was as quick as it was effective:

> Never mind what I'm doing here, you just quit yer swaggering and get me some fried chicken.

Andrew was eventually rescued by his brother-in-law, who braved the hostile countryside to bring him back to Iowa. As soon as he was fit, Andrew re-enlisted only to be wounded again at the Battle of Black River Bridge during the siege of Vicksburg in 1863.

But while he was away at war his plumbing interests were not forgotten. A few weeks before Vicksburg he was granted patent number 38316 for improvements in screw wrenches. In most respects his updated model was identical to the monkey-wrench used today. In 1886, Andrew was interviewed by a city slicker who had seen the advert for the wrench in *The Scientific American*. The fashionably dressed man refused to identify himself but offered 500 dollars for the patent, a vast sum for a struggling plumber. Only years after did Andrew find out that he had sold the patent to Coes and Co. of Worcester (MA), one of the country's leading wrench manufacturers.

Scotsman Tom Carson found himself on the wild frontier in New Mexico in 1880, and discovered a skill he didn't know he had: it turned out he was a dab hand at the gambling, whether in real estate or at cards. Having worked in India for four years as a tea-planter, Carson was a seasoned traveller and scarcely the typical immigrant Scot. After spending time at the British colony of Le Mars (IA) and finding that 'sport, not work occupied their whole time', he moved to New Mexico Territory. His original intention was to go into ranching, but other aspects of life on the frontier grabbed his attention.

He stopped over at Las Vegas (NM) which, according to his accounts, was every bit as lively as its spectacular successor in Nevada. Carson also saw his chance to make a killing in real estate. His description of Las Vegas:

> It was booming, full of life and all kinds of people; money was plentiful; saloons, gambling dens and dance halls were wide open. Real estate was moving freely, prices advancing, speculation rife—and infectious.

Carson relates how a few successful property deals encouraged him to try his luck in other towns. On reaching Santa Fe he would spend his evenings playing poker, faro and monte with the town's toughest citizens, and described this community as being as much a hell as Las Vegas. New Mexico, according to Carson, was probably the most lawless country in the world, and almost everyone who ventured into the area boasted of meeting the most notorious outlaw of them all Billy the Kid. Carson was no exception. His alleged encounter—a brief and peaceful one—took place at Fort Sumner. Reverting to his original plan of becoming a cattle-rancher, he managed New Mexican property for the Scottish Land and Mortgage Company for almost a decade.

Diversity and a talent for spotting opportunities always seemed to give the Scots that little head start over other ethnic incomers. James H. McCormick, who immigrated to the United States in 1862 from Kilmarnock, finally settled on a 100-acre farm in Lawrence County (PA). Having gained experience of the mining industry in Scotland, James developed agriculture and industry side by side—or more accurately, one on top of the other. He grew fruit trees at his farm at Slippery Rock township and operated a coal mine beneath his orchards.

In 1856, the year before the Indian mutiny, Harry Byng was born in Glasgow; he died the year President John F. Kennedy took office, 1960. In an unsually long and varied life, Harry sailed around the world seven times before coming to Washington in the Pacific Northwest. He was a barber to trade and was, by royal appointment, hairdresser to King Kalagas of Honolulu. In 1887, he settled in the community of Hoquiam, opened a barber's shop and married a French Huguenot girl from South Carolina—gossip in the district was that he had bought his wife. Whatever the truth, he outlived his bride by many years and died in a local nursing home aged 104.

Another versatile Scot who figures in the history of the north-west is James Urquhart, born at the hamlet of Ferintosh in Ross-shire, who sailed for New York in 1851 and joined an immigrant wagon-train on the Oregon Trail. He worked in a variety of jobs, from building to mining, and was in Washington in time to vote in the territory's first election. Settling at Eden Prairie, he sent for his wife and five children. Urquhart laid out the town of Napavine and, in addition to farming, had his own merchant's business and served as county treasurer and postmaster. He was elected on three occasions to the territorial legislature.

SPORTIVE SCOTS

Next time you see the American sprint relay team burning up the Tartan track, it's worth remembering that United States athletic success has its roots in some of the disciplines of the Highland Games of the 1800s. In sport, as in other areas of American life, Scots immigrants launched themselves into a wide variety of competitive activities, both traditional and new-fangled.

The Highland Society of New York held its first 'Sportive Meeting' in 1836, and by the Civil War Scots in Philadelphia, Boston and other major cities were organising their own Games. All the traditional contests, such as putting the heavy stone, vaulting with a pole, throwing the hammer and tossing the caber featured, as well as less muscular contests such as the wheelbarrow and sack-races.

It's generally agreed that modern track and field meets evolved directly from these gatherings, which can be traced as far back as contests between Scots soldiers and Indians in Georgia before the Revolutionary War. Colleges such as Princeton, with its strong Scottish links, showed the way to the rest of the nation by holding their first 'Caledonian Games' in 1873. Interestingly, caber-tossing, so beloved by those with Scottish ancestry, never caught on with the American people. If it had, we might have seen it as a major Olympic event today.

The Scots industrial immigrants brought their love of soccer to America and with it the conviction that it was they, rather than the English, who had given the world the game. Among the earliest teams were those in Fall River and Pawtucket (MA), who played their first matches against Canadian opposition. In the 1890s, Fall River alone had twenty-five teams and crowds were regularly numbered in the thousands. Within a few years teams could be found right across the country.

Detroit soccer team was founded by a Scot and included the McKendrick brothers from Greenock Morton in their earliest sides. Chicago Thistle and Chicago Colhours were out-and-out Scottish sides, and there were teams with a Scottish flavour in Pittsburgh, St Louis, Denver, San Francisco, Seattle, Tacoma, New York and Philadelphia. Workers in the heavy industries—stone-cutting, mining and steel—were in the forefront of the soccer

The Scottish pride of Oregon c.1925. The White Heather football team played in the Portland FA, its backbone being players of Scots origin, notably from the McCleary family. (Oregon Historical Society) *bottom* Jock Semple, an athlete who began his career with Clydesdale Harriers before immigrating to Massachusetts, was for decades the moving force behind the Boston Marathon. (Nan Small)

Highland Games in America provided the inspiration for modern track and field athletics. These engravings from *Harper's Weekly* in 1867 show the games at Jones's Wood in New York City. (Institute of Texan Cultures at San Antonio)

craze. American colleges soon developed their own rib-crushing version of rugby, and young, second-generation American Scots gradually drifted away from the beautiful game.

The nearest the American golf fraternity has to a martyr is a Mr Lockhart from Fife, who in 1887 brought his clubs and balls to America and was fined for practising his strokes among the sheep in New York's Central Park. Golf really took off in the early years of this century in America, and much of the credit for making it the people's game goes to another Fifer, John Reid from Dunfermline, who with a few loyal friends began playing on a vacant lot at Yonkers (NY) in the 1870s. From these humble beginnings grew the famous St Andrews Golf Club, Westchester County (NY), of which Reid was a founder.

At roughly the same time, Scots in Chicago were also knocking around the 'gutty' balls much to the amusement of their neighbours. In 1886, John Gillespie from Moffat, Dumfries-shire, developed the first golf course in the southern United States at Sarasota (FL), a town of which he was six times mayor. Among the all-time greats of American golf both Bobby Jones and Walter Hagen claimed Scottish ancestry.

By World War I there were thousands of golf clubs across the United States and Scots professionals were employed to pass on their skills. Despite the Scottish gift of golf to the United States, Americans still loved to have a joke at the expense of the canny Scots, even on the golf course. It was said that one of these pioneers was forced to quit the game he loved so dearly—because he lost his golf ball!

Wee Charlie Barr (1864–1911) was a Gourock-born yacht-racing captain who was brought up within sight of the busy shipping lanes at the Tail of the Bank. As a boy he watched the big ships leaving the Clyde for North America and gained his first sea-going experience during a season on a flounder trawler.

His brother, John, was a noted skipper and in 1884 they took the forty-foot cutter *Clara* to the United States and raced her. Their performances caused surprise and admiration in American racing circles, and Charlie, who fell in love with America even before his feet had touched dry land, decided to stay and became a naturalised American in 1889.

For the remainder of his life he was employed by a series of wealthy yacht-owners. Only five foot three inches in his stocking soles, Charlie became renowned for his skill as a skipper, particularly for his confidence in piling on sail during a race when others were flinching. His admirers suggested that a combination of daring, intelligence and constant study of the nautical charts, weather and wind statistics made 'Wee Charlie' king of the skippers. A man of few words, he was regarded as merciless in competition.

Jock Semple, a born runner who moved from pounding the streets of Clydebank to become known as Boston's 'Mr Marathon', is remembered internationally for one fleeting yet remarkable event which is now part of athletics folklore.

Stone Mountain Highland Games in Georgia, where the pipes and drums of the British Caledonian pipe band echo from the Confederate memorial carved into the mountainside. (The Herald Archives)

Kathy Switzer, a student from Syracuse University, decided to run the Boston Marathon in 1967, when women were still barred from the competition on the grounds that it was too punishing for female competitors. Kathy applied by signing 'K. Switzer' and Jock, who screened all the entries, assumed 'K' was male and posted off a number. On the press bus during the event, a sportswriter spotted Kathy among a crowd of runners and Jock set off in pursuit. As he tried to tear off her number, Kathy's giant boyfriend elbowed Jock into a ditch. The cameras clicked furiously.

Kathy, who later made up with Jock, ended up on the front page of newspapers the world over and made a guest appearance on the Johnny Carson show. The view of most experts is that Jock's determination to stick by the regulations, which many considered outmoded, did more in a few seconds for the cause of women's running than a thousand editorials.

Jock was born on the south side of Glasgow in 1903, and his family moved to Clydebank when he was four. There, while working in the Singer's factory, he was introduced to running and quickly accumulated a cabinet-full of trophies. Ironically, his first training partner was a girl of his own age. In his biography Jock put a new slant on the Switzer incident when, speaking of those early days in his running career, he complained:

> Even then I favoured women's athletics but today I still wear an 'anti-woman' label because of that one incident with Kathy Switzer.

Having learned the carpenter's trade in John Brown's shipyard, Jock sailed with his brother, Jim, for America in 1927; his father, having seen how despondent Jock was when a strike put him out of work, offered to lend him money for the trip to America. Jock jumped at the chance, and his father added: 'Use the opportunity. See what you can do for yourself with a new start.' Jock did not need a second telling.

America, however, was approaching the stock market crash and there was no work in Philadelphia. Jock braved it out, becoming a vegetarian and living off old fruit which he bought from the vendors at the docks. He persisted with his first love—road-running—in the days when the sport suffered public ridicule and even occasional hostility. After moving to Boston, he finished nine times in the top ten in the world's most famous marathon.

The gruff Scot was well-liked, and Walter Brown, whose father co-founded the Boston Marathon in 1897, set Jock up with a physiotherapy clinic after World War II, where he looked after the stars of American football, baseball and basket-ball, as well as boxing legends like Jack Dempsey and, of course, fellow-runners. By 1953 Jock, who also trained several Olympic marathon teams, was co-director of 'the Boston' and in the fifties and sixties did most of the clerical chores for the great event. In the seventies, with the marathon boom, his workload increased correspondingly.

No single natural catastrophe tested the versatility of the Scottish business community in America more than the Great Fire of Chicago, which began on 8 October 1871, after an exceptionally dry summer which saw mushroom clouds from prairie fires crowd the western horizon.

The Illinois Saint Andrew Society reckons that there were 8,000 Scots in the city that Sunday evening, and the annual report of the Society gives a graphic account of the blaze:

> . . . the flames, urged by a strong south-west wind and fed by blocks of wooden buildings and miles of wooden streets, rushed with irresistible fury over the river and through the heart of the city.

For more than twenty-four hours the fire, stayed only by the waters of Lake Michigan, raged. Rain on Tuesday morning brought the first relief. Call for aid was sent around the world and it is on record that the Scots responded warmly to an appeal to help sufferers 'in the hour of their trial and distress': the City of Glasgow, for instance, gave 5,000 pounds, but donations big and small flooded in from Scotland.

Only two fatalities were reported from the Scots community, although over 200 people are thought to have died. The Scots were Robert Clark Sr., aged seventy-one, recently returned from a visit to Scotland, who perished while trying to flee the fire; and William George, who died from his injuries a few days later.

Even an incomplete list of the major Scottish business losses gives some indication of the scale of the disaster: Robert Hervey, five times president of the Society lost his valuable law library; Thomas Dougall, his soap factory and houses on Elm Street; Hugh Ritchie, a soap factory and house on Grand Haven Street; John Alston lost his glass and paint manufacturing plant at 172 Randolph, valued at 200,000 dollars; Robert Fergus & Sons, offices and printing plant; Thomas Hastie, his shoe firm and 60,000 dollars in US bonds; John M'Glashan lost stock and furniture; Robert Richie, seven houses on Franklin and Maple Streets; A.M. Thomson lost his Western Coffee and Spice mills; James C. Stewart, the Thistle Saloon on Clark Street—the sad list goes on and on. Other Scots-owned premises burned down include a foundry, drug store, art gallery and glass-cutters. The Society itself lost its library, paintings and property.

The scene at the St Andrews Day dinner in Chicago the following month, with 120 guests present and the walls bare of flags, pictures and banners destroyed in the fire was a heart-rending one. Each member had been touched in some way by the disaster, and 'men once wealthy were now penniless'. Yet still the Scots continued to arrive in Chicago, one immigrant remarking in a letter home that, days after the blaze, the streets of Chicago were still warm to the touch.

For hundreds of Scots the fire was the collapse of their dreams. It's a tribute to the adaptability and resilience of these folk that they were among the first to roll up their sleeves and launch into the rebuilding of Chicago, their adopted home. To sum up the adaptability of the Scot in America there is no need to look further than the town of Tombstone (AZ). In 1884, a young Scots girl, Mary McGee, came to the West with her mining engineer husband and lived at a small inn until their home was built. A young Norwegian girl employed at the inn missed her homeland almost as much as Mary, and the two became firm friends. When Mary's house was completed, her relatives in Scotland sent her a box of native Scottish shrubs. As a gift, Mary gave several Lady Banksia rose-bushes to her new-found friend, and together the girls planted them beside the inn's woodshed. Today these roses cover nearly 7,000 square feet—the largest such plot in the world—and when it blooms each April it fills the air with the fragrance of thousands of tiny white flowers. Like the old country's transplanted sons and daughters, the rose flourished in its new home.

Trainload of logs ready for shipping from a Scots timber operation at Diboll (TX). Blairgowrie's William Cameron made his fortune as the rail network developed after the Civil War, eventually owning sixty retail lumber yards. (The Institute of Texan Cultures, San Antonio.)

# ✎ *Chapter 12* ✎
# LOG COLLEGES AND MEDICINE MEN

COLONIAL AMERICA WAS NO PLACE for the faint of heart. For the professional classes in particular conditions could seem very harsh, yet in significant numbers we do find Scots teachers (in the early days often ministers wearing the dominie's hat) and doctors (mostly trained in the Scottish universities) working along the eastern seaboard or scattered amongst the pioneer communities.

The fledgling Americans knew they were on to a good thing. As Thomas Jefferson once wrote of the Scots: 'from that country we are sure of having sober, attentive men'. Mostly this was true, but not always.

Self-help in matters medical was the order of the day in the 1600s, with only a handful of doctors, like the clerical circuit-riders, moving across country to deal with the aches and pains of the new Americans. For the pioneers, life was a difficult and often dangerous business. Disease (malaria, tuberculosis, dysentery, yellow fever, cholera and smallpox), Indian attack, falling trees, raging torrents and severe weather all took their toll. Traditional medicines were widely employed, and the settlers acquired some of the local knowledge and essential skills from their Indian neighbours. Patent cures became very popular, particularly 'snake oil', probably because of its alcoholic content.

Even in the 1700s and early 1800s a doctor was still a rare sight away from the towns, and so everyone had to learn how to prepare herbs, roots and barks for a variety of complaints. Hardy settlers could set broken legs and arms that mended well, knew how to remove bullets or arrowheads and how to tend wounds and birth babies. When the doctor did show up he was likely to be keen on 'bleeding' his patient or prescribing explosive purgatives.

Doctors who did make the Atlantic crossing in the first century of settlement were a dedicated group. There was no lucrative employment, only a hard slog. It was only in the 1700s, when the coastal towns began to expand rapidly and a relatively affluent merchant class developed, particularly in the tobacco states of the South, that opportunities for professional men, including doctors, started to materialise.

Up to 1765 there was no medical tuition whatsoever available in the American colonies. Even after the establishment of America's first medical school at Philadelphia, which was based on the Edinburgh model and dominated by Scots-trained teachers, many young Americans went back to Scotland to train, particularly at Edinburgh.

An early Scots arrival in America was William Vans Murray, cousin and ward of the Duke of Atholl, who escaped to Maryland after the 1715 Uprising, settled in Cambridge and made a fortune as a medical practitioner. Lionel C. Chalmers, born in 1715 in Campbeltown, Argyll, went to the Carolinas as a child, studied medicine and practised for more than forty years.

Dalkeith provided a remarkable dynasty of New World doctors in the shape of Dr Gustavus Brown (b.1689), his son by the same name, born in Maryland in 1747 and educated at Edinburgh University, and yet another Dr Gustavus Brown, one of the old Scot's grandsons, who was called on to attend to President George Washington in his last illness. Another Scots medical clan were the McCaws: James Brown McCaw (1772– 1846) was a leading surgeon in Virginia for over thirty years, and also studied at Edinburgh. He is thought to have been the first physician to tie the external carotid artery in the year 1807. He was the great-grandson of James McCaw, a surgeon who immigrated from Wigtownshire in 1771.

Dr John Moultrie, born in Culross in Fife, was the first citizen of South Carolina to obtain an MD from the University of Edinburgh; and although Philadelphia subsequently established itself as a centre of medical excellence, it was for many years rivalled by Charleston (SC), where between 1732 and 1736 thirty-six physicians were practising, many of them Scots.

PROFESSIONALS ON THE NEW FRONTIER

It was often the children of the better-off Scots immigrants to America in the 1700s who returned to the old country for a medical education. Tucker Harris (1715–1821), one of Charleston's most noted family doctors, was the son of Scots-born William Harris, who left for America as a young man. Tucker's early education in Charleston was obtained in one of the town's best schools, and after initially showing some interest in a career as a merchant, he left for Edinburgh in 1768, receiving his diploma as MD on 12 June 1771.

He married in Scotland and set off again for South Carolina from Gravesend in London. Tucker Harris cared for the sick of Charleston for over forty years, playing a significant role in the Revolutionary War as an army surgeon in charge of the Continental Army hospital. He was taken prisoner in 1780 when Charleston surrendered to the British, and his support for the Revolutionary cause is further confirmed by the fact that the Harris family were on the list of Patriots expelled by the British in 1782.

Most doctors who practised in America during the 1770s seem to have been men of very broad interests, and as we've noted were often pioneers in botany and zoology, filing detailed studies on insect populations, epidemics, plant colonies and weather statistics back to Europe for publication in medical journals.

In Pennsylvania, Dr Thomas Graeme, from Balgowan in Perthshire, was a leading physician for half a century and also an Associate Justice of the Supreme. He died in 1772.

Dr David Oliphant was born near Perth in 1720, and served as a surgeon with the Jacobite Army at Culloden before fleeing to South Carolina; Scots-born doctor, Peter Middleton, assisted in the first dissection in America in 1750; and Dr James Tillary is remembered for his self-sacrifice in remaining in New York in 1795 and 1798 to help victims of yellow fever outbreaks.

The island of Coll provided one of the first of the batch of medical immigrants from Scotland to New England. Neil MacLean was born around 1700, studied medicine and came to America in 1736, when he settled at Hartford (CT), married the daughter of a wealthy London merchant and had six children. His reputation as a trustworthy, understanding family doctor was immense. He was, according to a contemporary, 'a noted physician of extensive practice, a man of refined education, great dignity and ease of manner and of uncommon benevolence of heart'.

Gifford in East Lothian was the home village of William Douglass, who was destined to become one of the most well-known general practitioners in America during the first half of the eighteenth century. The son of the Marquis of Tweeddale's factor, he studied medicine at Edinburgh, Leyden and Paris before taking the giant step and moving to Boston (MA) in 1718.

Unfortunately, Douglass didn't get off to the most auspicious start when he argued vehemently with his colleagues against the use of innoculation during a severe smallpox epidemic in 1721. Thirty years were to pass before he would publicly admit the efficacy of the procedure. However, he built up a successful practice and provided a major service to his profession when, in 1735–36, he noted in great detail the progress of a scarlet fever outbreak which ravaged Boston.

Another East Lothian doctor, William Brown (1752–1792), immigrated to Alexandria (VA) with its influential Scots colony and (like many doctors with Scots roots) he served with the Revolutionary Army and was an acquaintance of Washington, Jefferson and Madison.

In his will the first President of the United States, George Washington, declared:

> To my compatriot in arms, an old intimate friend, Dr Craik, I give my bureau and the circular chair, an appendage of my study.

By Washington's deathbed was the trusty Dr James Craik, born at Arbigland, Dumfries-shire, on the same estate as the American naval hero, John Paul Jones. Craik had immigrated to America by way of the West Indies. He was one of Washington's closest associates, making a hazardous canoe and horseback journey with the future president into the wilds of the Ohio and Kanawua river valleys, to make a 'location' of land granted by the Crown to officers and men who had fought in the French and Indian War. Craik's career closely followed that of his illustrious friend, and his only published work relates to the national hero's final illness. Dr Craik died in 1814.

### NECKTIE CLUB FOR A MEDICAL PIONEER

On the public square in Danville (KY) stands a modest monument commemorating the world's first successful removal of an ovarian tumour by an Ulster-Scots doctor, Ephraim McDowell (1771–1830). This historic event took place under the most trying of conditions and even today is regarded as something of a medical miracle.

McDowell was the son of an Ulster-Scots judge who had settled in the Danville district. The young man had been apprenticed to a distinguished surgeon, Dr Alexander Humphreys, also an Ulster Scot, back east in Staunton in the great valley of Virginia. Like so many others, McDowell had gone to Edinburgh to complete his medical education; back in his home town he was to become perhaps the most distinguished surgeon west of the Alleghenies. In December 1809, doctors at Motley's Glen—some sixty miles and a two-day ride west of Danville, right on the edge of the

Ulster Scot Dr Ephraim McDowell, who was educated at Edinburgh University and performed the first successful operation to remove an ovarian tumor, on Christmas Day 1809. *right* Jane Todd Crawford, his forty-six year old patient, had neither anaesthetic nor antiseptic. (The McDowell House)

wilderness—had a pregnant woman they believed was expecting twins, but were unable to deliver her. McDowell had already established himself as a surgeon of repute, and an urgent request was made for his help.

Arriving at Motley's Glen on horseback he examined the patient, Mrs Crawford, mother of a sizeable brood of children, and quickly discovered that rather than expecting twins she was carrying a large ovarian tumour. The best medical opinion in Scotland and England had declared that the opening of the abdomen would result in inevitable death—but McDowell saw that the woman's case was otherwise hopeless and persuaded her to travel to Danville.

McDowell knew that if the operation failed the chances were that he would face a charge of murder. Rumours of the planned surgery spread quickly, and from the pulpit Ephraim was accused of being in league with the devil. Tempers got so heated that at one stage the Danville mob attached a rope to a tree with the intention of lynching the doctor. However, on Christmas Day, with only the crudest of anaesthetics, McDowell prepared Mrs Crawford for the operation and, as was his custom, he offered up a prayer. In this case the prayer has been preserved, and part of it pleads:

> Direct me, Oh! God, in performing this operation, for I am but an instrument in Thy hands and am but Thy servant, and if it is Thy will, Oh! spare this poor afflicted woman.

According to his own testimony, McDowell removed up to 20lb of gelatinous material; yet in a few weeks the patient was able to return to her family and lived to be almost eighty. In Edinburgh, London and Philadelphia the medically informed still refused to believe the operation had been carried out. But McDowell's pioneering effort and Mrs Crawford's courage had paved the way for surgery to be conducted on the uterus, spleen, kidneys, gall bladder and liver. Every operation for appendicitis or gall stones is a lineal descendant of that one daring experiment in the wilds of Kentucky. Ironically, McDowell died of appendicitis.

Brilliant and eccentric were just two of the adjectives applied to the career of the occasionally outrageous Glasgow-born anatomist, Granville Sharp Pattison (1791– 1851), who was educated at the University of Glasgow. He began his teaching career at the city's Andersonian Institution, where he rapidly built a reputation as a popular lecturer.

He had been at the centre of public anger when he and some students were accused of body-snatching, most notably from the Ramshorn Churchyard close to their quarters. After a mob attacked the university, smashing windows, Pattison and the others were put on trial in Edinburgh and, although cleared, there was so much ill-will persisting that Pattison decided to immigrate. Arriving in America with the expectation of landing the post of Chair of Anatomy at the University of Pennsylvania, he was disappointed but made an impression with a controversial series of lectures which resulted in the Scot issuing the challenge of a duel to the Professor of

Medicine at the university. The professor's brother took up the gauntlet and 'received a ball in his pistol arm for his trouble'. A ball passed harmlessly through Pattison's coat.

After teaching stints in Maryland, New Jersey and London—always tinged with controversy—he eventually secured the Chair of Anatomy at the University of the City of New York, where he founded the medical department and where his popularity among his students, partly on account of his eccentric style, was immense. Pattison edited medical journals, was fond of hunting and fishing, and loved music. He was the leader of a group who arranged for the first productions of grand opera in New York.

Throughout the 1800s and into the 1900s Scots and their descendants figured prominently not only in the development of medical and surgical techniques in the universities and hospitals, but also out on the wilderness frontline of the developing nation. Men like Forbes Barclay, born in 1812 in Lerwick, who was chief physician for the Hudson's Bay Company at their Columbia River headquarters at Fort Vancouver, and later became a civic leader in Oregon City. Men like Charles Smart, who studied medicine at the

The house at Danville (KY) where McDowell carried out his pioneering operation with a superstitious lynch mob waiting at the door. (The McDowell House)

University of Aberdeen before moving to the Wild West in 1862, where he served as an army surgeon; he was the compiler of the first Apache Indian vocabulary.

## DOC McCARTY: BULLET WOUNDS MY SPECIALITY

It was an Ulster-Scots doctor, Thomas McCarty, who landed one of the busiest postings in the Old West—Dodge City (KS), where gunplay was commonplace and a doctor could gather more experience with gunshot wounds than any military surgeon would in a dozen campaigns.

In 1872, Philadelphia-trained McCarty stopped in Dodge to look up a relative while on his way to Denver (CO) and decided to stay. The town was only three months old, and he set up shop in a drugstore. Over the years, he was involved in most aspects of life in the frontier town, becoming a school superintendent, founding a hospital and encouraging his own son to become a doctor.

For physicians in these frontier towns life was tough in the extreme. Epidemics were frequent, sanitation non-existent and operations, just as in the movies, were conducted with alcohol anaesthetic on the kitchen table.

When Glasgow-born Dr James Smith Gardiner took the decision to move to California after the Civil War, he soon built up a large and successful practice based in Anaheim. His family had immigrated to Tennessee in 1849, but it was in the Far West that Dr Gardiner found success. The Anaheim histories suggest that, like so many American doctors in the late 1800s, his services were often repaid with 'hay, wood, pork and promises', very seldom in hard cash. However, Dr Gardiner, who also served as postmaster of Anaheim, is best remembered as the man who performed the first Caesarean operation in Orange County. On this occasion he was paid in coin—twenty-five dollars.

Scots seem to have flourished in the pioneering environment when it came to matters medical and the need to improvise. In Battle Creek (MI), John Moreland and his wife, Catherine, both native-born Scots, settled. Around them in the locality were a number of black families who had fled from oppression in the South. Generations later, a member of one of those black families told a Moreland descendant that Catherine had bestowed so many kindnesses on her neighbours, and delivered so many black babies, that she was known in the Negro community as 'The White Angel'.

The story is also told in *The Palimpsest* of a minister's son at a Scots settlement in Iowa, who had been brought to the manse with a great ragged wound in his leg. The boy had been working for a neighbouring farmer when he fell through a thatched roof on to a barbed wire fence. Without the services of a doctor locally, one of the farmers volunteered to tackle the wound. There were no antiseptics, not even a general knowledge of them, but the farmer washed out the cut, laid the boy out on a table, heated a poker, cauterized the wound and sewed it up. The injury healed without infection.

The indomitable spirit of the American-Scots doctors is well illustrated by the saga of Blind Doc McCray, general practitioner for forty-seven years in the community of New Albany in Kansas. Moses Elias McCray, according to his granddaughter, Lela Tindle, was immensely proud of his Scots background and became so renowned locally that, despite his blindness, hundreds of people in south-eastern Kansas simply refused to go anywhere else for treatment.

Born in 1851 in Hancock County (IN), Doc McCray moved as a child with his family to Iowa, where his father, William, an itinerant minister, farmer and saddle-maker was also a 'conductor' on the famous Iowa Underground Railway Movement, hiding runaway slaves and passing them along the network to Canada. Harbouring runaways was a crime, and when Moses was only thirteen the family had to flee by sleigh at night when a group of rebel sympathisers learned the McCrays' house was being used to hide Negros.

By 1873, the family were in Kansas, where the township of New Albany was just developing. After studying at the American Medical College at St Louis (MO), Moses set off with his sisters and mother for Nebraska where he practised near Red Cloud, returning only briefly to Kansas to marry his school-teacher sweetheart. Nebraska was a severe posting for any doctor, and Moses McCray would often find himself floundering on horseback through snowdrifts fence-post high. Having lost two children to the harsh Nebraska climate, he decided to make Kansas his home; but those snowstorms, in which the Doc frequently got lost, had a debilitating effect on his eyesight. Pain which he suffered in Nebraska became worse and his vision deteriorated.

Despite his handicap the practice continued to grow, and in March 1889 he treated 225 people during a measles epidemic. Hazards, including hold-ups, were many. The family tell of the famous occasion when Doc McCray was stopped by two men as he crossed the railroad tracks in his buggy. Ordered at gunpoint to give up his money and watch, he gave them instead the biting end of his horsewhip and sped off.

Doc McCray was one who made full use of traditional methods, and once he was called out to see a farm boy whose leg had been spiked by a pitchfork. Unfortunately the incident had been kept a secret for some days and blood poisoning had set in. The Doc demanded the horn of a freshly dehorned cow, shaved it into vinegar and made a poultice for the injured knee. The boy recovered.

For years, as his eyesight finally disappeared, folk marvelled at how he continued his profession. But he mixed his own medical powders and ointments, carefully counting down a long row of brown medicine bottles until he came to the correct ingredient which was indexed in his mind. Blind Doc McCray died in May 1927, and the little community of New Albany never had another doctor.

Pin-pointing the start of education above the simple rudimentary levels in America leads us to the little hamlet of Neshaminy, twenty miles north of Philadelphia. An immigrant from Scottish roots was at the heart of activity, founding the first of the famous 'log colleges'. In 1716, William Tennent, a graduate of Edinburgh University and of Ulster-Scots stock, arrived in Pennsylvania and was given fifty acres of land. Here he erected his school, the first institution founded by Presbyterians to educate young men for the ministry, but which was to become a role model for the rest of the nation.

Tennent, who was the only teacher, was an exceptional scholar, speaking and writing Latin with unmatched fluency. Although his little school was only to last until 1742, it had a profound effect on the American educational system. In the earliest years of the college, Pennsylvania citizens were amazed at Tennent's efforts and the stoicism of the young men who attended the school. One leading figure in the church wrote:

> The place wherein the young men study is in contempt called The College. It is a log house, about twenty feet long, and as near as many broad and to me it seemed to resemble the school of prophets.

In reality it was not so much a school as a one-man training centre for ministers, the tuition fees coming from the 'graduates'. Eminent ministers such as Samuel and John Blair, Samuel Finley, Charles Beatty and John Rowland, as well as Tennent's four sons all studied at Neshaminy College, and the term 'log college' soon became a stamp of educational merit rather than derision.

Out on the frontier, parents tried to educate their children at elementary level as best they could with classes held in the log kirks for children who lived close enough to the settlements. Still at work here was the belief, implanted by the Reformation in Scotland, that education was the mark of the man. The desire to have a school in every parish, to achieve popular literacy, was carried with the Scots and Ulster Scots across the Atlantic, general education of the people being accepted not only as desirable but essential. It was expected that, in the Scottish communities, a school teaching the rudiments—reading, writing, spelling and arithmetic—would be established wherever the teacher's salary could be afforded. When it came to spreading their wings, this background often gave the Scots immigrants a head start over their fellow arrivals in America.

William and Thomas Gordon from Aberdeenshire founded a free school in Middlesex County (VA) in the late 1600s; and in 1691, Hugh Campbell gifted 200 acres of land in each of the Virginian counties of Norfolk, Isle of Wight, and Nansemond for free schools. James Innes, who came to America from Canisby in Caithness in 1734, left in his will his plantation, library and personal estate for the creation of a free school for 'the youth of North Carolina'. Gabriel Johnston, provincial governor of the same state, was a professor of languages at St Andrews before immigrating, and he insisted

Moses Elias McCray, or as folk in south-eastern Kansas knew him, 'Blind Doc McCray'. Despite all the odds, he continued to practice as a country GP after being blinded by Nebraska snowstorms. (Lela J. Tindle)

234

on the need for a proper school system as early as the 1730s.

The 'log college' was the seed from which the College of New Jersey, later Princeton University, sprang. Established in 1746, it began its most vigorous period of growth when Dr John Witherspoon immigrated to take charge and set the seal on its distinctly Scottish approach to education. The curriculum, general philosophy, dress and examinations reflected what was going on in the Scottish universities. Although its aim was to provide ministers for the expanding church, and cope with the very special educational needs of the frontiersfolk, it put a strong emphasis on maths, natural philosophy and science, as well as the classics.

Witherspoon (1723–1794), born at Gifford near Haddington, and educated at Edinburgh University, had ministerial charges at Beith and Paisley before answering the call to Princeton in 1768, and soon brought it to prominence as one of the foremost educational establishments in the land. He had gone to America somewhat reluctantly, but in time he actively encouraged Scots immigration. With him Witherspoon took as extensive a library as he could muster, but large numbers of his books were destroyed in the Revolutionary War when the British burned Nassau Hall.

Along with James Wilson, another native Scot, Witherspoon was a signatory to the Declaration of Independence: it was he who issued the clarion call when there was momentary hesitation in the final act of signing the Declaration. His address that day still stirs American hearts, and is reminiscent of another Declaration, at Arbroath in 1320, when a more ancient kingdom sought to assert its freedom. He told the gathering:

> He that will not respond to its accents and strain every nerve to carry into effect its provisions is unworthy of the name of freeman. For myself, although these grey hairs must soon descend into the sepulchre, I would infinitely prefer they descend thither by the hand of the public executioner than desert at this crisis the sacred cause of my country.

When it was suggested that the colonies were not ripe for independence, Witherspoon thundered: 'Not ripe, sir? In my judgement we are not only ripe but rotting.'

The success of his work at Princeton is reflected in the fact that, between 1766 and 1773, 230 students graduated—from this group emerged twelve members of the Continental Congress, twenty-four members of the Congress of the United States, three Justices of the Supreme Court, five cabinet members, one president and one vice-president.

Generally, outside the areas dominated by the English-style universities of Yale and Harvard, Scottish educational principles were most influential. Princeton graduates were especially active in the southern and Gulf states, but Scots were busy right across the colonies. The College of William and Mary at Williamsburg (VA), was founded by John Blair (1665–1743), who had been educated at Marischal College in Aberdeen and adopted teaching techniques and examination procedures from his days in the Granite City.

The most illustrious student from William and Mary was surely Thomas Jefferson, author of the Declaration of Independence. He attended for two years and was later to pay a glowing tribute to his Scots-born Professor of Mathematics, Dr William Small, who, said Jefferson, it was his good fortune to be taught by and who 'probably fixed the destinies of my life'. Small had taken the young Jefferson under his wing. The future president declared:

> From him I got my first views of the expansion of science and of the system of things in which we are placed.

Philadelphia College, which was to become the University of Pennsylvania, was also strongly influenced by the Scots. William Smith, a Scottish Episcopalian in the true Aberdonian tradition, and the Rev. Francis Alison, a Glasgow University-educated Ulster Scot, were considered the founding fathers, brought together by Benjamin Franklin, the American statesman and scientist. They helped his dream of a Pennsylvania university come to life.

Smith, remembered as one of the great educators in the New World in the 1700s, had one unspoken ambition—he wanted to become the first Episcopal bishop in America. Born in 1727 and educated at the University of Aberdeen as a charity student, Smith had a weakness that was to plague him throughout his life, a fondness for drink. As Thomas Jones explains in his biography of Smith, the Scot was nominated late in his career as the first Episcopal bishop; but before he could be consecrated he was chairman of a church convention in New York and got so drunk that no one suggested him for the 'lawn-sleeves' again.

Critics were never short of adjectives to describe this interesting man: bellicose, drunken, foul-mouthed, venal, niggardly, spiteful and mendacious. Having started his professional life as a poor school-teacher, he immigrated to America in 1751 and was soon well acquainted with the influential folk of colonial Pennsylvania, including the Penn family themselves, Franklin, and the future President Washington.

Jones's account also tells us that at the 1774 gathering of the Continental Congress, Smith was the Philadelphian most delegates wanted to meet. His colourful reputation had gone before him. Smith's most famous conflict was with Franklin, who, having agreed to hire the Scot as head of the College of Philadelphia, conducted a running battle with his new recruit, in private and public. Ironically, it was Smith who was asked to deliver a eulogy on Franklin's death and produced a stirring effort despite the long-standing personal animosity. Smith died in 1803.

Marischal College in Aberdeen was where mathematician John Kemp (1763–1812), born at Auchlossan, near Aboyne, first began to shine, and it was here that his professors and contemporaries first began to predict a bright future for him. By 1782 he was in America, and three years later he was given a year-long appointment to teach mathematics at Columbia College, New York.

An unusual end-of-session examination procedure, suggested by Kemp and adopted by the college, guaranteed his employment. Each student was required to draw a number from a box and demonstrate the problem or theorem in Euclid to which the number applied. John's pupils did spectacularly well. At the age of twenty-three he was appointed Professor of Mathematics and Natural Philsophy. He served the College for three decades and is given credit for having inspired one of his pupils, Dewitt Clinton, with the idea of constructing the Erie Canal across New York state.

## SHETLANDER'S STAMINA

John Harrower, a forty-year-old Shetland shopkeeper whose business failed, ended up teaching on a plantation on the eastern seaboard of America, the amazing journey that took him there, faithfully logged in his journal, being among the best-documented immigrant stories that we have.

Harrower set out in December 1773, with no intention of ever venturing across the Atlantic. Faced with poverty in Shetland, he decided to seek his fortune elsewhere in Europe and send for his family once he prospered. His only capital was a small supply of Shetland knitted stockings worth about three pounds, and using these he bartered his way across country. John's only advantages were that he was ambitious, literate . . . and determined.

Harrower tried and failed to secure passage to the Netherlands when he reached Dundee, and during his stay on Tayside rejected the opportunity to travel to North Carolina as an indentured servant. Reaching Newcastle, he tried again (unsuccessfully) to get across the North Sea to Holland. Living on a diet of bread, cheese and beer, he trudged through the snow to Sunderland. Eventually he got a berth on a boat destined for Holland but which ended up in Portsmouth.

Undaunted, John walked to London, where all the hustle and bustle stunned the man from the open spaces of Shetland. He tried and failed to secure several advertised jobs, including the post of book-keeper. By this time America had come firmly into the reckoning, but he was turned down for a clerk's job in Philadelphia. But John also believed that God would most willingly help those who helped themselves, and so armed with a testimonial he did the rounds of merchants and tradesmen, explaining his situation and offering to work for minimum wages. Black despair threatened to consume the Shetlander as he found himself among the vast legions of the unemployed, where 'many good people are begging'.

After writing to his wife with a full account of his adventures, he signed on as an indentured servant to go to Virginia for a four-year period. Although he was a bondsman for this period, his literary and numerical skills secured him the post of tutor at the home of Colonel William Daingerfield. He taught the sons of the house, some handicapped children, and even some Negro youngsters; but sadly, he died before he could accumulate enough capital to bring out his wife and children.

Securing a post as a tutor to a well-off family in the southern United States was a common method for teachers to find their way to America. Such was the route chosen by William Russell, born in Glasgow in 1798, who sailed for Georgia in 1817 after graduating from the city university, and he was soon at the home of John McPherson Berrien in Savannah (GA).

Russell may at one point have considered a permanent return to Scotland, but after a visit he finally decided that the damp Scottish climate was too severe for him. America's gain was our loss. By 1821 he had moved to New England, where he became principal of a number of leading academies, was the first editor of *The American Journal of Education* and helped found new schools and colleges all across the region. He consistently urged better teacher-training and improved textbooks, encouraged the entry of women into the teaching profession, and was convinced that teaching could transform American society for the better by utilising the old Scots virtues of charity, industry, fortitude and family stability. Despite ill health in his later years, Russell continued to hold regular study sessions for teachers.

Joanne Graham (1770–1860), born in Canada but educated at Paisley and Edinburgh, settled with her family in America in 1798 and became devoted to the cause of orphanages and Sunday schools. She has been described as the 'mother of American Sabbath schools' and was a co-founder of the New York Infant School Society.

INVERNESS ROYAL ACADEMY: THE ALABAMA CONNECTION

Inverness Royal Academy can take some credit for the early development of education in the state of Alabama. John Fraser (1801–1882) was the son of a Scots gentleman who immigrated to Petersburg in Virginia in the late 1700s. In 1815, John and his two brothers were offered an education in Scotland by an uncle, and the boys left Virginia on the first ship to sail to Great Britain after the war of 1812. They stayed with their grandmother, 'a true Presbyterian', and were taught at the Royal Academy in the Highland capital.

On returning to America, John studied at Cambridge (MA) with the writer Ralph Waldo Emerson and taught school before moving to Athens (AL) in 1832. He taught initially in the Masonic Hall, but after his marriage to Martha Wyche built a log house (which is still standing), followed quickly by a log schoolroom in a beautiful grove of trees near the house. Here he prepared young men for entry into college, many of them going to Alabama's first college at La Grange, fifty miles west of Athens. According to local historian Faye Axford, to enter La Grange the boys had to have an impressive knowledge of Latin and Greek, and scholars from Fraser's Classical Academy were future chief justices, publishers, writers and politicians.

John's beloved grove of trees was cut down by Union soldiers during the Civil War, but he continued teaching until 1875, when his three daughters Lizzie, Virgie and Cornelia were also conducting lessons.

Teachers with a Scottish background either in their ancestry or in their training helped spread education through the fast-growing communities of nineteenth-century America and were often dubbed the 'common sense philosophers'. Their down-to-earth approach to education found favour amid the vast social and moral upheaval brought about by America's industrial revolution and its consequent urbanisation, just as they had provided a solid foundation in the frontier outposts. However, it is not only in teaching itself that the Scots are remembered, but as much in the organisation and administration of education.

In the town of Aurora (CO), William Smith was the man who single-mindedly brought organised education into the district, after coming to Colorado from Scotland in 1878 under the sponsorship of Lord Barclay, owner of the Colorado Mortgage and Investment Company. Smith became involved with a company which built a canal, and by 1882 he had settled 320 acres bordering the canal, where, at his house—'a small, pioneer affair'—he raised sheep, pigs and had a small dairy operation as well as growing wheat and alfalfa. Smith and his wife, Anne, had four children and when Anne died he married her sister, Rachel, who had three children of her own.

Remembering his Scottish roots, Willie Smith was a strong advocate of the neighbourhood school system, echoing the parish schools of his native land, and whatever spare time he had he spent riding through the countryside (which at that time had more prairie dogs than inhabitants) trying to get people interested in organising School District 28. By 1885 he had enough signatures and the Aurora School District was born, Smith providing the land for the first school and serving on the school board for fifty years. In recognition of his contribution to Colorado's educational development, a high school was named after him and his timber-built house is now on the National Register of Historic Places.

Lindley Murray (1745–1826), the son of a Pennsylvania Scot, gave America its first English grammar; Henry Ivison published the first American series of school readers; and Joseph Ray and William McGuffey (both of Scottish descent) were names familiar to generations of American school children as producers of school books. Stoddart's arithmetic books were the work of a grandson of an Edinburgh Scot.

Schoolrooms, although more comfortable than Tennent's log college, were still very basic. Clarence Watson, in his memoirs of life in nineteenth-century Illinois, tells of his little one-room school which the children knew as Wiley College. It was a plain, rectangular building with a narrow entry where coats, overshoes and dinner buckets were deposited:

> Desks were in four rows facing the teacher and were plain wooden affairs, each accommodating two children and all the same height regardless of the age of the occupant.

Two pot-bellied stoves provided the heat for the entire room. Generally, it was a barren place with no decoration except for the occasional bunch of flowers left on the teacher's desk.

Frances 'Fanny' Wright, daughter of a Dundee linen merchant and one of Scotland's more sensational exports, was a radical feminist who took America by storm in the early 1800s. (The Herald Archives)

In Louisiana, John McNeese was the individual whose inspired work dramatically improved the quality of the region's education, but who only came to rest in the state because of a stock market crash and a disastrous drought. The son of a Scottish shipbuilder who had settled in New York in the early 1800s, John served in the Civil War before heading for Texas where he was involved in stock-raising.

As a cowboy, cattleman and store-owner, John flourished until the 'panic' of 1873 took its toll on Western businesses. When the depression forced McNeese to close his shop and resign his job as court clerk for Menard County, he decided to gather together what cattle he had and drive them to market in New Orleans. A drought scorched the trail to the coast, and when John reached the Sabine River in Louisiana catastrophe struck. Starving for food and dying of thirst, the ravenous herd gorged itself on switch cane which grew along the river bank—most of the herd died. For John McNeese, orphaned as a child and later stricken with tuberculosis, life must have seemed at a desperately low ebb. However, he shrugged off the calamity, sold the few beasts he had left, and started to carve out a new life for himself in south-west Louisiana.

In the community of Lake Charles he became a teacher in a rural school to earn a living, and ten years later in 1883 he was appointed to the Calcasieu Parish School Board, later becoming secretary. At this time, Louisiana had no coherent school system outside New Orleans; those who wanted education had to pay for it, and attendance at private schools far exceeded that of public schools. The situation in Calcasieu, a district of some 4,000 square miles, was particularly bad when John McNeese was appointed superintendent for education in 1888. But within two years he raised the total of public schools in the parish to twenty-four, and four years later the figure had grown to 114. His inspired ideas spread throughout the state, and perhaps his greatest contribution was the successful effort to levy the first public school taxes in Louisiana. He died in 1914.

One of Scotland's more sensational educational exports was undoubtedly the radical feminist Fanny Wright, daughter of a Dundee linen merchant. Fanny's out-spoken advocacy of women's rights and public education in the first half of the nineteenth century made her a social revolutionary of the first order, and a major US celebrity. She came to the attention of the American public with a series of lectures in 1828–29 which questioned many accepted social norms and outlined her dream of an ideal society in which education predominated. Her presence on the platform as a main speaker, at a time when women very much took a back seat, was a controversial event in itself.

Fanny was a colourful figure, having romantic associations with many of the leading intellectuals of the day, her name being linked at one time or another with Robert Owen, Thomas Jefferson and Jeremy Bentham. Under Owen's influence she founded an experimental community at Nashoba, near Memphis (TN) in the late 1820s, but it ended amid rumours of sexual scandal and failure of black and white members of the community to integrate; the experiment was also dubbed 'Fanny Wright's Free Love Colony'. Undaunted, she joined Owen at New Harmony, editing the community newspaper and then campaigned for labour rights, urging free, equal, universal and republican education. Amongst liberals she inspired undisguised admiration and at the same time contempt, occasionally hatred, from the more reactionary elements. Her opponents on one hand could brand her 'the red harlot of infidelity', while for her supporters she was the 'sweetest mind ever cased in a human body'.

~' *Chapter 13* ~'
# RIFLES BY THE PULPIT

W ITH SOME DEGREE OF ACCURACY it has been claimed that Scotland's two most significant gifts to America, apart from the immigrant legion itself, have been Presbyterianism ... and golf. Perhaps by the turn of the century a proper impact assessment might be carried out on the 'gift of golf'; but for Presbyterianism, introduced to America by Scots and Ulster Scots from the earliest days of settlement the case is surely well proved. From its first outposts in Pennsylvania, New Jersey and New York the faith reached out across the country, drawing its strength in this tough New World from its old Scots democratic forms and organised authority. It helped give shape and form to the young country and acted as a focus for the aspirations of the Scots settlers.

The Presbytery of Philadelphia, founded by Ulster-Scot Francis Makemie, whose parents were both Scots, was the strong root from which Presbyterianism in America flourished. Makemie arrived in 1683 as a missionary, along with another Presbyterian clergyman, John Hampton. Stopping over at New York, where the Anglican faith dominated, Makemie was invited to preach in a private home while Hampton conducted open-air services on Long Island, acts reminiscent of the house and field conventicles of the Covenanters. They were immediately arrested and brought before the governor, Lord Cornbury. For six weeks before trial Makemie was detained, and although acquitted he had to pay costs amounting to a (for the time) staggering eighty-three pounds. The Philadelphia Presbytery was founded in 1706, and by the following year the beginnings of a congregation in New York was reported. By 1717, New York's Old First Presbyterian Church was meeting under the Rev. James Anderson, a native of Montrose.

Studies suggest that, by 1760, of 200 ministers of the Church in America, fifty-five were Ulster Scots and twenty-six native Scots, but the bulk were already American-born. Among the native Scots preachers we find the names of Wilson, Taylor, Gillespie, Anderson, Patillo, and Latta. In the South the first Presbyterians were the refugees who were either transported or forced out of Scotland during the Covenanting struggles. Minister to the group who came after Bothwell Brig in 1679 and settled at Port Royal (SC) was the Rev. William Dunlop, who returned to Scotland to become Principal of the University of Glasgow.

243

The bulk of the Scots and Ulster-Scots newcomers to America, both before and after the Revolutionary War, were from a Presbyterian background; but regular schisms resulted in all sorts of shades of Protestants within their broad church.

In Pennsylvania, where a multitude of Scots names are found in the county records, it is said that at one time in Washington County alone there were twenty-three different kinds of Presbyterian, differing in some cases in only the most minute points of doctrine and practice.

Although from the outside these splits could seem very trivial, even petty, they were deeply felt by the people involved.

The story is told of a Pennsylvania couple, both avowedly Presbyterian, who had lived together for fifty years but never attended each other's churches. Every Sunday, when they came to a fork in the road, the father would take the sons to his church while the mother headed off in the opposite direction with the daughters to her own place of worship. One history of Pennsylvania describes these Scots and their approach to religion thus:

> Sandy may have been a bit bigoted to be sure, but he had the Scotch granite in his make-up, he was no reed shaken by the wind . . . the iron had entered his soul when called upon to do battle against the injustices of Church and State in Scotland and Ulster and it would take time to mellow and broaden him.

It's worth remembering that the bulk of Scots were not fleeing religious persecution: they were simply ordinary folk seeking a new start away from the economic ills of the old country. But what those early congregations lacked in numbers, they made up for in enthusiasm. Men, women and children would sometimes travel up to thirty miles to services, most of the men carrying a psalter and a rifle. In the church the rifles were stacked near the door in case of Indian attack, and the minister stood his at the foot of the pulpit steps.

One itinerant Presbyterian preacher summed up the problems of the developing church on the frontier in the 1700s by describing them as 'difficult days'—a masterpiece of understatement. Established settlements on the Atlantic coast sent missionaries into the backwoods communities, so pulpit supply was always a problem, and ministers in more prosperous areas were expected to take their turn on the outer edge. Frontier ministers usually served more than one congregation, going from church to church on horseback and facing all sorts of dangers and hardships. These were the famous circuit-riders.

The Rev. George Duffield, one of Pennsylvania's most noted circuit-riders, kept a detailed journal giving a colourful insight into life on the backwoods tracks. The preaching was occasionally in the rough cabins of settlers but more often, says Duffield, 'in the woods . . . at places designed for building houses of worship'.

Archibald Cameron, Lochaber-born circuit-rider, was brought up by his brother in Nelson County (KY). Ordained in 1796, his forty-year ministry left an indelible mark on the state. He spent most of his life in the saddle, crossing and re-crossing the Salt River to organise new churches and encourage struggling congregations. Described as being blunt and reserved in manner, careless in dress, he was also apparently in possession of a 'native eloquence' and keen powers of satire when the occasion demanded.

Another of this group of mounted ministers was the Rev. John Cuthbertson, a missionary for nearly forty years who travelled through the primitive settlements of Pennsylvania in the 1700s establishing churches and visiting the Presbyterian flock. He is reckoned to have ridden more than 60,000 miles, preached on 2,400 days, baptised between 1,600 and 1,800 children, married 250 couples and founded fifteen churches.

William Rainey, an Ulster-Scots Methodist circuit-rider took the gospel to remote areas of Mississippi in the early 1800s. Travelling rough, he often rested up in empty churches. Once, while sheltering from a storm in a remote building, an 'apparition' of an ashen-faced woman in a white robe wandered down the aisle towards him. Mr Rainey fled and rode through the teeth of the storm to the next settlement. Later he was to discover that the woman in white was a local 'crazy' who wandered the district at night.

AN ENDURANCE TEST

Services in the log kirks would be regarded today as endurance tests, suggests the American historian, Wayland Dunaway, but were submitted to with cheerful patience. Normally they began at 10 a.m. and lasted well into the afternoon. The day's programme consisted of sermons (sometimes lasting an hour and a half) and prayers, with a half-hour lunch break. This was a chance for young and old alike to swap gossip, Sunday service forming a vital news and information exchange in the often isolated frontier communities.

In the Ulster-Scots settlements of Pennsylvania the semi-annual communion service lasted several days, and because of the large numbers involved it was often held in the open air, with a stand for the pastor and visiting ministers. These ministers seemed to bear the hardships cheerfully, and there was spiritual reward despite the unpromising first impressions. Dr John McMillan came, with his new bride, to take over a backwoods charge in the late 1700s:

> We placed two boxes, one on another which served as a table, and two kegs served us for seats, and having committed ourselves to God in family worship we spread a bed on the floor and slept soundly

Ulster-Scots preacher, Francis Makemie, faces the wrath of the governor of New York, Lord Cornbury for preaching Presbyterianism in the Anglican heartland in 1683. (Presbyterian Church, USA)

till morning . . . we were in the place we believed God wanted us to be.

Unusual circumstances prevailed in the backwoods. For example, common-law marriage was temporarily permitted and the minster's salary was often paid partly in whisky. Although few Scots homes did not possess a Bible, they frequently felt hemmed in on all sides by settlers and native Americans whose moral and religious values seemed to contrast sharply with their own.

Another Ulster Scot, the Rev. Samuel Doak, travelled through eastern Tennessee with his gun and books. Pat Alderman's *The Overmountain Men* tells of how Doak came across a group of settlers felling trees and was promptly asked to lead them in worship. With his horse as a pulpit, he so impressed the company that he was asked to stay, and soon a church and school were built and the community of Salem was born. The minister's rifle was always at hand during services, and on more than one occasion he broke off the sermon to lead the pursuit of Indians.

Kingstree may have been luckier than most. When these pioneer congregations had erected their log meeting-houses, the next task—often a formidable one—was to try to persuade a minister to come and join them in the wilderness. The recently-settled Presbyterian folk of Kingstree (SC) made a call in 1736 to the Rev. John Willison of Dundee. Much serious discussion preceded the call.

Members of the Salem congregation included the Witherspoon family, originally from Lanarkshire, and their records note a very Scottish exchange on a backwoods path on the subject of the new minister. Mr Witherspoon was stressing the need for a pastor, and being pressed for a name by his neighbour, he replied: 'Wull, wha' but Mister Willison o' Dundee?'

'But the minister must have a muckle sight o' money for his living', pointed out the other. 'And that we must give him', came the Witherspoon response, suggesting that ten pounds would be an appropriate stipend. Asked where he intended to get that sort of money, Witherspoon had the answer: 'Weel, if wus comes to wus, I een can sell mi' coo.'

One of the first tasks for the frontier Scots was to select a site for their church, a location to build a lasting monument to their faith. At Alamance Creek, near Greensboro (NC), a group of Ulster-Scots Presbyterians settled in 1753. Calvin Wiley, a descendant of those first settlers, wrote of the great day when construction began:

> On a day appointed, the people, each with an axe, came together and it was proposed by Andrew Finley, a devout man and leader in public religious exercise, that before they began their work they should kneel in prayer for the divine blessing on their pious enterprise.

An early church with a particularly colourful history is the Old Tennent Church at Freehold (NJ). Scots Covenanter, William Ker, organised the first services in a log meeting-house only a few miles from the present church as early as 1692. Around this church on a Sunday in June 1778 raged a significant clash in the Revolutionary War, the Battle of Monmouth, in which Washington and his troops forced the British under Sir Henry Clinton back to the coast after a bloody, day-long struggle. During the battle the church served as a field hospital, but cannon shot still fell near the building. Records show that 107 Patriots are buried in a common grave alongside the British dead. Among the revolutionary soldiers whose names appear on a monument in the churchyard erected by the Daughters of the Revolution are three Andersons, two Bairds, a Campbell, five Craigs and four Gordons.

But even before organised Presybterianism began to be widely seen, Scots-educated ministers had been drifting across the Atlantic to serve with the Anglican and the Episcopalian Churches. Young James Keith left Marischal College in Aberdeen in 1661 to take up arguably the most challenging post yet offered to a Scots clergyman in the New World, at Bridgewater, the first inland settlement in the new Massachusetts colony. Remarkably, at the heart of modern-day West Bridgewater the parsonage built for this Aberdeen teenager, who had not yet been ordained, still stands. Built the year after James's arrival, it is said to be the oldest existing Episcopal parsonage in the United States.

From the town records it's clear that these early settlers were of an 'extraordinarily devout nature', and immediately after the community put down its first roots it was arranged for the divinity student (then about eighteen years of age) to cross the Atlantic. The Rev. Keith is said to have found a place in the affections of his flock from the moment the modest youngster preached his first sermon from the Pulpit Rock by the river, and chose for his text Jeremiah 1:6 'Behold I cannot speak, for I am a child.'

Into the 1800s a substantial number of ministers who had received their training in Glasgow and Edinburgh crossed the Atlantic as missionaries to serve in some of the wildest and woolliest outposts of the frontier. With their strong beliefs and an abhorrence of intemperance, slavery, lack of educational opportunities and corrupt or inefficient local government, they helped mould what was to be recognised as the classic American identity. Scots lay preachers were also highly valued, possibly owing to their better educational background.

The Scots industrial workers who began to arrive in the 1800s were by and large Protestant, although there were always groups of Episcopalians and Roman Catholics, especially if the latter were from parts of the western Highlands or the Glasgow area. By this time a small but steady movement of Catholic priests can be traced from the British Isles to America, but probably the most noted Scots Catholic immigrant of that period was Bishop Richard Gilmour, second Bishop of Cleveland (OH) from 1872 to 1891. Born in Glasgow of Presbyterian parents, he went first to Nova Scotia and then Pennsylvania, where he took the temperance pledge and studied for the priesthood. In Cincinnati he is remembered as the man who brought harmony to a Catholic community torn by ethnic strife.

Ulster-Scots chaplain, James Caldwell, hands out copies of the Watts psalm books to soldiers at the Battle of Springfield. The troops had run short of gun wadding and Caldwell's phrase, 'Give 'em Watts boys', lives on in the legends of the Revolutionary War. (Department of History, Presbyterian Church, USA)

The Scots valued their chosen form of worship and style of religion above most anything else in their lives. The McConnaughey family moved from Inverness to Pennsylvania in the mid-1700s, but by the 1830s had converted from Presbyterianism to the Baptist faith. About 1840, the McConnaughey clan—parents, children, in-laws and grandchildren—moved on to the expanding frontier, pulling up their Pennsylvania roots and trekking (appropriately) to Highland County, Ohio. On reaching their new home they presented a letter to the established Baptist congregation, but the Ohio church refused to accept their letters until they had been 'dunked', baptised in the riverside tradition. Patricia McConnaughey Gregory of Indianapolis (IN) explains:

> This didn't set well with my ancestors so they started their own church. There were certainly enough of them to do this. The twist to the story is that the original Baptist church is long gone but the one established by the bold McConnaugheys is still there.

Most Scots in the Midwest farming communities kept Sundays very strictly and courting on the Sabbath was frowned on. Many young men were told at the door when they came to pay their respects: 'Gang awa' hame boy, an' read yer Book.' It was common practice for all books and newspapers, except the Bible, to be put away on Saturday night. Twice daily on normal working days fathers would gather their families together for worship. They read chapters from the Bible verse about, even down to the long genealogies.

The story is told by Janette Murray in *The Palimpsest* of one Iowa farmer who had difficulty reconciling the need for worship with the fact that the wheat urgently wanted cutting. The family were laboriously reading through the infamous 'so-and-so begat so-and-so' verses. To the Scot, this seemed a wasteful exercise on such an important morning. He interrupted the reading:

> So-and-so begat so-and-so and so it continues to the foot of the page and a wee bit over. Let us pray.

They all knelt down and the boys were soon out in the wheatfield. The scene at Sunday services in the relatively prosperous parish of Tranquillity (IA) in the mid-1800s is also recalled by Murray, who remembered the girls sitting demurely in lace-trimmed dresses, pink and blue sashes and hair-ribbons.

> We were not so uncomfortable as the boys with their kilts and white starched blouses with wide embroidered frills. They were real little Lord Fauntleroys when they put on their velvet Tams. Great was their joy at seven when they were emancipated from their kilts and curls.

THE BLOSSOMING OF UNION CHURCH

Construction of a Scots kirk within a new settlement, whether in the first occupation of the tidewater colonies or the later movement west, was often

THE NEW

# TESTAMENT

Of our LORD and SAVIOUR

# JESUS CHRIST:

Newly Tranſlated out of the

## ORIGINAL GREEK

And with the former

## TRANSLATIONS

Diligently compared and reviſed.

*PHILADELPHIA:*

PRINTED AND SOLD BY R. AITKEN, BOOKSELLER,

OPPOSITE THE COFFEE-HOUSE, FRONT-STREET.

M.DCC.LXXXI.

Dalkeith-born printer and publisher, Robert Aitken, who was based in Phila-delphia, produced the first complete English Bible printed in America when the Revolutionary War halted imports from Britain. (Department of History, Presbyterian Church, USA) the signal for rapid growth. In the case of one southern community they were doubly blessed. In Mississippi, a 200-square mile oblong section of Jefferson County came to be known as the 'Scotch Settlement'.

In 1805, just after the United States had bought Louisiana, four Scots families came from North Carolina to Tennessee, and after a year moved into Mississippi. George Torrey, his son, Donald, Laughlin Currie and Robert Willis and their families started farming in Jefferson County in 1806 and were followed from the Carolinas by the Gilchrists, Galbraiths and Camerons.

Two Presbyterian churches soon flourished, the Ebenezer and the Union. The countryside around the kirks filled up with Scots, some still Gaelic speakers. The Ebenezer is remembered as a congregation of great wealth and influence; many prominent local families, including those first pioneers, were members and took an active role in state and county government. Union Church was organised in 1817, the first settlers in its vicinity having arrived a few years earlier, mainly from Robeson County (NC).

The 1820s was a period of great vitality in the Scotch Settlement; the land was fertile, the farming easy. Natchez, on the Mississippi River, was the market town for the entire settlement and a whole week could be spent by the Scots farmer in his ox-cart going to market and back. It was a grand occasion. According to Grafton, historian of the district, the farmers (or at least some of them) were not averse to a wee drink:

> On coming back with a jug of Scotch whisky their animal spirits would
> be stirred on the way and their homecoming loudly advertised.

When the Civil War broke out the first company that left Jefferson County for the seat of the war was the 'Charley Clark Rifles' from the Scotch Settlement around Union Church. Before leaving the men paraded in the shade of the old trees beside the church and were handed a silken banner of the Southern Confederacy from the hands of Miss Flora Buie. Few came home.

For the affluent Ebenezer folk, the Civil War was a disaster. They were big slave-owners and without the free labour their lands became useless. Cotton prices dropped away, the old men died and the young men left the farms for Natchez, Memphis, Jackson or even further afield. Scotch Settlement never regained its distinctive Scottish flavour. For a time it looked as if the same fate might overtake Union Church, but the kirk and the school held the community together into the twentieth century.

American Presbyterians, as we see elsewhere, were among the first to speak out against taxes imposed by Britain, and there is evidence of Presbyterian ministers of Scots origin urging the people to take up arms in the revolutionary cause. Even before the war, two Ulster-Scots ministers from Pennsylvania were making names for themselves, displaying formidable combat skills in the Indian war which preceded the fight for independence.

In 1755 the Rev. John Steel, pastor of East and West Conocheague Presbyterian churches, organised a company of rangers. Unanimously elected captain, he organised patrols to nip Indian risings in the bud. Even more famous was the 'Border Captain', the Rev. John Elder of Paxtang and Derry churches, who got together a band of raiders (mostly from his own congregations) who patrolled the vast area from their settlement to the Susquehanna River. Both men were a 'terror to the Indians', Christians who were merciless in their pursuit of the native American.

The reputation of the fighting Scots ministers persisted into the Civil War. When the Shaw family left Jura after the '45 Uprising, they took to America a tradition of bravery and religious dedication. After settling in North Carolina they fought in the Revolutionary War, and in the following century were firmly behind the Confederacy. The Rev. Colin Shaw of Bladen County (NC) was a military chaplain with the Confederate Army, and his exploits gained him the nickname of 'the Fighting Parson'. When Sherman's Northern Army was camped near Goldsboro (NC) in 1865, the Rev. Shaw—who 'loved a fight' and was exasperated by raids on the local community by Sherman's marauders—organised a 'home guard' of old men and boys to protect lives and property in the South River district. Despite being injured in a skirmish, Shaw put the Yankees to flight and subsequently led a raid in the vicinity of Burgaw (NC), where he cut communications on the Atlantic Coast Railroad in the rear of General Terry's army.

A 'Dead or Alive' order was issued by the Federal HQ against the minister, and one day a Union patrol appeared at the Shaw plantation in Bladen. Chaplain Shaw, having been warned, escaped to the woods while his wife and children were ordered out of the house before the detachment put it to the torch. A daughter, Mollie, insisted that she play for the last time on her piano and struck up with 'Dixie'. She refused to leave, even though the flames were licking round the drawing room, until she had completed the melody and eventually had to be dragged out through a window. Mollie, who was fourteen, has a special place in the Shaw family folklore.

ZION, CITY O' WIR JOHN

Founder of the impressively-titled Christian Catholic Apostolic Church in Zion was John Alexander Dowie, who was born in Edinburgh in 1847. His background was one of abject poverty and strict religious observance, perhaps explaining in part why he was to become one of Scotland's most eccentric religious exports. By the age of six he had taken the pledge and 'developed a fanatical hatred of alcohol'. His family moved to Melbourne in Australia, setting up an independent tabernacle in 1882, and it was around this time that John developed what he believed was the talent to cure diseases by prayer.

Arriving in San Francisco in 1888, he moved on to Chicago two years later, developing his mission of divine healing despite opposition from other

A FORTNIGHTLY PAPER PUBLISHED IN THE INTERESTS OF ZION CITY, NEAR CHICAGO.
EDITED BY THE REV. JOHN ALEXANDER DOWIE.

VOLUME I. NUMBER 2.                    CHICAGO, AUGUST 22, 1900.                    PRICE TEN CENTS.

Masthead of the newspaper published at John Dowie's Zion city. (Illinois State Historical Library)

clergy and the medical profession. The CCA Church in Zion was launched in 1896, with John's passionate and rousing sermons soon drawing in the crowds. One observer at a meeting described Dowie as follows:

> ... his enormous brow, large eyes and venerable beard gave him an impressive appearance while his bow legs were hidden in elaborate robes.

In 1901 this remarkable figure declared himself to his followers and the world as 'Elijah the Restorer'. Forty-two miles outside Chicago (IL) he built the most amazing town America had seen or was ever likely to see—Zion City. In this community lived 5,000 of his adherents, with banks, schools and industries all under Dowie's direct control. There was no theatre, no dance halls, no societies or lodges, no chemist or doctor's surgery. Smoking, drinking and pork-eating were banned and the faithful were summoned to prayer by the blast of a whistle. Thanks to the children of Zion, Dowie's personal fortune grew. In the first decade of the twentieth century his church claimed 50,000 followers worldwide, with missionaries at work across the globe and texts produced in a dozen languages.

First setback for the church came with the 'invasion' of New York. With an army of 5,000 supporters on ten special trains, he set off to convert the Big Apple to the faith; but the two-month campaign, according to city newspapers, first of all succeeded in amusing New Yorkers, disgusting and finally boring them. By this time, Dowie, as he set about trying to recover the hundreds of thousands of dollars lost in the New York campaign, was claiming that he was the son of a British nobleman. His megalomaniac tendencies had reached the surface.

When he took ill in 1905, his increasingly oppressed followers deposed him on account of 'polygamous teaching and other grave charges'. Dowie began a legal battle in Chicago for the restoration of his confiscated Zion City properties, but died within the year.

BY HANDCART TO UTAH

The prophet Joseph Smith's experience on a hillside in New York state, when he claimed to have been shown the Book of Mormon inscribed in gold tablets, was to have a profound effect on the lives of thousands of Scots who chose America and the Mormon faith as their future in the middle years of the nineteenth century. The Church of the Latter Day Saints is one of the greatest (perhaps *the* greatest) experiment in co-operative religious enterprise the world has ever seen. Hostility towards the church, however, and its unfamiliar doctrines (including plural marriage) meant that the Mormon community had to move steadily west in search of sanctuary, finally settling in an area now known as Utah, considered uninhabitable at the time.

During the period 1839–40, the church sent missionaries to the British Isles and they met with substantial recruiting success in Glasgow, Fife and Edinburgh, where the church flourished and where it offered hope for the great masses who thronged the industrial heartland of Scotland. It is estimated that some 5,000 Scots immigrated to America to join the Mormon community, and Professor Fred Buchanan of the University of Utah has concluded that they were solidly working class.

Apart from the Mormon capital of Salt Lake City, other communities such as Ogden and Logan developed with strong Scottish representation among the settlers. The town of Tooele, some thirty miles south-west of Salt Lake City, was a target for many Scots families. An examination of local histories and church records in this community alone gives a clear picture of the Scots folk who made this part of Utah—previously inhabited only by the Goshiute Indians (the poorest of them all, it seems)—their home. Many of these families came in heavily loaded ox-carts from large centres such as St Louis (MO), an arduous and dangerous overland trek.

An early arrival was David P. Adamson from Dunfermline, who pushed a hand-cart for 1,300 miles to reach his new home, followed by the rest of his family a few years later. Such tales of endurance were commonplace. Others came by a less direct route. Mary Bevan, born in Glasgow in 1837, arrived in the United States at the age of sixteen to work in the woollen mills

Rev. John Dowie, Edinburgh-born founder of the Christian Catholic Apostolic Church in Zion and of Zion City, a remarkable community north of Chicago (IL). (Illinois State Historical Library)

of Massachusetts. Having saved enough money to send for her widowed mother and little brother, they travelled to Tooele in 1859.

The Heggie family from the Aberdeenshire parish of Newhills came to America in the 1850s, making their way from New Orleans to Tooele. Son John had been a gardener in Arbroath but landed the sharply contrasting job of driving animals in and out of the nearby mud stockade, built as a protection against Indians. John was married in Tooele to Martha Smith, also from Aberdeenshire, with curious Indians peeking through the church doors to witness a marriage in the style of the white man.

Hardship characterised the lot of these immigrants, both before leaving Scotland and after reaching their promised land. The story of the Mormon Campbell family from Bo'ness is a long, unrelenting tale of tough times. We can assume that this is, as they say, a worst-case scenario.

Thomas Campbell was born in the Lothians, but moved to Lanarkshire with the first opening of the collieries and married there in 1844. With his wife, Elisabeth, he left for Saline in Fife after the death of their first child. It was at Dunfermline, in February 1848, that they were baptised into the Church of the Latter Day Saints. Between 1847 and 1851 five children were born, and the family moved to Bo'ness, where they lived in a single room with Thomas's widowed mother. By March 1864, they had drifted on to Bathgate, where, in a few short weeks during a smallpox outbreak, eight of their 13 children died.

In 1866 Thomas, his wife, and their five remaining children left for America. After two years in Pennsylvania they were next found in Salt Lake City, where for about three months they stayed in a covered wagon. The Mormon leaders asked them to move to American Fork, and they remained there for several years, trying their hand at farming in the difficult conditions. Thomas returned to Salt Lake City to help in quarrying stone for the Temple, and it was in this famous quarry that he was crushed by a huge rock which left him paralysed and bed-ridden. He died soon after and was buried at Salt Lake City. Sadly, the last we hear of Elisabeth is that she spent her later years 'working very hard doing washing for other people'.

It occasionally took Scots clergymen a little time to adjust to the circumstances of the New World. Haddington-born Presbyterian minister Charles Nisbet (1736–1804) went to America filled with confidence and expectation in 1785 to take over the role of president of Dickinson College in Pennsylvania. However, his enthusiasm for the job was soon tempered by the fact that, while the Revolutionary War had been won, Nisbet found 'illness, poverty, demoralisation and gloom' everywhere. The depressing effect of this post-war environment made him resign his post within a few months with the declared intention of returning straightaway to Scotland. His health had also suffered badly in his short stay in America.

Nisbet, it seems, held a strong prejudice against all things Irish, and when he discovered that the vessel on which he was scheduled to sail was commanded by an Irishman he refused to go anywhere near the dock.

During the subsequent delay in seeking alternative passage, Nisbet began to perk up. His health showed a marked improvement and he began to see the limitless possibilities of the new nation. Plans for a return to Scotland were abandoned, he accepted re-election to the college and taught there with 'unabating vigour' for the next eighteen years. Interestingly, Nisbet also seems to have been a pioneer of that sport which has (in the latter part of the twentieth century) taken America by storm—jogging. In his youth Nisbet liked to run twenty miles before breakfast, and encouraged his students to do likewise.

Apart from the serious business of religion the Scots ministers also brought much of the colour and character of the old country to America. A fascinating legend with it roots in Scotland is that of a Presbyterian minister, Colin Lindsay, who settled in the Sandhills area of North Carolina. Born in 1744, Colin was the first minister of Old Laurel Hill Presbyterian Church, and it's said that eight years before he was born, his mother had gone into a deep coma. Thought to be dead, she was buried near her Highland home. Thieves, anxious to steal her diamond rings, dug up the body that same night and when they couldn't prise a ring loose, they tried to cut off her finger. At this painful moment she regained consciousness and sat up. The terrified grave-robbers fled.

Colin Lindsay immigrated to America in 1790 and became one of Sandhills' most popular preachers. The strange tale he told of his mother's premature burial is now part of North Carolina folklore.

~ *Chapter 14* ~

# FROM CITY HALL TO WHITE HOUSE

F ROM 'SOCKLESS' JERRY SIMPSON, cycling champion of Pennsylvania
Avenue, to Alexander Hamilton, the ultimate statesman whose features stare out from the US ten-dollar bill, the influence of Scots on the
American political scene and decision-making processes has been immense.
Regardless of their profession—farmer, physician, minister or miner—no
matter their economic or social status, Scots took an interest in politics and
local government almost from the moment they set foot in America. With
the freedom of opportunity that so many saw in the young United States
there also came a belief that, by working politically, they would be able to
shape their own and their children's destiny in a way that would have been
unthinkable in the old country. The new Americans felt that they had a real
stake in the future.

On this basis, while most Scots were content to serve as councilmen, county
commissioners and school-board members, others aspired to higher office, to
the House of Representatives, to Congress and the Senate, to the cabinet, the
vice-presidency, even the presidency, wherein we find a surprisingly rich
Scottish contribution.

Of the vast, unsung army of American-Scots city hall politicians, the story
of Richard Melrose (1850–1924) has many classic elements. Apart from the
'rags to riches' aspect, his saga also displays the manner in which so many
public-spirited Scots helped to get new townships moving, even in locations
where there was no Scottish community to speak of. Melrose left Scotland
in 1864, a fourteen-year-old orphan immigrant, and first rode into Anaheim
(CA) (then a small collection of wooden buildings) in 1865, as part of an army
detachment searching for deserters. He immediately felt at home.

Melrose returned to the little German wine-growing settlement five years
later, when it was still surrounded by a high hedge to keep the livestock
out of the vineyards, and he gradually increased his influence in the town
and further afield by becoming a lawyer, state assemblyman, educator,
philanthropist and politician. To that impressive list should be added local
newspaper editor: he must have enjoyed running the story of the famous
day when the pavements of Anaheim caught fire. As a progressive civic
leader, Melrose had actively encouraged the idea of paving Center Street
and teams were organised to collect manure from every stable in town,
which was then compacted into a sidewalk. One hot summer's afternoon,

after someone had dropped a light, the pavements caught fire and the story went into Anaheim legend.

In 1877, Melrose was admitted to the Bar, and by the middle of the following decade he was the figure most associated with promoting Anaheim, and serving as assemblyman for Orange County by 1908. His Scottish heritage of fairness and a quest for equality shines through in his involvement with the thorny issue of Japanese immigration. The new assemblyman argued against a ban on Japanese ownership of property and segregation in schooling. Visiting a mine near La Paz during the Mexican Revolution, Melrose was reported killed by rebels; however, three weeks later his party emerged across the border at Nogales, having made their escape by horseback, boat and train. This adventurous politician died at his Tudor-style Anaheim home in 1924, and his story is mirrored in a thousand communities nationwide.

Lists of colonial office-bearers of Scottish origin are extensive. Most of these men never considered themselves as immigrants but as officers of the Crown on foreign duty, postings where pay was generally very poor but where there were opportunities to acquire land and enter trading ventures.

Sometimes these colonial administrators could over-step themselves. Such a man was John Stuart, who immigrated from Scotland in 1748 and became one of the staunchest advocates of British rule among the Indian tribes of the southern colonies. After campaigning against the Spanish in Florida, he was appointed a captain in the South Carolina Provincials, and by 1761 was Superintendent of Indian Affairs with a salary of £1,000 and a £3,000 annual allowance to buy presents for the Indians aimed at winning them over to the British cause. He was successful in arranging peace treaties and boundary agreements but was already being ticked off for lavish spending on Indian gifts. His expenses, according to his 'boss', Lord Shelburne, were 'running above all expectation and proportion'. Stuart successfully demanded that he be appointed 'councillor extraordinary' on all councils and official bodies within his district, increasing his personal status quite dramatically and bumping up his annual expenses to the staggering annual total of £19,000.

The Revolutionary War brought the good times to an end. Stuart was arrested in 1775 as an active British sympathiser accused of trying to incite the Catawba and Cherokee tribes to support the British cause. He is later found as a refugee in Florida, where he stayed for the remainder of his life. His wife and daughter were in house imprisonment during the war, but Mrs Stuart managed to escape and rejoin her husband at Pensacola.

GOVERNORS, LOYAL OR OTHERWISE
At the start of the Revolutionary War it was natural to expect governors in the British colonies to be staunchly loyal to George III, and generally this was the case. However, Jonathan Trumbull, whose family (the Turnbulls)

hailed from Philiphaugh near Selkirk, was governor of Connecticut and the descendant of New England settlers who arrived in 1638. He was to become an active supporter of the fight for freedom. George Washington considered Trumbull a staunch patriot and more than once referred to the fact that he could rely on 'Brother Jonathan'. Trumbull, who gave his name to the present-day town in Connecticut, was governor for fifteen years until his resignation from office in 1784. Historians have speculated on Trumbull's unusual decision to support the independence cause and have pointed to his Borders heritage, and the brave self-determination which was necessary in that region for survival, let alone freedom. He was tuned in to the cause of liberty. His son was also governor of Connecticut.

When Gabriel Johnston arrived in North Carolina as royal governor in October 1734, he was welcomed, according to the records, with 'much applause and goodwill'. There followed ten years in which Johnston, from Annandale, and a professor of Oriental languages at St Andrews before his posting, succeeded in making himself the most unpopular man in the Carolinas. The welcome he received on arrival at the Cape Fear River soon evaporated when he fell into open conflict with the Colony's general assembly. He wanted quit rents—upon which his own salary depended—paid in cash rather than commodities. Political chaos ensued, with Johnston dismissing one assembly after another without any legislation being passed.

Another intriguing Carolinas character was Samuel Johnston (1733–1816), a native of Dundee whose 'calm wisdom' was highly valued during the turmoil of the revolution. He was, according to the *Dictionary of American Biography*, 'revered for his integrity and thoroughly opposed to disorder and revolution, if revolution could be avoided without yielding to oppression'. He was North Carolina's sixth governor, four years a senator, and Justice of the Supreme Court from 1800 to 1803.

Born in 1701 in Linlithgow, James Glen was governor of South Carolina from 1743 to 1746, and had a busy and adventurous career as the local representative of the British government. At the start of his tenure most of his time was spent organising against the threat of Indian attack, but Glen was a confident individual who spoke of finding the colony defenceless and in ashes, and declared his intention of leaving it fortified and flourishing. He saw the key to this ambition in successful negotiation with the local Indian tribes, and he made a number of hazardous journeys into the interior for pow-wows with the chiefs. His reports were always awaited with great interest by the government officials in London.

One of the earliest reports of a Scot figuring in the civic affairs of a major east coast city comes after the arrival on 8 August 1678 of James Graham and his parents, from Auchinleck in Ayrshire. With a thorough grounding in the law, Graham was to be appointed one of six aldermen of the city and helped William Penn on a commission to buy the Upper Susquehanna Valley from the Indians. In 1691, he was appointed Speaker of the First

Thomas Sully's portrait of Andrew Jackson, seventh president of the United States and the first to be elected by the people. 'Old Hickory' claimed to have been born 'somewhere between Carrickfergus and the States'. (In the collection of the Corcoran Gallery of Art, gift of William Wilson Corcoran 69.49)

General Assembly of the Province of New York, holding this position on and off for eight years. A skilled wordsmith, Graham lived in the style of a colonial gentleman, as witnessed by the record noting that he had 'one overseer, two white servants and 33 slaves'.

Another of the Graham clan, John Graham (c. 1718–1795), immigrated to Georgia from Scotland in the 1750s, and steadily worked himself into a position of influence within the colony. He owned three large plantations and 262 slaves.

As a Loyalist and member of the ruling council Graham found, with the Revolutionary War looming, that he was in a delicate, even dangerous, situation. For a time, when his life was under threat, he hid in the swamps of the Savannah River until he escaped to the man-o-war *Scarborough* which lay offshore. His appointment as lieutenant-governor in those troubled times led to further misfortune when the revolutionaries burned his ship, *Inverness*, as well as his mansion in Savannah.

He fled to London, like so many of the Scots colonial hierarchy, but returned in time to witness a series of crucial engagements of the war, living in a tent as the British besieged Savannah in July 1779. When it became clear that the British cause was lost, he moved with his four sons to Florida (still under the control of Spain), and after the conflict spent much of his later years co-ordinating claims against the new free states for loss of and damage to property on behalf of the Georgia Loyalists.

But not everyone who left Scotland to taste of freedom on the other side of the Atlantic met with political success. James Thomson Callender was born in Scotland in 1758, but his radical views forced him (like many others) to immigrate in the wake of the French Revolution. He reached America in 1793 and impressed the founding fathers, and in particular Thomas Jefferson, who took him under his wing and commissioned him to write tracts and papers. Sadly he never made the grade in politics, and drowned while drunk.

HORNET'S NEST OF HIGHLANDERS

American histories are filled with stories and anecdotes of that great day, 4 July 1776, when the leaders of the American freedom movement finally declared themselves independent of Britain. Ever since the clash at Lexington the previous year, there had been an increasing clamour to make the break; but even before the initial skirmishes in Massachusetts in 1775, the Scots and the Ulster Scots had been flexing their new-found political confidence.

Many Highlanders had been directed to Mecklenburg County in North Carolina for permanent residence. Throughout this county there had been alarm at the hard-line reaction of the British authorities to events such as the Boston Tea Party, and a crisis conference was called at Charlotte (NC) on 19 May 1775. This meeting was chaired by Ulster-Scot Abraham Alexander (1717–86), who had arrived at New York before settling in the

Carolinas. The purpose of the conference originally had been to decide on ways of helping their brethren in Boston; but the deliberations were to be far more wide-ranging, and the communiqué, momentous. Representatives stayed in session all day and it was 2 a.m. the following morning when the historic outcome was disclosed. The key to the Mecklenburg Declaration lay in Article 2:

> We the citizens of Mecklenburg County do hereby dissolve the political bonds which have connected us with the mother country and hereby absolve ourselves from allegiance to the British Crown and abjure all political connections, contacts, associations with that nation who have wantonly trampled on our rights and liberties and inhumanely shed the innocent blood of American Patriots at Lexington.

In addition, the Scots descendants declared themselves a free and independent people and pledged to maintain this independence with 'our mutual co-operation, our lives, our futures and our most sacred honour'. Cornwallis, the British commander, was to describe this Scottish enclave as the 'hornet's nest of the Revolution'. Remarkably, this was the second such audacious declaration by the Scots in America, the first being at Fincastle County (VA) as early as January 1775, a certain indicator that while many Scots were still swithering over their allegiance to the King in London, large numbers had already thrown in their lot with the independence movement.

In Maryland, the lower house of their general assembly had been a stronghold of liberty, declaring annually for almost forty years up to the war that the King's subjects should not be liable to taxes unless they had some say in the framing of the law. Born in Scotland in 1720, William Murdoch was the main voice in this Maryland debate, leading resistance to the Stamp Tax and uniting the colony in opposition to the administration's attempts to levy such taxes.

The Presbyterian Church played its part, proclaiming in its significant Philadelphia 'pastoral letter' of 1775 that the people should bravely back future decisions of congress. This momentous epistle was sent to every legislature in the colonies, and it has been suggested that this circular was a principal factor in persuading many Americans to opt for resistance. This theme was later developed when some observers traced the roots of the Declaration of Independence to the National Covenant of Scotland. Certainly, the Church of Scotland receives—through the agency of the Rev. John Witherspoon—credit for having provided the framework for the American Constitution.

Above all the Scots voices raised in support of the cause of independence at this time, one is heard more clearly than any other. That is the voice of Patrick Henry of Virginia, who was that state's most outspoken advocate of severing ties with Britain once and for all.

As a farmer and storekeeper, Patrick Henry was simply a failure. But turning to the law, he swiftly became the most eloquent of pro-revolutionary

Patrick Henry, son of Aberdonian parents, was the orator who lit the spark of the Revolutionary War with his fiery 'liberty or death' speeches. (United States Postal Service)

orators. Many contend that a speech by Henry—made as early as 1759, when he had maintained the right of Virginia to make its own laws and warned the King that he was degenerating into a tyrant and forfeiting the right to obedience—had kindled the popular flame for independence. Later, according to Whitelaw Reid, an episode in the Virginia House of Burgesses fanned this flame into a furnace fire. Henry introduced resolutions which examined the basic civil rights of Americans. He argued that the inhabitants of Virginia inherited from the first adventurers and settlers equal franchises with the people of Great Britain; that taxation of the people by persons

265

chosen to represent them was the distinguishing characteristic of British freedom, and that the general assembly of the colony now had the sole right to lay taxes on its people, and that by vesting these tax-raising powers in others, British as well as American freedom was damaged. A clever and inspiring analysis, this caught the American imagination. His persuasive reasoning brought out into the open what many Americans had been pondering privately.

In March 1775, as the Scots and Ulster-Scots communities through the colonies were getting their independence act together, planting their feet firmly on the Loyalist side of the fence or simply awaiting developments, Henry spoke at St John's Church, Richmond (VA) and made his famous 'Give me liberty or give me death' speech, an address which set in train events which were to reverberate around the world. In 1776, he carried the vote of the Virginia convention for independence and was later created governor of his home state, being four times re-elected.

Of the fifty-six signatories to the Declaration of Independence, most historians trace nine with Scottish or Ulster-Scots roots. However, others, including John Hancock (whose huge signature was to ensure that 'George III wouldn't mistake it') and James Smith are also claimed by some in the Scottish camp. John Witherspoon, by far the most important Scottish contributor, is remembered for his lack of patience with advocates of the 'softly-softly' approach; the youngest signatory was John Rutledge, still in his mid-twenties and son of an immigrant to South Carolina from Ulster in 1735, the family having originated in Roxburghshire; William Hooper of North Carolina was the son of an immigrant Scots minister from Kelso; George Ross, also the son of Scots minister, was uncle to Betsy Ross from Delaware, who was given the honour of sewing the very first national flag and James Wilson, who was born in St Andrews, was a delegate from Pennsylvania to congress in 1776 and argued vehemently that independence was the only answer to America's turmoil and dissatisfaction.

FACE ON A TEN-DOLLAR BILL

When the Treaty of Paris finally confirmed American independence in 1783, and it came to framing a Constitution for the new nation, out of fifty-four members of the Convention twelve were of Scottish descent. Once again they carried far greater influence than this figure might indicate, because they counted for more than half of the college-educated representatives.

One Scot, in particular, stands tall in this company. Alexander Hamilton (1757–1804), claimed by many as the greatest Secretary of the Treasury that the United States has ever had, was also thought by many to be the most inspired statesman of his generation. Born on the island of Nevis in the West Indies, he was the grandson of his namesake from Grange in Ayrshire. Half Scottish and half Huguenot French, he came to America at the age of fifteen when agitation for change was already well under way.

At the outbreak of war, Hamilton was addressing noisy public meetings,

Lyndon B. Johnson was born into a Texas family steeped in politics, and intensely proud of their Scottish heritage, claiming ancestors who served for several generations in the Scottish parliament. *right* Thomas Woodrow Wilson's mother, Jane Woodrow, was the daughter of a Scots Presbyterian minister who immigrated to America in 1836. Some say his Ulster-Scots stubbornness, his inability to compromise, cost him his dream of taking the USA into the League of Nations. (The Herald Archive)

writing tracts and appeals; at the age of twenty he was private secretary to Washington, and four years later—with victory now inevitable—he was recalled as a dashing young officer who led the assault on Cornwallis's first redoubt at Yorktown. He was a friend and trusted advisor of Washington, but Hamilton's double-edged ambition for military glory and political power could draw him into conflict with his leader. Once he found the excuse to put down his pen and pick up the sword, when Washington scolded him for being late for a meeting and Hamilton rejoined his regiment.

Interestingly, Hamilton, at the age of twenty-five and a member of congress, did his best to restrain the persecution of defeated Loyalists, many of them sharing his Scottish blood. Statesmanship of the most delicate and brilliant stamp was required to create a strong central government, with so many competing interests within the States. Yet Hamilton's skilful hand was able to balance the jealousies of the various states and persuade them on the merits of the Constitution, guiding the United States of America into existence. With the help of Madison, he wrote a series of essays designed to commend the proposals for the new nation to its people. It is reckoned to be one of the most lucid and carefully structured presentations of the principles of successful popular government ever written. Treasury work next commanded his attention, and he set out to get the nation on a sound financial footing. When the Constitution was finally ratified, he was welcomed back to his home city of New York in a flag-waving procession of bands with many thousands lining the streets.

Before entering the political arena, Hamilton had been one of New York's most eminent lawyers, and when he resumed his practice he was still regularly consulted by Washington. He was actual leader of the Federal Party, and his political rivalry with Aaron Burr led to a duel on 11 July 1804. Mortally wounded, Hamilton died the next day—eye witnesses said he hadn't raised his pistol at his opponent. His views on the structure of government have influenced nations across the globe.

## THE SCOTS PRESIDENTS

It is possible to identify as many as fifteen presidents of the United States whose lines of heritage can be traced back to Scotland, ranging from James Monroe, fifth president who took office in 1817, to the 'cowboy' president, Ronald Reagan, who occupied the Oval Office as the fortieth incumbent in the 1980s.

James Monroe's family lived in the western reaches of Virginia, and the future president served in the Revolutionary War, emerging with the rank of lieutenant-colonel. Monroe (1758–1831) was descended from Andrew Monroe, who immigrated from Scotland in the middle of the seventeenth century. Occupying the offices of Secretary of State and Secretary of War before becoming the nation's leader, he is perhaps most famous for the 'Monroe Doctrine' which warned the nations of Europe who had colonial ambitions to keep their hands off the Americas.

Andrew Jackson (1767–1845), who claimed to have been born 'somewhere between Carrickfergus and the United States', was brought up in the back country of the Carolinas and was the first real people's choice. The seventh president had a sparkling military career, including a successful defence of New Orleans against the British in 1818. 'Old Hickory', it has been argued, is the most famous Ulster Scot of them all.

James Knox Polk (1795–1849) was the eleventh president, his family coming to America from the west of Scotland via Ulster. The Pollocks (as they were then) moved first to Pennsylvania and then settled in Mecklenburg County (NC), where James was born. During his term of office the United States acquired California and New Mexico, and the Oregon boundary was settled in a deal with the United Kingdom.

James Buchanan (1791–1868), whose grandparents were Ulster-Scots Presbyterians, was born at Stony Batter, near Mercersburg (PA), and was the nation's fifteenth president, serving under Jackson and Polk before being elected in 1856. During his administration the slavery question drew to a head, and Buchanan was always strongly in favour of the maintenance of the system, openly supporting attempts to establish Kansas as a slave state.

Andrew Johnson (1808–75) came from a humble background in the Scots communities of North Carolina, his father a porter and his mother a kitchen maid. He made his name as a politician in Tennessee, and at the outbreak of the Civil War he became leader of the Southern Union supporters and took office on Lincoln's assassination. As a result of his conflicts with congress, Johnson became the first and only president of the United States to be impeached, but was acquitted by a single vote and completed his term of office.

Ulysses Simpson Grant (1822–85), the eighteenth president, was the descendant of a Scot who came to Massachusetts as early as 1630. When the American Civil War began, Ohio-born Grant was working in a leather store in Illinois but he re-entered the Army (he had served with distinction in the Mexican War), and his wartime record saw him nominated as president by the Republicans. Although it was his administration that guaranteed the right of suffrage without regard to race, colour or previous servitude, his two terms of office were never as memorable as his exploits on the battlefield.

Rutherford Hayes (1822–1893), who was elected president in 1877, was descended from the Scot George Hayes, who came to Windsor (CT) about 1680. The nineteenth president was an Ohio-born lawyer, and his greatest achievement was in spearheading the commercial recovery of the United States.

Chester Alan Arthur (1830–1886), the twenty-first president was the son of a Belfast minister of Scottish descent and came to office in 1881, when James Garfield was shot and fatally wounded by a disappointed office-seeker. Arthur served until 1885.

Grover Cleveland (1837–1908), son of an Ulster-Scots mother and a Presbyterian minister, worked his way up the political ladder from sheriff of Erie County (NY) to the Oval Office. First elected in 1885, he was a great trade reformer and the only president to serve split terms of office.

Benjamin Harrison (1833–1901), the Ohio-born twenty-fifth president, was regarded as a highly successful politician, holding office from 1889 to 93. He was a grandson of a former president, William Harrison, and great-grandson of a signatory to the Declaration of Independence. On his mother's side, he was descended from an Ulster Scot called McDowell.

Ohio was also the home state of the twenty-fifth president, William McKinley (1843–1901), who was a man of few speeches and had big business behind his election success of 1896. He was descended from David McKinley, an Ulster Scot born about 1730, and the president was assassinated while attending an exhibition at Buffalo (NY) in 1901.

Theodore Roosevelt (1858–1919) was of Dutch descent on his father's side, but on the distaff side he was descended from the Bulloch family of Stirlingshire, who provided the first governor of Georgia after the Revolutionary War. An explorer and a hunter, he was elected to the

Ronald Reagan visiting the church at Castlehead, Paisley, in 1991. This was where
his great-great grandparents, Claud Wilson and Peggy Downie, were married in 1807.
(The Herald Archives)

presidency on the murder of McKinley and urged the entry of the United
States into World War I.

Woodrow Wilson (1856–1924) became the twenty-eighth president of the
United States in 1913. His paternal grandfather, the Rev. James Wilson,
had immigrated from County Down to Philadelphia in 1807; his mother,
Jane Woodrow, was the daughter of a Scots Presbyterian minister who
immigrated to America in 1836. Wilson's dream of a league of nations to
settle international disputes before they ignited was only partly successful,
his own Senate refusing to take part. His administration, which is notable
for the prohibition and women's suffrage amendments to the Constitution,
ended in his physical breakdown.

Lyndon Baines Johnson (1908–73), universally known as 'LBJ' and president for six years from 1963, was born into a Texan family steeped in
politicians, including a signatory to the Texas Declaration of Independence
and the founder of the patriotic Daughters of the Revolution. The Scots
ancestors of the family were said to have served in the parliament in
Edinburgh. Assuming the presidency on John F. Kennedy's assassination,
Johnson worked against poverty and discrimination during his tenure.

Most recent is Ronald Reagan, who became fortieth president of the United States in 1981, in the midst of the Iran hostages affair. The former Hollywood star of cowboy movies is the great-great grandson of the weaver and radical Claud Wilson, and his wife, Peggy Downie, who were married at Castıehead kirk in Paisley in 1807. The church was visited in 1991 by Ronald and Nancy Reagan during a Scottish tour. Reagan proudly sported a Wilson family tartan jacket and told his hosts with a grin:

> When my family arrived in America from Scotland, they were given a horse, a plough, 10 acres and two tickets for Frank Sinatra's farewell concert.

Beyond the Oval Office we find an array of Scots and Ulster-Scots cabinet members reaching down into the present century. Of the vice-presidents, the most intriguing is John Caldwell Calhoun (1782–1850), often described as a cold, humourless individual. Descended from the Colquhouns of Loch Lomondside, who had settled in Ulster, he had Scottish blood on both sides of his family.

Calhoun served as vice-president in the early years of the nineteenth century under both John Quincy Adams and Andrew Jackson, and was a product of the famous 'log colleges', having been brought up in the Abbeville District of South Carolina before going to Yale. His father was an up-country farmer and slave-owner, and Calhoun was to prove a great defender of the interests of the slave-holding states. After being admitted to the Bar, he married into the planting aristocracy of South Carolina then entered politics. Serving as Secretary of War and Secretary of State, and signing the treaty which annexed Texas, he found his hopes of the presidency dashed in 1829 by the tremendous popularity of Andrew Jackson.

His wife caused one of the century's biggest political scandals by organising the social ostracism of innkeeper's daughter, Peggy O'Neale, who had married a Tennessee senator. Calhoun, meanwhile, thought himself a poet in the making, but legend has it that he once tried to write a poem but gave up after scribbling 'Whereas', discovering that he had run out of inspiration. He died in 1850, having shortly before suggested that the South should withdraw from the Union.

From every part of Scotland came immigrants who served in local and national government. The valley of Wolf Creek in Tama County (IA) proved popular in the mid-1800s with settlers from Ayrshire. Scots accents, dress styles and customs were everywhere. Many hard-working Scots made their home here, but perhaps one of the best remembered is James Wilson, who etched his name into the history of the United States congress in the 1880s.

In the last few minutes of the forty-eighth congress, Republicans tried to put through a Bill restoring to the dying General Grant his old army rank and pension. However, Democrats (then in a majority) wanted a vote first on the election contest between Wilson and Benjamin Frederick

'Sockless' Jerry Simpson, the Kansas politican from a Scots heritage who was one of the most colourful characters in Washington during the late 1800s. (The Kansas State Historical Society, Topeka)

for the seat of United States representative for the fifth Iowa district—it looked as if there would be no time to consider the old general's position. Seeing this stalemate, Wilson offered to step down if the House would put General Grant on the retired list. This was done, and it seemed as if James Wilson's sacrifice had ended his political career. Great work lay ahead for him, however, and he bounced back to serve as Secretary for Agriculture for sixteen years under Presidents McKinley, Roosevelt and Taft.

## CONGRESSIONAL WHITTLER

'Sockless' Jerry Simpson, who shared Scots blood with many thousands of immigrants to Kansas, was one of the most interesting and outrageous figures to emerge on the American political scene in the late 1800s. Coming from Canada as a child, he gained his nickname when he was elected to congress in 1890. Having accused his opponent of being filthy rich, with legs encased in 'fine silk hosiery', he unveiled his own bare shanks at a campaign meeting, declaring that he had 'no socks at all save the natural buff my mother gave me'. Forever more he was 'Sockless' Simpson. Well-wishers sent him over 300 pairs of socks and he strode home to victory. His Washington career indicated that this clever, canny man was as much at home in the society drawing-room as he was rounding up cattle. One sedate Washington hostess once asked: 'Mr Simpson, would you mind showing me whether you really wear hosiery or not?' Simpson responded: 'Not in the least, madam, providing you will reciprocate.'

Jerry Simpson had been a skipper on the Great Lakes where he developed his physical and intellectual skills, becoming a formidable 'rough and tumble' fighter and once flooring a burly blacksmith in under a minute. The man became one of Simpson's staunchest political supporters.

Moving to Kansas in the early 1880s to take up ranching, he suffered a tragedy when his daughter was killed in a saw-mill accident. According to the American *Heritage Magazine*, by 1890 he was earning forty dollars a month as Medicine Lodge city marshall, bringing in a few extra dollars by digging sewers. His main political claim to fame is that he led a farmers' revolt against the 'Money Men' back East, after a series of disastrous droughts. By 1889, Kansas farmers found it more economical to burn corn for fuel rather than ship it. Thus Simpson's Kansas People's Party was born, set to 'raise less corn and more Hell!' With his memorable grin, pale blue eyes and skilled speech-making, Simpson soon became a Washington celebrity, falling victim to the cycling craze and reckoned to be one of the 'prominent wheelmen' of Pennsylvania Avenue. Ever the non-conformist, he loved to 'act the hick' and could be found whittling in the corridors of congress. He was a sartorial headliner, too, being seen in congress in a suit of yellow stripes. When the People's Party faded from prominence, 'Sockless' Simpson went back to farming.

*Chapter 15*

# THE STAR-SPANGLED SALTIRE

B EHIND THE SCENES IN INDUSTRY, the arts, sport and showbusiness, in
the military and finance, in most walks of life in fact, the native-born
and American Scots are as busy as ever. Today in the United States,
helping to foster ever-strengthening ties with Scotland, are over 200 Clan
Societies and Family Associations—the enormous Clan Donald and Clan
Donnachaidh Societies alone have thirty branches between them. There
are around a hundred Scottish Societies, from the Mother Lode Scots at
Sutter's Creek (CA) to the St Andrew's Society of Washington DC. Pipe
bands proliferate—125 across the United States at the last count, from the
New York City Department of Corrections Pipe Band to the splendidly titled
Nae Breeks Pipe Band from Millville, (NJ). Even in such a far-flung state as
Hawaii you'll find Scots celebrating their heritage. Six groups promote
Scottish culture and heritage mid-Pacific—The Honolulu Pipes and Drums,
the Celtic Pipes and Drums of Hawaii, the St Andrew's Society, a Royal
Scottish Country Dance Society, the Hawaiian Scottish Society and the
Caledonian Society of Hawaii.

Across mainland United States the picture is similar. Tack on the
numerous Scots cultural organisations, Burns clubs, country dance groups,
scores of Highland Games Associations and literally hundreds of shops
nationwide (including a supermarket in Seattle) specialising in the sale of
bagpipes, books, drums, kilts, swords, clan crests, travel and music videos
and Scots crafts and you'll see that not only is the Caledonian connection
thriving, it has also become a multi-million dollar business.

Directly or indirectly, tens of thousands of Americans are involved in a
range of Scots-interest activities, running family magazines, fund-raising
for projects in America and the old country, manning stalls at Highland
Games or researching family history. Many claim only the remotest Scots
ancestry, and in the case of the pipe bands, the only real entry qualification
is a love of the pipes and drums, hence the occasional Oriental or Middle-
Eastern found giving it laldy in the ranks.

The 1970s and 80s in particular witnessed a tremendous growth in interest
in all things Scottish on the other side of the Atlantic, the obvious triggers
being an increase in leisure time, a higher age-profile in the population,
and a compelling, almost infectious need among the American Scots to
track down their roots, even if the search leads only to a pile of stones

GI brides, like this cheery group of women leaving Glasgow in the 1940s, constituted the last major exodus from Scotland to America, although significant numbers were still taking the plunge a decade later, as seen in this shot of Scotsmen boarding a flight in the 1950s. (The Herald Archives)

at the end of some windswept glen or a refurbished tenement in Partick or Leith. Annually, a great army of American tourists—well over quarter of a million—not only see the sights but come in search of their Scottish heritage. Many go away disappointed, but enough have made connections to boost the genealogy business quite spectacularly.

Alex Beaton, Glasgow-born singer and guitarist formerly with The Cumberland Three in the 1960s, but now based in California, is well-placed to observe the Scottish scene in America as he travels the Games circuit playing concerts and entertaining at dinners:

> Today you can get crowds of up to 40,000 at the Games but the majority have really only taken off in the past fifteen or twenty years. Seeing the success of one event, people were encouraged to give it a try themselves and the whole thing has simply snowballed.

Issues which to most of us might seem obscure and relevant to a bygone era can arouse intense passions amongst the Scots enthusiasts. In 1992, trouble arose when the Southwest Chapter of the Clan Gregor Society in America and the Clan Gregor Centre at Balquhidder in Perthshire found themselves at odds over the background of John McGregor, a piper and one of five native-born Scots slain in the 1836 siege of the Alamo at San Antonio (TX). Society researchers insisted that McGregor was born at Dull, near Aberfeldy, and immigrated first of all to Canada's Prince Edward Island in 1808. On the other hand, the Clan Centre believe that he may have been a direct descendant of Rob Roy himself. This genealogical debate and many others will run and run.

Enthusiasm for the Scottish heritage can show itself in many unusual, even bizarre forms, and any summer in New England you're likely to meet a mobile Dunvegan Castle sweeping majestically along the leafy back-lanes. Dick MacLeod of Lake Massasecum (NH), regional vice-president of the MacLeod Society, established his Scottish pedigree long ago, even finding time during a convalescence to paint the shutters on his lakeside home with the splendid MacLeod tartan.

His great-great-grandfather came to America from Kilmuir on Skye, and a few years ago Dick decided on a unique tribute to the MacLeod home ground. In his backyard he constructed a splendid scale model of Dunvegan Castle—eight feet wide, twelve feet long and twelve feet high, to avoid low bridges—which he now regularly takes on the back of a trailer and proudly displays at Highland Games and gatherings. On a visit to Scotland, Dick discovered there were no plans of the MacLeod stronghold on Skye, so he photographed his wife standing in the impressive doorway and calculated the scale using her height against the building. During construction, Dick says a host of travellers stopped 'just to see what the hell I was putting together'. The castle is now a New Hampshire landmark, 'just past the castle' or 'third on the left after the castle' being commonly used along Lake Massasecum to pin-point a destination.

Dick MacLeod of Lake Massasecum (NH) tours the New England Highland Gatherings with his splendid model of Dunvegan Castle which always draws the crowds. (Dick MacLeod)

Apart from this consuming passion among the American Scots for all things tartan, the skirl of the pipes and the researching of family histories, can the legacy of the legions of Scots traced in previous chapters—their religion, desire for learning, and startling capacity for hard work—still be traced in American society today? It would seem so. A 1978 study by the United States Census Bureau turned up some remarkable statistics. Scottish descendants in the United States lead other European-based ethnic groups (English, French, German, Irish, Italian, Polish and Spanish) in both earning capacity and education. The Scots were the only group to record *nil* illiteracy, and they also had the lowest unemployment rate (2.1 percent) and the highest ratio of high school graduates (81.2 percent). The continuing quest for learning, a belief in the value of education, can be found in some unlikely corners of the vast American nation. In the town of Sallisaw (OK), is a family with their heritage steeped in the traditions of the Cherokee nation yet proudly declaring their centuries-old link with Scotland.

Mary Adair, artist and teacher, widow of the Pawnee Indian Samuel Horse Chief, teaches at the high school operated by the Cherokee nation. Two of her children also work among their own people: her oldest son,

Samuel, is recreational director and athletics coach at the Cherokee school, while her daughter, Catherine, is a technician in an alcohol/drug-prevention programme among the tribe.

The family look back to Robert Adair, who came to Galloway from Limerick and married a daughter of the House of Argyle, Arabella Campbell. For hundreds of years the Adairs flourished in the south-west maintaining strong connections with Ireland until Thomas Adair immigrated, first to Pennsylvania in 1730 then on to South Carolina. One of his family, John Adair (b. 1758), married a Cherokee girl called Gahoga, this couple being Mary Adair's great-great-great-grandparents. Many of her forebears were important figures in the Cherokee nation. Mary's grandfather, Oscar, was a Cherokee judge, her great-grandfather a chief justice of the Cherokee Nation Supreme Court, and her great-great-grandfather, Walter, was jailed along with other Cherokee chiefs by settlers in Georgia who were seeking more land and urging the removal of the Indians. Walter died in 1835 shortly before that sad trek, the forced resettlement of the tribes in the West, actually began. The Adair family have an annual reunion and Mary says, 'Although we have been Cherokee Nation citizens for generations, we remember our Scots heritage.'

Down in Florida, in the town of Orlando (now familiar to thousands of Scots visitors to Disney World) lives Bob Barr, a remarkable example of the Scot at work within the American-Scots community. Having retired from his job as a manager with the Eastman Kodak Company in the 'Journey into Imagination' feature at Disney World, Bob is now president of his own marketing firm but also serves as a key figure in 'Give Kids the World', a charity dedicated to helping terminally ill children from all over the world fulfil their greatest wish—to meet Mickey Mouse.

A Korean War veteran, Bob's parents left Glasgow for America in 1923, and he has been a lifelong enthusiast for his Scottish heritage, serving as MC at over a hundred Highland Games and Tattoos in the south-east United States during the past twenty years, including the famous International Scottish Gathering at Stone Mountain (GA). A regular speaker at Burns Night suppers and Scots banquets, he gives an audio-visual presentation to schools, churches and Scottish organisations. In 1990, he was elected a Fellow of the Scottish Highlands Society and the Society of Antiquaries of Scotland; in 1991, Stirling District Council honoured him for promoting friendship between Scotland and the United States.

Such stories of bridge-building between Scots interest-groups in America and the old country are commonplace, and it is not only the overtly Scottish organisations which seem to have been gripped by this curiosity and affection for Scotland. Today there are over 300 officially registered tartans, including individual tartans for the United States Navy, the United States Air Force, the United States Marine Corps, the United States Military Academy at West Point, the Citadel Military Academy at Charleston (SC), and even the state of Georgia.

It's a truism, of course, that whenever Scots wander they become more Scottish the further they are from their own backyard. In 1992, 7,500 immigrants from the United Kingdom, among them hundreds of Scots, settled to a new life in the United States. But what makes a modern-day Scot go to America and, more importantly, convinces him or her that it's worth staying?

Fiddler Alasdair Fraser, now basing himself on America's west coast, hails from Clackmannan and first went to the United States on a BBC tour. In 1981, he moved to San Francisco to work as a petro-physicist with British Petroleum. His fiddle was never far from his side, however, and Alasdair was constantly writing reels and playing more and more music. His decision to make his home in the United States came with the realisation that Americans—contrary to the popularly-held view—were not superficial and faddish but deeply interested in any subject to which they addressed themselves, anxious, for example, to explore fiddling in all its aspects. Alasdair had given himself two years in America, but found there was a steady and growing demand for the music he was playing. He now runs the Valley of the Moon Fiddling School, which is over-subscribed and

Singer-guitarist Alex Beaton from Glasgow, and fiddler Alasdair Fraser from Clackmannan are two of the most popular entertainers among the Scots communities in the United States today, and are always in demand at Scottish gatherings nationwide. (Juan Cabrera)

includes in its student body Scots who, ironically, are travelling to America to learn to play the fiddle in the traditional styles.

Every year Alasdair tries to get back to Scotland, to renew acquaintances and to 'check his sources'. As well as teaching the fiddle and playing at Highland Games, he is also in demand as an adjudicator. He recorded fiddle music for the hugely successful re-make of *The Last of the Mohicans*, and also plays in an early music consort. In America he has found an openness to ideas and a willingness to learn without, Alasdair says, any preconceived notion of the way things should be, a situation he finds refreshing and encouraging. Always he finds time to spend with fellow Scots and has sensed the unique character of these Stateside get-togethers:

> Whenever Scots gather in America there is this special bond—ties which are still strong, more so I would reckon than with any other ethnic group.

Effectively Scotland's independent efforts at colonisation were over by the early 1700s, the communities having dispersed and assimilated, and now held together by clan and family ties. However, there is one corner of New Jersey where a flavour of the Scots enclaves may still be savoured.

The Argyle Fish and Chip Restaurant founded in Kearny seventy years ago is run by John Nisbet, who has his roots in Musselburgh and has moved along with the changing social setting, his American clientele just as important now as his Scots customers. American fare is provided, as well as traditional Scots dishes. Walls are decorated with battle scenes and Highland panoramas, and around Burns Night the haggis is piped in twice nightly for a fortnight and the place is full to over-flowing. Every Friday a piper parades between the tables, and the Argyle has become a stopping-off point for celebrities both Scots and American.

From deep-fry catering in New Jersey to painting and decorating in California, from nursing in the Carolinas to running an opera company in Kentucky, there are Scots at work. On the arts and showbusiness front, the talented young Perth sculptor, Michael Craig, is completing his first year at New York Academy of Art thanks to sponsorship from *The Herald* newspaper, while in Hollywood Broxburn boy, Michael Caton-Thomas, is one of the most sought after directors. David Byrne, who emerged from design school in Rhode Island to help found the rock group, Talking Heads, is one of the most influential musicians of the late twentieth century, having been born in a tenement in Dumbarton in 1952.

As they have been for 300 years, graduates of Scottish universities are still in great demand in the United States. Heriot-Watt, one of Scotland's newer universities, has up to 200 graduates now working and resident in the United States. Napier University, also in Edinburgh, has close associations with the Clan Napier in America and works with American companies on research and consultancy projects. Student exchanges are common, Robert Gordon University in Aberdeen having ties with Illinois Institute of Technology and Oregon State University, while the University of Edinburgh has a long-standing exchange programme with the University of Pennsylvania, as well as Georgetown University in Washington and the University of California. Dr Tom Barron, director of the university's International Office, describes his institution's links with the States as 'close, deep and enduring'. Strathclyde University in Glasgow is involved in many joint research projects and has exchange links with the Universities of Iowa, Kansas, North Texas and Central Michigan, and many of their students go on to postgraduate study in the US.

A more subtle aspect of the Scots presence is seen in the 'door-knocking' activities of the US-based staff of Locate in Scotland, the inward investment arm of Scottish Enterprise. With small offices in Stamford (CT), Houston (TX), San Mateo (CA) and Chicago (IL), the organisation provides the initial link in persuading expansion-minded US companies to consider Scotland as an ideal base for their European operation.

As we've already seen, Scotswomen were never content to settle only for the traditional domestic role in America—they too felt they had a stake in the new freedom, and their contributions were immense. Suffragettes Maude Younger, sisters Jean and Kate Gordon, Nettie Shuler, Harriet Upton and the saloon-wrecking, bottle-smashing anti-drinks campaigner Carrie Nation, were all proud to proclaim their Scots ancestry. Juliette Magill Kenzie Gordon Low, founder of the Girl Scouts of America; Anita McGee, who brought the Army Nurse Corps into being; Ann Maxwell, who started the School of Nursing at New York Presbyterian Hospital, and Juliet Hopkins, a Confederate hospital administrator during the Civil War can be added to this catalogue of female achievement. Following in this impressive tradition today are two ladies from the Tail of The Bank with two generations separating them but having also a common desire to get things done.

Ellen Currie, now in her eighties, left Greenock in 1930 and settled eventually at Marshall (MI) with her Rothesay-born husband, Colin, now deceased. The Scots connection with Marshall is a deep one, the town having been named after Chief Justice John Marshall of Virginia. Together the Curries promoted the idea of senior citizens housing in the town, beginning in 1974 by attending meetings and working in committees until the local authority agreed to build a one hundred unit development for the elderly. Ellen and Colin were first to move in. Despite her years, Ellen is still involved in community fund-raising.

Very much in the jet-setting style of the 1990s, Fiona Ritchie, a champion of Celtic music, is one of the best-known radio voices in America. She presents a weekly radio show called 'The Thistle and the Shamrock', which is networked to 255 local radio stations by satellite. Fiona regularly crosses the Atlantic between her twin bases in Edinburgh and the University of North Carolina in Charlotte.

Bob Barr of Orlando (FL), who was born in Tarrytown (NY) of Scottish parents, typifies the twentieth-century American Scot. (Robert Barr Jr.) *right* Fiona Ritchie from Gourock has one of the best-known voices in the United States, her Celtic music programme being beamed by satellite to 270 radio stations. (Fiona Ritchie Productions)

This rich panoply of Scottish experience in America extends from our shadowy mercenary, Tam Blake, to astronaut Alan Bean, who took a yard of specially-woven tartan to the moon. The Scots tribes are more than just a footnote to American history, a stirring memory, they remain a potent force. However, apart from the considerable tourist revenue, what relevance do these centuries-old ties and this vast pool of goodwill and affection have for the old country today? Scotland is a nation torn between a longing for greater self-determination, a meaningful place in a changing Europe, and an understandable apprehension, after 300 years of the Union, about venturing off again under its own steam.

Critics of the tartan sub-culture regard contact with the American Scots as irrelevant, apart from the money-earning aspect. There's certainly a temptation to dismiss the Scottish-American scene as a superficial hotch-potch of bagpipes, caber-tossing and swirling kilts, peopled by groups of slightly eccentric enthusiasts trapped in a 'loch and glen' mentality, a past which effectively vanished after Culloden. And yet, each time our American cousins return to Des Moines or Dallas, Philadelphia or Portland, they carry with them an impression of Scotland. Native Scots are under an obligation to ensure that the image which travels overseas is an accurate and modern one, reaching beyond the gloss of the Highland Gatherings and the tartan cinema epics of the mid-1990s to more basic truths.

American Scots are tied emotionally—some would say over-sentimentally—to Scotland, or more accurately to the rediscovered clan culture. Paradoxically, the majority of resident Scots do not share this clan consciousness, this 'Celtomania', and operate in a world of unemployment, urban neglect and seemingly out-of-touch government. While the American Scots are well-versed and take pride in their family histories, this contemporary Scottish scene is less familiar to them. Genealogical exactitude does not always provide historical insight. For example, they are occasionally surprised to learn that Scotland no longer has a parliament, or that it was changed so fundamentally by the industrial revolution.

Would a broader picture damage their attachment to Scotland? I'd like to think not. Perhaps we've reached a crossroads where these misconceptions can be corrected and the Scots diaspora reminded that Scotland is a nation still, a complex people with complex aspirations, not a theme park. The broader history of Scotland—social, economic and political, as well as romantic—which has brought us to the current crisis of confidence, a history which takes in the politically radical weavers of Renfrewshire as well as the Jacobite Uprisings and personalities such as Muir, Maxton and MacLean as well as Mary Queen of Scots, must be more widely available. Writer Julie Davidson has observed:

> The great tartan monster has become our national mascot . . . like it or loathe it, it's become our corporate logo. We can't uninvent it. But at least we can try to make sure we understand the elements which went into its design.

Perhaps then the tourist trade, historical accuracy and contemporary issues can all be served. Broader loyalties, not just to the 'new' clan system but to the Scottish nation, with all its blemishes and self-doubt, would be welcome from our friends in America. The expatriates, the Scots descendants, need somehow to be bound closer to the practical realities of present-day Scotland so that the country's ambitions may be better transmitted and understood by the world at large. Scotland, for centuries as much a state of mind as a genuine political entity, has been and remains the spiritual home for countless Americans, and these links—arguably in need of some fine-tuning—are inescapable and important.

# SOURCES

*Scotland's Mark on America* by George Fraser Black, San Francisco R and E Research Associates (1972)

*Scottish and Scotch-Irish Contributions to Early American Life and Culture* by William Lehmann, Kennikat Press (1978)

*The Enterprising Scot* by W. Turrentine Jackson, Edinburgh University Press (1968)

*The Scots Overseas* by Gordon Donaldson, Hale (1966)

*The Scots and Scotch Irish in America* by James E. Johnson, Lerner Publications (1966)

*Andy Little: Idaho Sheep King* by Louise Shadduck, Caxton Printers (1990)

*The Scot in America and the Ulster Scot* by Whitelaw Reid, San Franscisco R and E Research Associates (1970)

*Scotch-Irish Presence in Pennsylvania* by James H. Smylie, Pennsylvania Historical Association.

*Dictionary of American Biography*, published by Charles Scribner's Sons, New York (1937)

*Scotch-Irish Pioneers in Ulster and America* by C.K. Bolton, Boston (1910)

*Portable Utopia: Glasgow and the United States 1820–1920* by Bernard Aspinwall, Aberdeen University Press (1984)

*Invisible Immigrants* by Charlotte Erickson, University of Miami Press (1972)

*Scotland and its first American Colony* by Ned C. Landsman, University of Princeton Press (1985)

*The Coming of the Scot* by John H. Finley, New York (1940)

*A Dictionary of Scottish Emigrants to the U.S.A.*, compiled and edited by Donald Black, Magna Carta Book Company (1981)

*Directory of Scottish Settlers in North America 1625–1825* by David Dobson, Genealogical Publishing Company (1984)

*The Scotch-Irish in America* by Henry J. Ford, Princeton (1915)

*British Immigrants in Industrial America 1790–1850* by Berthoff, Rowland and Tappan, Cambridge, Massachussetts (1953)

*The People's Clearance: Highland Emigration to North America* by J.M. Bumsted, Edinburgh (1982)

*Scotus Americanus* by W.R. Brock, Edinburgh University Press (1982)

*Scotland and America: A Study of Cultural Relations* by A. Hook, Blackie & Sons (1975)

*Scottish Colonial Schemes* by George Pratt Insh, Glasgow (1922)

*The Tobacco Lords* by Tom Devine, John Donald, Edinburgh (1975)

*A Scotch Paisano in Old Los Angeles* by Susan Bryant Dakin, Berkeley (1978)

*Scotsmen in Buckskin* by Porter and Davenport, New York (1963)

*Scots and Scots Descendants in America*, edited by D. MacDougall, Caledonian Publishing Company, New York (1917)

*The Journal of John Harrower*, edited by Edward M. Riley, Colonial Williamsburg (1965)

*The Scot in British North America* by W.J. Rattray, Toronto (1888)

*An Historical Account of the Settlements of Scottish Highlanders in America prior to 1783* by J.P. MacLean, Baltimore (1978)

*Biographical Dictionary of Rocky Mountain Naturalists* by Joseph Ewan, Utrecht (1981)

*The Mistress of the Mansion* by Alice D. Addenbrooke, Reno (1950)

*Hunting for Gold* by Major William Downie, American West Publishing Company.

*Encylopedia of Colonial and Revolutionary America* by John Mark Faragher.

*Voyagers to the West* by Bernard Bailyn, Knopf, New York (1986)

*Death Song: The Last of the Indian Wars* by John Edward Weems, Indian Head Books, New York (1991)

*Scots Most Active on the Frontier* by James Callaghan, The Tombstone Epitaph (1991)

*The Passing of the Arizona Copper Company* by James Colquhoun, held by the University of Arizona Library (1921)

*Old Scots Saga Tells All* by Nellie Duffy, Grand Junction Sentinel (1963)

*Scots and Scotch-Irish in Connecticut* by Frank Stone, University of Connecticut (1978)

*Lairds, Bards and Mariners* by Bruce Le Roy, Washington State Bicentennial Commission (1978)

*Florida History* by Hal Bamford, Great Outdoors Publishing Company.

*Scotch Grove Pioneers* by various authors, Centennial Booklet.

*Idaho's Ethnic Heritage* by Mercier Simon-Smolinski, Idaho Centennial Commission/ National Park Service (1990)

*Wabash County History*, edited by Lina Robertson, Wabash County Historical Society.

*The Kinnamon Family in America* by Lester Kinnamon (1982)

*Emigrant's Guide to the Western States of America* by John Regan (1852)

*The Palimpsest*, Journal of the State Historical Society of Iowa.

*The River and the Prairie* by Bill Roba (1986)

*Peopling the High Plains*, edited by Gordon Hendrickson, Wyoming State Archives and Historical Department (1977)

*Webster's American Biographies*, G.O. Merriam Co., Springfield, Massachusetts (1974).

*John Ritchie: Portrait of an Uncommon Man*, edited by Daniel Fitzgerald, Shawnee County Historical Society.

*Pioneers of Destiny* by W.D. Weatherford, Vulcan Press (1955)

*The Mountain People of Kentucky* by William H. Haney, The Robert Clarke Company, Cincinatti (1906)

*Just Call Me Jock* by Semple, Kelly and Murphy, Waterford Publishing Company (1981)

*The Overmountain Men* by Pat Alderman, The Overmountain Press (1970)

*Counting Sheep* by Alexander Campbell McGregor, University of Washington Press (1982)

*A Sense of Place*, edited by Marilyn Wright, St Andrews Press, Laurinburg, North Carolina (1991)

*Hurrah for Bonnie Iowa* by Murray and Fiske, Graphic Publishing Company (1963)

*Cattle, Horses and Men* by John H. Culley, University of Arizona Press (1940)

*They Chose Minnesota*, edited by June Holmquist, Minnesota Historical Society Press (1981)

*Kalispell, Montana and the Upper Flathead Valley* by Henry Elwood (1980)

*Dr John McLoughlin, Father of Oregon* by Frederick V. Holman, The Arthur H. Clark Company (1907)

*The Scotch-Irish of Colonial Pennsylvania* by Wayland F. Dunaway, University of North Carolina Press (1944)

*History of Williamsburg* by William W. Bodie, Columbia S.C., The State Company (1923)

*Alexander Mitchell* by Charles H. Buford, paper delivered in New York (1950)

*Scottish Texans and the Highland Games* by Harry Gordon, The Encino Press (1974)

*A Good Time Coming*, edited by Frederick Stewart Buchanan, University of Utah Press (1988)

*Glasgow Herald Book of Scotland*, edited by Arnold Kemp and Harry Reid, Mainstream Publishing (1990)

*From Rocking Horse to Cow Pony* by Jessie Macmillan, Alamogordo, New Mexico

*Chief William McIntosh: A Man of Two Worlds* by George Chapman, Cherokee Publishing Company, Marietta (GA)

*The Penguin History of the United States of America* by Hugh Brogan (1990)

*High Plains History of East-Central New Mexico* by Don McAlary and Harold Kilmer, High Plains Historical Press (1980)

# INDEX

Abercrombie, Lord James, 146
Aberdeenshire, 4, 17, 18, 25, 39, 46, 77-78, 128, 150, 168, 195, 199, 233, 236, 257
Adair, Mary, 277
Adamson, David, 255
Addison, Alexander, 99
Ainslie, Hew, 187
Airlie, Earl of, 38
Aitken, Robert and Jane, 192
Aitkins, Robert, 155
Alabama, 27, 165, 168, 170, 238
Alaska, 4, 11, 25, 65
Alexander, Abraham, 263
Alexander, Cosmo, 194
Alexander, James, 63
Alexander, John (TX), 62
Alexander, John (VA), 76
Alexander, Matilda, 156
Alexander, Sir William, 15
Alexander, William, 147-148
Alison, Rev. Francis, 236
Allan, Ebenezer, 135
Alston, John, 223
American Civil War, 14, 25, 36, 53, 59, 72, 74, 83, 86, 88, 90, 107-109, 111, 113, 133-134, 136, 144, 155-160, 162, 163, 179, 182, 191, 193, 195, 198-199, 206, 231, 252-253, 281
Anderson, Elizabeth and John, 178
Anderson, Rev. James, 243
Andrews, Timothy, 155
Anesi, Annie Jean, 46
Angus, 18, 60, 77, 81, 83, 85, 137, 243, 257
Arbuthnot, Alexander, 170
Argyllshire, 15, 20, 24, 30, 36, 70, 86, 147, 187, 226
Arizona, 6, 12, 43, 44, 45, 51, 57-58, 70, 90-91, 101-102, 115-116, 162, 164, 180-181, 224
Arkansas, 57, 118, 160, 171
Ayrshire, 15, 30, 34, 45-46, 49, 62, 70, 84, 99, 124, 128, 140,

187, 193, 195, 198, 203, 204, 207, 213, 216, 261, 266, 271

Baird, James, 24
Banffshire, 40, 54, 128, 146, 155, 189
Barclay, Forbes, 230
Barclay, Robert H., 155
Barclay, Robert, 17
Barr, Bob, 278
Barr, Charlie, 220
Battles: Bannockburn (1314), 128, 144; Beecher's Island (1868), 161; Bothwell Brig (1679), 19; Bunker Hill (1775), 76, 150; Concord (1775), 64; Culloden (1746), 20, 64, 72, 152, 158, 227, 282; Dunbar (1650), 18, 28, 84, 85; King's Mountain (1780), 150-151, 160; Lexington (1775), 64, 148-149; Little Big Horn (1876), 60, 94, 146, 179, 182; Mier (1843), 102; Monmouth (1778), 248; River Raisin (1813), 178; San Jacinto (1836), 160; Sheriffmuir (1715), 112; Ticonderoga (1758), 146; Waterloo (1815), 121, 132, 212; Worcester (1651), 29
Baxter, Nancy, 118
Bean, Alan, 282
Beaton, Alex, 276
Bell, Alexander Graham, 84
Bell, Robert, 202
Bell, W. K., 52
Bennett, James Gordon and James Jr., 189-191
Bevan, Mary, 255
Binnie, John, James and Andrew, 80
Blair, Duncan, 183
Blair, John, 111
Blake, Thomas, 2, 12, 13, 282

'Bluidy Clavers' (John Graham of Claverhouse), 7
Boston (MA), 6, 19, 23, 29, 36, 60, 76, 77, 81, 84, 112, 120, 126, 127, 128, 129, 148, 149, 187, 192, 194, 195, 199, 204, 217, 220, 221, 227
Boswell, James, 20
Bowers, Eilley Orrum, 92[93
Bowie, Jim, 102, 160
Brackenridge, Hugh, 187
Brendan, St., 11
Brice, John, 155
Brockie, Robert, 48
Brooks, Mattie Ellen, 71
Brown, George Mackay, 11
Brown, Gustavus, 226
Brown, William, 227
Bruce, James, 25
Bruce, Robert, 144
Buchanan, Franklin, 155
Buchanan, Jack, 202
Buchanan, John, 177
Burke, J. J., 190
Burmiss, John, 6
Burns, Robert, passim
Burt, John, 187
Burton, Sir Richard, 62
Byng, Harry, 216-217

Caithness, 128, 147, 155, 156, 233
California, 2, 4, 26, 38, 41, 42, 43, 44, 58, 65, 81, 90, 92, 94, 102, 105, 106, 107, 130, 142, 161, 162, 195, 196, 203, 209, 211, 231, 259, 269, 274, 276, 281
Calhoun, John Caldwell, 271
Callender, James T., 192, 263
Cameron, Archibald (SC), 86
Cameron, Archibald (KY), 245
Cameron, Colin and Brewster, 51
Cameron, Ewan, 52
Cameron, Francis, 128
Cameron, James, 158

Campbell, Duncan H., 84
Campbell, Hugh, 20
Campbell, John, 198
Campbell, John A., 59
Campbell, John, 40
Campbell, John, 188
Campbell, Lachlan, 22
Campbell, Peter, 182
Campbell, Sir George, 15
Campbell, Thomas and
  Elisabeth, 257
Campbell, Thomas, 90
Campbell, William, 150-151
Canada, 7, 11, 15, 24, 25, 37, 40,
  46, 60, 65, 66, 68, 72, 80, 81,
  116, 132, 141, 145, 147, 178,
  180, 183, 192, 207, 210, 217,
  232, 238, 248, 273, 276
Candlish, James, 35
Cardross, Lord, 16
Cargill, Andrew Hays, 103, 156
Carlyle, John, 75-76
Carmichael, Hoagy, 203
Carmichael, Neil, 103
Carnegie, Andrew, 1, 84, 87, 104,
  105, 113
Carolinas, 4, 15, 16, 17, 20, 22,
  103, 131, 150, 171, 192, 226,
  280
Carson, Christopher 'Kit', 57
Carson, Thomas S., 116-117, 216
Chalmers, Lionel, 120, 226
Charleston (SC), 36, 73, 86, 126,
  150, 157, 174, 189, 226, 279
Chicago (IL), 2, 24, 63, 77, 78, 80,
  113, 128, 143, 157, 173, 206,
  217, 220, 223, 253
Chisholm, Jesse, 52
Chisholm, Peter, 115
Christie, James, 60-61
Clackmannanshire, 89, 279
Clark, Christopher and
  James, 57
Clark, Robert, Sr., 223
Clark, William, 58
Clarke, Robert, 202
Cleveland, Moses, 173
Cochran, Sir John, 15
Colden, Cadwallader, 120
Colorado, 8, 38, 52, 58, 125, 127,
  130, 161, 183, 193, 217, 239
Columbus, Christopher, 11
Connecticut, 24, 28, 88, 134, 160,
  192, 199, 207, 227, 261, 269,
  281
Cooper, James Fenimore, 186
Cooper, Peter, 83
Coulter, Robert, 139
Covenanters, 2, 15, 109, *passim*
Cowan, John, 136

Craik, Dr James, 227-228
Crain, Jimmie, 105-106
Crawford, David, 213
Crawford, Jane, 229
Crawford, William, 173
Crockett, Davy, 1, 102, 160
Cromwell, Oliver, 18
Crook, George, 179-181
Crooks, Ramsay, 66-67
Cuming, Sir Archibald, 174-175
Cumming, John, 40
Cunning, Willis, 130
Currie, Ellen, 281
Cuthbertson, John, 245

Dalton, John, 75
Delaware, 90, 91
Detroit (MI), 39, 78, 177, 178
Dewey, George, 157
Dickie, George, 81, 157
Dickinson, Suzanna, 160
Dickson, Robert, 66
Dinwiddie, Robert, 145
Doak, Rev. Samuel, 151, 247
Donahue, Peter, 83
Donaldson, William and
  Lawrence, 78
Dougall, Thomas, 223
Douglas, David, 4
Douglas, William, 120
Douglass, Archibald T., 160
Douglass, Jimmy, 57
Douglass, William, 227
Dowie, John Alexander, 253-255
Drever, John, 2
Drummond, Fred, 140
Duffield, Rev. George, 244
Dumbartonshire, 30, 41, 42, 46,
  128, 193, 220, 271
Dumfriesshire, 9, 25, 66, 75, 99,
  157, 202, 206, 220, 227, 261
Dunbar, David, 197
Dunbar, Sir William, 67,
  110-111
Dunbar, William C., 128
Duncan, Bill, 198
Duncan, Donald and John, 29
Duncan, Isadora, 203
Duncan, Tom, Bill, James
  and Gavin, 46
Dundee, 30, 31, 50, 52, 53, 79, 80,
  83, 85, 113, 128, 206, 237, 247,
  261
Dunlop, Rev. William, 16, 243

East Lothian, 4, 5, 63, 107, 195,
  227, 235, 257, 280
Eastwood, Clint, 203
Eckford, Henry, 81

Edinburgh, 18, 24, 40, 50, 52, 55,
  63, 76, 77, 79, 80, 85, 96, 99,
  112, 152, 156, 174, 187, 192,
  194, 199, 203, 211, 226, 227,
  228, 229, 233, 235, 238, 239,
  248, 253, 255, 270, 276, 280,
  281
Elder, Rev. John, 253
Elliott, James, 110
Erikson, Leif, 11

Fergus, Robert, 223
Ferguson, Alexander, 136
Ferguson, Patrick, 150-151
Fergusson, Arthur, 105
Fife, 15, 20, 76, 80, 84, 104, 148,
  209, 220, 226, 233, 255, 257,
  261, 266
Fighting McCooks, 144
Finlayson, John, 204
Firth, Robert, 37
Fleming, John, 171
Florida, 1, 16, 36, 64-65, 72, 110,
  111, 156-157, 166-168, 178, 220,
  260, 263, 278
Forbes, George, 206
Forbes, Thomas, 168
Forbes, William, 20
Ford, James and Agnes, 71
Forfarshire, 80
Forgan, James, 80
Forrest, Edwin, 203-204
Forsyth, George, 161
Forsyth, James, 179
Foster, Stephen, 203
Fraser, Alasdair, 279
Fraser, John, 238
Frazier, Jimmy, 46
French and Indian War, 20, 144-
  147, 152, 171, 227
Frick, Henry, 113
Fulton, Robert, 84
Gallagher, Thomas, 112
Galloway, 48, 154, 278
Garden, Alexander, 4, 120
Gardiner, Dr James Smith, 231
Geddes, James Lorraine, 199
George, William, 223
Georgia, 22, 24, 64, 78, 90, 111,
  126, 130, 131, 147, 150, 168,
  192, 217, 221, 238, 263, 269,
  279
Gibson, James and Walter, 16
Gibson, James, 147
Gilchrist, Mary, 130
Gilchrist, William, 49
Gillespie, John, 220
Gillies, Alex, 46
Gilmour, Richard, 248

Glasgow, 28, 29, 38, 46, 50, 75, 76, 78, 79, 83, 84, 5, 88, 104, 112, 113, 128, 133, 137, 145, 158, 160, 163, 177, 178, 187, 198, 200, 202, 203, 204, 206, 207, 215, 216, 223, 229, 238, 243, 248, 255, 276, 278
Glen, James, 261
Goodfellow, David, 43-44
Gordon, Alexander, 121
Gordon, Jean and Kate, 281
Gordon, William and Thomas, 233
Gowan, David, 43, 45, 48
Gowans, William, 201-202
Graeme, Thomas, 227
Graham, Isabella, 63
Graham, James, 261
Graham, Joanne, 238
Graham, John, 75
Graham, John, 263
Grant, Ann M'Vicar, 187
Grant, George, 54-56
Grant, Matthew, 158
Gray, David, 187
Gray, Elish, 84
Greeley, Horace, 191
Greer, Joseph, 151
Greig, Alex, 46
Greig, James, 25
Guthrie, William, 52-53

Hall, Andy, 13, 14, 115
Hamilton, Alexander, 120, 259, 266-268
Hancock, John, 266
Hancock, Winfield, 158
Harkness, William, 206
Harper, Robert, 22
Harris, Joel Chandler, 187
Harris, Tucker, 226
Harrower, John, 237
Hart, James and William, 193-194
Hastie, Thomas, 223
Hawaii, 41, 141, 216, 274
Healy, David, 128
Hebron, John, 18
Heggie, John, 257
Henderson, James, 137
Henderson, Richard, 63
Henry, Alex, 211-212
Henry, Joseph, 84
Henry, Patrick, 264-265
Henry, William, 84
Hervey, Robert, 223
Hogben, John, 131
Hogg, James, 63-64
Hooper William, 266
Houston, Sam, 160

Hunter Robert, 63
Hunter, Robert D., 52

Idaho, 36, 48, 90, 96, 162, 180
Illinois, 2, 14, 24, 28, 30, 36, 70, 71, 77, 78, 80, 85, 88, 92, 113, 114, 127, 131, 138, 161, 203, 206, 213, 223, 239, 254, 274, 281
Imlay, Gilbert, 187
Indian Tribes and Chiefs: Ah-Ha-Chocher, 165; Apache, 43, 57, 102, 103, 180, 231; Arapahoe, 58; Big Foot, 179; Black Hawk, 67; Blackfeet, 166; Catabwa, 260; Cherokee, 63, 160, 165, 174, 175, 177, 260, 277, 278; Cheyenne, 161; Chickasaw, 166-168; Chinook, 185; Chippewa, 171, 180; Choctaw, 166-168; Crazy Horse, 180; Creek, 166-170, 177, 182; Crow, 121; Delaware, 177; Eskimenzin, 103; Geronimo, 180; Goshiute, 255; Iroquois, 99, 182; Koott-humpum, 177; Lone Walker, 166; Nisqually, 185; Osage, 140; Ottawa, 171; Ouray, 183; Pawnee, 277; Puyallup, 185; Red Jacket, 174; Roman Nose, 161; Sauk, 12; Selish, 183; Seminole, 166-168; Seneca, 135; Shawnee, 177, 178; Sioux, 60, 66, 94, 161, 172, 179, 181, 183; Sitting Bull, 60, 179; To-To-Win, 66; Tuscorora, 187; Ute, 183; Wea, 171; Yamasee, 16, 171; Young King, 174; Zuni, 12
Indiana, 24, 49, 52, 53, 63, 63, 71, 104, 111, 117, 118, 125, 189, 205, 206, 232
Inglis, Thomas, 176
Innes, James, 20, 233
Inverness, 31, 65, 165, 200, 238, 250
Inverness-shire, 15, 23, 39, 40, 51, 81, 128, 150, 245
Iowa, 8, 24, 30, 36, 38, 72, 88, 105, 124, 130, 210, 215, 216, 231, 232, 250, 271, 273, 281
Irvine, William, 147
Irving, Washington, 66, 186
Ivison, Henry, 239

Jackson, Thomas, 159
James VI of Scotland and I of England, 14, 18
James, Jesse, 113

James, William and Henry, 187
Japp, Margaret, 125
Jefferson, Thomas, 236, 241
Jeffrey, James, 155
Johnson, Catherine, 130-131
Johnson, Dr Samuel, 20
Johnson, James, 268
Johnson, William, 39-40
Johnston, Gabriel, 233, 261
Johnston, John, 48-49
Johnston, Joseph, 159
Johnston, Samuel, 261
Johnston, William, 63
Johnstone, John, 18
Jones, John Paul, 154, 227

Kansas, 10, 38, 39, 49, 52, 53, 55, 59, 71, 72, 77, 81, 85, 86, 94, 110, 111, 122, 171, 179, 200, 201, 206, 231, 232, 273, 281
Keith, James, 248
Keith, William, 195-196
Kemp, John, 236-237
Kennedy, Archibald, 80
Kennedy, David, 197
Kenton, Simon, 173
Kentucky, 7, 22, 27, 58, 63, 64, 76, 84, 109, 173, 176, 187, 189, 228, 245
Ker, William, 247
Kerr, Deborah, 204
Kerr, Rev. John, 62
Kidd, Captain William, 112
Killen, William, 99
Kincardineshire, 18, 43, 45, 46, 58
King, John Crookshanks, 195
Kinross-shire, 30, 78, 132
Kinzie, John, 24
Kirkcudbrightshire, 34, 154
Kirkpatrick, Andrew, 99
Knox, Henry, 147, 148, 168

Laidlaw, James, 48
Lanarkshire, 62, 63, 76, 88, 137, 194, 201, 206, 247, 257
Lauder, Sir Harry, 200
Law, John, 99-101
Lawson, Alexander, 194
Lawson, James, 206
Lawson, John, 187
Lee, Robert E., 158
Leiper, Thomas, 76
Leslie, John, 168
Lewis, Andrew, William and Charles, 173
Lewis, David, 62
Lincoln, Abraham, 113, 114, 155, 158, 191
Lindesay, John, 22

Lindsay, Colin, 258
Little, Andy, 48
Lochs and Lakes: George, 22; Great Salt, 66; Michigan, 2, 223; Ontario, 135; Seneca, 49; St Mary's, 166; Superior, 135, 138
Loftus, Cissie, 204
Logan, William and James, 200
London, 15, 29, 54, 55, 75, 78, 94, 100, 112, 168, 175, 186, 203, 226, 229, 237
Long, John, 203
Lothain, Leannah, 205
Louisiana, 28 58, 68, 99-101, 108, 145, 241, 252
Low, Juliette Magill Kenzie Gordon, 281
Lyle, William, 187

MacArthur, Douglas and Arthur, 163
Macbeth, Charles, 87
MacCoon, John, 18
Macdonald, Alexander, 88
MacDougall, Alexander, 147-148
Macfie, William and Alexander, 46
MacGregor, Rev. James, 6
MacInnes, Alexander, 155-156
MacIntosh, Daniel, 182
MacIntosh, Donald, 182
Mackay, Donald, 81
Mackay, James, 68
Mackenzie, Alexander, 68
Mackenzie, Donald, 68
Mackenzie, Finlay, 48
Mackenzie, George, 186
Mackenzie, Kenneth, 68
Mackenzie, Murdo, 52
Mackenzie, Robert, 193
Mackintosh, John
Mackintosh, Peter, 112
MacLean, Neil, 227
MacLeish, Archibald, 187
MacLennan, Frank P., 200-201
MacLeod, Dick, 276
Maclure, James, 71
Macmillan, Jessie, 207-209
MacNeill, Neill, 20
Macpherson, Allan, 171-173
Macpherson, Angus, 81
MacQuarrie, Robert, 128
Macrae, Jock, 142-143
Maine, 15, 23, 24, 88, 133, 136, 178
Makemie, Francis, 243
Malcolm, Daniel, 112
Malcolm, William Henry, 104
Mann, Eliza, 57

Manson, Donald, 155
Mantell, Robert Bruce, 204
Marjoribanks, Sir Dudley Coutts, 51
Maryland, 20, 23, 24, 29, 75, 76, 88, 115, 120, 155, 187, 191, 204, 226, 230, 264
Massachusetts, 11, 24, 29, 60, 84, 88, 112, 128, 129, 130, 147, 148, 163, 199, 206, 215, 217, 238, 248, 257, 263
Maxwell, Ann, 281
Maxwell, William, 203
McGillivray, Alexander, 166-167
McAllister, Doug, 46
McArthur, John, 157
McArthur, John, 206
McBrayne, Hugh, 160
McBroom, John, 58
McBroom, William Henry, 116-117
McCallum, Craig, 83
McCallum, John, 142
McCarty, Dr Thomas, 231
McCaw, James, 226
McClain, Alexander, 211
McClellan, George Brinton, 158, 179
McClellan, Robert, 66
McCollom, Fenelon, 199
McCormick, James H., 216
McCormick, Robert, 191
McCracken, Jackson, 90
McCray, 'Blind' Dr Moses, 232, 234
McDaniel, James, 59
McDonald, Andrew Y., 215
McDonald, Donald, 130-131
McDonald, Duncan, 183-184
McDonald, John, 165
McDougall, Alex 'Pee Wee', 96-97
McDougall, Alexander, 138
McDowell, Dr Ephraim, 228, 229
McDowell, Irwin, 158
McEvers, R. D., 179
McEwen, William, 138
McGlashan, John, 223
McGree, Mary, 224
McGregor, Dr Alexander, 46
McGregor, John, 160, 176
McGregor, Malcolm, 141
McGregor, Reuben, 90
McGregor, Thomas, Jane and Rob Roy, 161-163
McGuffey, William, 239
McIntosh, Archie, 180
McIntosh, John L., 199
McIntosh, John, 25
McIntosh, Lachlan, 147, 150

McIntosh, Waldo Emerson 'Dode', 170
McIntosh, William and John, 168-169
McKay, Alex, 90-92, 164
McKay, Charles, 66
McKay, James, 156
McKay, W. A., 46
Mckay, Gordon, 83
Mckay, James, 110
McKenzie, Jim, 8
McKenzie, Morodock Otis, 177
Mckenzie, David, 137
McKinley, Jim, 42
McLean, Andrew, 193
McLean, Duncan, 130
McLeod, Rev. Dr Alexander, 109
McLoughlin, Dr John, 41, 65-66, 132
McLure, Dave, 117
McMillan, John, 70
McMillan, Rev. John, 245
McNaughton, John, 136
McNeese, John, 241
McNeil, Andrew, 164
McQueen, William, 155
McRae, Ian, 140
McTammany, John, 198-199
McTavish, Donald, 66
Meekison, David, 226
Melish, John, 187
Melrose, Richard, 259-260
Melville, Hermann, 187
Mercer, Hugh, 152-153
Michigan, 24, 111, 126, 171, 178, 199, 231, 281
Middleton, Peter, 227
Miller, George, Robert and Josiah, 110
Miller, James, 62
Miller, T. F., 10
Milne, James and Jemima, 128
Minnesota, 24-26, 28, 30, 38, 62, 66, 79-80, 88, 126, 132, 135, 138-139, 181, 210
Minto, John, 40
Mississippi, 24, 28, 99, 100, 245, 252
Missouri, 27, 39, 41, 57, 68, 85, 102, 110, 173, 193
Mitchell, Alexander, 77-78
Mitchell, Elizabeth, 25
Montana, 46, 58, 105, 106, 122, 127, 166, 180, 183, 199
Montgomery, James, 111
Montrose, Marquis of, 85
Morayshire, 24, 31, 40, 60, 62, 67, 94, 110, 122, 123, 128
More, John and Betty, 22

Moreland, John and Catherine, 231
Mormons, 8, 26, 45, 66, 89, 92, 128, 137, 197, 203, 255, 257
Morrison, Charlie, 84
Morrison, David, 158
Morse, Samuel, 84
Moss, Sidney, 65
Moultrie, Dr John, 226
Mountains and Valleys: Alleghenies, 22, 147, 152, 177, 228; Appalachians, 28, 33; Chiricahuas, 162; Cumberland, V, 21; Rockies, 27, 44, 58, 67, 68, 120, 121, 127, 132, 166, 195; San Gabriel V, 41; San Rafael V, 51; Santa Cruz V, 57; Sierra Nevadas, 21, 92; Willamette V, 41
Muir, John, 4-5, 195
Muir, Samuel, 24
Mulhollin, Polly, 207
Munro, Alexander Bissett, 23
Munroe, Hugh, 166
Munroe, John and Ebenezer, 149
Murdoch, John, 45
Murdoch, William, 264
Murphy, John, 142
Murray, Alexander, 155
Murray, Lindley, 239
Murray, William Vans, 226

Nairne, Thomas, 171
Nation, Carrie, 281
Nebraska, 27, 34, 44, 45, 47, 66, 106, 182, 232
Neil, James, 128
Nevada, 91, 92, 95, 141-142
New Hampshire, 6, 24, 88, 135, 147, 148, 154, 276
New Jersey, 8, 15, 17, 18, 23, 24, 84, 99, 147, 187, 194, 230, 235, 243, 247, 280
New Mexico, 12, 50, 52, 58, 116, 117, 141, 179, 207-209, 216, 268
New York State, 20, 22, 24, 36, 39, 49, 120, 128, 135, 147, 148, 157, 164, 174, 178, 187, 192, 193, 217, 220, 243, 263, 269
New York City, 2, 3, 28, 39, 40, 43, 46, 60, 63, 70, 71, 75, 80, 81, 109, 112, 126, 127, 128, 129, 136, 147, 148, 155, 156, 157, 161, 196, 187, 189, 191, 194, 195, 197, 201, 203, 206, 207, 209, 217, 227, 230, 236, 238, 239, 255, 263, 274
Nisbet, Charles, 257-258
Nisbet, Eugenius Aristides, 99

Nisbet, John, 280
North Carolina, 20, 24, 63, 109, 110, 130, 156, 178, 187, 195, 197, 233, 237, 247, 252, 253, 258, 261, 263, 266, 268, 269, 281
North Dakota, 24, 28, 31, 38, 54, 129, 139, 199, 210, 213
Northern Isles, 1-2, 11, 18, 19, 37, 65, 110, 128, 186, 210, 230, 237
O'Neil, David, 60
Ohio, 24, 28, 59, 70, 84, 88, 118, 138, 145, 148, 173, 177, 179, 180, 198, 199, 200, 202, 203, 205, 206, 215, 248, 250, 269
Oklahoma, 27, 38, 52, 53, 54, 122, 140, 141, 190, 277
Oliphant, Dr David, 227
Oliver, James, 49-50
Oregon, 29, 38, 41, 46, 60, 65, 66, 67, 80, 132, 133, 162, 180, 181, 183, 217, 281
Orr, Bobette, 158
Oury, Will, 101-102
Owen, Robert and Robert Dale, 62, 189, 241

Paisley, 75, 161, 195, 207
Panton, William, 166-168
Paterson, John, 147
Penn, William, 17
Pennie, Daniel, 30
Pennie, Tom, 132
Pennsylvania, 20, 22, 24, 44, 63, 76, 83, 84, 88, 99, 102, 110, 131, 147, 150, 151, 152, 162, 171, 187, 216, 227, 239, 243, 244, 245, 250, 252, 257, 266, 268, 278
Perry, Oliver Hazard, 155
Perth, 90, 125, 227
Perthshire, 4, 41, 75, 111, 112, 119, 120, 132, 136, 171, 183, 187, 227, 276, 278
Philadelphia (PA), 20, 36, 76, 83, 126, 128, 136, 147, 151, 154, 164, 173, 192, 194, 202, 203, 204, 217, 222, 225, 226, 229, 231, 233, 236, 237, 264
Philip, James 'Scotty', 94, 95, 122-123, 172, 180
Pine Valley, 43
Pinkerton, Allan, 113-115
Pitcairn, John, 148-150
Pittsburgh (PA), 40, 70, 88, 97, 113, 131, 145, 173, 187, 203, 204, 217
Porteous, Jim, 106
Powell, John Wesley, 14
Presidents: Arthur, Chester, 269;

Buchanan, James, 268; Cleveland, Grover, 269; Grant, Ulysses S., 158, 162, 196, 209, 269; Harrison, Benjamin, 269; Hayes, Rutherford, 269; Jackson, Andrew, 160, 170, 268; Johnson, Andrew, 269; Johnson, Lyndon Baines, 270; McKinley, William, 269; Monroe, James, 268; Polk, James Knox, 268; Reagan, Ronald, 2, 268, 270-271; Roosevelt, Theodore, 52, 166; Wilson, Woodrow, 270

Quakers, 7, 15, 17, 18, 110, 147, 152, 187

Rainey, William, 245
Ramsay, William, 75, 76
Rankin, John, 109
Ray, Joseph, 239
'Red-Eyed' Ellen, 134
Redford, Robert, 203
Rees, David, 173-174
Regan, John, 70, 120
Reid, Hugo, 41-42
Reid, John, 220
Renfrewshire, 4, 16, 24, 40, 63, 68, 75, 83, 84, 112, 114, 137, 157, 206, 220, 235, 238, 281
Reston, James 'Scotty', 191
Revolutionary War, 7, 20, 22, 24, 26, 29, 32, 40, 63, 64, 76, 99, 102, 135, 140, 147-148, 152, 154, 158, 173, 176, 178, 192, 197, 202, 217, 226, 227, 235, 244, 263, 269
Reynolds, John F., 158
Rhode Island, 18, 84, 191, 194
Ritchie, Fiona, 281
Ritchie, Hugh, 223
Ritchie, John, 111
Ritchie, Robert, 223
Rivers: Clyde, 31, 75, 81, 83, 156; Colorado, 14; Columbia, 41, 58, 65, 66, 68, 132, 181; Connecticut, 84; Delaware, 40; Doon, 125; Forth, 137; Hudson, 22, 40; Kentucky, 57; Little Pee Dee, 103; Mississippi, 57, 68, 72, 100, 211, 252; Missouri, 57, 58, 66, 71, 105, 123, 145; Mohawk, 39; New, 177; Ohio, 57, 70, 145, 150, 227; Pecos, 116-117; Platte, 106, 121, 182; Potomac, 22, 75, 76; Raritan, 18; Red, 139, 140, 210-211; Royal, 14-16; Saskatchewan, 166; Savannah, 131;

Shenandoah, 22, 55, 59; Snake, 67, 68, 96; Susquehanna, 21, 22, 40, 171, 253, 261; Willamette, 65, 68; Withlacochee, 65
Robb, Rev. William, 34
Robertson, Bill, 198
Robertson, James and Alexander, 192
Robertson, James, 173
Robison, Robert, 81
Ross and Cromarty, 24, 52, 68, 81, 183, 186, 203, 217
Ross, John, 165
Roxburghshire, 13, 44, 49, 71, 81, 136, 137, 266
Rumsey, Robert, 84
Russell, William, 245
Rutledge, John, 99, 266

San Francisco (CA), 42, 81, 83, 92, 141, 157, 203, 213, 217, 253, 279
Scoon, William, 157
Scott, Charles, 147
Scott, Isaac, 135
Scott, Sir Walter, 128, 187
Selkirkshire, 136, 154, 261
Semple, Jock, 220-222
Sharp, John, 89
Shaw, Rev. Colin and Mollie, 253
Shirlaw, Walter, 195
Shorey, William, Ghigooie and Ann, 165
Simpson, 'Sockless' Jerry, 81, 259, 273
Sinclair, Earl Henry, 11
Sinclair, John F., 25
Sinclair, John Sutherland, 38
Small, Dr William, 236
Smart, Charles, 230
Smibert, James, 194
Smith, George, 77-78
Smith, Peter and Martha, 183
Smith, Peter S., 199
Smith, Russell, 204
Smith, William (CO), 239
Smith, William (PA), 236
South Carolina, 15, 16, 24, 73, 86, 99, 109, 118, 140, 150, 168, 205, 216, 226, 227, 243, 247, 260, 261, 271, 278
South Dakota, 24, 28, 38, 48, 52, 122, 123, 179
Spotswood, Alexander, 59

St Clair, Arthur, 147
St Louis (MO), 52, 66, 67, 68, 71, 128, 140, 215, 217, 232, 255
Stark, John, 147, 150
Steel, Rev. John, 253
Stevenson, Nathan, 6
Stewart, Archibald M., 191
Stewart, James C., 223
Stewart, James, 52
Stewart, John, 85
Stewart, Sir David, 144
Stewart, Sir William Drummond, 119-122, 132
Stewart, William, 26
Stirlingshire, 71, 136, 148, 204, 206, 269, 278
Stuart, Gilbert, 77, 194
Stuart, James 'Jeb', 159
Stuart, John, 260
Stuart, Robert, 67, 111, 171
Stuart, William, 155
Sutherland, 66, 68, 206, 210, 211
Swan, Alexander, 51
Swan, James, 76-77
Swinton, John and William, 195-196
Switzer, Kathy, 222

Taylor, Robert, 44-45, 47
Tennent, William, 233
Tennessee, 7, 22, 24, 27, 64, 107, 109, 151, 160, 165, 173, 176, 177, 198, 231, 241, 247, 269, 271
Texas, 38, 50, 51, 52, 62, 101, 102, 105, 117, 122, 140, 156, 160, 163, 178, 241, 270, 276, 281
Thom, William, 25
Thompson, Walter, 9
Thomson, A. M., 223
Tillary, Dr James, 227
Torrey, George, 252
Travis, Will, 102
Trumbull, Jonathon, 260-261
Turnbull, Andrew, 72
Twist, Allie, 165
Tytler, James, 112

Ulster and Ulster Scots, 2, 6-7, 15, 16, 20, 22, 24, 33, 39, 57, 58, 59, 63, 84, 92, 99, 109, 116, 130, 133, 138, 144, 147, 148, 150, 152, 155, 160, 171, 176-178, 187, 207, 228, 233, 236, 243, 245, 268, 269, 270

Utah, 26, 45, 66, 89, 90, 92, 137, 197, 203, 255

Vermont, 24, 88, 157
Victoria, Queen, 9, 94, 129
Virginia, 18, 20, 22, 24, 58, 59, 63, 64, 71, 75, 76, 99, 102, 104, 117, 118, 145, 147, 152, 156, 158, 159, 160, 173, 176, 177, 192, 196, 205, 207, 226, 227, 228, 233, 235, 237, 238, 264, 266, 268

Wallace, James Duncan, 77, 85-86
Wallace, William, 101, 144
Washington DC, 75, 105, 108, 113, 160, 189, 204, 273, 274, 281
Washington State, 28, 41, 46, 60, 65, 98, 128, 132, 142, 162, 183, 216, 217
Washington, George, 7, 76, 84, 98, 145, 147, 148, 151, 166, 173, 192, 227, 248, 261, 267
Watson, John, 194
Watt, Willie, 39
West Virginia, 104, 177
Western Isles, 11, 14, 15, 20, 22, 24, 128, 130, 139, 140, 148, 164, 227, 253, 276
White, Alexander, 24
White, James, 206
Wigtownshire, 80, 226
Willison, Rev. John, 247
Wilson, Alexander, 194
Wilson, James (IA), 271
Wilson, James, 99, 235, 266
Wilson, Jock, 127
Wilson, Peter, 83
Wisconsin, 25, 28, 36, 58, 62, 77, 78, 163, 165, 183
Witherspoon, Rev. John, 63, 235, 264
Wright, Fanny, 240-242
Wyoming, 34, 35, 45, 46, 48, 50, 52, 59, 60, 73, 96, 97, 121, 130, 180, 198, 205

Yellowstone, 105
Young, Brigham, 92, 197
Young, Robert, 128
Young, Robert, 151
Younger, Maude, 281